SPECIAL PROGRAMS IN REGULAR SCHOOLS

HISTORICAL FOUNDATIONS, STANDARDS, AND CONTEMPORARY ISSUES

SALLY J. ZEPEDA

University of Oklahoma

MICHAEL LANGENBACH

University of Oklahoma

ALLYN AND BACON

Boston • London • Toronto • Sydney • Tokyo • Singapore

Series Editor: Ray Short
Series Editorial Assistant: Karin Huang
Editorial-Production Service: Omegatype Typography, Inc.
Electronic Composition: Omegatype Typography, Inc.

Library of Congress Cataloging-in-Publication Data
Zepeda, Sally J.,
    Special programs in regular schools : historical foundations, standards, and contemporary issues / Sally J. Zepeda, Michael Langenbach.
        p.   cm.
    Includes bibliographical references and index.
    ISBN 0-205-26205-8
    1. Mainstreaming in education—United States.   2. Special education—United States.   I. Langenbach, Michael.   II. Title.
LC1201.Z46   1999
371.9'046'0973—dc21   98-20965
                                                                CIP

Printed in the United States of America

10   9   8   7   6   5   4   02

To the memory of my mother, the late Dolores A. Zepeda, and to my mentors, Judith A. Ponticell and Raymond Calabrese
SJZ

To my wonderful grandson, Jackson Clay Monroe (aka Jackman)
ML

Contents

PREFACE

School principals have many responsibilities. In addition to maintaining the regular school program, they now must manage a variety of special programs. Such programs make sense in today's schools; they are vital for our young people. To successfully facilitate the programs, however, principals must understand them—their rationale, the goals and standards by which they are judged, and the contemporary issues that surround them. Developing this understanding is often time-consuming.

In this book we provide the kind of information that will bring an administrator "up to speed" regarding the most common special programs in regular schools. For each type of program we offer a brief history, explain the specialized vocabulary, outline the goals, and discuss the major problems and issues.

Much has been written lately about democratic schools and site-based management, and much of that has been good. These writings provide myriad examples of administrators, teachers, and parents working together to make schools more responsive to students' needs and more effective in meeting those needs. We embrace the concept of mutual responsibilities for identifying and solving problems that schools encounter. The process by which an administrator seeks input from teachers and parents before making a decision is an important one. Implementing that process, however, is not easy. Soliciting the involvement of others is predicated on knowing the rudiments of what special programs are for, how they evolved, and what they require to be effective—all information clearly and concisely presented in this book.

In response to the Goals 2000: Educate America Act, passed in 1994, and the efforts of the National Assessment of Educational Progress to measure how well those goals are being accomplished, many special programs have developed standards enumerating what students should know and be able to do. For example, the visual arts, music, dance, drama/theatre, and physical education areas all have established such standards, and we have included some of those standards to give administrators an understanding of what kinds of resources and guidelines are available to them.

CHAPTER ORGANIZATION

The organization of the book is straightforward and very accessible to anyone interested in special programs. The topics are alphabetized, reflecting a source book approach. The book is made up of 17 chapters, each of which discusses a special program usually, but not always, requiring special teachers—either full time, itinerant, or consulting. Each chapter has three sections.

In the first section, we present a brief historical sketch of the program, including important milestones of the program's development. Often this section includes legislation or court cases that have had some impact in establishing or significantly affecting the direction of the program.

In the second section, we introduce, define, and describe special vocabulary. We also describe the current status of programs, sampling the professional literature. National standards and/or goals are presented here. Practitioners can turn to these standards for guidance in planning and evaluating special programs. The second section also contains reference works, including summaries of research, that are needed as a foundation for most special programs.

The third section of each chapter presents contemporary issues and concerns related to the special programs. Because the tradition and values associated with a school or district may affect the nature of a special program, our material is presented so that it can be applied in a wide range of settings.

Each chapter ends with a list, titled Illustrative Practices and Issues, that summarizes current research and articles addressing the program. Questions and suggested readings, designed to promote further thought and discussion and to deepen one's understanding of the programs presented, round out each chapter. The glossary at the end of the book is also an invaluable resource.

ACKNOWLEDGMENTS

We wish to thank the many students and colleagues who unselfishly provided resources and advice for this project. We also would like to thank four graduate assistants in the College of Education at the University of Oklahoma who assisted us—Linda Jones, Kristin Miller, Frances Patterson, and Clifford Pettersen. Our thanks also to the following reviewers for their comments on the manuscript: Irwin Blumer, Newton Public School System, and Judith A. Ponticell, Texas Tech University. A special thanks goes to our word processing expert, Susan Houck, and Mary Ann Langenbach for technical advice.

INTRODUCTION

Most new principals will be assailed immediately by special interest groups or individuals with special agendas. We agree with Walker & Soltis (1997) that the new administrator can make the best decisions only after all relevant parties have provided "fully and fairly considered judgment" about the issue at hand. Time and other conditions often make full and fair consideration very difficult, so administrators need to make decisions based on as much information as is readily available. This book is a foundation for decisions to be made about special programs; when this material is combined with information about the school and community as well as with input from teachers, parents, and students, a principal will be well-prepared to manage and facilitate special programs.

RATIONALE

Some years back, Postman and Weingartner wrote *The School Book* (1973), a sardonic, if not cynical, view of schools and many of their special programs. It was our intention to provide more useful information for the school administrator, who faces a multitude of challenges, many of which come in the form of special programs.

Typically a new principal does not have the luxury of developing for the first time this or that program. The new principal simply inherits what was already in place and is usually expected to maintain these programs. Essentially, new principals must play the cards that are dealt. In most cases it would be politically unwise to terminate quickly programs that have been in place for some time.

The basic principle, however, is the same. Whether reviewing an existing program or trying to generate interest in developing a new one, the principal needs to communicate with the staff and parents most directly involved or most likely to be affected by any change regarding any special program—extant or anticipated.

ACCOUNTABILITY

Many special programs require some form of accountability. An annual evaluation or some other form of documenting the use of special provisions may be required. Such *bureaucratic accountability* is to be expected, especially when continued funding or accreditation is desired.

Unfortunately, professionals frequently need to engage in bureaucratic accountability to assure others that ethical, responsible behavior is the norm. Often, funding sources will require accounting or evaluative procedures for assurance that allotted funds were spent appropriately. Parent groups also may request proof that special services or provisions were available for certain groups of children. Administrators need to resign themselves to the various requests for bureaucratic accountability and find ways, whenever possible, to streamline and expedite the necessary paperwork.

The increasingly litigious nature of our culture also makes it wise to protect ourselves with appropriate documentation whenever possible. Certainly such paperwork can be a distraction, taking up valuable time and energy that could be better spent attacking other problems, but often the forms simply must be filled out and filed.

Professional accountability begins in the education and training necessary to become a certified teacher and administrator and continues with the ongoing requirements of maintaining one's certification. In a more perfect world, professional accountability would be all anyone would need.

CERTIFICATION REQUIREMENTS

Certificate requirements will vary from state to state, and some may be driven almost entirely by professional organizations. Knowing the professional requirements to obtain certification for a specialized area, whether it be from a state or professional organization, can be helpful to an administrator. It could be helpful to know, for example, that a special education teacher is typically certified for grades kindergarten through 12. By learning what course work and other professional experiences each certificate requires, administrators can become better informed about the knowledge and skills necessary to carry out the various specialties. In addition, they can determine the full range of resources at the school.

MULTIDISCIPLINARY APPROACH

Children rarely have isolated needs. A poor reader, for instance, may have a vision problem or suffer from low self-esteem because of poor reading skills. Special programs and people—the school nurse who can check vision, the school psychologist who can treat low self-esteem, the after-school activities that can include tutoring—can all be brought to bear in serving the individual child. The multidisciplinary approach makes sense, but if principals are not aware of the special programs and all that they can do, children's needs will continue to be met in a less than satisfactory manner.

CHAPTER 1

ACTIVITIES PROGRAMS

Activities programs are more commonly found at the secondary level than at the elementary level. Frequently, such activities are called *extracurricular,* even though, when planned and carried out under the aegis of the school, they are technically part of the school's curriculum. Although terms, such as *extraclass, extraschool,* and *collateral,* have been used, *extracurricular* is commonly enough used by both the general public and many professional educators that any attempt to change the term now would be difficult.

Typical examples of extracurricular activities include athletics, both intramural and interscholastic; social, hobby, and service clubs; music groups, including band, orchestra, and chorus; student publications; drama/theatre; debate; student government; and assemblies (Berk, 1992). The above list, though not exhaustive, is virtually identical to one made by Trump in 1953 when he surveyed the same area. The activities program, hereinafter referred to as the *extracurricular program,* has been associated with public high schools since the turn of the century.

HISTORY

By the year 1900 about 8 percent of the population 14 through 17 years of age were in high school but, by 1920, that percentage increased to 24 (Connell, 1980). Cities were growing because of the continual industrialization begun in the nineteenth century. Immigration was high. Near the turn of the century about half the population were immigrants or children of immigrants. In 1890 four out of every five children in New York and Chicago had foreign-born parents (Violas, 1978).

At the beginning of this period, when only about 8 percent of high school age youth were actually in high school, the activities program (i.e., the extracurricular program) consisted mainly of loosely organized athletic clubs and fraternities, the latter being modeled after college fraternities (Trent & Braddock, 1992). Before compulsory school attendance laws were passed (in all states by 1919) and before child-labor laws were well enforced, one can imagine the class or socioeconomic status of the 8 percent of 14- through 17-year-olds who were in school. That the high school activities were athletic clubs and fraternities can hardly come as a surprise.

Reportedly, school teachers and administrators tried to rid the schools of these activities, especially the fraternities, frequently referred to at the time as "secret societies." In addition to the fear that these activities would take time away from regular studies, these organizations "were widely condemned by educators because of their exclusionary practices, anti-intellectual values, and promotion of undesirable habits, such as smoking, alcohol consumption, and monetary extravagance" (Berk, 1992, p. 1003). Interestingly, Trent and Braddock, writing in 1992, compare school personnel trying to rid the schools of fraternities in 1900 with similar efforts in the 1990s to rid the schools of gangs.

To formally establish school-sponsored extracurricular activities was the most effective way to counter the undesirable organizations around 1900. By 1920 extracurricular activities were well established: "[they] permeated virtually every American urban junior and senior high school" (Berk, 1992, p. 1003).

The urban scene in the United States in the years 1910 to 1920 was complex. It was growing rapidly—mostly by immigrants or former farmers, unable to make a living on the land. Many people lived in crowded conditions at work and home, and there were increasing numbers of young people on the streets, as a result of the eventual enforcement of child-labor laws.

According to Violas, in 1923 Henry Ford declared that "over 85 percent of the jobs in his factory could be learned in less than a month and almost half required less than one day's training" (p. 4). The nineteenth-century notion of years-long apprenticeships for artisans was, indeed, an idea of the past. The "new" workforce did not need many specialized skills and, more importantly, it was preferred that this workforce be compliant and uncomplaining. Violas (1978) explains the enthusiastic support for extracurricular activities as a way to train, indeed habituate, students—many of whom would be working in dull, monotonous jobs—in a way that they would likely tolerate such working conditions. Violas's thesis is that extracurricular activities were particularly well suited to accomplish these affective ends and were, therefore, supported by advocates for industry, including educational administrators, especially those from large urban centers.

Historical events, of course, always are open to many different interpretations. A more benign interpretation of the advent of extracurricular programs was provided by Connell (1980). In reviewing education in the twentieth century worldwide, Connell suggests that all countries pass through similar stages of educational purpose. The first stage is an effort to achieve solidarity. In 1900 the interest in the United States was in "the efforts to make good Americans out of a wide range of European immigrants" (Connell, 1980, p. 7). Citing practices in Japan, England, France, and Italy, Connell claims that schools were expected to instill "common sentiments and attitudes which would cement the people of a particular country together into a common allegiance" (1980, p. 7). With the advent of World War I, schools promoted nationalism even more.

It was not just that immigration continued unabated from the middle of the nineteenth century until the 1920s. Prior to 1900, most of the immigrants came from northwestern Europe—England, Germany, and Scandinavia—but by 1900 this pattern shifted dramatically to southeastern Europe. The people of Italy, Austria–Hungary, and Russia, unlike the people of northwestern Europe, "continued to view America as a promised land, and flocked there by the hundreds of thousands" (Butts & Cremin, 1953, p. 307).

The newer immigrants were different from earlier immigrants in important ways. The immigrants of the nineteenth century typically settled on farms; those from southeastern Europe typically remained in large cities in the Northeast: "There they served as a reservoir of unskilled labor for rapidly expanding industries, laboring at wages far below the acceptable minimum for native American workingmen" (Butts & Cremin, 1953, p. 307). The newer immigrants, more often than those of the nineteenth century, typically came over as single men—as opposed to men with families—and, in addition, the level of literacy for the newer immigrants was lower than that of the immigrants from northwestern Europe (Butts & Cremin, 1953).

There were three prevailing attitudes toward the influx of new immigrants (Violas, 1978):

> Exclusionists sought to prohibit the immigration of "undesirable" peoples . . . assimilationists, more complex in their prescriptions, called for changing the character of immigrants to fit them into the American social order. The least popular of the Americanizers were the cultural pluralists. They suggested a new conception of the national community, one that allowed diverse groups to exist and function within a broad, but comprehensive federation of ethnic enclaves. (p. 38)

These groups exerted mixed and varying kinds of influence throughout the twentieth century but, more importantly, it is of some interest to note that attitudes toward those who are different have not changed much over time. That one group predominated over the others in the ensuing decades is important to know, but just as important is the knowledge that such groups or categories of opinions existed and probably will continue to exist as long as some people are considered "different" by the majority.

Another view of the advent of extracurricular activities in the secondary schools is even more benign. Trump (1953) described the establishment of extracurricular activities (he called them extraclass activities) as a rational response of the high school teachers and administrators to the needs of secondary school students. At first blush, determining needs appears to be a straightforward proposition. It is not. First of all, one must decide whose needs are to be addressed—the individual student's or the society's? If individual and social needs are different, does that mean they are mutually exclusive? These curricular questions are not easily answered, nor are they usually answered once and for all. As Pratt (1980) concludes, determining needs is a value-laden activity.

Thus, the period from 1900 to 1920 can be characterized, especially in the urban centers of the Northeast and Midwest, as having a rapidly growing, general population, mainly as a result of the influx of immigrants from southeastern Europe and others drawn to the cities to work in factories. In addition, there was a rapidly growing school population because of increased enforcement of child-labor laws and compulsory school attendance laws. The influx of new students created problems for the high school system because it was expected to accommodate all of the new students. The high school curriculum in this period was largely college preparation, designed to serve students from families that expected their children to continue their education beyond high school. Two responses at the national level were made to address these problems.

The Smith-Hughes Act of 1917 provided funds and legitimation for vocational education at the high school level. This act made money available to school districts to broaden their high school curriculum beyond the relatively narrow, if not anachronistic, college preparation focus. The act also may have established tracking students at the secondary level but, at the time, tracking may have been the lesser of two evils—the other being the virtual inability of school personnel to accommodate a wider range of students.

The *Seven Cardinal Principles of Secondary Education,* expressed by the Commission on Reorganization of Secondary Education in 1918, were a significant departure from the European-based, mental discipline approach to the high school curriculum. The seven principles were health, command of fundamental processes, worthy home membership, vocational efficiency, civic participation, worthy use of leisure time, and ethical character. As Butts and Cremin observed, "The only one of the seven that could be considered a direct preparation for college was the command of fundamental processes; the other six were much more concerned with the personal and social competencies of life in general" (1953, p. 592).

To what extent the typical urban high school responded by broadening their regular curriculum is difficult to tell. Certainly, vocational education became a feature of the U.S. high school, but how much the teaching of English, history, and mathematics was changed is unclear. What is much more clear, however, is the advent of extracurricular activities, many, if not all, of which were justified on the grounds of satisfying the new personal and social dimensions of the seven cardinal principles.

If participation on an interscholastic or intramural sports team teaches team work or individual effort directed toward the greater good, that phenomenon is open to different interpretations. One interpretation is that by promoting team activities, school officials were carrying out the wishes of the capitalists, particularly by training a working class who would subjugate personal interests to the interests of the group. There appears to be ample evidence that special interest groups indeed promoted these ends (e.g., see Violas, 1978).

At the same time, one could justify participation in team sports to promote the importance of the group over the importance of the individual as necessary for day-to-day living in any kind of social order. If, for example, individuals choose not to obey traffic signals, the quality of life for the entire group will deteriorate.

The child study movement began around the turn of the century as did the progressive education movement, fueled, in part, by the former. The net effect of these two movements was the gradual (and still proceeding) shift to a child-centered approach to schooling. Up until the early part of the twentieth century, schools were essentially subject centered. As Cremin observed, although progressive education meant different things to different people, its impact on schools

> meant broadening the program and function of the
> school to include direct concern for health, vocation,
> and the quality of family and community life. (1961,
> p. viii)

Adding extracurricular activities to the school program was probably the easiest way for schools to respond to all the influences affecting them.

When the Great Depression affected the country, creating far more leisure time than most people wanted, recreational activities became more popular and, in turn, transformed intramural sports at the high school level from a highly competitive endeavor to one more recreational in nature—sport for sport's sake

(Barney, 1979). Wisconsin, Michigan, Illinois, and Indiana were the first states to organize high school intramurals. Before the organization of intramural sports, "Teachers, principals, and even janitors played on high school teams" (Rice, Hutchinson, & Lee, 1969, p. 190).

Despite the prefix "extra," some activities, such as band, orchestra, drama, debate, and athletics, have become part of the regular curriculum and are different in two important ways: Students have less control of them, and credit is earned by participating in them. Although these activities still may occur outside of regular school hours, the issues of control and credit make them different from the usual extracurricular activities.

CURRENT STATUS

Extracurricular activities still exist. As Goodlad (1984) discovered, most of the participation is in sports teams for both boys and girls at the middle and high school levels. He also found, however, that about a third of the students at both levels participated "in some sort of service activity pertaining either to the school or the community" (1984, p. 225).

Reviews of research conducted in 1987 and 1992 indicate a few generalizations about participation in extracurricular activities, but they are wrought with cautions about specific variables that appear to affect not only whether one chooses to participate, but how the particular variable (e.g., gender) may interact with the actual participation. In 1987 Holland and Andre concluded that:

> The available research indicates that participation in extracurricular activities, including both athletic and nonathletic activities, is positively correlated with desirable personality/social characteristics. (p. 447)

The inherent caution about correlations, however, is that such relationships do not mean that one causes the other. Students self-select into extracurricular activities, and they may have been predisposed to do that for any number of reasons. To note, for example, that students in a service club have higher grade point averages than students who are not in the club does not mean that participation caused higher grades. The high

grades may have contributed to the decision to join the club.

Berk made a comprehensive review of the research in 1992. Her conclusions stated that

> the weight of current evidence indicates that extracurricular activities contribute in vital ways to adolescent development and that they do not, as has often been assumed, undermine students' commitment to the academic side of secondary school life. (p. 1036)

She advises the reader to understand that pre-existing conditions such as the socioeconomic status of the family, measures of intelligence, and a variety of dispositions could affect whether a student participates in an activity. Simply taking a "snapshot" look at who is involved and a host of other variables that appear to be related to the involvement does not permit the inference that participation causes something.

Trent and Braddock (1992) also made a comprehensive review of research on extracurricular activity involvement in 1992 and were able to make similar cautionary generalizations. They found, for example:

> that participation in general is beneficial and that for many of these outcomes (educational aspirations and expectations), positive benefits have been found for males and females across race. (p. 478)

Trent and Braddock further observed that the goals of learning the value of teamwork and cooperation, sacrificing individual goals for group goals, learning the work ethic, integrating physical and mental health, and appreciating and respecting class, racial, and ethnic diversity have been virtually constant over the entire history of extracurricular activities in the schools.

CONTEMPORARY ISSUES

Two Supreme Court decisions have implications for extracurricular activities. One is related to free speech rights as they pertain to student publications and the other affects the rights of school personnel to decide what kinds of extracurricular clubs the school can allow.

In the *Hazelwood School District v. Kuhlmeier* case (1988), the Supreme Court found in favor of the school district, allowing the district to censor the school newspaper and thereby limit the freedom of speech of the students. Berk summarized the finding:

> The majority opinion justified the ruling as a necessary means for ensuring that educators maintain control over the curriculum (of which the school newspaper was judged to be a part), shield young people from sensitive material (in this case, on adolescent pregnancy and parental divorce), and dissociate the institution from student expression that school officials find objectionable. (1992, p. l033)

Berk suggests that the possible overuse of censorship by school personnel could work against learning responsible journalism, but the decision clearly is on the side of the school district.

The Equal Access Act was signed into law in 1984. The purpose of the act was to ensure that school facilities would be accessible to religious and political clubs in the same way that they are to other noncurricular clubs. The constitutionality of the act was challenged, and in 1990 the Supreme Court upheld its constitutionality in the *Westside Schools v. Mergens* case.

Two key terms integral to the Mergens case require explication. One is *limited open forum* and the other is *noncurricular related.* Limited open forum means that a group is permitted to meet on school premises. Noncurricular related means, according to the Supreme Court, that the subject matter of the group will not be taught in the regular curriculum; participation in the group is not required for a particular course; or participation does not result in academic credits (Mergens, 1990). In the Mergens case a chess club that existed at the school and was considered noncurricular had access to school facilities. Therefore, the school was forced to comply with the Equal Access Act and permit a Bible club to meet on school property.

Another issue is the use of extracurricular activities to address the changing needs of students and society. The school day is finite, and the curriculum for the vast majority of schools is filled with subject matter and activities that have been fought over for decades. Adding something to the curriculum usually means taking something else out. Teachers and administrators are well aware of the endless conflicts that determine the dynamic nature of the curriculum. To argue for adding something new and different usually means: "Take your place in line. There are many ahead of you." The extracurriculum, however, despite the misleading label (or maybe because of it), may be the best place to offer something new and different.

Berliner and Biddle (1995) suggest, for example, that schools broaden their content. They offer a menu that includes some familiar activities and some new ones:

> [the schools should appeal] to avocational interests, to recreation, and to creative use of leisure time. . . . These activities might include, for example: various kinds of community service; hobbies; sports; music; enjoying and performing the arts; reading philosophy or history; travel; studying comparative religions; and so forth. (p. 316)

We believe that the activities program—held before or after school hours on a voluntary basis—is the least difficult way to "add on" to what the school promotes. Supervising such activities may well have budgetary implications because teachers or other appropriately certified personnel will need to be paid, but the costs would be minuscule compared to the benefits of better meeting both individual and social needs.

ILLUSTRATIVE PRACTICES AND ISSUES

Fowler, R. C., & Corley, K. K. (1996). Linking families, building families. *Educational Leadership, 53*(7), 24–26.
> Fowler and Corley describe how an elementary school creates community in its building by establishing a parent center, Friday Clubs, and celebrations of learning. *Issues:* They use in-kind contributions from agencies and promotion of cooperative planning by teachers and others.

Thompson, S. (1995). The community as a classroom. *Educational Leadership, 52*(1), 17–20.
> Thompson describes a school district in rural Wisconsin that has family–school–community partnerships, projects, and interventions. *Issues:* How to gain support from parents and the community is described.

SUMMARY

The activities program typically goes by the more common name *extracurricular program.* Prior to the twentieth century, when less than 10 percent of youths age 14 to 17 were in school, extracurricular programs were virtually nonexistent. It was the combination of increased immigration, enforced child-labor and compulsory school attendance laws, and a national rethinking of the purposes of public school education (primarily the Seven Cardinal Principles and the progressive education movement) that began the shift from a subject-centered to a child-centered approach to schooling that facilitated the addition of extracurricular activities to the secondary schools.

The variety of clubs and organizations has changed very little over the years and, more importantly, the purposes and goals have remained rather constant as well. Participation in extracurricular activities has been and still is encouraged for students to learn leadership, teamwork, and, occasionally, subjugation of self for the greater good.

Most studies of student participation support the generalization that such participation does more good than harm. Cause–effect studies have not been conducted—nor have they been in any other realm of schooling—but virtually all of the relationship studies reveal positive associations between participation and a host of personal and social goals that schools try to promote.

QUESTIONS FOR FURTHER CONSIDERATION

Research

1. What effects have the "No Pass, No Play" laws had on extracurricular activities?

2. Desegregation and Title IX have had a direct impact on extracurricular sports in public schools. Examine old yearbooks and school newspapers from a school in your district and trace the development and impact of desegregation and Title IX over the past few decades.

Reflect

1. Based upon the context of your school, what benefits do children gain from participating in activities? Sports?

2. What can or should principals do to promote student involvement in the activities program?

Respond/React

1. Examine the idea that school programs have become a panacea for social problems. Can schools cure all the ills of society?

2. Examine the statement, "Dewey lost, Thorndike won," in light of what you know about the connection between schools and future factory workers.

SUGGESTED READINGS

Berk, L. E. (1992). The extracurriculum. In P. W. Jackson (Ed.), *Handbook of research on curriculum,* (pp. 1002–1043). New York: Macmillan.

Trent, W. T., & Braddock, J. H. II (1992). Extracurricular activities in secondary schools. In M. C. Alkin (Ed.), *Encyclopedia of educational research* (pp. 476–481). New York: Macmillan.

CHAPTER 2

ALTERNATIVE EDUCATIONAL OPPORTUNITIES

Educational opportunities for students have expanded with the inception of alternative schools and the alternative educational opportunities that they provide for myriad students whose ability levels range from the very talented to the very slow and from the average to the unmotivated. Alternative schools for the at-risk can provide students who have traditionally met with failure a sense of success, through an individualized curriculum delivered by teachers who are sensitive to the particular needs of students dealing with issues that have put them at-risk in traditional learning environments. Knutson (1996) views alternative schools as those that reflect "an understanding of programming for at-risk youth; those who are likely to not finish high school" (p. 119). The term *at-risk* is a difficult one to define because it represents a phenomenon that is tied to the social and emotional needs of students and how these needs interfere with success in school and possibly, in some instances, in life. The term at-risk can be applied to discouraged learners and students who have poor attendance, are truant, or are pregnant (Knutson, 1996). There are startling statistics about youth and the issues that put them at-risk from succeeding in the traditional educational setting. For example:

- More than 4 out of 10 young women become pregnant before they reach the age of 20—one million a year. (National Campaign to Prevent Teen Pregnancy, 1996, n.p.)
- By the 8th grade, 70% of youth have tried alcohol. (Community Intervention, Inc., 1996, n.p.)
- Twenty-five to thirty percent of America's students do not complete a high school education. (Dorrell, 1996, p. 15).

At-risk issues and behaviors are discussed in detail in Chapter 12, Prevention Education.

It is important to note, however, that modern alternative schools are not designed solely for at-risk students. Magnet schools offering specialized curricular programs for students who excel in such areas as math, science, and the fine and performing arts cater to the particular needs of students who have talents and abilities in these specialized areas. On the other hand, some alternative schools are for adjudicated youth, juvenile delinquents, and others who do not "fit" in with "regular" students in traditional settings. These types of alternative schools, according to Kelly (1993), "represent a dual response to: (1) students' need for flexibility and personalization with the stated aim of 'dropout prevention and recovery,' and (2) conventional high schools' need for mechanisms to isolate students who pose discipline and other problems and to provide specialized services efficiently" (pp. 216–217).

Some alternative programs are housed in traditional schools; other alternative programs are housed in their own schools. Alternative schools and their educational programs, regardless of their target population (e.g., at-risk, adjudicated youth, pregnant teens, and gifted and talented), serve a need or a purpose. It is this need or purpose that guides the development and operations of the alternative program or school. The term *alternative* is going to mean different things to those who use it, depending on the needs and goals it serves. Kellmayer (1995) provides this insight:

> Within the past 20 years, the term *alternative education* has been applied indiscriminately to such a wide variety of programs that its meaning has been clouded in confusion among educators, students, and the general public. Approximately 2,500 programs that are called "alternative" have been located across the United States. Researchers have estimated that the

actual number of alternative schools is probably closer to 5,000. (p. 2, emphasis in the original)

Charter schools, vouchers, full-service schools, and alternative schools and/or programs within traditional schools will likely become more commonplace as schools and their personnel work toward meeting more of the needs of all students.

HISTORY

Alternative educational opportunities can be traced to Dewey and the progressives in the 1920s (Kellmayer, 1995). More radical alternative educational approaches such as the "Summerhillian alternatives . . . organized around communal living situations and communitarian ideals" (Duke, 1978) were introduced by "radical romanticists" or "neoprogressives" (Ornstein & Hunkins, 1988, p. 40). A. S. Neill's book *Summerhill* (1960) is an account of his ideal alternative educational opportunity for children at Summerhill; an alternative school he and his wife began in Suffolk, England, in 1922. Neil's main objective was "to make the school fit the child" (1960, p. 4). Another 1960s neoprogressive, Holt, wrote the book, *How Children Fail* (1964), wherein he details how regular schools do not meet many of the needs of children. Holt's harsh criticism of schools can be summarized, "We destroy the disinterested love of learning in children . . ." (p. 208). Kohl's book, *The Open Classroom* (1969), calls for teachers to be able to teach "In an open situation . . . [where] the teacher tries to express what he feels and to deal with each situation as a communal problem" (p. 15).

Alternative schools began to surface in large numbers in the late 1960s as a reaction to the traditional bureaucratic structures, policies, and procedures that were in place in "regular" schools. The storm and stress of the 1960s and 1970s stimulated the need for alternative schools. Such markers as the Vietnam War and the Civil Rights movement sparked an intense challenge against the status quo and it was during this period that experimenting with what Kozol (1982) refers to as "Free Schools" started. The alternative school movement, according to Ascher (1982), "began . . . at a time when popular ideals emphasized egali-

tarianism and participatory decision-making, and when there was a great push to increase the participation of minorities in all phases of public life" (p. 65). Gold and Mann (1982) reported:

One learns after only a brief scan of alternative schools that there are many different kinds of alternatives, with differing philosophies, purposes, and methods. They serve a variety of kinds of students, not all of them by any means problematic. And, while some exist to address problems or deficiencies, others strive to open up new opportunities for their students. Alternative schools have been created for the gifted as well as the poor student, for the well-behaved as well as the disruptive. Some could be described as "permissive," others, as "strict"; some concentrate on basic scholastic skills while others pursue special talents and interests and so on. About all that alternative schools have in common is that their programs are somehow different from the curriculum followed by the large majority of the community's students. (p. 305)

The differences in alternative educational programs and schools alluded to by Gold and Mann (1982) are what Raywid (1994) speaks about as representing the current status of alternative schools, "early alternatives, like today's, represented innovation; small-scale, informal ambience; and departure from bureaucratic rules and procedures" (p. 26). Scherer's (1994) discussion with Deborah Meier, co-principal of Central Park East School in New York City, an alternative school that falls under the rubric of a charter school, underscores the evolution of what alternative has come to mean for the many interested in restructuring educational opportunities for children. The charter school movement began in the late 1980s and has sustained momentum into the 1990s, creating small, responsive schools for all children, clearly a departure from larger schools and systems. Scherer (1994) reports, "One of the reasons given for the resurgence in popularity of new kinds of schools, especially charter schools, is that the new models put decisions about education in the hands of parents" (p. 4).

Another alternative option, schools-within-schools, provide a structure of "smallness" in which students can be mentored by adults who care deeply about their personal, academic, and social success. Schools-within-schools were created, in part, due to the emergence of large and impersonalized school systems in which high numbers of students could potentially fall "through the cracks." With school sizes increasing, "the alienating effect . . . is more profound than ever" (Oxley, 1994, p. 521). Meier (1996) reports that "the vast majority of kids—probably 70–80 percent—belong to enclaves that include no grown-ups" (p. 12). Since schools-within-schools rely on "small unit organization" within the overall structure of an existing school, schools-within-schools have "the potential to bring about significant changes" for students (Oxley, 1994, p. 522).

Typically schools-within-schools are comprised of a small cadre of teachers who can provide more one-on-one assistance to students by using interdisciplinary curricular and instructional approaches. "Small schools allows for the creation of flexible, humane, self-directed learning communities. They can be places of direct accountability, thoughtfulness, safety, intimacy, and common purpose" (Klonsky & Ford, 1994, p. 66). Similarly, Testerman's (1996) research on the effects of schools-within-schools in large high schools indicates that this type of arrangement can have numerous positive effects for students, "improved grades, more consistent attendance, increased studying, less sleeping in class, and more dedication to schoolwork" (p. 365). Essentially, changing the structure of the day and encouraging more meaningful interactions between students and teachers yields positive results.

The theme of change keeps recurring with alternative schools and program options. Duke (1978) explored the quandary of defining the term *alternative school*. He believed that alternative schools emerged under the rubric of change tied to reforming schools. Early labels that were used to describe alternative schools and/or their options included, "Free schools, storefront schools, continuation schools, three R's schools, magnet schools, minischools, street academies, schools-without-walls, and schools-within-schools . . ." (Duke, 1978, p. 4). For the purposes of our examination of alternative educational opportunities and the alternative school movement, we will return to the 1970s and Duke's (1978) definition of the alternative school, "An alternative school simply is a school accessible by choice, not assignment" (p. 4). This definition might be misleading. As indicated ear-lier, not all children attend alternative schools by choice, given that many alternative educational opportunities signal the last opportunity for some children, especially the disruptive and adjudicated youth.

CURRENT STATUS

Due to the myriad possibilities of alternative educational programming, our discussions will cover the most common types of alternative options. Alternative schools and educational opportunities rely on nontraditional or more progressive and appropriate methods to reach the typically at-risk populations that are served by them. Chalker (1996) details the four most common types of alternative education frameworks in which students are served. Although alternative education can mean just about anything, program formats include most commonly "a separate alternative school, [the] schools-within-a-school, the continuation school, and alternative classroom settings" (p. 9). Table 2.1 represents an overview of each one of these types based on Chalker's (1996) book *Effective Alternative Education Programs: Best Practices from Planning through Evaluating.*

There are, of course, other alternative educational frameworks such as shopping mall schools and storefront schools. Raywid (1994) developed a way of analyzing the scope and function of alternative schools and programs by classifying the types of services provided as Type I, Type II, and Type III alternatives. According to Raywid, Type I alternatives or popular innovations, "seek to make school challenging and fulfilling for all involved" (p. 27). Type I alternative schools could include magnet schools for math, science, or the performing arts, and "they are likely to reflect programmatic themes or emphases pertaining to content or instructional strategy, or both" (Raywid, 1994, p. 27). In Type II alternative schools or last-chance programs, "students are sentenced—usually as one last chance prior to expulsion. . . . They have been likened to 'soft jails,' and they have nothing to do with options or choice" (Raywid, 1994, p. 27). Type III alternative schools "are for students who are presumed to need remediation or rehabilitation—academic, social/emotional, or both" (Raywid, 1994, p. 27).

TABLE 2.1   Selected Alternative Educational Programming Formats

ALTERNATIVE SCHOOL PROGRAM TYPES	PURPOSE AND FUNCTIONS	UNIQUE FEATURES
Separate alternative school	• Serves "chronically" disruptive students (p. 10) • Eliminates failures • Personalizes education • Improves basic skills • Provides . . . opportunities for problem resolution, adjustment, and change (p. 10)	Isolated and self-contained structure (p. 10) Innovative strategies • Individualized, competency-based instruction • Curricular integration • Structured environments • Basic skill emphasis • Small pupil-teacher ratios • Work study programs • Flexible schedule options • Nongraded work; mastery opportunities
School-within-a-school	• Reduces size and number of students into humanistic units (p. 11)	• Access to regular options and resources, electives, and special programs (p. 11) • Interrelated courses • Individualized competency-based instruction • Curricular integration • Student contracting • Low student-teacher ratios • Team and peer teaching • School-community collaboration • Individual and group counseling (p. 12)
Continuation school	• Preparation of individuals for high school diploma or GED certificate (p. 13)	• Less competitive, less structured, more personalized atmosphere (p. 13) • Reduced school schedule • Individualized instruction • Extra counseling • Open-entry/open-exit • Curricular emphasis on personal growth and vocational and academic goals (Kelly, 1993, p. 12)
Alternative classrooms in regular schools	• Improved self-image, enhanced academic and social skills, accelerated grade promotion or opportunities for additional Carnegie Units, and alternatives to graduation (p. 13)	• Individualized and self-paced course work.

Unless otherwise indicated, information was adapted from *Effective alternative education programs: Best practices from planning through evaluating* (p. 10–13), by C. S. Chalker, 1996, Lancaster, PA: Technomic, to illustrate the purposes and functions and unique features of each of the alternative school program types.

Raywid's discussion of how an alternative school or its program can be classified simultaneously as a Type I, II, or III underscores the complex work with youth that alternative schools seek to accomplish. An alternative school's classification is perhaps best understood by examining several elements: the objectives and goals of the program, how children are chosen to participate in the alternative school (choice or mandatory), the instructional methods employed, the way the day or time is arranged, and how student work is assessed. By examining these elements, more accurate appraisals of the workings of the alternative school and/or program can be made.

Features of Effective Alternative Schools and Programs

According to Fuller and Sabatino (1996), "to be effective, alternative school programs should include intensive individual and group counseling focusing on self-esteem, self-concept, personal responsibility, appropriate expression, vocational assessment, and career preparation" (p. 296). Ascher's (1982) analysis of alternative school programs indicated similar patterns or features as noted by Fuller and Sabatino. Ascher isolated specific aspects of alternative schools that were useful to student progress:

- Small size—brings about pride of ownership and experimentation
- Flexibility—allows for matching student learning styles with instruction
- Strong leadership—generates needed morale and energy, whether this leadership is exerted by a principal or the teachers
- Student participation in decision making—results in an atmosphere of respect, trust, and caring
- Learning designed to create student success and to enhance student self-concept—promotes lowered truancy and vandalism levels. (p. 67)

Raywid (1994) indicated that there were 11 features that made alternative educational programs successful:

1. They were small.
2. Both the program and organization were designed by those who were going to operate them.

3. They took their character, theme, or emphasis from the strengths and interests of the teachers who conceived them.
4. Their teachers all chose the program, with subsequent teachers selected with the input of present staff.
5. Their students and families chose the program.
6. A teacher–director administered each program.
7. Their small size denied them much auxiliary or specialized staff, such as librarians, counselors, or deans.
8. All the early programs were housed in mini-schools in buildings that were dominated by larger programs.
9. The superintendent sustained the autonomy and protected the integrity of the mini-schools.
10. All of the programs were relatively free from district interference, and the administration also buffered them from demands of central school officials.
11. The continuity in leadership has been considerable. (p. 29)

From examining the work of Fuller and Sabatino (1996), Ascher (1982), and Raywind (1994), it is apparent that effective alternative school programs are configured in such a way that both at-risk and accelerated (gifted and talented) students become the focus of education, that disruptions from outside sources are minimized, and that more humane and developmentally appropriate instructional methods are used to ensure higher levels of success. Moreover, it appears that in these types of programs the curriculum, the pacing of the curriculum, and the assessment of student progress are more individualized and responsive to the learning styles of the students.

Kellmayer (1995) believes that "as much as possible, participation in the alternative program should be voluntary for both students and staff. Especially in the case of staff, teachers should not be assigned to a program in which they do not wish to teach" (p. 26). As Chalker (1996) and others indicate, alternative education should be more humane and responsive. Humaneness and responsiveness cannot be mandated through union agreements and other contractual agreements (Kellmayer, 1995). The concept of power and control with which teachers influence children becomes an issue here. Kellmayer (1995) believes, "You can gain more influence over teenagers the less you try to control them. . . . Teachers who do not understand and accept this premise do not belong in an alternative program" (p. 26).

Kellmayer (1995) identified access to social services as a desirable and much needed attribute found in effective alternative programs. This is especially true in Type II and Type III alternative programs attended by last-chance students and students in need of intensive remedial assistance.

CONTEMPORARY ISSUES

The identification of students who would most benefit from alternative educational opportunities is problematic. This is true for students at both ends of the spectrum—the very brightest and those most at-risk of dropping or being pushed out of schools. Many schools have long waiting lists of students who could benefit from the services offered by the alternative program. Some alternative schools and/or programs (e.g., magnet schools) use selection criteria that could include, for example, taking an exam or participating in a performance audition. In the same vein, other alternative programs use selection criteria, but students who attend these schools have relatively little choice —they are on their way out of the traditional system as a result of their behavior or lack of motivation. Attendance for these students is mandatory. Some alternative programs offered within schools and districts are open to all students and provide choice. Decisions on whether to attend or not are made by parents and students. Alternative programs that utilize an open and voluntary attendance policy are reported to be more effective. On the one hand, disruptive students, if they are interfering with the educational rights of others, need to be removed to preserve the overall learning environment. On the other hand, one must wonder if student behavior once removed from the traditional setting will improve.

As the negative characteristics of children and the severity of the issues they face increase (e.g., poverty and disintegrating family and home environments), the likelihood of success in school decreases. Respon-

sive schools create alternative educational opportunities to assist at-risk students. The problem is that a student can be considered at-risk at intermittent times throughout adolescence. Without specified goals and objectives, alternative educational programs can become "revolving door" programs, with students moving in and out quickly without the benefit of time needed to address the underlying problems they face.

As indicated earlier, staffing alternative programs with qualified and interested teachers is best left to voluntary measures. Forcing teachers to accept an assignment in an alternative educational program and/or school can be fatal to the success of such programs. The selection of teachers, especially new hires, becomes a priority to find teachers (1) who have the interest and empathy to work with at-risk students; (2) who have the training and/or experience (e.g., interdisciplinary curriculum development); and, (3) who are willing to accept the challenges of developing caring relationships with their students.

If alternative schools and/or programs are best established by those who will be working closest with the students—teachers—in a bottom-up fashion, then critical decisions need to be made by teachers and administrators working together. Decisions that have traditionally been made by the principal will need to shaped and then made by teachers. This includes involving teachers in making more than curricular decisions. Decisions on policies, procedures, and the configuration of the master schedule need to include the voices of teachers. Time is an essential component in this process.

Innovations in course offerings and curricular design should be encouraged. Involving the student with the community through curricular modification can be achieved through service learning. There is a growing body of research that indicates community involvement and service learning opportunities can have a positive effect on students who are considered at-risk. Chapter 5, Community Service and Service-Learning, details curricular components of service learning programs that are appropriate for both alternative and traditional schools.

Regardless of the type of alternative setting or option (e.g., magnet school or a school-within-a-school), articulation between faculty and staff at the alternative school and feeder/sending school needs to be coordinated so that students entering or leaving can have a smoother transition. The needs of the student should be established both at the onset of placement in an alternative school and when returning to the sending school. The principal should assemble teachers and others, such as the school nurse, social worker, psychologist, and counselor, in addition to the student and parent and/or legal guardian. These professionals will be monitoring the progress of the student. A multidisciplinary approach can better identify and meet the needs of the student and ensure a much smoother transition.

The ongoing evaluation of alternative schools and programs is an absolute requirement. Many alternative programs are funded through local, state, and federal grant money and then subsidized by the school district. Future funding often depends upon results that must indicate that needs are being met. Because no two alternative school programs or initiatives are the same, evaluation of results becomes critical to assess for effectiveness and impact on targeted populations. The evaluation process should include the stakeholders—teachers, support staff, students, parents, and anyone else who is involved with the program. Involvement in planning and evaluation reduces fear and anxiety in all parties.

ILLUSTRATIVE PRACTICES AND ISSUES

Davis, S. M. (1994). How the Gateway Program helps troubled teens. *Educational Leadership, 52*(1), 17–19.

   Davis details how he and a colleague developed an alternative school for students who were continually being suspended from school for disciplinary reasons. Although the program "emphasizes academics . . . work with students' emotional conflicts and behaviors takes priority" (p. 17). The Gateway program has an admission procedure, which ensures that students have a voice in whether they attend the school. The Gateway Program relies on the students' sending school for assignments. Gateway personnel work with sending schools when students are transitioned back. *Issues:* Articulation between sending schools and alternative placement centers in critical, but often "tangled." Children in alternative education programs should receive the same quality and quantity of lessons.

Funk, G., & Brown, D. (1996). A store front school: A grassroots approach to educational reform. *Educational Horizons, 74*(2), 89–95.

   Funk and Brown detail the development of an elementary store front school, which was funded by the school district and a university, forming a partnership. The store front School features (1) a holistic/integrated curriculum, (2) a decentralized decision-making process, (3) a strong community orientation with mandatory parental involvement, and interagency cooperation (p. 91). The store front school has become a haven that allows children who have traditionally fallen through the typical structures of schools to succeed. *Issues:* Involvement of a broadbase of the public sector in planning a school is essential. Selection criteria and mandatory parental involvement are discussed.

Meixner, C. (1994). Teaching with love at Oasis High. *Educational Leadership, 52*(1), 24–26.

   Meixner conveys the message that high school students need an environment of love in order to thrive. Oasis High serves 150 at-risk students who have not done well in regular school. The philosophy of the school is that children need adults who are willing to "involve ourselves at an emotional level to nurture and strengthen our students' growth" (p. 32). The features of Oasis High are listed. *Issues:* Affective needs of children need to be met before academics. Flexible scheduling is needed as is partnership within the community, including local universities, and an emphasis on the individual, for alternative schools and/or programs to be effective.

Oxley, D. (1994). Organizing schools into small units: Alternatives to homogeneous grouping. *Phi Delta Kappan, 75*(7), 521–526.

   Oxley profiles two schools-within-schools (smaller units)—one high school in Germany and one in Philadelphia—to illustrate the benefits of creating alternatives to children being only a number, susceptible to "falling through the cracks." Both of these schools, although a country away from one another, were able to implement "cross-disciplinary approaches . . . take collective responsibility for their students' success . [provide students with the opportunity to] . . . work together to unify instruction and allow students to exercise skills and knowledge across subjects" (p. 522). *Issues:* Departure from school norms creates friction. Barriers to reform are identified.

SUMMARY

We believe that for alternative educational programming to be successful it needs to focus systemically on changing and restructuring the very schools in which alternative educational opportunities are offered. A tall order, to be sure, but one that has great potential as is evidenced in such schools as Central Park East and other District 4 schools in New York City.

QUESTIONS FOR FURTHER CONSIDERATION

Research

1. Explore Jonathan Kozol's "Free Schools" idea from his book. Have the emergence of alternative schools and educational opportunities met this original intent?

2. Charter schools, school choice, and vouchers are much-debated topics. What does the research say about their effectiveness and/or desirability?

3. What elements would the *ideal* alternative school for "troubled" students need for success? Design your own school, using your creativity, this text, and other research to support your ideas.

4. Raywid (1994) identified eleven features that make alternative educational programs successful. Analyze one alternative school and/or program, according to the criteria on page xx of this text. Report your findings and suggestions.

Reflect

1. What is it about public schools that is insufficient?

2. How can the suggestions for "alternative schools" identified by Raywid (1994) apply to all schools?

3. Discuss this statement, "Teachers do everything out of love or fear." How are issues of control/discipline reflected in this statement?

Respond/React

1. As an administrator, how would you evaluate student achievement if assessment instruments are nontraditional in an alternative setting? How would you report this type of nontraditional data to parents, the school board, and the community?

2. As the principal of a school-within-a-school, teachers have been complaining to you that students enrolled in this type of arrangement are disrupting students in the mainstream. Moreover, a group of these teachers has written a letter to the superintendent urging her to eliminate this program. How would you handle this situation?

SUGGESTED READINGS

Chalker, C. S. (1996). *Effective alternative education programs: Best practices from planning through evaluating.* Lancaster, PA: Technomic Publishing Company.

Kellmayer, J. (1995). *How to establish an alternative school.* Thousand Oaks, CA: Corwin Press.

Kelly, D. M. (1993). *Last chance high school: How girls and boys drop in and out of alternative schools.* New Haven, CT: Yale University Press.

CHAPTER 3

BILINGUAL EDUCATION

BY HERMAN F. CURIEL, PH.D., ACSW
ASSOCIATE PROFESSOR OF SOCIAL WORK
UNIVERSITY OF OKLAHOMA

Bilingual education is commonly viewed as the use of two languages for the purpose of instruction. The following are questions that are frequently the focus of debate. Is bilingual–bicultural education an effective vehicle for limited english proficient (LEP) children to become literate in their native language? Does literacy in one language facilitate learning a second language? Is it detrimental for children to delay learning English while they master reading and writing skills in their native language? Is there educational or psychological value in linking formal school learning with home learning? What exactly is bilingual education? How does bilingual education differ from English as a Second Language (ESL) programs? These are valid and complex questions that educators, legislators, and parents pose when making decisions on how best to meet the needs of a growing number of LEP children who commence school as monolingual native speakers.

The U.S. Department of Education National Center for Education Statistics (NCES) (1996) predicts an increase of 5 percent in public elementary school enrollments from 1994 through the year 2006 due to a combination of immigration and rising birth rates that started in 1977 (NCES, 1996, p. 661). The anticipated growth of LEP children and the varied existing educational approaches used by schools to meet federal mandates (Title VII of the Elementary and Secondary Education Act, PL 90-247) pose a true challenge for both faculty and school administrators.

The goal of this chapter is to facilitate the decision making process for decision-makers by highlighting the strengths and weaknesses of the most common approaches to learning English for children who commence school as monolingual native speakers. The chapter will address numerous questions like the ones presented in the introduction. Specifically

this chapter will propose a rationale for a strengths approach to empower the learner; provide a brief history of bilingual–bicultural education in the United States; relate key legislation; discuss research issues; describe bilingual education programs by types and intended educational outcomes; relate how English as a Second Language differs from the bilingual–bicultural approach; discuss staff and personnel considerations; and end with a list of recommended considerations and suggested readings.

EMPHASIZING LEARNER STRENGTHS

The students who are the target of alternative programs such as bilingual education or English as a Second Language are considered at high risk of academic failure because they start school as monolingual speakers in a nonschool language. Teachers who teach in the various forms of bilingual education need to have a strong commitment to their profession and to their students who look up to them for approval. Teachers need to feel hopeful that their efforts are helpful. Teachers, like social workers, face similar challenges with children whose families frequently are unable to help themselves or their children because of their limited formal education and deprived environmental circumstances. Working with LEP students can be both rewarding and challenging. The author recommends that teachers adopt a strengths' perspective from the field of social work to help them in dealing with their own self-esteem and that of their students. Teachers frequently feel that their efforts are not appreciated by administrators and the general public. Teachers in bilingual education may feel personally responsible for the attacks on bilingual education that are critical of the various approaches used to teach. There are good reasons for teachers to emphasize their own strengths when they need to feel hopeful about their work. Emphasizing and incorporating the students' strengths when developing strategies for teaching is useful in several ways. First, strengths provide blocks upon which to build teaching strategies. Instead of focusing on deficits, the strengths that learners bring to the classroom, for example, their speaking knowledge of the home language, should be emphasized. Second, emphasizing the students's strengths provides the teacher with a source of positive feedback for the student. Emphasizing strengths can be used to convey the teacher's respect for students and their heritage. Third, incorporating a strengths perspective provides teachers with something concrete, the student's motivation or enthusiasm for learning, to work with and think about.

In this discussion, a student who is bilingual when starting school is not considered to be at risk of academic failure. Such students, it is assumed, have the same or better formal learning advantages than their monolingual English peer cohorts. The whole purpose of what Senator Ralph W. Yarborough, D-Texas, had in mind when he sponsored the Bilingual Education Act of 1968 (Title VII of the Elementary and Secondary Education Act) was to reduce the risk of academic failure for non-English speaking children whose parents are non-English speakers and poor. The goal of the early bilingual–bicultural program was to afford the learner a curriculum that was supportive and used the student's knowledge of home language and cultural frameworks as strengths that the learner brought to the school. The learner's native language and parents' native culture were to be used as building blocks for promoting a path to native language literacy and as a bridge for learning English. The educational rationale is that children who experience an educational approach that builds on previous home learning reinforces a learner's sense of self-respect and self-value. If a child's limited English proficiency is viewed as a problem as opposed to an asset, we accentuate the learning issue and create a web of pessimistic expectations of, and predictions about, the student, the student's academic environment, and the student's capacity to cope with that environment. Furthermore, if we, through verbal and nonverbal messages, communicate to LEP students that their lack of

fit with the school language is a problem, we alter how students view themselves and how their peers see them. In the long run, these perceptions seep into the individual's identity. A sound bilingual education program initiates formal school learning by building cognitive and psychological bridges with the learner's home learning. Literacy in the native language provides a cognitive foundation for learning English.

Cummins (1978, 1981) is probably the principal proponent of the language facilitation theory. Cummins's initial (1978) theoretical work was designed to explain the inconsistent findings in the bilingual education empirical research. Cummins (1981, 1985) posits that the mixed findings reported in the literature are explained by two factors: (1) the "threshold" hypothesis, which states that the cognitive and academic benefits of bilingualism are mediated by the levels of competence attained in the native language and the second language—specifically that there is a threshold level of linguistic competence that a bilingual child must attain to avoid cognitive disadvantages, and (2) the "developmental interdependence" hypothesis that states that the development of skills in a second language is facilitated by skills already developed in the first language. Making use of the learner's native language to facilitate reading and writing skills in the first (native) language reduces the potential for developing the long-term negative learner associations with formal school learning that often results from "sink or swim" approaches to learning to speak, read, and write English.

The ultimate goal of bilingual–bicultural programs is for the learner to master English. The process for learning English in bilingual programs is delayed until the learner has acquired a level of native language literacy that becomes the foundation for learning the English language. Approaches that honor and value the learner's home language promote psychological nurturance that is critical for success in lifelong learning. A bilingual–bicultural education approach is one way to ensure that children who commence school as monolingual non-English speakers are given an equal opportunity to succeed in school. An educational approach that initiates formal learning for the non-English–speaking child by starting and building the learning process on what the child knows, that is, his or her native speaking language, supports the kind of emphasis on learner strengths that provides both teachers and students the rays of hope that are missing in otherwise sink or swim approaches to learning English.

HISTORY

Today's debate over bilingual education was spawned, ultimately, by the old controversy about what it means to be a U.S. citizen. Since the early days of the United States, a philosophical gulf has divided cultural assimilationists and pluralists (Worsnop, 1993). The former believe that the mission of the schools is to promote a common language and common national identity. In the social science literature this perspective is frequently referred to this as the "melting pot" ideology. Assimilationists believe that the best way to accomplish national assimilation is for non-English–speaking immigrants and Native Americans to discard their language and cultural roots and adopt the majority culture and its language, English, as soon as possible. Pluralists, on the other hand, may agree that the school mission is to promote a common language and common national identity. They, however, take a position that U.S. society as a whole benefits from the cultural and language diversity these groups represent. They would argue that the development of a national identity in a democratic society is an ongoing process that permits individual groups to retain a connection with their cultural roots. They view the acculturation process in phases in which individuals may start with a native identity, progress to a bicultural identity, and move to a U.S. identity with a positive experience with the host culture. Given these different perspectives, the role of the school and its mission in the education of children from non-English–speaking homes has been a source of controversy since the beginning of the Republic. "Out of necessity, bilingualism, and even multilingualism, remained the norm in North America throughout most of the nineteenth century. Before 1800, private schools for German-English bilingual education were common in the United States, French-language schools sprang up in the Northeast, and Dutch-language schools in the middle states" (Donegan, 1996, p. 60). Additionally, there were French–English programs in Louisiana, Spanish–English pro-

grams in the territory of New Mexico, and scattered Norwegian, Czech, Italian, Polish, and Dutch programs throughout the Midwest. (Secada, 1990). Some Native American tribes were among the nation's pacesetters. Castellanos (1983) relates that the Cherokees established and operated an educational system of 21 schools and two academies, which enrolled 1,100 pupils and produced a population that was 90 percent literate in its native language. They used bilingual materials to such an extent that by 1852 Oklahoma Cherokees had a higher English literacy level than the white population of either Texas or Arkansas.

U.S. entry into World War I brought an end to bilingual education in the United States. The surviving foreign language schools, most of them German, were forced to shut down by laws either mandating English-only instruction or reserving public education funds for English-only schools. By 1923, 34 of the 48 states had adopted English-only laws (Worsnop, 1993). In 1923 the Supreme Court ruled in *Meyer v. Nebraska* that the state's interest in fostering "a homogeneous people with American ideals" is not adequate justification for outlawing foreign language instruction in the public schools. In 1927 the Supreme Court in *Farrington v. Tokushige* struck down territorial legislation in Hawaii that regulated the islands' private foreign schools (Zirkel, 1977). Notwithstanding the two United States Supreme Court restraining actions, between "World War I through the early 1950s, bilingual education lay dormant while a number of states passed laws forbidding the use of languages other than English at school. In Texas, where until the 1960s most Hispanic students attended segregated schools, it was against the law to teach the lower grades in any language but English. After integration, and until the late 1960s, many districts forbade children to speak Spanish anywhere on school property" (Donegan, 1996, p. 62).

Following World War II, in response to the sudden discovery that U.S. children had fallen behind their Russian counterparts in response to the Soviet launching of Sputnik, Congress passed the National Defense Education Act in 1958, which included funds for teaching of foreign languages. In 1963 the refugees of Fidel Castro who fled to Miami revitalized bilingual education and temporarily modified its emphasis from a transitional to a maintenance orientation largely influenced by their belief that their children would be returning to Cuba once Castro was overthrown. In 1968 Senator Ralph W. Yarborough, D-Texas, sponsored the Bilingual Education Act, which was rooted in the Civil Rights Act of 1964 and outlawed discrimination based on a student's limited ability to use English (Donegan, 1996).

In 1968 President Lyndon B. Johnson signaled the nation's first commitment to addressing the needs of non-English–speaking children by signing into law Title VII of the Elementary and Secondary Education Act: The Bilingual Education Act. Focusing primarily on children who were both poor and, because of their inability to speak English educationally disadvantaged, Title VII authorized federal funding to support educational programs and to develop necessary instructional resources (Contreras & Valverde, 1994). On January 21, 1974, the U.S. Supreme Court, in a unanimous ruling, stated in *Lau v. Nichols* that San Francisco's school district's failure to provide special educational services to non-English–speaking Chinese students violated both the equal protection clause of the Fourteenth Amendment and Title VII of the Civil Rights Act of 1964 (Birman & Gingsburg, 1983). The ruling implicitly outlawed submersion programs in which language minority children are enrolled in ordinary classrooms in which lessons are taught in English and no vehicle exists for addressing the children's difficulties.

"Funding for bilingual education fell nearly 50 percent in the 1980s. During the 1995 budget-rescission process, Congress cut $38.5 million from programs. . . . The cuts took funds from some new programs that the Improving Americas' Schools Act of 1994 created when it modified the Bilingual Education Act and the 1984 Emergency Immigrant Education Act" (Donegan, 1996, p. 64). The reduced support for bilingual education represented a new wave of anti-immigrant and xenophobia forces that is embraced by conservative groups such as the English-only movement. Donegan (1996) notes that 22 states have passed English-only laws and at least six bills have been introduced in Congress either to make English the official U.S. language or to abolish government-mandated bilingual education. Once again, history was repeated in the 9th U.S. Circuit Court of Appeals ruling on October 5, 1995, that found in *Yniguez v. Mofford* that Arizona's official English law, which required legislators, judges, and other state employees to conduct official business in English, violates the free-speech provision of the U.S. Constitution's First Amendment. In California, Proposition 187, approved by voters in 1994 and that sought to end most government services to illegal or undocumented aliens, was dealt a severe blow when a U.S. federal court ruled in 1995 that the state could not deny public education to resident children regardless of their status (Donegan, 1996).

This brief history of bilingual–bicultural education practices in the United States suggests that the controversy that surrounds bilingual education has once again polarized well-meaning lay and professional groups who disagree on how best to help children who commence school as non-English speakers. Pluralism and assimilation do not have to be opposites. To be bilingual is an appropriate outcome when diverse cultures and languages are respected and value is placed on multilingual skills. The opponents of bilingual education obviously find little merit in children becoming literate in their native language. They believe that bilingual education reinforces the child's and family's identity with their culture of origin and weakens their identity with the U.S. culture. They believe that time spent in learning a native language takes time from learning English. The controversy has intensified, in part, by court rulings that have framed the bilingual education issue as a civil rights matter. Budget cuts proposed for fiscal 1996 amplify the ill effects of the $38.5 million cut from the $195.2 million for bilingual programs in fiscal year 1995 and attest to the existing power structure of dominant forces opposed to bilingual education (Donegan, 1996).

Before we discuss the current status of bilingual and bicultural education, it is essential to define these and related concepts:

• Biculturalism is the ability to behave on occasion according to selected patterns of culture other than one's own.

- Bilingualism means, very simply, the ability to function in another language in addition to one's native language.
- Bilingual schooling means the particular organizational scheme of instruction that is used to teach courses in the native language and in another language.
- Bilingual education is the process by which the leaning experiences provided in the home and in other educational and societal institutions enables a person to achieve total self-development as well as to function in another language in addition to the native language.
- Bilingual and bicultural education is a process of total self-development by which a person learns and reinforces his or her own language and culture while at the same time acquiring the ability to function in another language and to behave on occasion according to patterns of the second culture. (Rodriguez, 1975, p. 3)

The intent of bilingual–bicultural education is to develop an educational system that will adequately develop the intellectual abilities of each child by utilizing the child's native language to enable that child to acquire proficiency in English. An original goal of bilingual and bilcultural education that receives less emphasis today is to give attention to the cultural dimensions of the child's language.

CURRENT STATUS

The Bilingual Education Act of 1968, also known as Title VII of the Elementary and Secondary Education Act of 1965 (PL 89-10), acknowledges that the educational needs of children who are LEP cannot be met effectively by traditional schooling in which English is the only medium of instruction (Padilla, 1984). This landmark legislation was revised in 1974, 1978, 1984, and 1988 and is part of the Improving America's School Act of 1994 (PL 103-382). This legislation has provided funding to state education agencies and local school districts to encourage the development and implementation of bilingual education programs designed to meet the needs of LEP students. In Section 7112 of Public Law 103-382 a statement of policy reads:

The Congress declares it to be the policy of the United States, in order to ensure equal educational opportunity for all children and youth and to promote educational excellence, to assist State and local educational agencies, institutions of higher education and community based organizations to build their capacity to establish, implement, and sustain programs of instruction for children and youth of limited English proficiency. (Sec. 7112, 108 Stat. 3719)

The reauthorized Title VII strengthens the comprehensive approach of funded programs; streamlines program definitions to enhance flexibility; strengthens the state administrative role; improves research and evaluation; and emphasizes professional development (U.S. Department of Education, 1994). The following is a summary of new provisions noted by the U.S. Department of Education:

[The new Title VII] Establishes four functional discretionary grant categories. The restructured programs are (1) three-year development and implementation grants to initiate new programs (Sec. 7112); (2) two-year enhancement grants to improve existing programs (Sec. 7113); (3) five-year comprehensive school grants to develop projects integrated with the overall school program (Sec. 7114); and (4) five-year systemwide improvement grants for districtwide projects that serve all or most LEP students. (Sec. 7115, 108 Stats. 3719-3723) Improves local program evaluations and promotes the use of appropriate assessments linked to instructional practices that build upon the strengths of linguistically and culturally diverse students to help them achieve to high standards. It supports field-initiated research, enhanced national dissemination efforts, and growth in Academic Excellence programs. (Sec. 7133, 108 Stat. 3730-3731)

Section 7133 of Public Law 103-382 describes the Academic Excellence Awards criteria:

(c) Use of Funds—Funds under this section shall be used to enhance the capacity of States and local education agencies to provide high quality academic programs for children and youth of limited English proficiency, which may include—(1) completing the development of such programs; (2) professional development of staff participating in bilingual education programs; (3) sharing strategies and materials; and (4) supporting professional networks. (Sec. 7133, 108 Stat. 3730)

Five other new provisions of note cited in the U.S. Department of Education (1994) report indicate that the new Title VII:

> Strengthens the State role by requiring State Education Agencies (SEAs) to review Title VII applications within the context of their State reform plans. The new Title VII promotes partnerships between SEAs, Local Education Agencies (LEAs), and other entities for purposes of improving design, assessment of student performance, and capacity building to meet the educational services of linguistically and culturally diverse students. (Sec. 7115, 108 Stat. 3722-3723) Redesigns and strengthens professional development programs and ensures their integration with broader school curricula and reforms to improve the knowledge base and practices of educational personnel serving linguistically and culturally diverse students. (Sec. 71442, 108 Stat. 3732-3733)
>
> Authorizes the Foreign Language Assistance Program as a discretionary grant program to help local educational agencies establish and improve foreign language instruction in elementary and secondary schools. This program aims to develop the foreign language proficiency of our students to face the challenges, as a Nation, of the increasingly competitive global economy. (Sec. 7205, 108 Stat. 3738)

Donegan (1996) suggests that this new provision may reflect the influence of a 1993 Stanford University document entitled "Blueprint for Second Generation," which endorses equal opportunity for language-minority students and the right of all U.S. students to acquire proficiency in more than one language. The language in the provision suggests market forces and corporate interests may have an equal influence in this new interest in foreign languages. The legislation authorizes the Foreign Language Assistance Program, which provides discretionary grants to help local educational agencies establish and improve foreign language instruction in elementary and secondary schools. The program aims to develop the foreign language proficiency of students in general. This may prove to be a positive turn for acceptance of bilingual education as conservative forces yield to pressure for greater ethnic pluralism in the interest of expanded world markets.

Another key provision in Title VII of the Act of 1994 is reflected in the new expanded title: "Bilingual Education, Language Enhancement, and Language Acquisition Programs." This title describes the incorporation of the Emergency Immigrant Education Act, which provides funds to assist in providing educational services in local educational agencies that experience large increases in their student enrollment due to immigration. A statement of rationale for this provision is stated in Statue 108-3739, which reads,

> in the case of *Plyer v. Doe,* the Supreme Court held that States have a responsibility under the Equal Protection Clause of the Constitution to educate all children, regardless of immigration status; and immigration policy is solely a responsibility of the Federal Government. (Section 7301, 108 Stat. 3739)

For school districts serving Native American children, Sections 7102 and 7104 describes language that addresses the special status and eligible entities for those programs serving Native American and Alaska Native children in school. Section 7102 describes the special status:

> Native Americans and Native American languages (as such terms are defined in section 103 of the Native American Languages Act), including native residents of the outlying areas, have a unique status under Federal law that requires special policies within the broad purposes of this Act to serve the education needs of language minority students in the United States. (108 Stat. 3716)

Section 7104 describes the eligible entities for funding, which may include a tribal-sanctioned educational authority, a Native Hawaiian or Native American Pacific Islander native language education organization, or an elementary or secondary school that is operated or funded by the Bureau of Indian Affairs. The Bilingual Education Act of 1994 collapsed its 1984 definition of transitional bilingual and developmental bilingual education into a single category and added a provision for special alternative instructional programs. Section 7501 of Public Law 103-382 describes the new language:

> (15) SPECIAL ALTERNATIVE INSTRUCTIONAL PROGRAM—The term "special alternative instructional program" means an educational program for limited English proficient students—(A) utilizes spe-

cially designed English curricula and services but does not use the student's native language for instructional purposes; (B) enables limited English proficient students to achieve English proficiency and academic mastery of subject matter content and higher order skills, including critical thinking so as to meet age-appropriate grade-promotion and graduation standards in concert with the National Education Goals; and (C) is particularly appropriate for schools where the diversity of the limited English proficient students' native languages and the small number of students speaking each respective language makes bilingual education impractical and where there is a critical shortage of bilingual education teachers. (108 Stat. 3748)

The transitional bilingual education provision mandating that teachers in schools that receive federal bilingual education funds "incorporate the cultural heritage of [LEP] children and other children in American society" is no longer in the language of the 1994 act. Under the 1994 provisions, bilingual education instructs LEP students in English and their native languages; is geared toward making them proficient in English while mastering subject matter at the appropriate grade level; allows for development of native or ancestral languages of LEP students along with special groups of people including Native Americans, Alaska Natives, and Native Hawaiians; and sanctions two-way bilingual programs (Crawford, 1995).

The trend in federal bilingual education legislation has evolved from simply guaranteeing equal access to public education to ensuring native-language instruction and the teaching of LEP students' cultural heritage to the approval of a wider variety of approaches. These allow for, among other things, English-only instruction, teaching LEP students in both English and their native languages, and encouraging language maintenance and bilingual learning among LEP and native-English speakers enrolled together in two-way classes (Crawford, 1995).

EVALUATION RESEARCH

The debate about the benefits of bilingual education in the United States has continued for more than two decades. During this period, the controversy has largely focused on identifying the types of programs that work best in helping LEP students to succeed in school. Research results over these two decades have increasingly supported the notion that the most effective school programs for LEP students are those that use the child's native language as well as English (Medina, 1993; Medina & Escamilla, 1994; Snow, 1992). This section will address questions that were posed in the chapter introduction. The reader is reminded that the status of empirical research in this area is problematic given the diversity or variability found in the kinds of research that are done and the lack of consistency in the implementation of program designs. In response to the first question, "Is bilingual–bicultural education an effective vehicle for LEP children to become literate in their native language?", we call attention to the primary goal of present day bilingual education in the United States. With few exceptions, existing bilingual education programs are designed to be "transitional" as opposed to "maintenance"; the goal is for children to learn English, therefore, native language literacy is not a measure given high priority in determining program outcomes.

During the 1970s and into the 1980s when there was more congressional and popular support for bilingual education, a number of programs were maintenance bilingual education programs, and therefore literacy in both languages were the focus of investigation. Studies by Medina and Escamilla (1992a; 1992b) established that MBE programs promote English language acquisition for Spanish-speaking students who begin school with limited Spanish language skills as well as for those fluent in Spanish when they enter school. Another study by Escamilla and Medina (1993) established that maintenance bilingual education programs successfully develop both Spanish and English language skills for students who begin school with limited proficiency in both languages.

Critics of bilingual education emphasize the time required to provide native language instruction in both maintenance and transitional programs and conclude that students in these programs do poorly in English tests because they spend too much time in becoming literate in the native language. They argue that learning English is determined almost entirely by the time spent studying (Porter, 1990). The implication is that some level of literacy in the first language may have been attained at the expense of learning English.

A second question, "Does literacy in one language facilitate learning a second language?", is still not certain given the mixed findings in the empirical literature; however, Cummins (1978, 1981, 1985), who uses the facilitation theory described earlier to explain mixed findings, supports the author's view and therefore would respond in the affirmative. It is true that it is easier to teach a second language to individuals who are literate in their native language. A number of studies show that children can transfer skills learned in one language to another language (Barik & Swain, 1975; Bruck, Lambert, & Tucker, 1977; Lambert & Tucker, 1972) and that older children are more "efficient" learners of languages (Ausubel, 1964; Ervin-Tripp, 1974; Ramirez & Politzer, 1978; Stern, Burstall, & Harley, 1975). Hence, when it is observed that older learners who already knew how to read in their native tongue acquired a second language faster than younger learners, some individuals have interpreted this as support for the facilitation effect (Rossell & Baker, 1996).

A third question, "Is it detrimental for children to delay learning English while they master reading and writing skills in their native language?", also is subject to debate. Critics of transitional bilingual education allege that children emerge from these programs not knowing English, while supporters claim that the alternative—all English instruction in a regular classroom—is detrimental to LEP children's intellectual development and self-esteem. A number of longitudinal studies have reported positive long-term results for LEP students enrolled in bilingual programs during elementary grades (Curiel, Rosenthal, & Richek, 1986; Leyba, 1978; Powers & Rossman, 1984; Saldate, Mishra, & Medina, 1985).

A fourth question, "Is there educational or psychological value in linking formal school learning with home learning?", is assumed to be an accepted fact that explains why children do better when parents support the school's efforts. It is assumed that school learning that is reinforced by home learning and vice versa are the key ingredients in successful learner outcomes. Section 7307 of Public Law 103-382 authorizes funds to promote family literacy, parent outreach, and training activities designed to assist parents to become more active participants in the education of their children. A fifth question, "What exactly is bilingual education?", is an important question, the answer to which seems to mean different things to different program designers. The best response for this question is to cite the language of the 1994 act, which is stated in Section 7501:

> The term "bilingual education program" means an educational program for limited English proficient students that—(A) makes instructional use of both English and a student's native language; (B) enables limited English proficient students to achieve English proficiency and academic mastery of subject matter content and higher order skills, including critical thinking, so as to meet age-appropriate grade-promotion and graduation standards in concert with the National Education Goals; (C) may also develop the native language skills of limited English proficient students, or ancestral languages of American Indians, Alaska Natives, Native Hawaiians and native residents of the outlying areas; and (D) may include the participation of English-proficient students if such program is designed to enable all enrolled students to become proficient in English and a second language. (108 Stats. 3745-3746, PL 103-382)

The final question posed in the introduction is frequently a source of confusion for both educators and the lay public. "How does a bilingual education program differ from programs referred to as English as a Second Language (ESL)?" Both programs are used to work with LEP students. Bilingual programs are typically elementary school comprehensive programs that use native language instruction. ESL is typically made up of pull-out programs that may be a component of bilingual programs and available in secondary schools too. School districts serving heterogeneous linguistic populations may elect to offer ESL instruction if there are not enough children of the same first language background enrolled to make bilingual education practical (ESL Information Packet, 1988). The teaching of English as a second language is based on the principles and methodology of foreign language teaching. Literacy in the first language is a prerequisite for learning a second language. Early bilingual education programs were mandated to include content on various cultures, which the 1994 Act omitted. In ESL programs, students receive English instruction one or two periods a day, or in some districts two or three periods a week, and concurrently participate in the regular classroom for the rest of the time. ESL is a required component of bilingual education in the United States.

The merits of bilingual education are still being debated. Rossell and Baker's (1996) extensive survey of 300 bilingual program evaluations found that only 72 (25 percent) were methodologically acceptable. Their findings indicate that on standardized achievement tests, transitional bilingual education (TBE) is better than regular classroom instruction in only 22 percent of the acceptable studies when the outcome is reading, 7 percent when the outcome is language, and 9 percent when the outcome is math. They found that structured immersion, a special program for LEP children in which the children are in a self-contained classroom composed solely of English learners and English taught at a pace LEP students can understand, to be superior.

This limited survey of the empirical literature found what other researchers consistently report, that it is almost impossible to conclude that one approach to teaching children who are LEP is superior to another due to a variety of factors, which include the variety of program interpretations, discontinuity of bilingual education programs, and problems with the research designs that make interpretation of findings problematic. Defusing the controversy surrounding bilingual education will require continued research and concrete analysis of the effectiveness of alternative teaching models to support or refute theoretical and emotional posturing (Foster, 1982).

BILINGUAL EDUCATION PROGRAMS BY TYPES AND OUTCOMES

Although bilingual education is controversial, all levels of government—federal, state, and local—have for the most part accepted it as the preferred method of instruction for LEP children. Nevertheless, researchers continue to ask whether "it works" (Rossell & Baker, 1996). The Association for Supervision and Curriculum Development noted in its 1987 report on bilingual education that it is unclear which approach is better, teaching children in their native language or in English. The primary goal of bilingual education in the United States is to teach English to LEP students.

Several approaches are used to teach LEP students; some borrow methodology from or overlap with others (Crawford, 1995). The most common bilingual education approach is TBE. The goal of this approach is to move LEP students into regular (mainstream) classes within 2 or 3 years. In transitional bilingual education, the student is taught to read and write in the native language, and subject matter also is taught in the same language. English is initially taught for only a small portion of the day. As the child progresses in English, the amount of instructional time in the native language is reduced and English is increased until the student is proficient enough in English to join the regular instructional program (Rossell & Baker, 1996). Most bilingual classes are taught using the transitional method, which does not aim to preserve or enhance students' native language while teaching them English (Crawford, 1995).

A variation of transitional bilingual education is bilingual maintenance. These programs also are referred to as developmental bilingual education. The goal of these programs is to produce students who are fluent in two languages. The most sophisticated developmental approach is called two-way bilingual education. In this approach equal numbers of LEP students and English-speaking students are instructed in one language half of the day and the second language the other half of the day. The approach aims to make both sets of students fluent in two languages. Such programs are rare, but are considered superior when compared to other approaches (Crawford, 1995). Although bilingual maintenance programs enjoy a great deal of support from the intellectual community, they are not implemented widely because they do not enjoy political support from the state and federal legislatures that fund bilingual education (Rossell & Baker, 1996).

Immersion education sits near the other end of the bilingual-teaching spectrum. In these classes, commonly known as "special alternative instructional programs", and the most popular of which is "structured immersion," instruction is in the language being learned (L2), but the teacher speaks the students' native language (L1). Teaching is geared toward the child's ability to comprehend the lessons based on clues instructors give to coax the students through their lessons. The native language is used only in the rare instances in which the student cannot complete a task without it (Rossell & Baker, 1996). Although immersion is based on instruction in the student's second language, it is not "submersion" or what is commonly known as "sink or swim," in which teachers offer no special help (Crawford, 1995).

One popular offshoot of immersion education is called "alternate immersion," also known as "sheltered English" or "sheltered subject-matter instruction." In sheltered classes, children learn their second language first by studying subjects such as math, which are less language-intensive. As they learn more English, they move to more language-intensive subjects such as social studies.

ESL, described earlier, is an alternative instructional program that is used widely because of a severe shortage of qualified bilingual teachers. ESL is a pull-out program typically based on a special curriculum for teaching English to LEP children. The students attend one or two periods a day, or in some districts two or three periods a week, while they attend simultaneously regular classes. Instructors do not have to speak the child's language (Rossell & Baker, 1996). ESL is frequently a component of transitional bilingual programs.

In the school year 1993 to 1994, the National Center for Education Statistics of the U.S. Department of Education (1996) reported a 3.03 percent enrollment in bilingual classes and 3.97 percent in ESL classes for a total public school enrollment of 41,621,660. The National Association for Bilingual Education (1996) reports that bilingual education is used to instruct only about one in four LEP students. ESL is used to teach just less than half of LEP students. Over a quarter of LEP students do not receive services to teach them English or assistance to help them understand what is being taught to them. Also, according to the National Center (1996), 60 percent of the 1991 to 1992 state and locally funded programs with LEP students were labeled *bilingual education.* Thus, nominally, Rossell and Baker (1996) suggest that TBE appears to be the dominant special language instructional program in the United States. However, based on their on-site program observations, only Spanish-speaking children and Creole-speaking Haitian children were learning to read and write in their native languages.

This survey of the bilingual education literature indicates that there are a variety of approaches used to teach LEP students and that some borrow methodology from or overlap with others. The reauthorized 1994 Bilingual Education Act sanctions a wider variety of approaches that allow for more creativity and also can be a means to undermine the traditional approaches. This wider latitude of potential programs for addressing the needs of LEP children will present true challenges for future teachers, administrators, and investigators.

PROFESSIONAL STANDARDS FOR PREPARATION OF BILINGUAL/ MULTICULTURAL TEACHERS

Standard Three in Professional Standards for the Preparation of Multicultural Teachers, National Association for Bilingual Education (1996), describes the coursework that should be offered to ensure professional competence. Such preparation includes the following:

1. Pre-professional academic preparation
2. History and foundations of education with an emphasis in bilingual–multicultural education
3. Curriculum development, including the need to adapt and revise curriculum for diverse populations
4. Classroom management and instructional methods and techniques with a focus on methods and materials for bilingual/ESL classrooms
5. Assessment
6. Theories and application of second language teaching
7. Linguistic and cultural issues related to language-minority students in the United States

CONTEMPORARY ISSUES

Personnel who work with young children regardless of educational level or age of children must share basic philosophies about how young children develop. They must understand and be able to articulate how young children's vulnerabilities affect the nature and content of pedagogy. There must be congruence in their attitudes and values on the roles that expectation and motivation play in learning. They must share an understanding of the role of the teacher and the parent in the educational process. Personnel who work with LEP students need to communicate in verbal and nonverbal messages to all children, but in particular to LEP children, positive regard for their personhood and acceptance of their language difference. The ideal teacher or teacher aide is one who loves children and is enthusiastic about teaching encounters. In many schools teachers work closely with teacher aides who have native language skills that the teacher may not have. The roles of these two teaching partners should be characterized by mutual respect and appreciation for what each contributes to the teaching partnership. It is not uncommon for teachers who have invested many years of study and time in acquiring an education to feel threatened by the teacher aide or paraprofessional who lacks formal education, but who has the students' native language skills. The teacher may fear that the teacher aide will undermine the teacher's position. A secure teacher does not have to have such fears and welcomes the opportunity to learn from the teacher aide. Children can sense when there is a teacher–aide power conflict. It is unfair for children to be placed in the middle of a power struggle between two adults to whom they look up. The teacher has the authority and responsibility for resolving team member conflicts. In the context of a strengths perspective, both the teacher and teacher aide are team members and colleagues who share a common goal—to help students learn. They need to coordinate the different skills that they bring to their partnership so that they become an effective pair for teaching LEP students.

To encourage more positive working relationships with colleagues and students, three personal qualities commonly used by social workers, counselors, psychologist, psychiatrists, and members of the clergy should be developed. The three specific relationship-enhancing traits or qualities are warmth, empathy, and genuineness. It is assumed that those who practice these traits will experience more satisfying personal and professional relationships. The remainder of the discussion will focus on how to enhance teacher–student relationships.

Displaying warmth involves conveying a feeling of interest, concern, well-being, and affection for the student. Warmth can be communicated to the student both verbally and nonverbally. Warmth promotes a sense of comfort and well-being in both the student and the teacher. Empathy is the second trait that has been found to be an essential dimension of relationship building between helpers and helpees. Empathy, in therapeutic encounters, involves being in tune with how the helpee, or recipient of help, feels and requires that the caretaker convey to the recipient that the helpee's situation is understood (Hepworth & Larsen, 1987). In the context of teacher–LEP student relationships, the teacher may convey in both verbal and nonverbal ways an understanding of how the student may feel torn between what is being taught in school and how this is different from what is being learned at home. All that is required in practicing this trait is for the teacher to understand the student's situation. In social work this skill means being able to mentally visualize how it must be to walk in that other person's shoes.

The third trait used in therapeutic encounters to enhance relationships is genuineness. This means being authentic or real. This involves the sharing of self by relating in a natural, sincere, spontaneous, open, and genuine manner (Hepworth & Larsen, 1987, p. 998). Genuineness, in the context of teacher–student relationships, simply means that teachers continue to be themselves despite their teaching roles. Teachers are individuals who have unique and definitive qualities and attributes. We would hope that this would include an appreciation and respect for their own cultural heritage and that of their students.

ILLUSTRATIVE PRACTICES AND ISSUES

D'Angelo, D. A., & Adler, C. R. (1991). Chapter 1: A catalyst for improving parent involvement. *Phi Delta Kappan, 72,* 350–354.

> D'Angelo and Alder highlight communication barriers that often interfere with parents being involved with their child's life in school, and then shift to Chapter 1 regulations and the Hawkins-Stafford School Improvement Amendments of 1988 that require schools to "broaden the definition of parent involvement to promote more comprehensive programs" (p. 350). The Chapter 1 parental involvement programs highlighted ". . . fall into three main categories: face-to-face, technological, and written communication" (pp. 350–351). This article provides ideas on how to effectively remove

a barrier to communication with parents who speak a language other than English. All ideas presented can be replicated, although, D'Angelo and Adler emphasize that "each school has its own set of values that need to be responsive to the culture, to the qualities, characteristics, and needs of the parents" (p. 350). *Issues:* School personnel need to be trained in "cultural sensitivity" when communicating with the parents of Chapter 1 students. Ongoing evaluation of efforts and the results of efforts is critical to the success of parental involvement on behalf of the parents of Chapter 1 students.

James, D. C. S. (1997). Coping with a new society: The unique psychosocial problems of immigrant youth. *Journal of School Health, 67*(3), 98–102.

Although James does not describe any particular bilingual programs, she does discuss the unique needs of immigrant children and adolescents. James also provides insights on adjustments to (1) the mainstream society, (2) home and family life, and (3) school. James provides a solid discussion about the services within schools that are needed to assist immigrant children: culturally appropriate counseling, health services, and psychological and social work services. *Issues:* Factors that affect immigrant children and adolescents from being successful in school. The personnel needed to work with immigrant children are described. Building resilience in immigrant children and adolescents is discussed.

SUMMARY

We have indicated that the teacher is a very important person in a student's life. Teaching variables that we have suggested affect LEP student outcomes include the type of bilingual education program the student experiences, personal characteristics such as attitudes of both the student and the teacher, the teacher's teaching experience, the teacher's relationship with the teacher aide, teacher authenticity, teacher knowledge of subject matter, and measures of self-esteem of both teacher and student.

Dewey (1916), our most heuristic educational philosopher, advised, "We must continuously add meaning to one's experiences and use these experiences to direct subsequent experience" (p. 377). Growth, for John Dewey, meant beginning with the present experience and adding meaning to it. He spoke of culture as traits that a person cultivated; it represented a person's capacity to constantly expand the range and accuracy of their perceptions of human behavior and its meanings. Certainly, this is a constant challenge for bilingual education teachers.

QUESTIONS FOR FURTHER CONSIDERATION

Research

1. What are some strategies you can use in your school to build self-esteem in your LEP students? Develop a staff development program to sensitize adults who work with LEP students in your building.

2. What is behind the "English-Only Movement?" Whom would the movement benefit and why?

Reflect

1. Explain how you could help develop a bilingual–bicultural program in your school. What are the roadblocks?

2. How would you assess whether a teacher's personal philosophy about learning was negatively affecting that teacher's ability to offer developmentally appropriate instruction for bilingual students?

Respond/React

1. How would you deal with individuals or groups who believe that families of LEP students do not care or are somehow inferior?

2. Should the U.S. make English our official language? Why or why not?

SUGGESTED READINGS

Holt, D. et al. (1992). *Cooperative learning in the secondary school: Maximizing language acquisition, academic achievement, and social development.* Washington, DC: NCBE Publications.

Zehler, A. M. (1994). *Working with English language learners: Strategies for elementary and middle school teachers.* Washington, DC: NCBE Publications.

CHAPTER 4

CHILD CARE

Child care means, as a minimum, taking care of children. The phrase is misleading, however, because it implies that children can be cared for in a physical way that is somehow separate from and unrelated to an education. Such care is not possible. There always are educational effects on young children, wherever, whenever, and however they are cared for. The difference, typically, is between planned and unplanned educational effects. The separation of child care from early childhood education is artificial, and we regret that we appear to also see them as separate and distinct. We address early childhood education in Chapter 6 and devote more attention to history and guidelines for developmentally appropriate practices there. This chapter is a separate topic only because we can devote more attention to child care for those school-age children who are also known as "latchkey" children.

HISTORY

Child care for school-age children began with the advent of World War II, during which many women with school-age children went to work in defense-related industries (RMC Research Corporation, 1993). Federal funds were provided to public schools to provide extended day care for school-age children. During the war years (1941–1945),

> some 95 percent of all day care centers were under the auspices of the Federal Office of Education, and most of the school-age programs were located in the new schools built in the 1930s by the Works Project Administration. (RMC Research Corporation, 1993, p. 2)

When the war ended in 1945, so did the vast majority of such programs. Interest in providing care for school-age children did not resurface until the 1970s.

A number of demographic facts account for the relatively recent emergence of the need for school-age child care. Increasing rates of divorce, teen pregnancy, single parenthood, and both parents working full time have created an increasing need for care of school-age children. A host of explanations have been put forth detailing how and why these changes occurred. Suffice it here to simply acknowledge that by the 1970s and 1980s more young children than ever before needed care, and school-age children were among them.

CURRENT STATUS

Caring for school-age children can take a variety of forms. There can be before- and after-school programs that include breakfast and snacks, programs that provide help with school work through the use of tutors, and less formalized systems that provide only recreation and games. The most conceptually complete arrangement for school-age child care is Zigler's School of the 21st Century (Zigler, Finn-Stevenson, & Marsland, 1995).

> The School of the 21st Century is a school-based/ school-linked family support program designed to promote children's optimal development by providing high quality child day care and support services to children from birth through age 12. At its core are two child care components: before- and after-school and vacation care for school-age children and full-day child care for three-to-five-year old children. (p. 1302)

Another feature of the school is that "the child day care components operate year-round, including holidays, snow days, school vacations, and inservice days when schools are not in session" (p. 1302). The School of the 21st Century is of the genre called full-service schools, wherein a variety of social, health, and educational services are provided for the children and their families. (See, for example, Dryfoos, 1994.)

As of late 1995 there were over 300 21st Century schools located in 14 states. The nature of these schools and further elaboration of the conceptual model are described by Zigler and colleagues (1995).

Essentially, according to Zigler and colleagues, there are four systems that have an impact on children's development: the family, the child day care environment, the school, and health care services. These systems may or may not be formally interrelated. The primary purpose of the School of the 21st Century is to serve as the hub for these services to ensure that they are connected formally and that they are providing optimal benefit for the children.

As a conceptual model, the School of the 21st Century (hereinafter, simply, the School) is adaptable to different community settings. For example, if a community has an adequate number of high-quality child day care facilities (a rather rare condition, to be sure), the School would serve as a referral agency when parents needing such care made inquiries. The more likely scenario, however, would be discovering, through a needs assessment, a shortage of such child day care centers. In this case, the school could provide the care or provide professional development training to existing child care staff so they would provide care. In either event, whether providing the care or the training, the School would be addressing an important need for young children—at least down to age 3. For infants, and for prenatal care as well, the School would arrange for home visits to assist parents or parents-to-be by providing them with information about child development and parenting skills. It is important to note that all of the parent and family involvement is of a voluntary nature. In no way is the School, or any other early childhood education endeavor for that matter, intended to encroach upon the sanctity of the family. Home visits are by invitation only.

The volunteer aspect of home visits or any kind of family service is but one of six guiding principles for the School. Another of the guiding principles is "universal access to high-quality child day care . . .

based on a parental fee for services, with a sliding scale and subsidies built in to ensure access by middle- and low-income families" (p. 1309).

The nature of the child care is another principle. All aspects of development—social, cognitive, physical, and emotional—will be addressed, but particular attention for the 3- to 5-year-olds will be on social and emotional development. These preschool-age children will be engaged primarily in play and social interaction. School-age children, however, will have a program that "provides children with experiences that are qualitatively different from the academic day, such as physical activities, organized recreation, or quiet times to relax" (p. 1310).

Providing professional development for child day care workers, whether they be employed by the school or within another setting, is another guiding principle. The School could initiate career ladders, provide salary and other benefits, establish a professional lending library, and in many other ways provide support for child day care workers, whether they be at the school or at a different site.

Another guiding principle is promoting and encouraging parental involvement. Citing evidence from Head Start studies, Zigler and colleagues claim that the School must respond to families' needs, and the best assurance that those needs will be articulated and responded to is to have parents involved in the planning of programs.

The last guiding principle is that there must be integration with the community. The social, political, and economic aspects of the community must be harnessed to provide or coordinate all the services that could help families. The assumption is simply that the public school is the most easily accessible institution to provide the integration.

The technical assistance available for the schools or school districts wishing to implement at least a version of the model, i.e., for the School of the 21st Century, is housed at the Bush Center in Child Development and Social Policy at Yale University in New Haven, Connecticut. Interested parties are required to write to the center to demonstrate their commitment to the six guiding principles previously discussed. Such correspondence is responded to with visits to estimate the school's or district's capacity and commitment to implement the model or an appropriate version thereof.

Preliminary evaluations of schools that have adapted the model indicate the following benefits:

- Reductions in the number of hours children remain unsupervised
- Increased consistency of care
- Reductions in the number of different child day care arrangements that children must tolerate
- Reductions in children's risk of developing behavioral problems
- Reduced absenteeism
- Reduced risk, over time, for the need for special services
- Enhanced school readiness
- Reduced parental guilt and stress
- Increased parental satisfaction with the public school
- Increased availability of affordable child day care
- Improved family child care (Zigler et al., 1995, p. 1321)

The School of the 21st Century appears to hold much promise for fulfilling two of the eight goals in *Goals 2000: Educate America Act*—the first goal that speaks to children being ready for school and the eighth goal that addresses parental involvement. The majority of before- and after-school programs for school-age children, however, are not as close to a full-service school as the School of the 21st Century. A review of typical before- and after-school programs appears below.

In 1991 the RMC Research Corporation initiated a study of before- and after-school programs for the U.S. Department of Education. Using an elaborate sampling and selection technique, RMC gathered data from before- and after-school programs from all regions of the United States. Thirty-five states and the District of Columbia were involved in the study. Site visits by a team of trained researchers were conducted at 12 settings in three different regions of the country. The study also included phone call surveys to collect data from 1300 sites that provided before- and after-school care. The study appeared to be comprehensive and thorough and yielded what should be reliable information on the state of the practice of providing such care.

The specific definition of before- and after-school care the RMC study used was:

formal, institutional programs that provide before- and/or after-school care within the age range 5 through 13 (i.e., enrolled in kindergarten through eighth grade) for at least two hours per day, four days per week. (p. 16)

The sample, then, included licensed school-age child care programs, public school-based programs, church-operated programs, programs operated by private schools, and programs operated by youth organizations. Home-based programs and those offered by family day care providers, or group day care homes were excluded. Also excluded were any drop-in–only arrangements as well as individually arranged instances of music lessons, scout meetings, or the like. The results from the study of all the facilities will be followed by the findings related to only the school-based sites. (About 35 percent of the children enrolled in such programs were at school-based sites.)

Overall, in 1993 the study found the following:

- An estimated 1.7 million children in kindergarten through eighth grade were regularly enrolled in before- and after-school programs.
- About 85 percent of these enrollments were children from prekindergarten age through grade 3.
- The average program enrolled 23 children in before-school programs and 35 in after-school sessions.
- Before- and after-school programs are underutilized nationally—enrollments average only 59 percent of capacity in programs that are licensed, with one-third of the programs overall operating at 75 percent or more of their licensed capacity. (pp. 15–16)

The last finding, the underutilization of program space, is a curiosity, given the fact that the National Child Care Survey 1990 (Hofferth, Brayfield, Deich, & Holcomb, 1991) found that care arrangements for school-age children (ages 5 to 12) in families where the mother was employed outside the home were care by relatives (25 percent); centers (14 percent); family day care (7 percent); in-home care (3 percent); and no arrangement (44 percent). At least five reasons may explain underutilization (RMC Research Corporation, 1993).

Licensed care facilities are inspected for a variety of qualities, not the least of which is physical space. If, for example, a school houses its program in the gymnasium with access to a playground, the site could be licensed for a relatively large number of children, assuming certain children-to-staff ratios would be maintained. Administrators of programs may prefer to cap enrollments to achieve an optimum size rather than a maximum one.

RMC found that only 12 percent of all the children enrolled were from families receiving public assistance and that 21 percent in the public school-based programs were receiving free or reduced lunches. The cost of transportation also could be an inhibiting factor for enrollment. Especially in districts where bussing of children is routine, before- and after-school programs may literally be out of reach for some families.

Another possible barrier to participation may be not knowing that such programs are available. Little evidence was found that existing programs do very much advertising. In addition, it must be noted that parents of children 5 to 12 may simply not consider formal programs important. (This last point, of course, flies in the face of most national surveys.)

The vast majority of children (about 84 percent) enrolled in after-school programs were prekindergarten through third grade. Seventy percent were kindergarten through third grade. Only about 9 percent of the children were in fourth grade or above.

Gender proportions were equal in programs and other demographics included the following: 68 percent European American; 19 percent African American; 8 percent Hispanic American; and 6 percent Asian American, Pacific Islander, Native American, or other. About half of the publicly sponsored programs served children primarily from low-income families.

Most programs were nonprofit (about 66 percent). Only 18 percent of all programs were sponsored by public schools. (Some public school sites were actually sponsored by another agency.)

The average program operated almost two hours in the morning and a little more than three hours after school. The average hourly fee for combined before- and afterschool sessions was $1.77. Overall, 86 percent of the parents paid the full fee for enrolling their children, but over half of the publicly sponsored programs and over a third of the private nonprofit programs indicated a willingness to adjust fees according to family income.

Nearly all (84 percent) of the programs were regulated or licensed by a child care licensing agency or approved by a state department of education. Included in these were 23 percent that were accredited by a state or national accrediting agency.

Two thirds (66 percent) of all programs for children age 5 to 12 were either public or private nonprofit organizations. The 34 percent remainder were typically for-profit national chains and proprietary schools.

Among all the programs only 7 percent reported any kind of formal "partnership arrangement in which other organizations play a key role in maintaining the program" (RMC Research Corporation, p. 41). Public school sponsored programs were more likely to be engaged in partnerships, but the rate was only 14 percent.

Overall, 82 percent of the programs operated full days during the summer. Only 62 percent of the public school–based programs operated in the summer; 62 percent were open on school holidays; 65 percent on school vacations; and 46 percent on snow days.

Providing adult supervision and a safe environment was the overarching purpose of virtually all programs. The most frequently available activities for children were socializing (97 percent of programs); free time (95 percent); board or card games (89 percent); reading (86 percent); time for homework (81 percent); physically active play (81 percent); block building (80 percent); and creative arts and crafts (61 percent). "More than half of the programs never offer computer games, television viewing, or formal counseling/therapy as activities" (p. 63).

Parent involvement in programs took several forms. Over 60 percent of programs used parents at least occasionally as volunteers. Thirty-six percent of all programs included parents on advisory boards, but nonprofit programs were three times as likely to have such parental input as were for-profit programs.

Public School Programs

In 1991 over 600,000 children in grades K through 8 were enrolled in 13,500 before- and after-school programs based in public school facilities. These numbers correspond to 35 percent of all children served and 28 percent of all existing programs. Thus, it is almost as likely that another nonprofit private organization or nonprofit private social-service/youth serving agency will sponsor a school-based program as it would be for the school to sponsor it. Other organizations that based their programs in public schools include for-profit organizations (11 percent); state, county, or local governments (12 percent); nonprofit private schools (6 percent); and church or religious groups (2 percent).

Regardless of the sponsor, public school–based programs typically had the following characteristics:

- Three-fourths enrolled by children in grades K–3; 17 to 22 percent were in grades 4–7; and less than 5 percent were in prekindergarten or grade 8 or higher.
- About 17 percent operated as some sort of partnership arrangement.
- More than half offered both before- and after-school sessions. Few operate after 6 P.M. or on weekends.
- About 80 percent of parents of enrolled children paid full fees.
- The primary space used included cafeterias and lunchrooms, classrooms, and gymnasiums, with three-fourths also having at least weekly access to a playground or park.
- Over half (58 percent) experienced staff turnover in the past year.
- Three fourths report that parents participated in program planning or evaluation activities. (pp. 111–112)

And finally, public school–based programs that are sponsored by the public schools had the following characteristics:

- They enrolled more in before-school programs (average of 33 versus 19 that are school-based but sponsored by another organization).
- They enrolled an average of 50 in after-school programs, compared with an average of 36 in the others.
- They were less likely to offer care during the summer (53 percent versus 69 percent); school holidays (54 percent versus 67 percent); school vacations (56 percent versus 69 percent); or on teacher in-service days (70 percent versus 82 percent).

- They were less likely to offer movement and dance (61 percent versus 78 percent) at least weekly and more likely to offer dramatic play (61 percent versus 50 percent), tutoring (53 percent versus 38 percent), videos/movies (41 percent versus 29 percent), or computer games (39 percent versus 29 percent) at least weekly.
- They were more likely to make special provisions for older children (76 percent versus 59 percent).
- They were more likely to have a higher child-to-staff ratio (averaging 14.2 to 1 versus 10.5 to 1). (pp. 112–113)

In addition to compiling all of the quantitative descriptors of programs listed above, and more, RMC addressed a variety of other attributes of school-based programs.

The administrative structure may be headed by the school principal or a program manager or supervisor who is a school district employee. The manager may even be from another agency. In some instances, the manager was supervised by the principal and in other cases, the manager was supervised by another administrator.

Resources also were shared in a variety of ways. At some sites an office and multipurpose room might be dedicated to the program, and in others, the school's facilities may be jealously guarded by the school principal.

The RMC study utilized a specially adapted version of an observation tool developed by the School-Age Child Care Project at Wellesley College. The instrument—Assessing School-Age Child Care Quality—guides the observer through four areas and has specific standards for each. The areas and standards are listed below:

1. Safety, Health, and Nutrition
   a. *Safety and health.* The program takes all possible steps to protect the safety and health of the children.
   b. *Nutrition.* Snacks and meals are nutritious.
2. Human Relationships
   a. *Staff–child interactions.* Staff are warm and respectful with children as they guide children to make friends and trust others.

b. *Ratio and group sizes.* These are small enough so that staff can meet the needs of children.

c. *Child–child interactions.* Children interact with each other in a positive way.

d. *Staff–parent interactions.* Staff and parents work as a team by communicating frequently, setting goals, and solving problems.

e. *Staff–staff interactions.* Staff support each other and work together as a team to meet the needs of children.

3. Space

a. *Indoor space.* Space is cozy, adequate in size, clean, and well organized.

b. *Outdoor space.* Space is safe, adequate in size, and provides a choice of activities.

4. Activities and Time

a. *Materials, supplies, and equipment.* These are interesting to children of all ages.

b. *Scheduling.* The daily schedule is flexible and reflects the individual and developmental needs of children.

c. *Choices.* Children of all ages are free to make choices about activities and friends.

d. *Learning.* The program includes things to do that are fun, educational, and enriching.

e. *Programming for all ages.* The program activities reflect the fact that children's needs, interests, and abilities change with age. (pp. 133–134)

In an effort to determine the benefits, if any, associated with low-income children's involvement in formal after-school programs, Posner and Vandell (1994) studied a sample of 216 third-grade children in Milwaukee. The children were in one of four groups: a formal after-school program; mother care; informal adult supervision; and self-care.

Great care was taken to account for family environments that might affect selection decisions. Because self-selection into programs rules out random assignment to different groups, researchers need to compare members of groups on those variables that could have an effect on their decisions. Posner and Vandell found a few differences associated with choice of after school activity but, more importantly, found "extensive positive effects for low-income children who attended formal after-school programs" (p. 454).

The positive outcomes included "better grades and conduct in school, as well as better peer relations and emotional adjustment" (p. 454). In addition, they found that those who participated in formal after-school programs would spend more time with academic activities and other learning opportunities and have more time in supervised activities with adults and peers when compared with children in other care arrangements.

One of the care arrangements included in the Posner and Vandell study was self-care. Despite the relatively small number in this subgroup (n = 15), the researchers found important associations. Children in self-care were found to spend "more time watching television after school and less time under adult supervision than children in other arrangements" (p. 454). The association with lack of adult supervision that stood out in this study was antisocial behavior. Although self-care arrangements usually meant these children were at home, watching television; those in the group called "informal adult supervision" (n = 46) often had as little adult supervision as those in self-care.

The researchers concluded that

the results of the current study suggest that formal after-school programs are one way to alleviate some of the negative effects of urban poverty on children. The after-school programs provided children with experiences and activities that enhanced their development. (p. 455)

The researchers note that their findings are consistent with the notion that after-school programs have a great potential for protecting children in high-risk environments (Posner & Vandell, 1994).

CONTEMPORARY ISSUES

Several issues were identified by the RMC researchers (1993) in their Department of Education report, and because their study was so comprehensive we believe the issues are especially credible. The degree to which they apply to any particular local setting, however, is a function of the specific characteristics of that setting.

The issues, though credible generally, ultimately must be examined with regard to a specific setting.

One issue is the lack of collaboration among organizations and agencies that ostensibly exist to serve children and families. Perhaps for-profit organizations can be forgiven because of their self-interests, but non-profit agencies would seem to have little to lose and much to gain by collaborating with others in providing services. Public schools, for instance, reported partnership arrangements at a level of only 17 percent. It may be that school personnel have a much too narrow vision of what schools are for.

Costs are an issue as well. The RMC researchers found that 86 percent of families pay full fees and that these fees were the largest source of income for 83 percent of the programs. Some kind of subsidy should be provided to make before- and after-school programs more affordable for low-income families. The effect of program costs, both for parents and programs, are the levels of salaries paid to program staff. On average, the hourly rate was $6.77 for senior staff (other than directors), and this was lower than the average hourly wage for preschool workers! The salary issue, as might be expected, is a factor in the issue of staff turnover.

The RMC researchers found that 58 percent of all programs reported an average staff turnover rate of 60 percent. Program stability and continuity are seriously threatened when administrators and others spend too much time in orienting new staff to the program. Again, some form of subsidy would address this nearly universal aspect of child care for all ages of children.

Finally, and this is an important caution for school-based programs, the after- school activities should not simply be an extension of the school day, that is, the children should be experiencing a qualitatively different environment. Certainly, adult supervision is a critical factor in such programs but, and this is especially true for older children in these programs, the children should have latitude regarding decisions about what they do and with whom. A variety of possible activities related to the age range of participants should be available for students who can then choose from activities that can entertain and enrich.

ILLUSTRATIVE PRACTICES AND ISSUES

Schoen, T. M., Arien, J., & Arvanitis, M. A. (1997). Children blossom in a special and general education integration program: A private child care center and a public school collaborate. *Young Children, 52*(2), 58–63.

> A public school and private care center find ways to include children with special needs. *Issues:* Learning how to collaborate is important for public school administrators and private child care center managers if children are to benefit.

Webb, C. N. (1997). Working with parents from cradle to preschool: A university collaborates with an urban public school. *Young Children, 52*(4), 15–19.

> This article describes efforts (and successes) in involving parents in their children's school. *Issues:* Recruiting and retaining parents and families are discussed.

SUMMARY

Child care is the rubric under which before- and after-school care falls. The implication, unfortunately, is that care does not include education. Clearly, it does. Therefore, the before- and after-school programs need to be developmentally appropriate and all that that means is discussed in Chapter 6.

The need for before- and after-school programs intensified in the 1970s and 1980s because of the country's changing demographics. The slight blip in the history of schooling when the federal government subsidized such care during World War II is all but forgotten now.

Reforming the vision of schools to be much more comprehensive and "full service" has been the most recent innovation that attempts to address the current needs. These new models promise to provide a variety of services, or at least coordinate them, to assist families in their education and health care concerns.

The current scene suggests that the overall need is beginning to be met, but there is still a long way to go. The greatest disappointment is within the public school sector; in many ways the closest, most logical facility to provide before- and after-school care, but seemingly quite resistant. Costs are a factor, to be sure, and that affects the larger social order in terms of taxes and other sources of revenue to subsidize efforts to provide these services.

Research, in addition to common sense, strongly suggests that young children need supervision when school is out. To disregard the increasing needs appears to us to be an action the school community takes at its own peril.

QUESTIONS FOR FURTHER CONSIDERATION

Research

1. Investigate countries that have a federal system for child care. What are some of the strengths? Limitations? In your opinion, should the U.S. government create a system of child care?

2. Locate a copy of child care standards from your state department. Visit a privately owned day care center. What are the indications that the standards are in place and being met?

3. Using the child care standards that emerged from the RMC study, compare and contrast two child care programs in your area. How do these child care centers live up to the standards? What improvements could be made?

Reflect

1. How can the strengths of the community be used to create better child care programs?

2. What are the likely causes of staff turnover in child care settings?

Respond/React

1. Should public schools provide day care within schools so that young mothers can finish their high school education?

2. Are child care and baby-sitting the same? Defend your answer.

SUGGESTED READINGS

Caldwell, B. M. (1991). Continuity in the early years: Transitions between grades and systems. In S. L. Kagan (Ed.), *The care and education of America's young children: Obstacles and opportunities* (pp. 69–90). Chicago: The National Society for the Study of Education.

RMC Research Corporation (1993). *National study of before & after school programs: Final report.* Washington, DC: U.S. Department of Education.

Zigler, E. F., Finn-Stevenson, M., & Marsland, K. W. (1995, November/December). Child day care in the schools: The school of the 21st century. *Child Welfare: Journal of Policy, Practice, and Program, 74*(6) 1301–1326.

CHAPTER 5

COMMUNITY SERVICE
AND SERVICE-LEARNING

Community service initiatives are increasing in K–12 schools across the nation. Zinser (1993) reports that, "More than a million high school students are participating in a variety of community service programs through their schools" (p. 30). Community service has been linked historically as a way of "doing good deeds" for those who need assistance. Throughout its history, community service has been viewed as altruistic and democratic. Community service in schools is now beginning to evolve as a curriculum, an extension of a curriculum, and as an add-on to the curricular program. Some community service programs are voluntary; others are mandatory and tied to graduation requirements. In a few states, community service is legislated. There are staunch supporters for the volunteerism connected to community service and, likewise, there are opponents who believe community service is even unconstitutional.

Although community service is more prevalent in high schools, formalized programs can be found in elementary and middle schools. Community service programs take many different forms, and there is no uniform curriculum. Some community service initiatives are tied to the school's formalized curriculum through coursework. When community service is directly tied to a curriculum, then it is referred to as service-learning. Other community service initiatives are subsumed within the school activities program. And yet other community service initiatives are linked to clubs and other community organizations such as churches and youth groups.

The basic premise behind community service is to provide opportunities for students to expand their learning experiences beyond the perimeter of the school so that they can "make the connection between knowing and doing" (Nebgen & McPherson, 1990,

p. 94) while at the same time giving something back to the community. Conversely, "Service learning is a teaching/learning method that connects meaningful community service experiences with academic learning, personal growth, and civic responsibility" (National Dropout Prevention Center, 1995, p. 1).

HISTORY

Community service has had a long but sporadic history up until the late 1980s to the present. Kinsley and McPherson (1995) report that reference to community service can be found in the work of Alexis de Tocqueville (1830) who wrote *Democracy in America* and coined the term *habits of the heart* through his descriptions of "the civic and social support citizens gave to their young nation" (p. 2). "The term 'habits of the heart' has been revived in the past decade to help refocus our thinking and to remind us that a fundamental and natural part of democracy is based on people helping and caring for one another" (Kinsley & McPherson, 1995, p. 2).

Four U.S. presidents—Franklin Roosevelt, John Kennedy, George Bush, and Bill Clinton—influenced the development of community service. In addition to the work of these presidents and their initiatives, community service also can be traced to John Dewey's *Experience and Education* (1936).

In addition, community service can be traced to the Great Depression and Roosevelt's creation of the Civilian Conservation Corps, the Public Works Administration, and the National Youth Administration. Bhaerman, Cordell, and Gomez (1995) reported that during the Depression and as a result of Roosevelt's efforts "Thousands of unemployed young people found work as well as a sense of well being" (p. 2). It is perhaps the sense of well-being and productivity that has, coupled with the progressive push for experiences beyond the classroom, sustained the community service movement to the present day.

Dewey's contribution to community service can be found within the pages of *Experience and Education*. Dewey believed that experiences, past and present, had a relationship to present and future learning: "every experience lives on in further experiences" (p. 27). Dewey called for a "coherent theory of experience" that could give "positive direction to selection and organization of appropriate educational methods and materials . . ." (p. 30). Conrad and Hedin (1991) indicated that Dewey's work did not necessarily advocate "service as an educational method as his ideas on how learning takes place and for what purpose suggest the possibility of stimulating academic and social development through actions directed toward the welfare of others" (p. 744). Dewey also believed that education was a social process and that "through education the individual had his or her capacities freed so as to achieve social aims" (Ornstein & Hunkins, 1988, p. 178).

Dewey's contribution was his unyielding call for experience. In community service models and programs (regardless of how organized) experience is the major component of learning that is strengthened by activities prior to, during, and after the experience.

Experience as a part of the educative process was part of the progressive movement. The progressive, William Kilpatrick, developed the project method that is thought to be the first foothold in combining community service as part of a formalized curriculum in schools. Projects could range "from school classroom projects to community projects" (Ornstein & Hunkins, 1988, p. 178). Kilpatrick's belief was that experience had to have " 'social purpose' whereas the experience-centered curriculum had only 'child purpose' " (Ornstein & Hunkins, 1988, p. 178).

Little activity in community service and volunteerism occurred in the 1940s. Conrad and Hedin (1991) report that the Citizenship Education Project was developed by Columbia University's Teachers College in the 1950s. The Citizenship Education Project "stressed participation and direct community involvement" (p. 744). Through this project and its "Brown Box" kit, "hundreds of detailed guides to social investigation and social/political action" (Conrad & Hedin, 1991, p. 744) were distributed to teachers.

Community service and experience drifted without much enthusiasm until the 1960s and 1970s. The idealism that followed the turbulent era of the 1960s was due, in part, to the efforts of the late President John F. Kennedy. Harrison (1987) cites a 1966 speech by Lyndon Johnson in which he said, "I hope to see a day when some form of voluntary service to the community and the nation and the world is as common in America as going to school" (p. 12).

During the 1970s, altruism, community involvement, and service through volunteerism were on the rise, due to two noteworthy initiatives from the 1960s —the Peace Corps and the Volunteers in Service to America (VISTA) (Bhaerman et al., 1995). Through VISTA, a youth-centered initiative, the National Student Volunteer Program, emerged. The National Student Volunteer Program provided an outlet to getting youth involved in their communities through volunteerism.

The 1980s have often been referred to as a decade of self-study and fact finding on the state of educational affairs. Numerous books and reports emerged to address the perception that young people were isolated from their communities and that a large number of students were apathetic and were not altruistic about their community. It was during the 1980s that the term the *Me Too generation* emerged.

The report *Turning Points: Preparing American Youth for the 21st Century,* published by the Carnegie Corporation (1989), advocated students to volunteer: "Students can volunteer to work at senior citizen centers, nursing homes, soup kitchens, child care centers, parks or environmental centers" (p. 70). The message was clear: students volunteering their time within the community could develop connections not only between the school and the community, but also, between children and their futures.

Several books written in the 1980s called for increased community involvement for young people through service. For example, "Ernest Boyer's (1983) *High School* . . . recommends that high schools require 120 hours of community service for graduation" (Conrad & Hedin, 1991, p. 744). Boyer, in the foreword to the book *Student Service: The New Carnegie Unit* by Harrison (1987), wrote,

> To encourage young people to become more fully involved in the communities of which they are a part, we proposed . . . that every student complete a service requirement—a new "Carnegie unit" that would involve them in work in the community or at school. We believe such a service program would tap an enormous source of talent, let young people know that they are needed, and help students see a connection between what they learn and how they live. (p. viii)

Another book, *A Place Called School* by John Goodlad (1984), "includes community service among suggested practices to improve education" (Conrad & Hedin, 1991, p. 744). In 1987 the Carnegie Foundation for the Advancement of Teaching published Harrison's (1987) book *Student Service: The New Carnegie Unit*. Ernest Boyer, who wrote the foreword to Harrison's book, brings to the forefront that throughout the Carnegie Foundation's research on the U.S. high school that students reported feeling, "isolated [and] . . . unconnected to the larger world" (p. vii). The national report, *The Forgotten Half: Pathways to Success for America's Youth and Young Families* (1988), offered, according to Sandler and Vandegrift (1993):

> a recommendation to "create quality student service opportunities as central to the fundamental educational program of every public school . . . during each year from kindergarten through twelfth grade." The recommendation was specifically focused on all young people—whether college bound or members of the 'forgotten half' who do not attend college. (p. 4)

In 1989 President George Bush oversaw the beginnings of the development of *Goals 2000: Educate America Act,* which eventually became a law in 1994. Goal three supports community service: "By the year 2000 . . . every school in America will ensure that all students learn to use their minds well, so they may be prepared for responsible citizenship, further learning, and productive employment in our Nation's economy" (The National Education Goals Report: Building a Nation of Learners, 1995, p. 11). Within this goal is offered an objective that specifically addresses community service: "All students will be involved in activities that promote and demonstrate good citizenship, good health, community service, and personal responsibility" (p. 11).

Federal policy and legislation have had a marked impact on community service in the 1990s. Following the currents of policy and legislation has been another initiative to establish within the curriculum of schools a more solid connection between community service and learning through experiences—service-learning. Silcox (1993) believes:

> There is a growing conviction that the nation must restore and inculpate in its youth a greater commitment to service. A realization that government alone cannot begin to solve all the problems of the local communities of the nation has prompted national leaders to call for a new emphasis on community service. (p. 58)

At both the state and federal levels, legislators in the 1980s and 1990s have promoted community service for youth. At the federal level, the National and Community Service Act of 1990, Public Law 101-610, was enacted. Emerging from this act was the Commission on National and Community Service. Over 28 million dollars was granted to support the development of community service opportunities. The aim of Public Law 101-610 was to promote citizenship, volunteerism, and the development of an ethic of community giving in both youth and adults. Several programs throughout school districts have evolved under Public Law 101-610 through Learn and Serve America. Learn and Serve America is a federally sponsored national service program that provides grants to K–12 schools through the Corporation for National Service. The goals of Public Law 101-610 are the following:

- Renew the ethic of civic responsibility in the United States
- Ask citizens of the United States, regardless of age or income, to engage in full-time or part-time service to the nation
- Begin to call on young people to serve in programs that will benefit the nation and improve the life chances of the young through acquisition of literacy and job skills
- Enable young U.S. citizens to make a sustained commitment to service by removing barriers to

service that have been created by high education costs, loan indebtedness, and the cost of housing

- Build on the existing organization framework of federal, state, and local programs and agencies to expand full-time and part-time service opportunities for all citizens, particularly youth and older U.S. citizens
- Involve participants in activities that would not otherwise be performed by employed workers
- Generate additional service hours each year to help meet human, educational, environmental, and public safety needs, particularly those needs relating to poverty. (National and Community Service Act, 1990)

In 1992 Maryland became the first state to establish a mandatory service-learning/ community service graduation requirement. The Maryland Board of Education, taking its lead from state statute, established a 75-hour community service requirement for high school students. In 1993 President Bill Clinton, in his inaugural speech, said the following, "I challenge a new generation into a season of service—to act on your idealism by helping troubled children, keeping company with those in need, and reconnecting our torn communities."

The National Service Trust Program was enacted in 1993. Like Public Law 101-610, the National Service Trust Program promotes and provides incentives for students who participate in school-based service activities at the elementary, secondary, and postsecondary levels (National Service Trust Program Act, 1993). As a result of the passage of these acts, some districts have instituted community service graduation requirements.

CURRENT STATUS

Community service and service-learning, although different, both can have a profound impact on schools and the students they serve. Shumer (n.d.) postulates that "Schools are changing from management dominated institutions to places where parents, teachers, administrators, and students share in decision-making. They are shifting from isolated, uninvolved organiza-

tions to institutions integrally connected to the workplace, the community and the world" (F1).

Community Service and Service-Learning Defined

The Alliance for Service-Learning in Education Reform (1995), the organization that set the Standards of Quality for School-Based Service Learning, made clear the differences between community service and service-learning:

> Although the terms are sometimes used interchangeably, service-learning and community service are not synonymous. Community service can be, and often is, a powerful experience for young people, but community service ripens to service-learning when there is a deliberate and explicit connection made between service and learning opportunities which are then accompanied by conscious and thoughtful occasions to prepare for and reflect on the service experience. (n.p.)

The South Carolina Department of Education (1994) defines service-learning as "an educational method which engages young people in service to their communities as a means of enriching the academic learning, promoting personal growth, and helping them to develop the skills needed for productive citizenship" (n.p.). The Washington, D.C. organization Points of Light Foundation (1995) believes that "service learning deliberately links young people's service in the community with their learning, particularly their learning in school. Through service learning, young people help others in their community while also enhancing their own education" (p. 9).

Sandler and Vandergrift (1993) report that

> students in community service projects . . . can apply academic concepts and learn about themselves and how to care about others and their community. It integrates study and reflection about the experience of youth service activities into the curriculum. (p. 3)

Regardless of the term used (community service or service-learning), students involved in these initiatives work without remuneration on behalf of an individual, group, or organization in need of assistance. To this end, students give of themselves so that others may benefit. Community service then is altruistic in nature (Boyer, 1983).

There are three types of service that children typically participate in—direct service, indirect service, and civic action (Fertman, 1994). Direct service consists of personal "contact with individuals in need" (Fertman, 1994, p. 13). Direct services "put students face to face helping someone" (Townsend & O'Neil, 1993, p. 1). Indirect service "involves channeling resources to solve the problem, rather than direct involvement with the individual in need" (Fertman, 1994, p. 13). Put another way, indirect service activities are "behind the scenes, channeling resources to alleviate a problem" (Townsend & O'Neil, 1993, p. 2). Throughout history, school children have risen to the occasion by providing indirect services to those less fortunate by engaging in such activities as canned food drives during the holidays and collecting money to assist victims of natural disasters. Civic action "emphasizes active participation in democratic citizenship. It includes two main activities: informing the public about a problem to be addressed and working toward solving the problem" (Fertman, 1994, p. 14). To this end, advocacy service projects "require students to lend their voices and talents to the disenfranchised or to correct an injustice" (p. 4).

All three types of service activities—direct, indirect, and civic action—engage students in extending a part of themselves on behalf of others. One type of service activity is not more important than the others. They are on equal footing. The ideal service-learning and/or community service program affords students the opportunity to be involved in a variety of service activities regardless of their type. Circumstance (i.e., age level of student, commitment of the school, flexibility of the school's curricular program, and the willingness of the community to embrace students working within the community itself) will guide the types of service activities with which the students will be involved.

Curriculum, Instruction, and Service-Learning

Richard Riley (1995), the U.S. Secretary of Education, said, "Service learning is about young people using classroom skills to solve real life problems. In Learn and Serve America programs, youth learn about community and citizenship in ways that can't be understood through textbooks" (n.p.). The connections that can be made between the work of the classroom and the work within the community can strengthen the overall curriculum.

The underpinnings of Public Law 101-610 are based upon the premise that service-learning means a method

- under which students learn and develop through active participation in thoughtfully organized service experiences that meet actual community needs and that are coordinated in collaboration with the school and the community.
- that is integrated into the student's academic curriculum or provides structured time for a student to think, talk, or write about what the student did and saw during the actual service activity.
- that provides students with opportunities to use newly acquired skills and knowledge in real-life situations in their own communities.
- that enhances what is taught in school by extending student learning beyond the classroom and into the community and helps to foster the development of a sense of caring for others. (National and Community Service Act, 1990)

In the school and classroom that incorporates service-learning as a part of the curriculum, changes occur in the relationships between students and the teacher. Kinsley (1994) indicates that "when using the service-learning process, teachers become coaches and students become actively engaged in their education. In essence, service-learning provides teachers with a way to help students construct their own learning environments and helps them navigate their way through content areas" (J3).

Duckenfield and Swanson (1992), cited by Duckenfield and Wright (1995), presented a four part service-learning framework for developing a service-learning curriculum. The elements for learning activities within this framework include preparation, action, reflection, and celebration (p. 7).

Preparation positions students to "understand what is expected of them as well as what they can expect from the service project" (p. 7). Service-learning has the capacity to encourage students and teachers to work in more cooperative ways with one another. Very much like the project method, service-learning preparation includes students in "selecting and planning the project" (p. 7).

Action, according to Duckenfield and Wright (1995), "is the service itself" that "needs to meet certain criteria" (p. 7). The criteria must posses the following characteristics:

- Be meaningful
- Have academic integrity
- Have adequate supervision
- Provide for student ownership
- Be developmentally appropriate

These criteria are broad but specific enough to accommodate all student grade levels (e.g., elementary, middle, and high school).

Reflection, which is discussed at length later, can be achieved through a variety of post service-learning activities, which could include the following:

- Discussion
- Reading
- Writing
- Projects (p. 7)

Because reflection is a critical aspect of service-learning activities, time for these types of activities needs to be built into the process. Reflection is a powerful tool and can help students increase their understanding of their experiences and see how the service is a vital part of classroom instruction.

The last component of the service-learning framework developed by Duckenfield and Wright (1995) is celebration: "Celebration is the component of service learning which recognizes students for their contributions. It also provides closure to ongoing activity" (p. 7).

Attributes of Service-Learning and Community Service Programs

Ernest Boyer, in the foreword to the book *Student Service: The New Carnegie Unit* by Harrison (1987), indicated that through the research and study of the high schools portrayed in this book, it was found that service programs had five attributes:

1. A service program begins with clearly stated educational objectives.
2. A service program should be carefully introduced and creatively promoted.
3. Service activity should be directed not just to the community but also toward the school itself.
4. A service program should be something more than preparation for a career.
5. Students should not only go out to serve, they also should be asked to write about their experience and, if possible, discuss with others the lessons they have learned. (pp. ix–xi)

The fifth attribute Boyer identified in 1987 has been expanded since then to include reflection as a critical aspect of service-learning. Witmer and Anderson's (1994) discussion and definition of service-learning, like numerous others, includes the process of reflection as a way for students to make sense of their service-learning and/or community service experiences. Service-learning should be "grounded" in experience and *"reflecting upon the experience"* (Witmer & Anderson, 1994, p. 3, emphasis in the original) is essential for students to make sense of their experiences, regardless if they occur in the school or in the larger community.

The grounding that Witmer and Anderson (1994) identified helps to promote democratic principles by encouraging students "to work together with their teachers in planning educational strategies for the students' own learning" (p. 5). Through incorporating service-learning into course offerings and the school's curriculum, teachers and students can forge ahead into more cooperative ventures with one another—one of the underlying premises of democratic schools.

The Johnson Foundation hosted a conference on service-learning in 1989. Over 70 organizations convened, and at the end of the conference the following 10 principles were found in effective service-learning programs: An effective program, according to Honnet & Poulson (1989), achieves the following:

- Engages people in responsible and challenging actions for the common good

- Provides structured opportunities for people to reflect critically on their service experience
- Articulates clear service and learning goals for everyone involved
- Allows for those with needs to define those needs
- Clarifies the responsibilities of each person and organization
- Watches service providers and service needs through a process that recognizes changing circumstances
- Expects genuine, active, and sustained organizational commitment
- Includes training, supervision, monitoring, support, recognition, and evaluation to meet service and learning goals
- Insures that the time commitment for service and learning is flexible, appropriate, and in the best interest of all involved
- Is committed to program participation by and with diverse populations (p. 2)

The Points of Light Foundation (1995) identifies three elements of service learning that need to be in place:

1. *Careful planning and preparation.* Young people, schools and agencies must be part of planning service-learning opportunities and each should be prepared for their role.
2. *Meeting real community needs.* The service performed by youth must be seen as relevant and timely. The service must be valued by agencies and youth.
3. *Reflection.* Structured time is provided for students to reflect on their service, or their service is related to their academic work. (p. 9)

Both the principles offered by Honnet and Poulsen (1989) and the Points of Light Foundation (1995) on the attributes of effective service-learning programs emphasize the involvement of students. Hedin and Conrad (1987) believe that "a good program can be defined simply as one in which the student plays a significant role in working with others to perform tasks that both the young person and the community regard as worthwhile and needed" (p. 10).

Standards of Quality

The Alliance for Service-Learning in Education Reform (1995) developed the *Standards of Quality for School-Based and Community-Based Service-Learning.* The framers of these standards underscore that these standards are "not absolutes" but rather points of departure for schools that are in the process of developing or refining community service and/or service-learning initiatives. There are many variables within schools and the communities they serve. It is these variables that will help school officials apply and modify these standards as they work to lead their schools in the development, design, and evaluation of service-learning initiatives. The standards are the following:*

I. Effective service-learning efforts strengthen service and academic learning.
II. Model service-learning provides concrete opportunities for youth to learn new skills, to think critically, and to test new roles in an environment that encourages risk-taking and rewards competence.
III. Preparation and reflection are essential elements in service-learning.
IV. Youths' efforts are recognized by those served, including their peers, the school, and the community.
V. Youth are involved in the planning.
VI. The service students perform makes a meaningful contribution to the community.
VII. Effective service-learning integrates systematic formative and summative evaluation.
VIII. Service-learning connects the school or sponsoring organization and its community in new and positive ways.
IX. Service-learning is understood and supported as an integral element in the life of a school or sponsoring organization and its community.
X. Skilled adult guidance and supervision are essential to the success of service-learning.

*Adapted, with permission, from "Standards of Quality for School-Based and Community-Based Service-Learning" (March 1995), published by the Close Up Foundation, Alexandria, VA. © 1995 Close Up Foundation.

XI. Preservice training, orientation, and staff development that include the philosophy and methodology of service-learning best ensure that program quality and continuity are maintained. (n.p.)

CONTEMPORARY ISSUES

Developing effective community service and/or service-learning programs within schools is a time-consuming task that requires examination of the structure of the school. Very often, curriculum needs to be restructured so that service and learning can be integrated. This process requires support from the principal. Support needs to be provided through staff development, coordination of services, resource allocation, and time.

Community service and service-learning initiatives should, ideally, be based on democratic principles. Therefore, for these types of programs to work, teachers need to be involved in the process of planning, implementing, and evaluating efforts. Because many service-learning initiatives are funded through the Learn and Serve America Act, a full-time coordinator can assume responsibility for establishing and monitoring the day-to-day activities of such programs. According to Eberly (1993): "It has been demonstrated that the single most important feature of a service learning program is a service learning coordinator. This is someone who integrates the community's interest in meeting its needs with the faculty's interest in education and the student's interest in serving" (p. 53).

However, this does not mean that the principal is not involved with the development of a community service/service-learning initiative. To begin building support for community service and service-learning, the principal must understand the goals and objectives of the program so that the principal may

- work with teachers and staff in designing program parameters (e.g., number of contact hours required to complement curricular components, goals and objectives).
- enlist the support and assistance of parents, community leaders, and university personnel.

- find resources (e.g., funding for a full-time coordinator, release time for teachers to work on developing curriculum, and plan activities that are consistent with objectives).
- monitor progress by conducting both formative and summative evaluation of the program.

Before beginning a community service/service learning program, the principal needs to assess the willingness of the faculty to begin such an endeavor. This assessment process will take time. Time is needed to let faculty members investigate the possible benefits for children, the school community, and the curricular connections that can be made by implementing a community service/service learning program. Principals need to engage teachers in open and ongoing discussions. Experts in the field should be consulted to provide inservice training, and teachers should be encouraged to visit with schools systems that have implemented community service/service-learning programs. The principal also is advised to visit with school administrators who have implemented community service/service learning programs to discover lessons learned from practice.

If no other schools in the district are implementing a community service/service-learning initiative, the principal needs to keep central administrators updated on efforts. The principal, along with others in the school community, should be prepared to make a presentation to the board of education. The support and endorsement of the board of education will determine, to a large extent, whether such a program will succeed. The principal needs to extend communication with others as well. Parents need to be involved in the process of developing a community service/service-learning program. Without parental support, the probability is increased that efforts could be met with opposition. The principal should have an open meeting, along with teachers and school counselors, where parents can respond by having the opportunity to ask questions, voice concerns, and share insights.

While goals are being established and support is being obtained from parents, students, and the board of education, school personnel need to determine what types of assistance the community can offer to the school and its students. This inquiry needs to occur simultaneously with assessing and gaining the support of teachers, students, parents, and the board of education. As the spokesperson for the school, the principal needs to communicate with local business people and community agencies to determine what resources are available (e.g., nursing homes, pet shelters, hospitals, and youth agencies). Without support from these people and agencies, success is not likely to occur.

Found within the *Standards of Quality for School-Based Service Learning* developed by the Alliance for Service Learning in Education Reform (1993) are suggestions for both formative and summative evaluation. Because community service/service-learning programs will vary, depending on the context of the school and community, there are no "fixed" ways of assessing results, although

> systematic methods for assessing a program's impact are needed, particularly since the field of service-learning is growing rapidly and demand for in-depth understanding of models and approaches is high. Such assessment includes detailed documentation of the model components and processes; the outcomes identified by, and expected of, all participants (i.e., students, community members, schools); and the impact of the service-learning program on individual participants, schools, and community. (p. 72)

As with other curricular programs, assessment needs to be based on the goals and objectives, the impact of the service-learning activities on participants (students, teachers, and community members) to (1) profile the program, (2) make modifications to the existing program based upon assessment, and (3) keep the community informed. Through newsletters, parent bulletins, and presentations to the community, the principal can not only keep stakeholders informed, but also can enhance public relations efforts.

Controversies Surrounding Community Service and Service-Learning

Although the intent of community service and service-learning is altruistic in nature (i.e., teaching social skills, building community and social responsibility, and building self-esteem and feelings of worth through

a sense of accomplishment), there have been controversies surrounding the mandating of community service. Morris (1992) raises the following concerns for the mandating of community service and service learning and its volunteerism aspects:

- Do we have adequate resources to ensure the teacher training necessary to make service-learning a successful education program?
- Mandating that service programs be available to, rather than required of, every student for credit may be a more effective method for encouraging present and continued community service in our youth.
- Mandates of any kind are unpopular and invite political dissention and judicial action.
- Scarce resources make it essential that individual school districts be given as much leeway as possible in designing programs that will be most beneficial to their student populations. (p. 4)

Funding.   Although federal and state grants are available to develop service-learning programs in schools, these funds, we suspect, are not enough to completely infuse service-learning into the content of all courses in any given school. Additional sources of funding need to be secured to finance such an initiative. For example, funds are needed to train teachers and to purchase new resource materials and supplementary materials. Many schools and districts create partnerships with community agencies and businesses. These partnerships can help defray the cost incurred in establishing service-learning programs, but they might not be enough. Parental support and backing from their organizations (e.g., the PTA or the PTO) also can be a source of funding, albeit a much smaller one. The district also should assist individual schools in securing funding and other types of support.

Legal Issues.   Of late, mandatory graduation requirements tied to community service and service learning have undergone judicial scrutiny. Many claim that this type of graduation requirement is unconstitutional. Bittner (1994) reports that the Bethlehem, Pennsylvania, School District has been challenged on their mandatory community service graduation requirement, which was passed in 1990. In *Steirer v. Bethlehem Area School District* (1993), the plaintiffs alleged,

> (1) the graduation requirement violated the free speech clause of the First Amendment by forcing them to engage in a particular form of expression; in this instance, the belief was altruism, and
>   (2) the graduation requirement violated the Thirteenth Amendment because participation in the program constituted involuntary servitude. (p. 115)

Although the court system ruled on behalf of the school district, Bittner (1994) believes that this case "established a precedent that helps to answer questions that students, parents, school boards, and administrators may have about community service programs (p. 116). In the *Steirer* case, the Bethlehem District was supported because students had the opportunity to pick and choose what agency they would do their service-learning in; therefore, they had free choice (Bittner, 1994). Moreover, "these students were not *forced* to believe in the concept of altruism" (p. 116, emphasis in the original).

In regard to the Thirteenth Amendment and involuntary servitude, the court also ruled in favor of the Bethlehem District because, as in other cases, "there was not a threat of physical force or the threat of imprisonment" (Bittner, 1994, p. 118).

As service-learning initiatives continue, it is likely that additional litigation will be encountered. Hence school principals, as they are constructing service-learning and/or community service initiatives, need to work closely with the district legal counsel to ensure that fundamental rights as protected by the Constitution are not violated.

Some might believe that community service compromises a student's time to seek gainful employment given that most community service occurs after school, on weekends, or during the summer. Although "More than a million high school students are estimated to be participating in . . . community service programs" (Zinser, 1993, p. 33), not all students are pleased with the "mandatory" aspects of required service. Zinser (1993) reports that "A Gallup poll released in December found that 61 percent of the 1,400 youths (age 12–17) surveyed were doing volunteer work. But more than half of them

thought it was wrong to mandate community service in school" (p. 31).

Schools and districts with mandatory service requirements need to monitor student progress toward meeting the required amount of service time. If the school employs a full-time coordinator this task can be assumed by this person. Otherwise, the principal will need to assign another person to tend to this duty. If classroom teachers are asked to track student hours, placement, and evaluation and develop this new program's curriculum on top of their other responsibilities, enthusiasm for this endeavor will dim.

Placement can cause concern for parents in that their children will be working closely with an adult who has not undergone the scrutiny involved in the hiring of school personnel. Principals need to develop ways of assessing the suitability of outside agencies, the range and scope of work students will be doing, and the acceptability of nonschool supervisors who will be working with students. Many principals handle this issue and others by forming an advisory board to help direct investigations to the questions and issues that emerge in the development and ongoing refinement of community service and service learning initiatives.

Building Support for Programs

As indicated earlier, the Points of Light Foundation (1995) suggests that service-learning and/or community service programs need to meet community needs. Without meeting such basic needs, support for service-learning and/or community service programs will not be widespread within the school and perhaps, more importantly, within those agencies who can provide the opportunity for learning through service. Building support for such an undertaking is a complex, multifaceted process. The principal must be in a position to show how such a program can benefit the school while, at the same time, showing how this type of program can benefit the larger community. Some might believe that what might be good for the community might not necessarily be good for the school. Some teachers might feel that business and other outside agency involvement is an intrusion. Articulation between those who work inside and those who work outside the school is a critical component for the success of service-learning and community service initiatives.

Benefits of Community Service and Service-Learning

Empirical data is sparse about the direct benefits to students, schools, and communities that engage in service-learning activities. This is indeed a quandary in an era of accountability. However, Watkins and Wilkes (1993), through their work with the South-Eastern Regional Vision for Education (SERVE) that profiles 30 programs in the Southeast, indicate that children who are involved with community service and service-learning:

- Learn more
- Earn better grades
- Come to school more often
- Demonstrate better behavior
- Become more civic-minded
- Gain first-hand appreciation and understanding of people from other cultures, races, and generations
- See the connections between school and "real life"
- Feel better about themselves
- Learn skills they can use after leaving school (pp. v–vi)

We believe intuitively that community service is good, that it builds a sense of volunteerism in people, that it helps build and develop skills, and that a plethora of other benefits can be reaped by students and school systems alike. It is difficult to track effectiveness, however, for several reasons. First, if school systems (i.e., unified districts) begin community service/service-learning initiatives when children are in high school, the benefits (and we think there are benefits) evolve over time. After graduation, schools typically do not track students. Second, we believe it is difficult to assess benefits because of the affective nature of community service. How does one measure altruism? We do not have the answer to this question or others. Principals, as they evaluate and assess their programs, might want to consider working with teachers, community service vendors, and higher education organizations in developing action research studies. Such

investigations can help evaluate the overall impact of such programs, activities, and outcomes.

Knauft (1992) indicated that "the most important outcome of teen volunteering is not the number of hours given, but the impact of this activity on the young person. The focus on helping others, of achieving success as a member of a group that serves the community and being able to broaden one's horizons are the rewards of the teen volunteer" (p. 15).

ILLUSTRATIVE PRACTICES AND ISSUES

Anderson, V., Kinsley, C., Negroni, P., & Price, C. (1991). Community service learning and school improvement in Springfield, Massachusetts. *Phi Delta Kappan, 72*(10), 761–764.

Anderson et al. explore the relationship between community service-learning (CSL) and school improvement across the Springfield, Massachusetts district. The process and people involved in conceptualizing, designing, and implementing the CSL are identified. Philosophical and curricular underpinning are discussed. Because the CSL initiative spanned a multi-school district, the framers realized that each building needed flexibility in developing their own CSL program. The following components organize schools in designing and implementing CSL: (1) establish an individual school or classroom service learning theme, (2) determine school or classroom objectives, (3) meet with community representatives, (4) develop a repertoire of activities, (5) develop learning experiences, (6) establish a time line, (7) reflect, and (8) celebrate (p. 762). The CSL efforts of two elementary schools are highlighted. *Issues:* The need to have guiding principles in place before launching CSL is addressed. The immediate benefits of CSL for children, families, and the community of this district were underscored. CSL initiatives are viewed as an integrated component of each school. CSL is viewed as part of the daily, lived curriculum.

Checkoway, B. (1996). Combining service and learning on campus and in the community. *Kappan, 77*(9), 600–606.

Checkoway highlights three student workshops: (1) Community Planning Workshop, (2) Neighborhood Development Workshop, and (3) Voter Participation Workshop. Each workshop is detailed and provides the social awareness to improve society. Sample activities within each workshop also are highlighted. The details of each type of workshop include descriptive accounts of the planning and designing of activities. At the end of workshop descriptions, Checkoway details the lessons learned from participating in service learning workshops. *Issues:* How to involve community members and university faculty members in student workshops is discussed. The relationship between service and learning is addressed.

SUMMARY

Community service and service-learning initiatives are on the rise and are being developed at the elementary, middle, and high school levels. The increase in the numbers of programs stem from a variety of factors—legislation, altruism, and reform efforts—to name just a few. Regardless of the reasons, the power of community service will be seen in the future as our youth progress through their adult lives.

QUESTIONS FOR FURTHER CONSIDERATION

Research

1. What would need to be done to begin a community service or service-learning program in your school? Outline the people to involve, the process needed to involve these people, and when to involve these people.

2. What is the role of the principal, teachers, and community in developing community service and service-learning programs?

3. Visit a school that has an established community service and service-learning program. Assess whether community service or service-learning is part of the curriculum or just an add-on.

4. Identify the legal issues involved in developing community service and service-learning programs.

Reflect

1. Should community service and service-learning be mandated? Why or why not?

2. One of the characteristics of youth is idealism. How can schools draw on that strength through community service and service-learning?

3. What traits would you want to look for in a service-learning coordinator? Why would it be advisable to hire a service-learning coordinator?

4. What ways could you integrate community service into the standard curriculum without having to mandate it?

5. How can you quantitatively measure the effects of service-learning?

6. Is elementary school too early to develop community service or service-learning?

Respond/React

1. Should school size dictate the community service or service learning program?

2. PL 101-610, The National and Community Service Act (1990), postulates many benefits. What arguments do the opponents of service-learning indicate?

SUGGESTED READINGS

Duckenfield, M., & Wright, J. (Eds.). (1995). *Pocket guide to service learning.* Clemson, SC: National Dropout Prevention Center.

Fertman, C. I. (1994). *Service learning for all students.* Bloomington, IN: Phi Delta Kappa Educational Foundation.

Harrison, C. H. (1987). *Student service: The new Carnegie unit.* Princeton, NJ: The Carnegie Foundation for the Advancement of Teaching.

Kinsley, C. & McPherson, K. (1995). Introduction: Changing perceptions to integrate community service learning into education. In C. Kinsley & K. McPherson (Eds.), *Enriching the curriculum through service learning* (pp. 1–6). Alexandria, VA: Association for Supervision and Curriculum Development.

Points of Light Foundation. (1995). *Everyone wins when youth serve: Building agency/school partnerships for service learning.* Washington, DC: Points of Light Foundation.

CHAPTER 6

EARLY CHILDHOOD EDUCATION

Early childhood education has a rich intellectual history that has been greatly influenced by philosophy, theology, and psychology. Actual programs for young children have a much shorter history, but all of them display at least remnants of how children have been, and now are, viewed by society.

HISTORY

As early as the fourth and third centuries BC, both Plato and Aristotle made references to the importance of teaching young children. Plato believed that most parents were not fit for childrearing and, therefore, the children should be brought up in state nurseries (Osborn, 1991). Plato even thought females should receive the same educational opportunities as males. Osborn (1991) noted:

> Aristotle said that training should begin early and that recognition should be given to the fact that each child possessed specific talents and skills. Aristotle would appear to be the first person to detail the idea of individual differences in children. (p. 12)

Both Plato and Aristotle were well ahead of their times.

Despite the high sounding rhetoric, the practice in ancient Greece left a great deal to be desired. Typically, only children from well-to-do homes and, even then, only the boys, received much formal education. Indeed, infanticide, the killing of newborns and infants, usually girls, was practiced in ancient Greece. This abhorrent practice continued well into the nineteenth century throughout the world, and one could make the sobering observation that the twentieth century instances of child abuse are simply modern manifestations of the practice (Osborn, 1991).

Plato and Aristotle notwithstanding, well into the nineteenth century most of the literature and art depicted young children as simply small adults. How children were viewed and how they were treated have some correlation. When children were viewed as small adults, it made sense they should work in the factories and mines. (Young children were especially well suited as chimney sweeps.) And such abuse of children did not suddenly cease. Child-labor laws typically existed years before they were enforced. Only gradually, through a combination of events and efforts, was childhood seen as a distinctive period, qualitatively different from adulthood. The variety of programs for children over the years reflected different views of children and revealed disagreement over issues such as the effects of heredity and environment and the consequent nature of children.

Views of the Inherent Nature of Children

John Locke (1632–1704), an English philosopher and political theorist, wrote about human understanding (1690) and education (1693). Unlike his contemporaries, Locke believed that children were born with minds that were like blank slates (*tabula rasa*). At birth then, according to Locke, all children were equal. Whatever differences there were between and among people were the result of experiences—sense experiences, to be exact. Locke's emphasis on the importance of sense experiences continues to have a profound effect on educational practices.

Johann Pestalozzi (1746–1827), the Swiss educational reformer, and Maria Montessori (1870–1952), the Italian doctor turned educational reformer, both used special objects and sense exercises to teach young children. Even *Sesame Street,* the well-known television program for children, has as its aim, "to give underprivileged children, especially in the inner cities, the simple ideas and basic experiences that their environment normally does not provide" (Cleverley & Phillips, 1986, p. 26). Such emphasis on environmental experiences, however, does have its detractors.

Arthur Jensen, an educational psychologist at Berkeley, had an article published in the *Harvard Educational Review* (1969) wherein he challenged the environmentalists' explanation for discrepancies in intelligence (as measured by IQ tests) among young children. Jensen claimed heredity played a larger role, but conceded that ". . . a genetic hypothesis . . . does not exclude the influence of environment or its interaction with genetic factors" (p. 84). Herrnstein and Murray (1994), likewise, challenged the environmentalists by promoting the idea that differences in intelligence (again, only as measured through standardized tests) are explained more by race than by experiences.

Two other opposing camps that are rooted in the hereditarian/environmental split are the maturationists and interactionists. The maturationists grew out of the early child development work of Arnold Gesell (1880–1961), who established norms for developmental milestones and believed maturation was the genetically driven "unfolding" of skills and abilities. Such development was impervious to environmental influences. Only time was a variable for maturationists. Development was from within. The interactionists, however, as the name implies, believed interacting with the environment would affect development. Interactionists were proactive compared with maturationists who could be characterized as passive, waiting for time to pass before children would be considered ready to learn.

The point is that the environmentalist/hereditarian and, to a lesser extent, the maturationist/interactionist debates continue and show little sign of abating. Neither side, however, totally excludes the possibility of effects from the other. Perhaps just as important as Locke in affecting views of young children were two other forces that began in the eighteenth century.

The eighteenth-century Puritans of Britain and the United States believed that children were inherently sinful. John Wesley, founder of the Methodist church, was raised by the rule, according to his mother, that "the first task of upbringing was the restraint of self-will in the child. Self-will had led Adam astray, and it was at the heart of all sin and misery in the world"

(Cleverley & Phillips, 1986, p. 29). Such beliefs in original sin and the inherent wickedness of all children gave rise to all kinds of strict regimens in the families and schools of this period and these beliefs and assumptions have lasted well into the twentieth century.

Cleverley and Phillips (1986) note that the renewed interest in Christian fundamentalism of the 1970s and 1980s reflect a retention in these same beliefs and assumptions. Quoting from *Family Life* (1976) they relate, "all children—not just certain children, *all* children—are born delinquent" (Stedman et al., 1976 in Cleverley & Phillips, 1986, p. 32, emphasis in original). In the 1990s, the ultrafundamentalists continue this view, and it is evident in Blumenfeld (1996) and Gaddy, Hall, and Marzano (1996).

In stark contrast to notions of original sin and the inherent depravity of all humans is the romantic view of children as being inherently good. Rousseau (1712–1778) is credited with articulating the romantic vision of childhood with his depiction of child rearing in his novel *Emile* (1762).

Rousseau blamed the cities or city life for all that was evil in the world. He believed a child should be raised in freedom. Much as Locke emphasized the importance of experience in shaping children, as opposed to a hereditary view, Rousseau went even further in promoting inherent goodness before any experience occurred.

> Let us lay it down as an incontrovertible rule that the first impulses of nature are always right; there is no original sin in the human heart, the how and why of the entrance of every vice can be traced. (Rousseau, 1955, p. 5 quoted in Cleverley & Phillips, 1986, p. 34)

Rousseau's assumption that children were innately good had an influence on a number of educators of the nineteenth and twentieth century.

Nineteenth- and Twentieth-Century Early Childhood Educators

Pestalozzi was impressed with Rousseau's ideas, believing that "all persons should have the right to develop skills which would make them successful and enable them to fulfill their own potential" (Osborn, 1991, p. 40). Friedrich Froebel (1782–1852) worked under the direction of Pestalozzi and is credited with developing the first kindergarten in Germany in 1837. One of Froebel's students, Margarethe Schurz, migrated to the United States and established the first U.S. kindergarten in 1855 in Watertown, Wisconsin. Her venture was private, not public, and the language used was German, not English, but the humane setting that promoted play attracted attention. By 1860 Elizabeth Peabody had opened the first English-speaking kindergarten in Boston.

In 1873, Susan Blow, under the leadership of Superintendent William Harris, established the first public school kindergarten in St. Louis, Missouri. By the turn of the century, however, the emphasis on play as an avenue for learning waned. Kindergartens became quite formal and rigid. Froebel died in 1852 and by 1900, with his influence diminished in the United States, kindergartens began looking more like elementary schools where a no-nonsense attitude and a heavy dose of the work mentality prevailed.

Two influential women, Margaret McMillan (1860–1931) from England and Maria Montessori (1870–1952) from Italy, further shaped early childhood education by adding a health component to their schools. Both women initially worked with children of the poor whose mothers worked outside the home. McMillan called her school for children, ages 2 to 7, a day nursery. The nursery promoted cleanliness, nutrition, and play. McMillan's teachers were called "nurse-teachers" to emphasize the dual responsibilities of health care and education (Maxim, 1985).

Montessori, a medical doctor by training, worked initially with the children of the psychiatric clinic at the University of Rome. She devised teaching materials, many of which are still in use today, to help the children overcome their retarded conditions. Her educational program, established in what she called a children's house, became more formalized when she began working in the slums of Rome.

In light of current efforts to combine special education initiatives with early childhood, it is interesting to note that both McMillan and Montessori were influenced by Edward Seguin, a prominent educator of the nineteenth century who believed a combination of medical treatment and education was needed for an effective therapy for children who were labeled *feeble-minded*. Seguin was a student of Jean Itard, who was instrumental in considering mental deficiency an educational problem and not a mental one (Osborn, 1991).

By the early twentieth century in the United States, kindergartens were beginning to flourish and a few nursery schools were established. The latter, when accommodating children of working parents, shifted to physical care almost exclusively and became known as day or child care centers. When nursery schools maintained educational priorities and served children of the more affluent for a few hours a day, 2 or 3 days a week, they retained the nursery school name.

Early in the twentieth century, another early childhood agency was established with additional purposes. The university-based child development laboratory schools provided teaching, research, and service functions. Most were begun by philanthropic organizations. Between 1924 and 1930, child development laboratories were established at Columbia University, the University of Minnesota, Iowa State University, Ohio State University, Cornell University, the University of Georgia, Spellman College, Bennett College, and Michigan State University. These laboratories were designed to promote children's welfare and physical well-being and to be settings for the observation of children—consistent with the growing interest in child development—and training centers for prospective teachers of young children (McBride & Lee, 1995). The child development laboratories were evidence of the special focus on young children that had begun to take hold in the early part of the twentieth century, building on the works of Freud, Erikson, and Piaget.

Views of How Children Learn and Develop

At the turn of the twentieth century, the views of Locke (children were a blank slate), the Puritans (children were depraved), and Rousseau (children were inherently good) were augmented by Sigmund Freud (1856–1939) and his interest in the emotional underpinnings associated with sexual development. Without getting into much detail, suffice it to say that Freud called attention to very early child development, especially regarding relationships between sons and mothers, daughters and fathers, and older and younger siblings. According to Freud, a great deal of emotional baggage was packed in the early years and often was not manifested in behavior until well into adulthood.

Informed by Freud's work, Erik Erikson (1902–1994) established a psychosocial stage theory of personality development that was more comprehensive than Freud's and revolved around a series of conflicts roughly corresponding to various ages. For example, from birth to 1, children generate a sense of trust or mistrust. From 1 to 3, they are between achieving autonomy or feeling shame or doubt. Between 3 and 5, it is initiative versus guilt. And between 6 and 12, it is industry versus inferiority. The next four stages go through older adulthood.

Erikson cautioned that successful completion of a stage (i.e., having more positive than negative experiences regarding trust, autonomy, and initiative) does not mean that a permanent character trait has been achieved. Successful completion simply means the individual is better prepared to enter the next stage and pass through it successfully (Erikson, 1963).

Jean Piaget (1896–1980) studied how intelligence develops. He developed a stage theory of cognitive development. Essentially, Piaget believed that children interact with the environment and experience three states—assimilation, accommodation, and equilibration. Assimilation is the processing of information. Adjusting mental structures, in effect, changing the very way processing occurs, is called accommodation. Equilibration is the attainment of sharper mental structures that add clarity to concepts. The state of equilibrium is dynamic in that "it carries with it the seeds of its own destruction, for the child's activities are thenceforth directed toward reducing those inconsistencies (that were made sharper and more clear earlier)" (Phillips, 1969, p. 20).

Piaget emphasized the child's interaction with the material environment, trying to make sense of the environment and the child's conceptions of it. Knowledge resides neither out there in the objective world nor exclusively within the individual; rather, it is "the mutual relation of the knower to the known" (Furth, 1969, p. 44).

Whereas Piaget regarded the child as a solitary inquirer, others, for example, Lev Vygotsky, have emphasized social aspects of learning. Parents, teachers, siblings, and peers can and do have an influence on what and how children learn (Cleverley & Phillips, 1986). Both Piaget and Vygotsky assert that children actively attempt to make sense of their world. Children actually construct their knowledge, hence a constructivist view of education is predicated on children being actively engaged in learning. This is in stark contrast to the behaviorists.

B. F. Skinner, undoubtedly the most well-known behaviorist, built on the work of Watson and Thorndyke, earlier psychologists who worked first with animals and then with children, believing that learning was basically a stimulus–response proposition. Skinner and other behaviorists developed the theory of operant conditioning, meaning the gradual shaping of responses or behavior by the environment. This belief in behavior (and learning) being shaped by the environment also has been known as environmentalism and determinism.

Finally, although not a learning theorist, Bloom published *Stability and Change in Human Characteristics* in 1964. His thesis was that the early years of childhood were critical to later achievements in a variety of developmental areas. The clear implication of Bloom's work was that it was more likely a child's intellectual, emotional, and social development could be affected during the first 5 years of life than the second or third 5 years. Changing behavior, dispositions, and attitudes can occur at any time (examples abound in anonymous self-help groups such as Alcoholics Anonymous), but such changes later in life are difficult and problematic. Better to have young children begin their life-long journeys with a good start and avoid, if possible, efforts at remediation and correction later.

National Initiatives in Early Childhood Education

Two major events that affected early childhood education in the United States were the Great Depression of 1929 and World War II. Except for the establishment of the Children's Bureau in 1912 as part of the U.S. Department of Commerce and Labor, and now under the Department of Health and Human Services, there was virtually no activity at the national level regarding young children. In 1933, during the Great Depression, the Federal Emergency Relief Administration established nursery schools for children ages 2 to 6. By 1935, nearly 2,000 such schools were serving 74,000 children. The dual purpose was to provide jobs for unemployed teachers and needed services for children of unemployed parents (Osborn, 1991). These nurseries remained open until the beginning of World War II in 1941.

In 1942, the Lanham Act, which was passed earlier to provide funds to war-impacted communities, was the vehicle for funding day care facilities for mothers working in defense related factories. Forty-one states had such centers, usually operated by the public schools. About 2,000 centers were in operation, typically from 6 A.M. to 6 P.M., and they served about 600,000 children. The centers ceased to exist by 1946, within a year of the end of World War II (Osborn, 1991).

The mid-1960s was a time for great additions to the early childhood landscape. In the summer of 1965, Project Head Start was launched. Initially serving 4 and 5 year olds during the summer, it has continued on a year-round basis to this date. Head Start, part of President Johnson's War on Poverty, was designed to break the vicious cycle of poverty. In the first summer alone, 652,000 children were served in 2,500 centers that employed 41,000 teachers (Osborn, 1991).

Head Start was and still is a comprehensive service, providing medical and dental examinations and corrections, immunizations, social services, nutritional care, and psychological services to 3 to 5 year olds who qualify by virtue of their family's income. Opportunities for volunteering and employment for parents were and are part of the program. Parents also have been involved as members of boards and in other decision-making capacities and work in non-professional positions as well (Leeper, Witherspoon, & Day, 1984).

In 1995, Head Start served about 752,000 children, estimated by the Children's Defense Fund (CDF) to be only about 36 percent of those who were eligible (CDF, 1996). The CDF figures for 1994, the latest available, indicate the following percentages of children served: 41 percent African American; 36 percent European American; 19 percent Hispanic American; 2 percent Asian American; and 2 percent Native American (CDF, 1996, p. 91). Since 1972, when it was mandated that at least 10 percent of the Head Start enrollments be reserved for children with handicaps, about 13 percent of those served were handicapped. Finally, the sponsorship for Head Start, funded 90 percent by federal sources and 10 percent by local agencies, is usually spread among community action agencies, not-for-profit agencies, and public schools.

CURRENT STATUS

Professional Status

The field of early childhood education is broader than either elementary or secondary education. This fact is both a strength and a weakness. The strength is the diversity of disciplines that lay claim and contribute to various aspects of the field. For example, health and nutrition experts, child development specialists, human services professionals, and myriad others provide services to young children. Early childhood education needs to be a big tent to accommodate all those who serve and advocate for young children. The heterogeneity of the field, however, also is a weakness.

Early childhood educators do not speak with one voice. The educators working within a public school facility may be at odds with day care teachers working in a for-profit agency. Of course all want what "is best" for children, but they can and do disagree on how to accomplish their goals. Kindergarten teachers, for example, may believe what is best is a sound preparation for the rigors of first grade, including learning the beginning skills associated with reading. Nursery school teachers may believe improving self-confidence and social interactions are what is best for young children—and they may both be right.

These divergent points of view can erode professionalism in other ways too. Day care, for example, is too often thought of as the providing of physical care only; as if education or, more specifically, learning, does not occur when we do not want it to. Because of this low expectation, qualifications for personnel are correspondingly low. Minimum wage "salaries" are not unusual for day care teachers. Even Head Start teachers, many of whom have far more training than day care teachers, earn considerably less money than public school teachers. In 1990, for example, Head Start teachers' average salaries ranged from a low of $7,863 in Mississippi to a high of $16,926 in Michigan, when public school average teachers' salaries ranged from $21,300 in South Dakota to $48,153 in Alaska. Overall averages were $11,859 for Head Start and over $30,000 for public school teachers (Hymes, 1991, p. 402).

Early childhood specialists suffer twice what public school teachers experience from the lay public. Teachers frequently contend with self-appointed experts who achieved their status simply by experiencing school themselves. Early childhood teachers must contend with all who have been children and the many who have been parents. Early childhood specialists have an enormous challenge in convincing or persuading some parents that the study of child development and related areas does make one more of an expert in the field than those who have not so studied.

The variety of explanations for early childhood education not being as much of a profession as, say, elementary education, may provide insight into the dilemma, but the explanations do not automatically solve the dilemma. In 1987, with the publication of *Developmentally Appropriate Practice in Early Childhood Programs Serving Children from Birth through Age 8* edited by Sue Bredekamp, the National Association for the Education of Young Children (NAEYC) hoped to accomplish two objectives. One was to improve the quality of education and care children these ages were receiving in all kinds of settings and the other was to provide a knowledge base for early childhood educators. "The statement addresses the field's fundamental problem, the perceived absence of a distinctive knowledge base, by setting forth a series of recommended practices in early childhood programs" (Powell, 1994, p. 178). The hope was and is to make early childhood education less of a marginal profession (Powell, 1994). To what extent that hope will be realized remains to be seen.

Developmentally Appropriate Practice

As indicated in the earlier historical sections, the field of child development closely followed and, in some cases, led the creation of childhood as a separate period of development in the early twentieth century. By the 1920s child-labor laws, followed by compulsory school attendance laws and the establishment of the federal Children's Bureau and numerous child development laboratories, all contributed to the growing interest in studying child growth and development. By the 1980s, the NAEYC felt it was time to capitalize on the accumulated research findings and to fashion a set of guidelines for early childhood educators. The basic premise upon which developmentally appropriate practice (DAP) is based is that "a major determinant of program quality (for children from birth through age 8) is the extent to which knowledge of child development is applied in program practices—the degree to which the program is *developmentally appropriate*" (Bredekamp, 1987, pp. 1–2, emphasis in the original).

Developmental appropriateness has two dimensions: age appropriateness and individual appropriateness. Regarding age, the guidelines claim "that there are universal, predictable sequences of growth and change that occur in children during the first 9 years of life" (Bredekamp, 1987, p. 2). All areas of growth and development—physical, emotional, social, and cognitive—have been studied and knowledge of these changes "provides a framework from which teachers prepare the learning environment and plan appropriate experiences" (Bredekamp, 1987, p. 2). Individual appropriateness includes variables such as personality, learning style, and family background. Knowledge of the individual differences regarding these variables, combined with the age variables of physical, emotional, social, and cognitive growth, should contribute to well-designed educational environments for children. Attention also needs to be paid to "tradition, the subject matter of the disciplines, social or cultural values, and parental desires" to plan developmentally appropriate practices (Bredekamp, 1987, p. 3).

The Curriculum.   Ten guidelines for DAP and the curriculum are suggested by Bredekamp. Each will be briefly described below. (For more complete description, see Bredekamp, 1987, pp. 3–8.)

1. The curriculum should accommodate all areas of growth and development—physical, emo-

tional, social, and cognitive—and do so in an integrated manner. No one area can be affected without affecting one or more of the others. All of the areas are legitimate concerns for early childhood educators.

2. Curriculum planning should be based on teachers' observations of children. For example, every child has needs, strengths, weaknesses, and interests. In addition, children's families and cultural backgrounds should be taken into account when planning appropriate activities.

3. The emphasis should be on active learning. Children should have ample opportunities to interact with materials, other children, and adults.

4. The activities in which the children engage and the materials with which they interact should be "concrete, real, and relevant to the lives of young children" (p. 4). Work sheets and coloring books are especially inappropriate for children under 6. Recommended materials for ages 3 to 8 include, but are not limited to sand, water, clay, table and unit blocks, puzzles, games, and dramatic play props.

5. The range of appropriate activities and materials should be wide enough to encompass the age and individual differences within the group. At least 2 years would be an appropriate range for a single age group. If children are grouped in a family or vertical style (e.g., 3, 4, and 5 year olds together) the range of activities and materials would have to be correspondingly broader.

6. All activities and materials should be robust, that is, children can be engaged at different levels of difficulty and complexity. Activities and materials should be such that children will be challenged and not so unidimensional that children are either frustrated or bored.

7. Children should have opportunities to choose from a variety of activities and materials. Teachers engage the children by asking questions and making suggestions.

8. Multicultural and nonsexist activities and materials should be provided for children of all ages. Stereotyping of any kind is to be avoided. The intent here is to promote the child's self-concept and self-esteem and the integrity of the child's family.

9. A balance of active and quiet activities should exist. Most 4 and 5 year olds still need naps, but even older children will benefit from alternating periods of high and low activity.

10. Outdoor activities should be a part of the regular program. Beyond the traditional school recess, it is important for children to exercise large muscles and to learn about the environment in ways not possible indoors.

Adult–Child Interactions. Seven guidelines address adult–child interactions. (As with curriculum guidelines, see Bredekamp, 1987, for more detail.)

1. Adults should respond quickly and directly to children whenever possible. The children's needs, desires, and messages should be responded to in a manner that is consistent with the children's differing styles and abilities. Adults should "move quietly and circulate among individuals in groups to communicate with children in a friendly and relaxed manner" (p. 9). Teachers may have to sit low or kneel in order to make comfortable eye contact with children.

2. Many opportunities should be provided to promote communication. Individual and small group interactions are particularly useful for children ages 4 to 8. Opportunities for children these ages to communicate with one another also are important. Open-ended questions permit responses that reveal the child's level of understanding of various concepts.

3. Opportunities for success should be plentiful, and adults should encourage children to stay with tasks until completed. Children learn from mistakes, and adults need to be supportive of children when mistakes occur.

4. Teachers should recognize and respond to children's stress. Children can be unduly stressed as a result of classroom or other circumstances, and teachers need to respond with understanding and comforting behaviors.

5. Teachers should nurture children's development of self-esteem "by respecting, accepting, and comforting children, regardless of the child's behavior" (p. 11). Teachers should never inflict

physical or emotional pain, ridicule, insult, or threaten children.

6. Teachers should help children develop self-control. Rules may be cooperatively developed with older children, but always should be clear and reasonably consistent.
7. Teachers should help children become more independent in all endeavors, but as the responsible adult, a teacher at all times must supervise the children. Children 5 and older may be able to leave the group to run an errand, but only if the teacher believes the child is responsible enough to do it without incident.

Home and Program Relationships.   Three guidelines cover the relationship between the child's home and the early childhood program. (See Bredekamp, 1987, for more detail.)

1. "Parents have both the right and the responsibility to share in decisions about their children's care and education" (p. 12). Teachers should initiate and maintain the communication with parents. (This particular guideline has the potential for undoing all of the others.) As Powell (1994) has indicated, it is possible that parents may not approve of or desire developmentally appropriate practices. We will return to this under Contemporary Issues.
2. "Teachers share child development knowledge, insights, and resources as part of regular communication and conferences with family members" (p. 12). Parents should provide information about individual children and this mutual sharing (teacher and parent) will strengthen the family and the program. (This guideline comes close to suggesting a professional–client relationship to which some parents take umbrage. It too will be addressed under Contemporary Issues.)
3. All agencies and their personnel who are responsible for children—teachers, consultants, aides—along with parents, should share relevant educational and developmental information about children as they proceed from one level to another. Children can move horizontally, for example, from a morning day care center to an afternoon kinder-

garten, or vertically, from first grade to second. The parents and "receiving" teachers will be able to plan better when they have relevant information from other teachers. (This is called developmental continuity (Barbour & Seefeldt, 1993) and will be discussed under Contemporary Issues.)

Assessment/Evaluation.   Finally, there are four guidelines for developmental evaluation of children. (See Bredekamp, 1987, for more detail.)

1. Decisions about a child's enrollment, retention, or placement should never be made on the basis of a single assessment. Observations by teachers and parents are more valid and reliable guides for developing appropriate activities as well as placements.
2. Multiple assessments and observations are needed to make decisions about children who may have special needs and require special programming. Parents, too, should realize that a single assessment leaves a lot to be desired.
3. Whenever assessments are from standardized instruments the norms need to be appropriate to the age, gender, culture, and socioeconomics of the child. The validity of comparisons of children who are not so matched is questionable.
4. Public schools should have a developmentally appropriate placement for every child of legal entry age. Institutions should serve the people, not vice versa.

In addition to taking the lead to establish developmentally appropriate practices, the NAEYC, also in the 1980s, established accreditation standards for early childhood settings. The two primary goals of the NAEYC accreditation project are the following:

1. to help program personnel become involved in a process that will facilitate real and lasting improvements in the quality of the program and
2. to evaluate the quality of the program for the purpose of accrediting those programs that demonstrate substantial compliance with criteria for high quality. (Bredekamp & Glowacki, 1996, p. 2)

The accreditation is appropriate for all kinds of early childhood centers, and includes, but is not limited to, public school prekindergartens, Head Start centers, kindergartens, and school-age child care centers.

Teacher Certification

For day care teachers, sadly, there is little preparation, if any, required by most states. This situation undoubtedly reflects the cycle of low wages that precludes attracting and keeping highly qualified applicants. In addition, it reflects the erroneous assumption that anyone can provide appropriate care and education to young children.

The Child Development Associate (CDA) program was begun in 1972 to provide a middle level group of early childhood professionals—neither to replace a college-trained teacher nor to serve as an aide (Powell & Dunn, 1990). The CDA credential program was "designed to accommodate individuals who might not qualify for or succeed in traditional baccalaureate teacher education programs. It does so by focusing on performance (with children) rather than on the completion of course work . . ." (Powell & Dunn, 1990, p. 48).

CDA candidates are required to have 480 hours of work with children, from birth through age 5 and to complete 120 clock hours of formal training in early childhood education. A team of early childhood professionals then assesses the candidate in the following six goal areas of competence and determine if the candidate can

1. establish and maintain a safe, healthy learning environment
2. advance physical and intellectual competence
3. support social and emotional development and provide positive guidance
4. establish positive and productive relationships with families
5. ensure a well-run, purposeful program responsive to participant needs
6. maintain a commitment to professionalism (Powell & Dunn, 1990, p. 47)

In addition to the CDA credential and sometimes as a variant of it, aspiring early childhood teachers can complete 1- or 2-year associate degree or vocational training programs. The CDA credential and other pre-baccalaureate programs can be viewed as steps on a career ladder for those aspiring to more advanced positions within the field.

Currently, only about half of the states require early childhood certification or endorsement for their baccalaureate-level teachers (Cooper & Eisenhart, 1990). A great deal of variation exists even among the states that do require special preparation. In 1982 the NAEYC published *Early Childhood Teacher Education Guidelines* to address the variance in existing programs. Gleaning from the Guidelines, Cooper and Eisenhart (1990) list 10 areas in which theoretical and research knowledge, as well as practical skills, are recommended:

1. Human development
2. Historical, philosophical, psychological, and social foundations of early childhood education
3. Curriculum for teaching young children
4. Observation and recording of children's behavior
5. Working with atypical children
6. Interpersonal communication
7. Family and community relations
8. Values and ethics
9. Comprehension of cultural diversity
10. Legislation and public policy as it affects children, families, and programs for children. (Cooper & Eisenhart, 1990, p. 178)

Learning within any of the 10 areas can be and is quite variable. Learning, for example, about different curriculum models could supplant opportunities for learning about the variety of teaching strategies. But the list is a beginning for establishing a kind of standardization or knowledge base necessary for a profession.

CONTEMPORARY ISSUES

Great Need for Care and Education

Contributing to the single, most important contemporary issue is the fact that over 60 percent of the parents of children under 6 years of age are employed outside the home and, according to a large scale study of child care centers conducted through the University of Colorado at Denver, University of California at Los Angeles, University of North Carolina, and Yale

University (1995), the care offered at about 75 percent of the centers is custodial only. As indicated earlier, children learn all of the time. To claim only custodial care is occurring is tantamount to saying whatever learning is occurring does not matter—a totally untenable statement for educators. The same study found 12 percent of the child care centers provided such poor care that it jeopardized children's safety and development. Only 14 percent appeared to be on the plus side, that is, offering care that would promote growth and development (Children's Defense Fund, 1996).

About a third of the child care is provided by centers in the form of group care. About a quarter is provided by family care homes. These two sources of care typically are regulated by state-level human services or welfare agencies. Education agencies usually have no authority to affect group centers or family care homes. Licensing requirements, enforced by human service and welfare personnel, include group size, staff-child ratios, physical space, health and nutrition, and general safety concerns.

The preeminent issue then, the one that supersedes all others, is the availability and provision of quality care and education for the 7 million children of working parents who are cared for by someone other than a parent (Children's Defense Fund, 1996). In 1995 Head Start served 752,000 children, about one-tenth of the 7 million children of working parents, and only about one third of those eligible, based on family income. But Head Start, like public schools, cares for children for only a portion of the typical work day.

Public school administrators must be advocates for young children. If they are not, they should find other work. It is the frequently overlooked and routinely underfunded care and education of young children—from birth to age 5 especially, but including older, latchkey children—that must be improved. Public schools have always prided themselves in taking children "as they are." The commitment to providing the best education possible is unwavering. But that commitment can be challenged and tested when children arrive at the schoolhouse door ill-prepared to be at their best because they have had 4 to 5 years of less-than-optimum care and virtually random education. What better way to improve the quality of the K–12 school experience than to improve the beginner's chances of success?

The principal should take the lead in advocating for high-quality care and education for all children anywhere, but especially for those who soon will be entering the public school. Kindergarten and primary grade teachers, along with the principal, could be a formidable group of advocates. And such advocacy need not be adversarial. Public school personnel should be concerned with developmental continuity, that is, easing the transitions across and between all early childhood settings.

Developmental Continuity

Another issue especially relevant to public schools is establishing and maintaining developmental continuity (Barbour & Seefeldt, 1993). As one of the DAP guidelines stated, children's development is continuous and should not be unnecessarily interrupted by the horizontal or vertical movement between agencies. Where half-day kindergartens exist, it is not unusual for children to spend the other half of the day in a day care facility. And even if kindergarten were "all" day, unless the schools have before- and after-school programs, the children will likely be spending as much, if not more, time within another facility. These are examples of horizontal movement.

When children move from a nursery school, day care, or Head Start program and enter the public school, the transition is considered vertical and needs to be made as comfortable as possible. Kindergarten and primary grade teachers need to realize the children they are receiving may have spent 4 or 5 years of their young lives in other facilities. The public school teachers are more likely to provide an appropriate transition for these children when they understand more completely the nature of the previous educational experiences.

Barbour and Seefeldt (1993) have numerous suggestions for creating and maintaining developmental continuity. Working toward developmental continuity could be a bottom-up proposition—a few teachers and parents initiating the process—or one that is top-down, where a principal or another administrator takes the lead. The end result of either approach would be greater communication between and among teachers and parents from all kinds of early childhood settings. There could be changes at all levels as well.

Preschool programs could become more sensitive to educational issues, in addition to providing care (Langenbach & Neskora, 1977). Elementary schools could consider restructuring their primary grades to accommodate better the continuous growth and development of young children. Multiple age or family grouping, as was the case in the 1950s in some nongraded primaries, could be established. Nongraded settings also typically improve reporting and promotion practices as well.

Challenges to Developmentally Appropriate Practice (DAP)

Another contemporary issue is the challenge to DAP. Walsh (1991), Kessler and Swadener (1992), and Mallory and New (1994), have raised a number of objections to DAP. Walsh (1991) challenges the notion that there is a consensus on children's development, as claimed by NAEYC in its 1987 publication (Bredekamp). He also suggests that the emphasis on development has been misinterpreted by many early childhood educators as an emphasis on maturation and a return to the ubiquitous "readiness" so prevalent in primary grades whenever learning to read is mentioned. The implication of an emphasis on maturation—that development is exclusively from within and that time alone is the only variable—includes both delaying any schooling activity until the child is ready and assuming a relatively passive role for teachers. Ample evidence exists that both practices are unwise. Walsh also believes the DAP emphasis on Piaget has reinforced notions of the "solitary learner" instead of Vygotsky's and Bruner's beliefs in socially mediated learning, that is, emphasizing the roles of other children and adults.

Kessler and Swadener (1992) have edited an entire book that challenges DAP from a variety of perspectives. They include a critical sociology that considers the political context of the school, especially in regard to what knowledge is brought by students compared with the knowledge promoted by the school. The Tyler rationale for curriculum development also is challenged as is the idea that child development theory actually prescribes what to teach. On this latter point, they quote Spodek, "What children need to know or ought to know is not determined by what children are

capable of knowing" (p. xx). In addition, Kessler and Swadener draw from feminist perspectives and examples of qualitative research traditions, for example, life histories and autobiography, as possible sources for informing curriculum.

Most recently, Mallory and New (1994) have assembled challenges to DAP in the belief that the "current conceptualization is overly narrow in its general interpretation of the role of the teacher, and specifically with respect to acknowledging variations associated with cultural and developmental diversity" (Mallory & New, 1994, p. 2). New (1994) takes exception to the allegation that the DAPs are natural extensions of child development research findings. She claims that the preponderance of child development studies has involved only white, middle-class American children. Less than 10 percent of child development research, in her view, has included culturally or linguistically diverse populations.

Lubeck (1994) suggests that DAP is unduly focused on the immediate environment of the classroom and materials. She believes such a focus precludes, or at least obfuscates, being concerned with social issues of equality, justice, and giving voice to the disenfranchised. She makes a good point, but it represents a view many practitioners simply dismiss by saying, "It's not my job." Early childhood educators should be concerned with issues of racism, injustice, poverty, and inequities in school and society (Apple & Beane, 1995).

The DAP guideline concerning parents sharing in decisions about care and education was cited earlier as having a built-in seed of potential self-destruction (Powell, 1994). Schools committed to democratic principles always tread perilously close to creative anarchy. As Apple and Beane (1995) observe,

> Proponents of democratic schools also realize, sometimes painfully, that exercising democracy involves tensions and contradictions. Democratic participation in decision making, for example, opens the way for antidemocratic ideas such as the continuing demands for censorship of materials, the use of public tax vouchers for private school tuition, and the maintenance of historical inequities in school life. . . . Such contradictions and tensions point to the fact that bringing democracy to life is always a struggle. (p. 8)

Only by working together can professional educators and parents, as well as other community members, create and maintain schools that serve the common good of the whole community (Apple & Beane, 1995).

Lubeck (1994) considers the DAP guideline about teachers sharing child development knowledge objectionable. "[Parents] are expected to listen to those who make claims to greater knowledge and authority" (p. 33). Her objection makes sense if those who are making such claims do not really have more knowledge and authority. But it also makes sense in that it reflects, possibly, a bad version of a professional–client relationship. The medical profession, for example, has been charged with treating patients as objects (Cousins, 1979). If early childhood educators, irrespective of their training and educational accomplishments, treat parents as unenlightened observers, Lubeck's resentment is warranted.

Comparing Curriculums

One of the features of Head Start shortly after it began was the idea of planned variation. Program planners were encouraged to experiment with different approaches to teaching young children. The intent was to compare, over time, which programs, if any, were "better" than others. Many attempts were made to assess program accomplishments, but because of the comprehensive nature of program objectives and the shortcomings of most research designs that attempted to account for them, the results from most investigations have been mixed, that is, some models do well with what they emphasize but not so well with regard to other objectives. In short, no clear "winner" in terms of an early childhood model has emerged.

Instead of global, conclusive pronouncements of curriculum approaches that "do it all," some more focused generalizations do seem appropriate. For example, whereas cognitive gains appear to be short term, that is, they wash out 3 or 4 years later, performance and social indicators have been found to be positively affected. Low-income minority children who were regarded as likely candidates for school-age placement in special education "were significantly less likely to be retained in elementary school, less likely to be placed in special education programs, and more likely to graduate from high school" (Mallory, 1994, p. 51).

An important observation related to evaluation of early childhood settings is the influence of the evaluation on the curriculum (Shepard, 1991). If, for example, the only assessment of a program is an achievement test, it is quite possible that the emphasis in teaching will be achievement, at the expense of other, likely more worthwhile, goals (Spodek & Brown, 1993).

Illustrative Practices and Issues

Dunn, L., and Kontos, S. (1997). What have we learned about developmentally appropriate practice? *Young Children, 52*(5), 6–13.

> This article discusses the state of practice in early childhood settings: DAP is not the norm, despite the research that supports DAP. *Issues:* How can teachers be more successful in implementing DAP? How can administrators assist in the implementation?

Kamii, C., & Ewing, J. E. (1996). Basing teaching on Piaget's constructivism. *Childhood Education, 1996 Annual Theme,* 260–264.

> This article explores Piaget's theories on the way children learn and examine Piaget's contributions to constructivism. *Issues:* How do constructivism, associationism, and behaviorism differ?

SUMMARY

It has been less than 100 years that young children have not been thought of as simply small adults. Infanticide and abusive child-labor practices characterized life for the vast majority of children well into the nineteenth century. More enlightened views of children, and how they develop and learn, have evolved over the last century, while some other views have persisted.

Perhaps there has even been a kind of cycling in the last 50 years. Indeed, developmentally appropriate practices are, as Apple and Beane (1995) observe, a lot like the child-centered progressive ideas of the 1940s and 1950s. And the non-graded primaries of the 1950s may need to be revisited as Barbour and Seefeldt (1993) suggest.

The counterpoints, however, may be in similar cycles. The launching of Sputnik in 1957 and the ensuing clamor for more math and science spelled the end of non-graded primaries and the back-to-basics movement, precipitated by the 1983 publication of *A Nation at Risk,* and effectively put an end to open education.

One of the lessons from the recent past may be that schools were not sufficiently protected by those most closely associated with them—the parents, teachers, and administrators. Perhaps schools were too quickly affected by the vagaries of national concerns. It may be that parents, teachers, and administrators, working together for the common good of the school and community, can be an effective buffer for the school, permitting such schools to serve well what those closest to them consider to be important.

QUESTIONS FOR FURTHER CONSIDERATION

Research

1. Research shows that "catch-up" programs found in schools do not give students an advantage, rather these programs just keep students from falling further behind. How does this statement relate to the Goals 2000 mandate that children will come to school ready to learn?

2. Examine Piaget's and Vygotsky's theories of learning. How can these theories be applied in the development of early childhood education programs?

Reflect

1. How can you build upon the strengths children bring to school?

2. In what ways could developmentally appropriate practices promote multiculturalism?

Respond/React

1. How would you explain the finding that only about one third of the early childhood programs are developmentally appropriate?

2. What kinds of compromises may be necessary to reconcile the proponents of developmentally appropriate practices with those who object to them?

SUGGESTED READINGS

Barbour, N. H., & Seefeldt, C. (1993). *Developmental continuity across preschool and primary grades.* Wheaton, MD: Association for Childhood Education International.

Bredekamp, S. (Ed.). (1987). *Developmentally appropriate practice in early childhood programs serving children from birth through age 8.* Washington, DC: National Association for the Education of Young Children.

Hymes, J. L. Jr. (1991). *Early childhood education: Twenty years in review.* Washington, DC: National Association for the Education of Young Children.

CHAPTER 7

FINE ARTS EDUCATION

The fine arts include art, music, drama/theatre, dance, and creative writing. In terms of special programs, art and music are the most prevalent, especially at the elementary level, while drama/theatre and dance are nearly exclusively at the secondary level (Leonhard, 1991). Creative writing typically is included in language arts in elementary schools and in English or writing courses in secondary schools. Thus, our emphasis in this chapter will be on art, music, drama/theatre, and dance. After a brief review of each of the fine art's histories, the standards for that art will be presented.

The visual arts and music are offered in more than 95 percent of elementary, middle, and secondary schools, while drama/theatre and dance are rare entities at the elementary level, and though present in the middle school and secondary schools, their presence is substantially less than visual arts and music (Leonhard, 1991). Drama activities are provided to elementary children through other subject areas such as language arts and social studies in about 80 percent of elementary schools, but actual drama/theatre programs are found in less than 5 percent. However, more than half of middle schools and about 60 percent of secondary schools have special programs or courses in drama/theatre.

Dance has slightly more presence than drama/theatre at the elementary level (about 8 percent), but considerably less than drama/theatre at the middle and secondary levels where only about 30 percent report having special programs or courses in dance (Leonhard, 1991). Speculating why the percentages of emphasis differ among these four fine arts will be left to others. Our interest is to provide some rudimentary history and description of each of these fine arts.

Art or the arts have carried a number of different meanings since antiquity. For Plato, art was most often used in reference to artisans and craftsmen, who ranked only one class higher than slaves and consequently were held in relatively low regard. Art also meant imitation of nature (as in artifice and artificial). More often, however, art has meant the highest level of accomplishment within any endeavor. When used in the context of the fine arts, art means "creative works and the process of producing them and the whole body of work in the art forms that make up the entire human intellectual and cultural heritage" (Consortium of National Arts Education Associations, 1994, p. 1).

A major boost for the fine arts occurred when they were included as core subjects in *Goals 2000: Educate America Act.* It may be that because the fine arts were included as core subjects in *Goals 2000,* along with mathematics, science, English, and the other traditional disciplines, that the marginalization of the arts in schools may be history, but it was not always so.

VISUAL ARTS EDUCATION

History

Currently, art is taken to mean one of the fine arts, but until the last two centuries, the more common meaning was as in the useful arts. Art education, specifically, education in the visual arts, was influenced by both conceptions of art. The church, private academies, and guilds were important to keeping all manner of visual arts alive through the Middle Ages.

In the late sixteenth and early seventeenth centuries, private academies promoted visual art in the tradition of the great masters while guilds trained craftsmen in the useful arts. The early art academies of the Renaissance period, usually sponsored by a prince or member of the clergy, were inspired by Michelangelo. Such a genius could not have been nurtured by a guild master—the dominant "art education" until the sixteenth century. But even academies became stultified by their own methods of copying masters. In the academies, the teaching method was soon formalized. According to Efland,

> The sequence of drawing from drawings, drawing from casts, and drawing from the model was viewed as the heart and core of the method from the latter years of the seventeenth century to the latter years of the nineteenth century. (1990, p. 37)

Artists had been elevated from the skilled craftsmen idea that persisted from the time of Plato through the medieval period to the cultural elite, and the academies were developed to train new artists by the study of the past masters. This adoration and virtual emulation of the past found its way to colonial America in the seventeenth century.

The Boston Latin School, established by the Puritans in 1635 and still in operation, was designed to carry on the classical teaching prevalent in the "old" world. The classical approach to schooling was challenged, however, with the advent of the Industrial Revolution, the full impact of which was felt in the nineteenth century.

Efland (1990) attributes changes in visual arts education to three forces: industrialization, the resistance to and eventual overthrow of autocratic rule, and the cultural revolution known as romanticism. Undoubtedly, all three affected education, but industrialization appears to us to have had the greatest impact on teaching the visual arts.

Benjamin Franklin's interest in making all education more practical included the notion that drawing was a particularly useful skill. When manufacturing rapidly advanced during the nineteenth century, Franklin's ideas for the practical arts were finally incorporated, and teaching industrial and mechanical drawing became very common in the schools.

At the same time that this positive interest in drawing for industrial and manufacturing purposes became evident a more philosophical rationale for marginalizing art as a fine art occurred. In 1861, Herbert Spencer, a promoter of Social Darwinism, asked and answered what has become a perennial question for

schools, "What knowledge is of most worth?" His answer centered around logical extensions of Darwinism to schooling. In effect, he positioned knowledge that dealt with self-preservation first, followed by knowledge to help secure the necessities of life, and then that which is necessary for raising children in a family was of "most worth." Last on his list was knowledge associated with gratification of tastes and feelings. As Efland observed,

> Thus the doctrine of evolution was invoked to provide a rational basis for determining the relative importance of the subjects in the curriculum . . . by Spencer's reckoning, the arts assume a minor role. (1990, p. 157)

By the turn of the century, art education typically meant industrial drawing, and to the extent that it might include the study and appreciation of great art or the learning associated with actually producing works of art, it was considered an extra, if not a frill. Exceptions to this state of affairs did exist but seldom deterred the relegation of art, as in fine art, to the margins of the basic curriculum.

One exception was William Harris, superintendent of the St. Louis schools, who is credited with establishing the first public school kindergarten. Harris became U.S. Commissioner of Education in 1889 and promoted the idea that art was a result of a spiritual evolution and that by studying great art up to the then current era, one would develop "a deep respect for social institutions that would impose a degree of constraint upon personal action" (Efland, 1990, p. 133). A century later this socially conservative purpose of art education was echoed by the former Secretary of Education, William Bennett (1984), and by Edward Hirsch (1987).

Early in the twentieth century, several forces began to influence art education. The child study movement, the arts and crafts movement, and progressive education all affected art education for most of the rest of the century.

The interest in childhood as a distinct period, qualitatively different from adulthood, had its beginning around the turn of the century. Many child development specialists were, and still are, stage theorists—believing that children's development is a progression through distinct stages. The child study movement eventually became the groundwork for Victor Lowenfeld's text, *Creative and Mental Growth* (1947), which was the most influential art education textbook throughout the 1950s, 1960s, and 1970s (Efland, 1990).

The arts and crafts movement began in England in response to the perceived excesses of the Industrial Revolution and was transported to the United States near the turn of the century. One major objective of the movement was to provide art experiences to the working class. The arts and crafts movement found its way into the public schools to edify "the union of art with craft, lost since the Renaissance" (Efland, 1990, p. 15). In addition, the child study movement emphasized the importance of children's interests and their need to be active learners—ideas that were precursors to the progressive education movement.

Progressive education promoted the idea that children learn best what they live, that is, meaning is rooted in their daily lives. Progressive educators insisted that children be active learners who attended to their tasks, but also expressed themselves through gesture, voice, speech, music, making, modeling, painting, drawing, and writing—in short, the arts were central to progressive education.

Many have debated the degree to which progressive education actually changed the typical school. There is no doubt that the professional literature was affected, but the actual practices of ordinary classrooms may have been sufficiently insulated from the implications of any shift in educational philosophy. And there were setbacks to progressivism.

In 1918 the Cardinal Principles of Secondary Education were issued by the National Education Association's Commission on the Reorganization of Secondary Education. The principles were a reaction to the intellectual emphasis of the secondary schools and in that sense represented some tenets of progressive education but relegated the arts to leisure pursuits (Elfand, 1990).

By the 1920s industrial education became vocational education and consequently was out of the art education realm. The utility purpose of much of art education remained, however, in the guise of arts and crafts.

The Great Depression actually helped the visual arts in two ways. First, to provide work for artists, some were paid by the federal government to be artists-in-residence in both elementary and secondary schools (Martin & Ross, 1988). In addition, because jobs were so scarce, more young people stayed in school longer, thereby increasing the number of students encountering the arts. The G.I. Bill that provided tuition for veterans, had a similar effect after World War II when colleges and universities experienced large increases in enrollments.

In the 1950s Victor Lowenfeld's text, *Creative and Mental Growth* (1947), had a major impact on the practice of art education. Influenced by Freud, Lowenfeld believed that free expression was necessary for healthy growth and development. Lowenfeld believed that children's artistic development occurred in stages, and he illustrated his text with examples of the various stages. He is credited with giving more teachers confidence in teaching art than anyone in this century (Efland, 1990). His emphasis on stages of development and the attendant appropriate expectations teachers should have may make him one of the first to promote developmentally appropriate practices, a full 40 years before that phrase became the mantra for early childhood and special education teachers.

As noted earlier throughout discussions of the 1950s and 1960s, here and elsewhere, the launching of the then Soviet Union's space satellite in 1957 had profound effects on schooling. In essence, the mood was to abandon any activity that smacked of "life-adjustment" or promoted self-expression or in anyway detracted from the basics. Furthermore, because of our apparent "failure" in the space race, it was thought we should especially concentrate on the sciences. Indeed science "provided the model of curriculum reform for the whole of general education, including art education" (Efland, 1991, p. 240).

A great deal of curriculum development occurred in the 1960s, and most of it was outside of schools. University faculty were the primary movers in establishing approaches to the various disciplines, packaging them, and expecting schools to adopt them. Math, biology, chemistry, and physics were the most affected because the principle operating was that only subject matter disciplines warranted study. A discipline has "an organized body of knowledge, specific methods of inquiry, and a community of scholars who generally agree on the fundamental ideas of their field" (Efland, 1990, p. 241).

The interest in art as a discipline did not take effect, however, until 1984. More about that later. The 1960s also was a time for the arts-in-education movement—one that promoted the idea that "art was not a discipline. Rather it was an experience, to be had by participating in the artistic process or by witnessing this process in the work of performing artists" (Efland, 1990, pp. 244–245). The arts-in-education movement often included community artists and agencies— bringing them into the schools to promote the teaching of all of the arts. The emphasis was on performance, and although there was criticism for the heavy reliance on federal agencies and private foundations, "the arts-in-education program enjoyed a good press, reminding people that the arts belonged in the school" (Efland, 1990, p. 247).

The 1970s and 1980s were a time for competency-based education and the excellence movement respectively. The competency movement emphasized writing specific behavioral objectives to focus the teacher's attention on students' skills and to facilitate their measurement. Such words as *know, understand,* and *appreciate* were anathema to the competency advocates. In the place of general words came more specific ones such as *identify, describe,* and *demonstrate.* These more specific words are amenable to measurement—for example, "The student will identify, with 90 percent accuracy . . ."

Much of the competency movement can be explained by the increasing interest in accountability— from state departments of education, professional accrediting agencies, and various funding sources for special programs. The excessive use of measurable terms, however, led to the cynical observation that if it cannot be counted, it does not count (Pratt, 1980).

The excellence movement was a result of the 1983 report, *A Nation at Risk,* that charged, among other things, that our schools were mired in mediocrity. " 'Excellence,' 'substance,' and 'rigor' have been the watchwords of the education reform movements of the eighties" (Pankratz, 1989, p. 1). Although a variety of responses occurred to the call for excellence, the discipline-based art education movement was one of the best known (Pankratz, 1989).

Discipline-based art education (DBAE) got its impetus from the J. Paul Getty Trust in 1982. A group of art educators began summer institutes in California to help elementary classroom teachers teach art. DBAE proposes that content be drawn from four art sources: the art studio (production); art criticism (theory); art history (exemplars); and aesthetics (philosophy). The Getty initiative in DBAE has been promulgated in school districts throughout the states (DiBlasio, 1989).

Standards and Goals

In 1992 a consortium of fine arts associations was formed to develop standards in the arts. Funding was provided by the U.S. Department of Education, the National Endowment for the Arts, and the National Endowment for the Humanities through a grant administered by the Music Educators National Conference. The Consortium of National Arts Education Associations is made up of the American Alliance for Theatre and Education, the Music Educators National Conference, the National Art Education Association, and the National Dance Association.

The standards are written for all four of the fine arts for three levels of schooling: K–4, 5–8, and 9–12. Two types of standards are used, content standards— those that specify what should be known and done— and achievement standards—those that signify what level of achievement is expected. There are six content standards for the visual arts. These six content standards are common across all three grade-level categories. The achievement standards, of course, become more sophisticated as one proceeds from the K–4 through the 9–12 level. At the 9–12 level, the achievement standards are divided into two categories —proficient and advanced. All students at the 9–12 level are expected to be proficient in at least one art, whereas the advanced level would be expected only of those students who selected specialized courses in that art area.

Below are the six content standards for the visual arts, followed, for the purpose of illustration, by just one achievement standard from each grade cluster. For a complete listing of all achievement standards, as well as a lucid description and explanation of all of the fine arts and why they are important, please see the Consortium of National Arts Education Associations (1994).*

Content standard

1. Understand and apply media, techniques, and processes.

Achievement standard

K–4   Know the difference between materials, techniques, and processes

5–8   Select media, techniques, and processes; analyze what makes them effective or not effective in communicating ideas; and reflect upon the effectiveness of their choices

9–12   Proficient level—Apply media, techniques, and processes with sufficient skill, confidence, and sensitivity that their intentions are carried out in their art works

Advanced level—Communicate ideas regularly at a high level of effectiveness in at least one visual arts medium

Content standard

2. Using knowledge of structures and functions

Achievement standard

K–4   Know the differences among visual characteristics and purposes of art in order to convey ideas

5–8   Generalize about the effects of visual structures and functions and reflect upon these effects in [the students'] own work

9–12   Proficient level—Demonstrate the ability to form and defend judgments about the characteristics and structures to accomplish commercial, personal, communal, or other purposes of art

Advanced level—Demonstrate the ability to compare two or more perspectives about the use of organizational principles and functions in artwork and to defend personal evaluations of these perspectives

*Excerpted from *National Standards for Arts Education,* published by Music Educators National Conference (MENC). Copyright © 1994 by MENC. Reproduced with permission. The complete National Standards and additional materials relating to the Standards are available from Music Educators National Conference, 1806 Robert Fulton Drive, Reston, VA 20191 (telephone 800-336-3768).

Content standard

3. Choosing and evaluating a range of subject matter, symbols, and ideas

Achievement standard

K–4   Explore and understand prospective contents for works of art

5–8   Integrate visual, spatial, and temporal concepts with content to communicate intended meaning in their artworks

9–12   Proficient level—Reflect on how artworks differ visually, spatially, temporally, and functionally, and describe how these are related to history

Advanced level—Describe the origins of specific images and ideas and explain why they are of value in [the students'] artwork and in the work of others

Content standard

4. Understanding the visual arts in relation to history and cultures

Achievement standard

K–4   Know that the visual arts have both a history and specific relationships to various cultures

5–8   Know and compare the characteristics of artworks in various eras and cultures.

9–12   Proficient level—Differentiate among a variety of historical and cultural contexts in terms of characteristics and purposes of works of art

Advanced level—Analyze and interpret artworks for relationships among form, context, purposes, and critical models, showing understanding of the work of critics, historians, aestheticians, and artists

Content standard

5. Reflecting upon and assessing the characteristics and merits of their work and the work of others.

Achievement standard

K–4   Understand there are various purposes for creating works of visual art

5–8   Compare multiple purposes for creating works of art

9–12   Proficient level—Identify intentions of those creating artworks, explore the implications of various purposes, and justify their analyses of purposes in particular works
Advanced level—Correlate responses to works of visual art with various techniques for communicating meanings, ideas, attitudes, views, and intentions

Content standard

6. Making connections between visual arts and other disciplines

Achievement standard

K–4   Understand and use similarities and differences between characteristics of the visual arts and other arts disciplines

5–8   Compare the characteristics of works in two or more art forms that share similar subject matter, historical periods, or cultural context

9–12   Proficient level—Compare the materials, technologies, media, and processes of the visual arts with those of other arts disciplines as they are used in creation and types of analysis
Advanced level—Synthesize the creative and analytical principles and techniques of the visual arts and selected other arts disciplines, the humanities, or sciences

Contemporary Issues

Variety of Approaches.   There are various approaches to teaching the visual arts. Lehman and Sinatra (1988) identify three main approaches: creative self-expression (also called traditional); competency based arts education; and discipline-based art education. Regarding the creative self-expression approach, Lehman and Sinatra suggest that there is "something to be learned in the arts beyond superficial pleasure, warm feelings and a vague belief in their inherent goodness. . . . The arts are not merely fun and games" (1988, p. 55).

The competency approach typically divides skills and content into discrete elements. The teaching strategy for such an approach usually is a "parts-specific" one, proceeding from isolated skills because mastery of specific objectives is the overall goal (Lehman & Sinatra, 1988, p. 69). The problem is that specific competencies, even if mastered, do not necessarily equal the whole. Put another way, the whole is greater than the sum of its parts. The approach that appears to have the most promise to Lehman and Sinatra (and others, see McLaughlin, 1988, and Fowler, 1988) is DBAE.

The issue of which approach is best may never be resolved. Conducting surveys of teachers, however, can provide evidence of which approach is reported as most common. A 1989 survey of 843 schools (elementary, middle, and secondary) from across the United States revealed that more than 95 percent of the respondents indicated that DBAE was incorporated "to a great extent" or "to some extent" in teaching the visual arts (Leonhard, 1991, p. 205).

Marginalization.   As will be seen with all of the fine arts, the primary issue for the visual arts is to improve their status within the school curriculum. In the past, the visual arts may have been seen as an extra because of their emphasis on self-expression and the senses, while the schools were seen as places where reason was to be emphasized. The recent shift to treating the visual arts as a discipline-based enterprise may be an effective counter to the previous emphases (Fowler, 1988). Gardner's multiple intelligences (1993), for example, include spatial intelligence, lending more credence to a mind-centered origin of the visual arts. And a careful reading of the Consortium's Standards reveals a host of cognitive verbs, e.g., identify, compare, apply, and analyze. All of this is not to mean creativity is being overlooked; it simply means a balance between the creative and the rational is approaching in the visual arts. Such a balance bodes well for strengthening the visual arts' position in the curriculum.

MUSIC EDUCATION

History

Music, like any art, appeals to the senses. As a form of expression, music has been about as universal in humankind as speech. In early times and throughout most of history, music was, and is, important to religion, especially to religious services. Unlike the other fine arts, however, music was the source of more rational inquiry as well.

The Greeks of antiquity viewed music in two ways and that division lasted for nearly a thousand years. One view of music appealed entirely to reason. This view claimed that music embodied mathematical principles; that it was, in effect, a science. The Greeks believed that the study of music as a science could reveal the secrets of the physical universe. That music was considered a science is evidenced by the fact that music was one of the original liberal arts, included with arithmetic, geometry, and astronomy.

The other view of music was more utilitarian and less theoretical. This view of music—as an art, communicated through voice or instruments—was different from the view of music as a science. Mark and Gary (1992) claim the utilitarian view was the antithesis of the theoretical view because "[music as an art] was known through the senses rather than by reason . . . (and) it appealed to the emotions and influenced behavior" (p. 19). Simply put, the Greeks, and the Romans and others thereafter, did not trust the senses. Unlike reason, the senses could be fooled.

During medieval times music was especially important to the Church, and those who wished to serve the Church needed to know about music. By the eleventh century, musical notation was developed and that made it possible for the teaching of singing to shift from rote learning to singing by sight.

At the beginning of the Reformation in the sixteenth century, the teaching of music as a science at the university level had declined and was no longer accorded the prestige of other liberal arts. The decline in the influence of the Catholic Church resulted in the closing of many Catholic Church schools. But the advent of Protestantism had other, more positive effects on music. Martin Luther, credited with starting the Reformation, "wanted children to study music and to enjoy it. He believed that teachers should be musicians, and the schools established under the influence of his religious teachings include music in the curriculum" (Mark & Gary, 1992, p. 29). Whereas music in the Church before the Reformation involved only the clergy, Luther believed that the entire congregation should participate in singing. To this end, he, with the assistance of others, published a songbook (Mark & Gary, 1992).

The progression of any kind of music education through the seventeenth and eighteenth centuries was uneven. Although Luther's promotion of singing influenced many of his German followers, some of whom would eventually emigrate to America and bring such customs with them, John Calvin's influence was to subdue the use of music in church services, and this practice persisted with the Puritans, who founded the Massachusetts Bay Colony in 1630.

Music education began formally in North America in the 1720s with the establishment of singing schools. Despite the Puritan disregard for music in religious services, many other ministers were concerned with the quality of singing in church. Music texts, called "tune books," were originally written by ministers who hoped to improve the quality of their congregation's singing. Improvements were made in the notational systems that were sufficient enough for children, as well as adults, to learn to read the music.

Singing schools, although inspired by the clergy, were typically independent enterprises, unrelated to church or government. Singing masters, usually itinerant, would "hold class" in a courthouse, home, church, or tavern in the evening, meeting one to five times a week for a period of a few weeks to several months (Mark & Gary, 1992). The singing schools were the forerunners to public school music education. Indeed, these singing masters were oftentimes the first public school music teachers.

The formal beginning of music education in the public schools was in Boston in 1839. Lowell Mason, an accomplished musician, author, educator, and indefatigable advocate for music education, was appointed Boston's first superintendent of music. He hired the music teachers, many of whom were former students, and within seven years, was teaching in six schools and supervising ten teachers in ten other schools in the Boston area.

In the North, music education found its way into the public schools of the larger cities by the time of the Civil War. Keene observed that the introduction of music education was "always a grass-roots effort . . . and always, when it succeeded, the promotion was led by a well-trained musician especially interested in the education of children" (1982, p. 119).

In the South, the development of public schools and subsequent inclusion of music education came later, near the end of the nineteenth century. The delay has been attributed to the absence of large, teeming cities, as existed in the North; a more class conscious culture; and, of course, the Civil War and its devastating aftermath (Keene, 1982).

An important European influence on at least the writings of early music educators was the work of Swiss-born Pestalozzi. (Froebel, credited with the development of the kindergarten and a major influence on early childhood education in Europe and the United States, was a mentee of Pestalozzi.) Although Pestalozzi did not address music education methods per se, he nonetheless influenced a number of nineteenth century music educators with his ideas about teaching and learning of young children.

Among Pestalozzi's major beliefs were "that the subject matter to which the learner was exposed had to be compatible with the growth and development of the child," and that because "knowledge enters the mind through the senses," lessons should be such that "the child sees, handles, or otherwise makes direct acquaintance with the object" (Keene, 1982, p. 82). Some doubt exists about consistent application of all that Pestalozzi recommended (see Keene, 1982), but he is nonetheless credited with influencing music education in the United States.

Despite the availability of musical notation that could be read, Lowell Mason, and other early music educators influenced by Pestalozzi, promoted learning the songs first that is, "the thing before the sign" or "rote before note" (Keene, 1982, p. 188). As recently as 1982, Keene claims that the battle between those who promote rote or note learning first is still unresolved (p. 188). By 1900 music education was virtually universal in the United States and, like all of education, was affected by other forces such as the child study movement and progressive education. Unique to music education in the twentieth century, however, were three influences from Europe—Dalcroze, Kodály, and Orff—as well as U.S. music educators'

own interest in improving the stature and effectiveness of music education.

Dalcroze.   The founder of the Dalcroze method was Emile Jaques-Dalcroze (1865–1950), a Swiss musician who believed music education should include bodily activity. This activity, or rhythm, was important, he believed, to train the nerve centers of the body. His formal training included "rhythmic movement; solfeggio, including ear training; and pianoforte improvisation," but, according to Keene, "only rhythmic movement has influenced American music education to any extent" (1982, p. 335).

More than other music educators, Dalcroze emphasized the importance of rhythmical movements in learning music; he called them *eurhythmics*. Landis and Carder describe Dalcroze's rationale by noting, "of the three basic elements in music—melody, rhythm, and dynamics—the latter two are closely related to the physical nature of human beings and therefore a logical way to study music is through active physical response to it" (1972, p. 31). Landis, who has made use of eurhythmics with students from kindergarten through high school, claims that

> Movement should be as natural and untaught as possible. Natural movements of children are exceedingly beautiful and expressive. It almost never is necessary to demonstrate movements or to have them demonstrated by someone from outside the class. Instead, movement will be improved by pointing out the work of children who achieve freedom and originality. (1972, p. 184)

The rhythmic emphasis of Dalcroze has had a sustained impact on U.S. music education (Mark & Gary, 1992).

Kodály.   Zolton Kodály (1882–1967), an Hungarian music educator, was a strong advocate for music in early childhood "that begins with singing and leads to the development of musically independent individuals who can read and write with ease" (Campbell & Scott-Kasner, 1995, p. 51). Kodály's goal was "to provide skills in music reading and writing to the entire population of a country" (Landis & Carder, 1972, p. 41). He believed that just as young children are expected and taught to learn to read and write their native language they should be, at the same time, taught and expected to read and write music.

Kodály's method is called *sol-fa teaching* and, according to Landis and Carder (1972),

> It [the Kodály method] is primarily a plan for teaching choral musicianship, it stresses the skills of music reading and writing, including sightsinging and diction; it is meant to begin as early as possible in the life of the student and to prepare (the student) for life long enjoyment of music. (p. 41)

Kodály's success in Hungary may be attributable to the four to six weekly sessions from kindergarten through secondary school (Campbell & Scott-Kasner, 1995). Because of the relative brevity of school time devoted to music education, music teachers in the United States typically pick and choose the "best" aspects of Kodály for their music teaching (Mark & Gary, 1992).

Orff. Carl Orff (1895–1982) was a German composer who promoted the integration of music and movement. "He believed children to be naturally musical, uninhibited in their expressive movement, and more receptive to his brand of musical training than adults" (Campbell & Scott-Kasner, 1995, p. 54).

Orff "observed that when children express themselves in natural and unstructured situations, they use music, movement, and speech together, rather than separately" (Landis & Carder, 1972, p. 71). He was something of a recapitulationist in that he believed children pass through the historical stages of music development. Although recapitulation theory currently has few adherents, many music educators have been enamored with Orff's structured plan of proceeding with small, incremental steps from the simple to the complex.

Orff was influenced by Dalcroze and his approach to combining movement with music was, and is, the key element to Orff's method. There are specially constructed Orff instruments and a five-volume set of books titled *Music for Children* that has been adapted for English-speaking children and contains the progression of subject matter referred to above (Mark & Gary, 1992).

All three of the European influences—Dalcroze, Kodály, and Orff—found various degrees of acceptance among U.S. music educators. Three impediments to complete adoption are articulated by Landis and Carder (1972): (1) the common practice at the elementary level of singing in informal groups; (2) the development of a large listening repertoire; and (3) the entirely inadequate amount of time devoted to music instruction. The variety of methods in music education in the United States represented both a fertile ground for new approaches and a vulnerability to forces outside of music education.

The child study movement and progressive education combined to promote a more child-centered, activity-oriented approach to education in general. The degree to which the typical school was transformed by these movements is arguable. Certainly, movable desks became ubiquitous, but so did standardized tests. The launching of Sputnik in 1957 and the ensuing national concern for education have led to a number of conferences, commissions, and reports that have fueled the controversies over education in general and the fine arts in particular. Music educators have been active players in those deliberations and have helped to forge a consensus among fine arts advocates on standards and goals.

Standards and Goals

Below are the nine content standards for music education, followed, for the purpose of illustration, by just one achievement standard from each grade cluster. For a complete listing of all achievement standards, as well as a lucid description and explanation of all of the fine arts and why they are important, please see the Consortium of National Arts Education Associations (1994).*

Content standard

1. Singing, alone and with others, a varied repertoire of music.

*Excerpted from *National Standards for Arts Education,* published by Music Educators National Conference (MENC). Copyright © 1994 by MENC. Reproduced with permission. The complete National Standards and additional materials relating to the Standards are available from Music Educators National Conference, 1806 Robert Fulton Drive, Reston, VA 20191 (telephone 800-336-3768).

Achievement standard

K–4 Sing independently, on pitch and in rhythm, with appropriate diction, and posture, and maintain a steady tempo

5–8 Sing accurately and with good breath control throughout their singing ranges, alone and in small and large ensembles

9–12 Proficient level—Sing with expression and technical accuracy a large and varied repertoire of vocal literature with a level of difficulty of 4, on a scale of 1 to 6, including some songs performed from memory

Advanced level—Sing with expression and technical accuracy a large and varied repertoire of vocal literature with a level of difficulty of 5, on a scale of 1 to 6

Content standard

2. Performing on instruments, alone and with others, a varied repertoire of music

Achievement standard

K–4 Perform on pitch, in rhythm, with appropriate dynamics and timbre, and maintain a steady tempo

5–8 Perform on at least one instrument (e.g., band or orchestra instrument, key-board instrument, fretted instrument, electronic instrument) accurately and independently, alone and in small and large ensembles, with good posture, good playing position, and good breath, bow, or stick control

9–12 Proficient level—Perform with expression and technical accuracy a large and varied repertoire of instrumental literature with a level of difficulty of 4, on a scale of 1 to 6

Advanced level—Perform with expression and technical accuracy a large and varied repertoire of instrumental literature with a level of difficulty of 5, on a scale of 1 to 6

Content standard

3. Improvising melodies, variations, and accompaniments

Achievement standard

K–4 Improvise "answers" in the same style to given rhythmic and melodic phrases

5–8 Improvise simple harmonic accompaniments

9–12 Proficient level—Improvise stylistically appropriate harmonizing parts

Advanced level—Improvise stylistically appropriate harmonizing parts in a variety of styles

Content standard

4. Composing and arranging music within specified guidelines

Achievement standard

K–4 Create and arrange music to accompany readings or dramatizations

5–8 Compose short pieces within specified guidelines, (e.g., a particular style, form, instrumentation, compositional technique) demonstrating how the elements of music are used to achieve unity and variety, tension and release, and balance

9–12 Proficient level—Compose music in several distinct styles, demonstrating creativity in using the elements of music for expressive effect

Advanced level—Compose music, demonstrating imagination and technical skill in applying the principles of composition

Content standard

5. Reading and notating music

Achievement standard

K–4 Read whole, half, dotted half, quarter, and eighth notes and rests in 2/4, 3/4, and 4/4 meter signatures

5–8 Read whole, half, quarter, eighth, sixteenth, and dotted notes and rests in 2/4, 3/4, 4/4, 6/8, 3/8, and alla breve meter signatures

9–12 Proficient level—Demonstrate the ability to read an instrumental or vocal score of up to four staves by describing how the elements of music are used

Advanced level—Demonstrate the ability to read a full instrumental or vocal score by describing how the elements of music are used and explaining all transpositions and clefs

Content standard

6. Listening to, analyzing, and describing music

Achievement standard

K–4   Identify simple music forms when presented aurally

5–8   Describe specific music events in a given aural example, using appropriate terminology

9–12   Proficient level—Analyze aural examples of a varied repertoire of music, representing diverse genres and cultures, by describing the uses of elements of music and expressive devices

Advanced level—Demonstrate the ability to perceive and remember music events by describing in detail significant events (e.g., fugal entrances, chromatic modulations, developmental devices) occurring in a given aural example

Content standard

7.   Evaluating music and music performances

Achievement standard

K–4   Devise criteria for evaluating performances and compositions

5–8   Develop criteria for evaluating the quality and effectiveness of music performances and compositions and apply the criteria in their personal listening and performing

9–12   Proficient level—Evolve specific criteria for making informed, critical evaluations of the quality and effectiveness of performances, compositions, arrangements, and improvisations and apply the criteria in their personal participation in music

Advanced level—Evaluate a given musical work in terms of its aesthetic qualities and explain the musical means it uses to evoke feelings and emotions

Content standard

8.   Understanding relationships between music, the other arts, and disciplines outside the arts

Achievement standard

K–4   Identify similarities and differences in the meanings of common terms (e.g., form, line, contrast) used in the various arts

5–8   Compare in two or more arts how the characteristic materials of each art (that is, sound in music, visual stimuli in visual arts, movement in dance, human interrelationships in theatre) can be used to transform similar events, scenes, emotions, or ideas into works of art

9–12   Proficient level—Explain how elements, artistic processes (such as imagination or craftsmanship), and organizational principles (such as unity and variety or repetition and contrast) are used in similar and distinctive ways in the various arts and cite examples

Advanced level—Compare the uses of characteristic elements, artistic processes, and organizational principles among the arts in different historical periods and different cultures

Content standard

9.   Understanding music in relation to history and culture

Achievement standard

K–4   Identify by genre or style aural examples of music from various historical periods and cultures

5–8   Describe distinguishing characteristics of representative music genres and styles from a variety of cultures

9–12   Proficient level—Classify by genre or style and by historical period or culture unfamiliar but representative aural examples of music and explain the reasoning behind their classifications

Advanced level—Identify and explain the stylistic features of a given musical work that serve to define its aesthetic tradition and its historical or cultural context

Contemporary Issues

The General Current Scene.   It is always difficult to claim what is "out there" now in terms of current practices, but a few generalizations seem safe and, in total, constitute a contemporary issue for music education. Typical music experiences begin with singing at the elementary level and proceed to performance ensembles at the secondary level. Through the progression, fewer and fewer children participate. At both levels, the study of music history, theory, appreciation, composition, and improvisation is almost negligible (Patchen, 1994).

Discipline-Based Music Education. "The discipline-based approach is a conceptual framework for learning and teaching music; it is not a fixed curriculum or method" (Fowler, 1994, p. 4). Discipline-based music education (DBME) is based on the four disciplines of production, aesthetics, history, and criticism. Broadening the content by adding aesthetics, history, and criticism, and expanding performance to include improvisation and composition, is intended to help students develop their reasoning skills vis-à-vis music that will, in turn, enhance the educational value of performing, whether the performing be at the elementary or secondary level.

Just as the visual arts have been reconfigured into a discipline-based endeavor, so too has music education (Fowler, 1994a). DBME is intended to be the solution to the problem of the current scene but given its newness, it is an issue in its own right. It is too early to know if DBME will be embraced by music educators and, if so, what effects, if any, it will have on music's place in the curriculum.

Marginalization. In a national comparison of music education in 1962 and 1989, Leonhard (1991) found average minutes per week to be reduced in grades 1–3 from 75 in 1962 to 55 in 1989. In grades 4–6, the 1962 average was 80 minutes and in 1989 it was 62. At both levels that reduction is about 25 percent. An even greater decline from 1962 to 1989 was apparent in the offering of instruction in piano, wind/percussion, and strings. These comparisons reflect a weakening impact at the elementary level. It remains to be seen the extent to which DBME can reverse this trend.

Itinerant Teachers. Another issue associated with fine arts education is the practice of using itinerant teachers. This practice is most common at the elementary level with visual art and music teachers and further marginalizes these fine arts. Itinerant teachers move from building to building, with some finding themselves placed in as many as three different buildings a day and working with students at multiple age and grade levels. Regardless of the number of buildings itinerant teachers are placed in per day, they have special needs that arise from their movement from one building to another.

Communication between principal and itinerant teacher has to be open. Great care needs to be taken to keep the itinerant teacher informed of schedule changes, assemblies, and special events that can interfere with teaching. Communication can become fragmented due to scheduling and traveling time between buildings.

Often, a principal in one building is designated as the official supervisor of the itinerant teacher. This principal is responsible for the ongoing supervision and evaluation of the itinerant teacher. Typically, the principal charged with supervising and evaluating the itinerant teacher has direct experience with the performance of the itinerant teacher only in his or her building. If an itinerant teacher performs well in one building and not as well in another building, the principal responsible for evaluation may not be aware of the deficiencies of the itinerant in other assigned buildings. Coordination between principals is critical if the evaluating principal is to have a fair, accurate, and comprehensive view of the overall performance of the itinerant.

Coordination of the itinerant's schedule also needs careful attention. Itinerants need time to travel between buildings. Because itinerants typically hold a regular teaching contract, there are other provisions that must be built into the itinerant's schedule: duty period, professional preparation period, and lunch period. To fulfill the intent of the teaching contract, the principal needs to consult with district policy guidelines for itinerant teachers to see, for example, if they are excluded from the duty period typically part of a teacher's workday.

Special consideration also needs to be made for scheduling attendance at such routine activities as weekly or monthly faculty meetings, parent–teacher conferences, and staff development activities during professional development days. Coordination can be achieved by the building principal's examination of the scheduled classes the itinerant will be teaching, travel time and distance between buildings, and contract requirements.

Many itinerant teachers believe that they are professionally isolated from the faculty because they travel. They might not feel as if they belong to any one community they serve. This isolation can become even more intense if the itinerant is new to the district and a first-year teacher. There also is the danger that the itinerant teacher will not be included in social activities such as holiday celebrations and other faculty gatherings. Principals who utilize itinerant teachers need to ensure that these teachers are made to feel a part of the community of the school.

DRAMA/THEATRE EDUCATION

History

Just as the visual arts and music can be traced to earliest forms of human behavior, so too can drama. At the risk of oversimplifying, drama is usually thought of as a process. As such, it can be seen as a natural extension of play, as in the play of young children, wherein they learn about the world and themselves. Drama, like play, is inherently educative.

Theatre can be seen as a product. Theatre always has an audience; drama typically has no audience as such. All theatre involves drama, but all drama need not result in theatre.

When discussed in the context of schooling, drama/theatre is really educational drama/theatre, where the emphasis is on process more than product. The following historical accounts of theatre, however, assume the product conception, until the late nineteenth century in America when our discussion of theatre is within the context of schooling.

The Origins of Theatre. Brockett (1995) claims that the most common theory of the origin of theatre is that it evolved from ritual. Early humans engaged in many rituals to influence the supernatural powers that they believed affected their lives. Often masks and costumes, as well as rhythmical sounds and dance, were used in performing the ritual. Aspects of the performance were retained and reproduced long after the ritual was no longer believed to be relevant because audiences developed an appreciation for the performance itself. In other words, autonomous theatre emerged from ritual. Theatre created, or at least appealed to, aesthetic tastes, that, in turn, created the need for theatre.

Another theory of the origin of theatre is based on the fundamental human pleasure of storytelling. Events such as hunts, battles, or other feats are recounted through impersonation and eventual role-taking by others. Whatever the origin, and there are various other competing theories, suffice it here to say that theatre, in some form or other, has been around for as long as any other classified human behavior.

Ancient Greece. The Greeks are credited with being the first to have government provide official sanction and financial support to theatre in 534 B.C. when Athens created a contest for the best tragedy (Brockett, 1995). Sophocles (*c.* 496–406 B.C.) won 24 of these contests and, according to Brockett, introduced having as many as 3 actors, fixed the size of the chorus at 15, and was the first to use scene painting (1995, p. 18). In addition, Sophocles was one of the first playwrights not to act in his plays. Up until his time, the writer and actor were the same. Other characteristics of early Greek plays included the use of masks, that one actor would play several roles, and that men played all roles, including those of women.

Plato and Aristotle wrote about theatre in the fourth century B.C. Plato urged censorship because of the theatre's profound influence (Brockett, 1995). This is consistent with his view of visual art and music performance in that they too appealed to the senses and were not reliable means for finding truth. Aristotle's influence was on critical theory. "Aristotle states . . . that every drama has six parts: plot, character, thought, diction, music, and spectacle. He discussed unity of action, probability, the requirements of plot, characteristics of the tragic hero, problems of diction, and many other topics . . . [that] continue to be informative and controversial" (Brockett, 1995, p. 40).

Theatre in Rome. Roman theatre retained much of the Greek influence and added its own by the third and second century B.C. Many more performances were held at festivals of pagan gods. Roman influence took the form of variety of entertainment. Brockett summarized it thusly:

> We can probably grasp the essence of Roman theatre more readily by comparing it with American television programming, for it encompassed acrobatics, trained animals, jugglers, athletic events, music and

dance, dramatic skits, short farces, and full-length dramas. (1995, p. 49)

The high point of Roman theatre was the fourth century A.D. The decline of Roman theatre is attributed to three factors: the forces of the rising Christian Church, the leaders of which denounced the theatre; the breakdown of the Roman Empire from within; and pressures from barbarians from without (Brockett, 1995).

The Middle Ages.   The church dominated during the Middle Ages and most of the remnants of Greek and Roman theatre were effectively diminished. The Church itself, however, incorporated aspects of theatre in its services and by the tenth century, church music–drama appeared. This liturgical drama typically was performed in churches and monasteries; in the latter to help establish uniform practices and educate the monks (Brockett, 1995).

By the twelfth century, religious plays were performed outside the church and frequently lengthened as well as translated into the vernacular; hence the name, vernacular religious drama. But by the sixteenth century, when the Church's influence was weakened by corruption and the advent of universities that questioned Church dogma, religious plays were out of favor and dramatists rediscovered Greek and Roman works. Brockett (1995) suggests the dissolution of the force of the Church meant the end of the basis for any international drama, that is, from that point forward, each country would develop its own national style of theatre with its own characteristics.

To continue to trace the development of theatre one needs to examine the development of Italian, French, German, Spanish, Russian, and British theatre traditions, as Brockett (1995) does well. Suffice it here to say U.S. theatre was affected by all of these influences. By the early twentieth century theatre was well established in the United States and was just beginning to make an impact on schools.

Visual arts and music were part of the K–12 curriculum in the United States by the beginning of the twentieth century. Dance, too, had come to be included, via physical education, as will be discussed in the next section. Drama was included around 1900.

Progressive Education's Influence.   The proponents of progressive education, near the turn of the century, advocated the expansion of the traditional K–12 curriculum to include what was to become the progressives' mantra—educating the whole child. Slight inroads had been made by the visual arts, music, dance via physical education, and even some semblances of vocational education, but educators interested in drama/theatre had been, up to that time, effectively shut out. This changed, according to Ward (1930) for a number of reasons. Kindergartens were typically more open to new methods and therefore creative dramatics, that is, acting out different roles was easily absorbed by kindergarten teachers. Upper grade teachers used drama to help teach a variety of subjects, such as health, English, geography, and history. Exactly when secondary schools began producing "the senior play" is unclear. As Coggin observed, "Of the situation of American school drama, it is impossible to generalize" (1956, p. 204). According to Ward, drama was not initially appreciated as an art (1930).

Drama/Theatre Education.   Drama/theatre education includes at least two uses of the word "drama." One use is dramatic play. Dramatic play is the uninhibited natural play in which young children (ages 2–6) engage without prompting. It is their way to help make sense of their environment. Dramatic play involves the imagination. It is the make-believe world "of their own in which to master reality. They try in this imaginative world to solve real-life problems that, until now, they have been unable to solve" (McCaslin, 1987, p. 5). Dramatic play is not drama; it is not a performance; and it has no beginning and no end (McCaslin, 1987). Landy (1982) considers dramatic play "a natural process of role-taking and role-playing. It is inborn and one of the properties that defines one's humanness" (p. 259). Although Landy (1982) uses the term *drama* generically, he suggests, like McCaslin, that creative drama is an extension of dramatic play:

> [creative] drama is not a new skill to be taught, but a natural process that often becomes blocked as the instinct to play gets buried under the cloak of academics, rational thinking, and socially acceptable behavior. (p. 14)

To McCaslin (1987) creative drama is synonymous with playmaking, with a few caveats, that is, it is informal drama; it is always improvised, that is, no lines are written down or memorized; and it is not designed for an audience. McCaslin makes the further distinctions that creative drama (or playmaking) is "guided by a leader rather than a director . . . and that the goal is the optimal growth and development of the players" (1987, p. 6).

Winifred Ward is credited with developing creative drama in the United States. She was the supervisor of dramatics in the Evanston Public Schools and an instructor in dramatic production at Northwestern University in the early part of the twentieth century. To Ward (1930), creative drama meant the same as educational drama:

> [creative drama] is dramatic expression which comes from within, rather than the imitative expression which so often characterizes the rehearsing of plays for public exhibition. (p. 3)

Ward envisioned the change in emphasis from exhibitional drama—the ubiquitous school play, even at the elementary level—to educational drama—that which emphasizes process more than product. She believed the shift would reveal the inherent value of creative drama as a subject in its own right. She did not doubt creative drama's instrumental value in helping to teach literature and history, for example, but she advocated its unique value for helping middle school age students.

The children in grades 6, 7, 8, and 9, Ward believed, more than those in any other grade level, experienced the most difficult problems of growth and development. She considered creative drama the perfect outlet for students to express their feelings without risk of ridicule (1930). Material for dramatization could come from the students, or from any number of sources, but Ward thought "no material offers so many possibilities for artistic growth, however, as literature" (1930, p. 4). Almost by definition, literature is "closest to drama and to life itself" (p. 6).

Even though creative drama could be justified in its own right, that is, to foster and advance imagination, creativity, and self-expression, it has additional benefits for children. Besides being a wholesome, relatively risk-free outlet for expressing emotions for all

children, and especially those of middle school ages, creative drama can assist in vocabulary development, voice, and diction. It can be a supplement to physical education by promoting good bodily expression, poise, and grace. And finally, creative drama can contribute to personality and leadership development by fostering independence, resourcefulness, and ingenuity (Ward, 1930).

By the 1980s, drama was used in three ways at the secondary level. The most common was the performance or formal theatre; next was as an occasional method of teaching other subjects, most usually history and English; and, least of all, as a means of enhancing social and emotional development (Landy, 1982). Beginning with the least used way, we address each below.

Ward (1930) understood progressive educators' realization "that the creative is the richest life, both for the individual and society . . . and as drama is the integration of all the arts, it offers, probably, the greatest possible opportunity for creative self-expression" (pp. 8–9). Ward and others who advocated for the inclusion of creative drama were convinced of its inherent educational benefit. Its inclusion in the curriculum, however, was typically for its more utilitarian aspect.

Teaching reading through creative drama is, according to Landy (1982), one of the most widely used techniques in U.S. schools. In regular reading, students need only to "figure out" what the author meant in the use of the words of the text. When creative drama is used in teaching reading, a technique sometimes called reader's theatre, is utilized in which "students are asked to translate the author's words into their own words, movements, and images. To do this, students must understand the author's intention, a process that fosters the development of reading comprehension and interpretation skills" (Landy, 1982, p. 48). Applying a dramatic technique to the teaching of reading does not require stage sets, costumes, or the memorization of lines. It is not a play (Landy, 1982).

"The school play is undoubtedly the most widely practiced form of drama and theatre in education" (Landy, 1982, p. 77). There appears to be consensus among drama/theatre educators that formal productions before an audience are unwise for children under the age of 12. Such performance is thought to "divert the children's attention from learning about themselves to pleasing an audience" (Landy, 1982, pp. 79–80). The concern, it seems, is that the situation will encourage pandering to the audience.

The most negative aspect of the school play is when it is likened to a typical athletic event with excessive competition that creates a hierarchy of roles. Ideally, the school play is noncompetitive and promotes a fully developed characterization for each actor, no matter how big or small the role (Landy, 1982). The play experience should promote growth in self-confidence, self-understanding, and understanding of others. Landy (1982) discusses several potential benefits of the school play. Students should learn to expand their repertory of roles by taking on the roles of others. They can learn to overcome performance anxiety. Social skills should be enhanced because the students must learn to listen and to share praise and responsibility with others. At the intellectual level, students can begin to understand a dramatic text by interpreting it into verbal and physical action, thereby improving their language skills. Gaining insight into human behavior and motivation is another intellectual benefit. Finally, students can learn empathy by entering into the life and experiencing the world view of another.

In 1979 the Secondary School Theatre Association developed a list of criteria for selecting school plays (Landy, 1982):

1. Characters worth doing—challenging to the performers
2. Theme worth expressing—of lasting value to the audience as well as the cast and production staff
3. Lines worth learning—good literary quality
4. Suitable cast size
5. Audience appeal
6. Capable of production within the budget and with the facilities. (pp. 81–82)

Two additional criteria Landy offers are "appropriateness of material to the varied interests, abilities, and maturity levels of all involved . . . and the provision for presenting opposing viewpoints on controversial issues" (1982, p. 82).

Standards and Goals

Below are the eight content standards for drama and theatre, followed, for the purpose of illustration, by one achievement standard from each grade cluster. For a complete listing of all achievement standards, as well as a lucid description and explanation of all of the fine arts and why they are important, please refer to the Consortium of National Arts Education Associations (1994).*

Content standard

1a. Script writing by planning and recording improvisations based on personal experience and heritage, imagination, literature, and history

Achievement standard

K–4 Collaborate to select interrelated characters, environments, and situations for classroom dramatizations

Content standard

1b. Script writing by the creation of improvisations and scripted scenes based on personal experience and heritage, imagination, literature, and history

Achievement standard

5–8 Individually and in groups, create characters, environments, and actions that create tension and suspense

Content standard

1c. Script writing through improvising, writing, and refining scripts based on personal experience and heritage, imagination, literature, and history

Achievement standard

9–12 Proficient level—Construct imaginative scripts and collaborate with actors to refine scripts so that story and meaning are conveyed to an audience
  Advanced level—Write theatre, film, television, or electronic media scripts in a variety of

*Excerpted from *National Standards for Arts Education,* published by Music Educators National Conference (MENC). Copyright © 1994 by MENC. Reproduced with permission. The complete National Standards and additional materials relating to the Standards are available from Music Educators National Conference, 1806 Robert Fulton Drive, Reston, VA 20191 (telephone 800-336-3768).

traditional and new forms that include original characters with unique dialogue that motivates action

Content standard

2a. Acting by assuming roles and interacting in improvisations

Achievement standard

K–4 Imagine and clearly describe characters, their relationships, and their environments

Content standard

2b. Acting by developing basic acting skills to portray characters who interact in improvised and scripted scenes

Achievement standard

5–8 Analyze descriptions, dialogue, and actions to discover, articulate, and justify character motivation and invent character behaviors based on the observation of interactions, ethical choices, and emotional responses of people

Content standard

2c. Acting by developing, communicating, and sustaining characters in improvisations and informal or formal productions

Achievement standard

9–12 Proficient level—Analyze the physical, emotional, and social dimensions of characters found in dramatic texts from various genres
Advanced level—Demonstrate artistic discipline to achieve an ensemble in rehearsal and performance

Content standard

3a. Designing by visualizing and arranging environments for classroom dramatizations

Achievement standard

K–4 Visualize environments and construct designs to communicate locale and mood using visual elements (such as space, color, line, shape, texture) and aural aspects using a variety of sound sources

Content standard

3b. Designing by developing environments for improvised and scripted scenes

Achievement standard

5–8 Explain the functions and interrelated nature of scenery, properties, lighting, sound, costumes, and makeup in creating an environment appropriate for the drama

Content standard

3c. Designing and producing by conceptualizing and realizing artistic interpretations for informal or formal productions

Achievement standards

9–12 Proficient level—Explain the basic physical and chemical properties of the technical aspects of theatre (such as light, color, electricity, paint, and makeup)
Advanced level—Explain how scientific and technological advances have impacted set, light, sound, and costume design and implementation for theatre, film, television, and electronic media productions

Content standard

4a. Directing by planning classroom dramatizations

Achievement standard

K–4 Collaboratively plan and prepare improvisations and demonstrate various ways of staging classroom dramatizations

Content standard

4b. Directing by organizing rehearsals for improvised and scripted scenes

Achievement standard

5–8 Lead small groups in planning visual and aural elements and in rehearsing improvised and scripted scenes, demonstrating social, group, and consensus skills

Content standard

4c. Directing by interpreting dramatic texts and organizing and conducting rehearsals for informal or formal productions

Achievement standards

9–12 Proficient level—Develop multiple interpretations and visual and aural production choices for scripts and production ideas and choose those that are most interesting

Advanced level—Explain and compare the roles and interrelated responsibilities of the various personnel involved in theatre, film, television, and electronic media productions

Content standard

5a. Researching by finding information to support classroom dramatizations

Achievement standard

K–4   Communicate information to peers about people, events, time, and place related to classroom dramatizations

Content standard

5b. Researching by using cultural and historical information to support improvised and scripted scenes

Achievement standard

5–8   Apply research from print and nonprint sources to script writing, acting, design, and directing choices

Content standard

5c. Researching by evaluating and synthesizing cultural and historical information to support artistic choices

Achievement standards

9–12   Proficient level—Identify and research cultural, historical, and symbolic clues in dramatic texts and evaluate the validity and practicality of the information to assist in making artistic choices for informal and formal productions
Advanced level—Research and describe appropriate historical production designs, techniques, and performances from various cultures to assist in making artistic choices for informal and formal theatre, film, television, or electronic media productions

Content standard

6a. Comparing and connecting art forms by describing theatre, dramatic media (such as film, television, and electronic media), and other art forms

Achievement standard

K–4   Describe visual, aural, oral, and kinetic elements in theatre, dramatic media, dance, music, and visual arts

Content standard

6b. Comparing and incorporating art forms by analyzing methods of presentation and audience response for theatre, dramatic media (such as film, television, and electronic media), and other art forms

Achievement standard

5–8   Describe characteristics and compare the presentation of characters, environments, and actions in theatre, musical theatre, dramatic media, dance, and visual arts

Content standard

6c. Comparing and integrating art forms by analyzing traditional theatre, dance, music, visual arts, and new art forms

Achievement standard

9–12   Proficient level—Describe and compare the basic nature, materials, elements, and means of communicating in theatre, dramatic media, musical theatre, dance, music, and the visual arts
Advanced level—Compare the interpretive and expressive natures of several art forms in a specific culture or historical period

Content standard

7a. Analyzing and explaining personal preferences and constructing meanings from classroom dramatizations and from theatre, film, television, and electronic media productions

Achievement standard

K–4   Identify and describe the visual, aural, oral, and kinetic elements of classroom dramatizations and dramatic performances

Content standard

7b. Analyzing, evaluating, and constructing meanings from improvised and scripted scenes and from theatre, film, television, and electronic media productions

Achievement standard

5–8   Describe and analyze the effect of publicity, study guides, programs, and physical environments on audience response and appreciation of dramatic performances

Content standard

7c. Analyzing, critiquing, and constructing meanings from informal and formal theatre, film, television, and electronic media productions

Achievement standard

9–12   Proficient level—Construct social meanings from informal and formal productions and from dramatic performances from a variety of cultures and historical periods and relate these to current personal, national, and international issues
Advanced level—Construct personal meanings from nontraditional dramatic performances

Content standard

8a. Understanding context by recognizing the role of theatre, film, television, and electronic media in daily life

Achievement standard

K–4   Identify and compare similar characters and situations in stories and dramas from and about various cultures, illustrate with classroom dramatizations, and discuss how theatre reflects life

Content standard

8b. Understanding context by analyzing the role of theatre, film, television, and electronic media in the community and in other cultures

Achievement standard

5–8   Describe and compare universal characters and situations in dramas from and about various cultures and historical periods, illustrate in improvised and scripted scenes, and discuss how theatre reflects a culture

Content standard

8c. Understanding context by analyzing the role of theatre, film, television, and electronic media in the past and the present

Achievement standard

9–12   Proficient level—Compare how similar themes are treated in drama from various cultures and historical periods, illustrate with informal performances, and discuss how theatre can reveal universal concepts

Advanced level—Analyze the social and aesthetic impact of underrepresented theatre and film artists

Contemporary Issues

Participation.   The major issue with drama/theatre is that it does not appear to be widely embraced in K–12 settings. Leonhard (1991) found that about 60 percent of the secondary schools reported teaching subjects such as acting, creative drama, improvisation, pantomime, puppetry, childrens theatre, directing, and radio, television, and film. Where drama/theatre is present, it seems to suffer, albeit on a much smaller scale, what music suffers, and that is the specialization at the secondary school level. Only a relatively small number of students are typically involved in formal performances and, even then, the emphasis is usually on the production rather than the process, not to mention history, aesthetics, and criticism, the topics that discipline-based advocates promote.

Although dramatizations within other subjects, especially below the high school level, may be prevalent, such instrumental use of creative drama does not address the primary purpose of this fine art. Creative drama and theatre should promote creative self-expression and help each child make his or her life richer and happier.

Marginalization.   The advent of the standards in 1994 may contribute to the idea that drama/theatre is a discipline and the same kind of discipline-based approach promulgated for the visual arts in 1984 and music in 1994 may rescue drama/theatre from its precarious position in the K–12 curriculum. Like the other fine arts, however, drama/theatre has an uphill battle against the tradition of the public school to occupy itself with cognitive interests.

DANCE EDUCATION

History

Dance may be the oldest of the fine arts and certainly the only one to claim linkages to birds and animals (Kraus, Hilsendager, & Dixon, 1991). Pagan rituals for an abundant harvest or victory over an enemy often involved dancing as an expression of celebration. With regard to the birds and animal sources, Kraus and colleagues explain:

> Without question, the dance-like movements of other living creatures were one of the inspirations for the dances of early humans. It is true that many insects, birds, animals, and even fish carry out ritualized movement patterns that appear to be much like our conception of dance. (p. 29)

Religion and courtship were probably among the first reasons for dance. The review by Kraus and colleagues suggests that early Egyptians and Hebrews held dance in great esteem, as did the Greeks and Romans. The pantomime dance was perfected in Rome because of the variety of languages spoken by the audiences and the poor acoustics of the large theaters.

With the fall of Rome and the ensuing Dark Ages, all of the arts suffered decline. Curiously, dance was simultaneously denounced by the Church because of the view that the body was a source of immoral pleasure and yet also considered legitimate in the form of "prayerful dance that propitiates God" (Kraus, Hilsendager, & Dixon, 1996, p. 53). Apparently the church leaders believed that conversion of the pagans to Christianity would more likely prevail if such rituals as dance were maintained.

The Renaissance that followed the Middle Ages was the period during which the Church lost its stranglehold and the secular pursuits of the arts were reinvigorated. The fourteenth, fifteenth, and sixteenth centuries were thus influenced by the Greeks who had written about education 1,500 years earlier.

Both Plato and Aristotle considered dance an important part of physical development. Renaissance writers, inspired by the writings of Plato and Aristotle, encouraged dance instruction as both a social skill and an important means of physical training (Kraus, Hilsendager, & Dixon, 1991). John Locke, who was influential in promoting the blank slate notion regarding the importance of environment and experience over heredity, encouraged the learning of dance for its beneficial effects of gracefulness, manliness, and confidence (Mark & Gray, 1992).

Froebel, the father of the kindergarten movement in Germany, also had an effect on eighteenth and nineteenth century U.S. education through his concern for development beyond the intellectual. He was concerned with social and physical development, as well. Although the development of dance grew out of the physical education movement in this country and was found more often in programs for girls, Kraus and colleagues note that the West Point military academy had dance as a required course by the early part of the nineteenth century. "Its rationale . . . was that each officer had to be able to conduct himself as a gentleman and that instruction in dancing would help him do this and would provide poise and social competence" (Kraus et al., 1991, p. 195).

Among common schools, that is, the public elementary and secondary schools, dance became more evident from the middle of the nineteenth century to its end. Typically, dance during this period was cast as a kind of physical exercise and was generally accepted by all levels of social class as an appropriate social pastime.

The turn of the century marked the beginning of the child study movement's influence on education. In addition, progressive education, with its emphasis on children being more active in school settings, was beginning to make an impact on common schools.

G. Stanley Hall, the first major child study scholar, advocated the teaching of music appreciation through dance because he "believed music should be felt in order to be understood . . . and this was to be done through rhythmic movement" (Keene, 1982, p. 336). Although some in the child study movement believed rhythmic activity was innate and not teachable, the author of *Principles of Music Education* (Mursell, 1927) also believed there was a natural tendency to move to music and, more importantly, that this rhythmic sensitivity was teachable. Keene (1982) credits Mursell with the "universal acceptance of rhythmic instruction as a part of the elementary music curriculum" (p. 339).

In addition to child study specialists and music educators, dance was promoted by many physical educators as well. There were two forms, however: gymnastic dance for boys and aesthetic dance for girls (Kraus et al., 1991). Folk dancing was part of gymnastic dance and as it grew in popularity, it began to be seen as not just good exercise, but what many now would consider a precursor to multicultural education.

With immigration from Europe at its peak in the early decades of the twentieth century, folk and national dancing had to have made at least these aspects of schooling more connected with the lives of many of the children.

Dance as an expressive art form began in the 1920s and 1930s. Originally called natural dance, it became known as creative dance and was intended "to emphasize free and unstructured movement, self-discovery, and spontaneous response to music" (Kraus et al., 1991, p. 301). Soon, professional dancers helped to emphasize technical mastery "in expanding the range of dance movement, and in developing a recognition of dance as an art form—rather than a means of catharsis or naive self-expression" (Krause et al., 1991, p. 301). The blending of the natural response with the discipline of technique gives rise to Gray's definition (1989) of dance:

> Dance is the pure art form of body movement, the creation or reproduction of movement forms that do not necessarily serve a practical purpose yet can provide a deep sense of satisfaction and achievement. (p. 9)

This more aesthetic and technical definition of dance did not prevail by mid-century and the degree to which it will be achieved in the future remains to be seen.

The curricular reforms of the 1960s onward have emphasized the traditional disciplines of math and science, creating a hierarchy of goals that typically places the arts near the bottom. Physical education was becoming marginalized as well, but Kraus and colleagues note that physical educators during the 1960s and 1970s began to underscore the importance of kinesiology and body mechanics, as well as the physiology of exercise, neuromotor coordination, and other scientific aspects to reshape their area as a discipline. And in the 1980s many physical educators responded to the national concern for the poor state of physical fitness of many youth. Many advocates of dance education who were within the ranks of physical educators felt the need to justify the inclusion of dance in the K–12 curriculum.

Kraus and colleagues offer eight goals for dance (listed below) that provide a rationale for including dance in elementary, middle, and secondary schools. In their text, *History of the Dance in Art and Educa-tion,* they elaborate the contribution of each to the educational value of dance (see pp. 312–318).

1. Movement education
2. Development of personal creativity
3. Aesthetic experience
4. Intercultural and integrative experience
5. Social involvement
6. Carryover values (worthy use of leisure time)
7. Dance as exercise
8. Career goals in dance

These eight goals are similar to the seven standards for dance education published in 1994.

Standards and Goals

Below are seven content standards for dance, followed, for the purpose of illustration, by just one achievement standard from each grade cluster. For a complete listing of all achievement standards, as well as a lucid description and explanation of all of the fine arts and why they are important, please refer to the Consortium of National Arts Education Associations (1994).*

Content standard
1. Identifying and demonstrating movement elements and skills in performing dance

Achievement standard
K–4 Accurately demonstrate nonlocomotor/axial movements (such as bend, twist, stretch, swing)
5–8 Demonstrate the following movement skills and explain the underlying principles: alignment, balance, initiation of movement, articulation of isolated body parts, weight shift, elevation and landing, fall and recovery
9–12 Proficient level—Demonstrate appropriate skeletal alignment, body-part articulation, strength, flexibility, agility, and coordination in locomotor and nonlocomotor/axial movements

*Excerpted from *National Standards for Arts Education,* published by Music Educators National Conference (MENC). Copyright © 1994 by MENC. Reproduced with permission. The complete National Standards and additional materials relating to the Standards are available from Music Educators National Conference, 1806 Robert Fulton Drive, Reston, VA 20191 (telephone 800-336-3768).

Advanced level—Demonstrate a high level of consistency and reliability in performing technical skills

Content standard

2. Understanding choreographic principles, processes, and structures

Achievement standard

K–4   Create a sequence with a beginning, middle, and end, both with and without a rhythmic accompaniment; identify each of these parts of the sequence

5–8   Clearly demonstrate the principles of contrast and transition

9–12   Proficient level—Use improvisation to generate movement for choreography
Advanced level—Demonstrate further development and refinement of the proficient skills to create a small group dance with coherence and aesthetic unity

Content standard

3. Understanding dance as a way to create and communicate meaning

Achievement standard

K–4   Observe and discuss how dance is different from other forms of human movement (such as sports, everyday gestures)

5–8   Effectively demonstrate the difference between pantomiming and abstracting a gesture

9–12   Proficient level—Formulate and answer questions about how movement choices communicate abstract ideas in dance
Advanced level—Examine ways that a dance creates and conveys meaning by considering the dance from a variety of perspectives

Content standard

4. Applying and demonstrating critical and creative thinking skills in dance

Achievement standard

K–4   Explore, discover, and realize multiple solutions to a given movement problem; choose their favorite solution and discuss the reasons for that choice

5–8   Create a movement problem and demonstrate multiple solutions; choose the most interesting solutions and discuss the reasons for their choice

9–12   Proficient level—Create a dance and revise it over time, articulating the reasons for their artistic decisions and what was lost and gained by those decisions
Advanced level—Discuss how skills developed in dance are applicable to a variety of careers

Content standard

5. Demonstrating and understanding dance in various cultures and historical periods

Achievement standard

K–4   Perform folk dances from various cultures with competence and confidence

5–8   Competently perform folk and/or classical dances from various cultures; describe similarities and differences in steps and movement styles

9–12   Proficient level—Perform and describe similarities and differences between two contemporary theatrical forms of dance
Advanced level—Create a time line illustrating important dance events in the twentieth century, placing them in their social/historical/ cultural and political contexts

Content standard

6. Making connections between dance and healthful living

Achievement standard

K–4   Identify at least three personal goals to improve themselves as dancers

5–8   Identify at least three personal goals to improve themselves as dancers and steps they are taking to reach those goals

9–12   Proficient level—Reflect upon their own progress and personal growth during their study of dance
Advanced level—Discuss challenges facing professional performers in maintaining healthy lifestyles

Content standard

7. Making connections between dance and other disciplines

Achievement standard

K–4   Create a dance project that reveals understanding of a concept or idea from another discipline (such as pattern in dance and science)

5–8   Create a project that reveals similarities and differences between the arts

9–12   Proficient level—Create an interdisciplinary project based on a theme identified by the student, including dance and two other disciplines

Advanced level—Compare one choreographic work to one other artwork from the same culture and time period in terms of how those works reflect the artistic/cultural/historical context

Contemporary Issues

Sex-Role Stereotyping.   Reflecting either social values or the prejudices of teachers, it appears as if boys at the secondary level are disinclined to enroll in dance when the opportunity is available (Kraus et al., 1991). Overcoming this kind of obstacle will always be a challenge, but the growing interest in dance in the culture is bound to have an incremental effect. Schools could require a course in dance, offer an activity club after school, or simply promote it as an especially effective means of physical exercise.

Marginalization.   Leonhard (1991) suggests dance is as rare as it is in public schools because it is the "least highly developed of the specializations in art education" (p. 205). Although it is the oldest of the arts, it has come into the public schools later than the others and consequently many states do not yet have certification requirements in place. Compared with the other arts, there are fewer specialized teacher education programs in dance. In Leonhard's view, however, "Dance education is making real progress" (1991, p. 206).

ILLUSTRATIVE PRACTICES AND ISSUES

Fowler, C. (1994). Strong arts, strong schools. *Educational Leadership, 52*(3), 4–8.

Fowler articulates how the arts support a cohesive curriculum and illustrates how the arts develop the human spirit and sustain civilization. *Issues:* Should the fine arts be considered ancillary to other areas of the curriculum?

SUMMARY

The fine arts include visual art, music, drama/theatre, and dance. Each can be traced back to the very origin of preliterate societies, yet each has only a relatively brief history in the K–12 curriculum. The forces of tradition and an excessive preoccupation with the cognitive and rational subjects and skills have effectively impeded a more complete embrace of the fine arts. To expand what is currently in the K–12 curriculum, however, does not mean that one is promoting something that is irrational.

The mind–body dualism may have given way to the divisions of educational objectives, wherein distinctions are made between and among the cognitive, affective, and psychomotor. Such a taxonomy is useful for analysis and discussion, but it suggests a separation that is artificial, that contributes little to the ideal of educating the whole child—except to make it more clear that by overemphasizing the cognitive, we are not.

A careful reading of all of the standards revels two aspects. One is that the standards can be read as goals. The consortium admits this and further states that the intention is to have local schools and districts decide on how to reach them. "[The] arts standards provide a vision of both competence and educational effectiveness, but without creating a mold into which all arts programs must fit" (Consortium of National Arts Education Associations, 1994, p. 12).

The other aspect to note is the frequent use of verbs that reflect measurable behavior, for example, select, apply, communicate, convey, generalize, reflect, and demonstrate. The more traditional know and understand are present, to be sure, reflecting perhaps the tortuous undertaking it is to reduce to behavioral terms those goals that are not amendable to such reduction. That the consortium managed to use as many behavioral terms as it did is commendable; that consensus was reached among all parties is astounding.

QUESTIONS FOR FURTHER CONSIDERATION

Research

1. What does research indicate about children who study music?

2. Visit a school that has an artist-in-residence program. What steps did the principal take to develop or institute this program?

Reflect

1. How can principals prevent the marginalization of the arts when so few students take advantage of curricular and/or co-curricular activities?

2. Examine the subjects and courses taught at your site. Examine high school graduation requirements and college entrance standards. Do these requirements and standards discourage students from taking courses in the arts?

3. What role does the principal play in promoting the integration of the arts into the school's curriculum?

Respond/React

1. React to this question. Are the arts necessary as part of public school curriculum, or are they still "just for fun?"

2. As a building principal or a district-level administrator, how would you react to a community whose obsession with "back to basics" motivates them to marginalize the fine arts?

SUGGESTED READINGS

Consortium of National Arts Education Associations. (1994). *What every young American should know and be able to do in the arts.* Reston, VA: Music Educators National Conference.

Fowler, C. (1994). *Discipline-based music education: A conceptual framework for the teaching of music.* Chattanooga, TN: University of Tennessee at Chattanooga.

Kraus, R., Hilsendager, S. C., & Dixon, B. (1991). *History of the dance in art and education* (3rd ed.). Englewood Cliffs, NJ: Prentice-Hall.

Landy, R. J. (1982). *Handbook of educational drama and theatre.* Westport, CT: Greenwood Press.

Leonhard, C. (1991). *The status of arts education in American public schools.* Urbana, IL: Council for Research in Music Education.

CHAPTER 8

GIFTED AND TALENTED

The special programs that serve gifted and talented youth can take several forms. Whatever the form, however, gifted and talented (GT) programs have come under increasing criticism for their very existence. It has even been suggested, for example, that interest in such programs started as a reaction by the upper classes to the great influx of lower class immigrant children in the early part of the century (Margolin, 1994) and that an abiding elitism, if not racism, is continuing to undergird them (Berliner & Biddle, 1995; Sapon-Shevin, 1994). The issues of class and racial bias are woven into much of the discussion regarding whether GT programs are appropriate for public schools in a democracy.

Whereas research should be the basis for much of what is done in school settings, providing separate programs for the gifted or, for that matter, ability grouping and tracking, can be opposed on the grounds of moral imperative. For example, according to Hastings (1992), ability grouping in a democratic society is ethically unacceptable.

Ethics notwithstanding, GT programs currently exist and probably will for some time. What is important is to understand a bit of their history and their various current forms to manage and evaluate them in a manner that makes sense and is defensible.

HISTORY

A history of gifted education requires attention to the history of intelligence testing. Entire books are devoted to such histories, so our treatment here will be limited to milestones in the testing of intelligence and the gifted education movement.

Intelligence Testing

Alfred Binet, a French psychologist, developed the first test of intelligence in 1908. His primary purpose

for developing the test was to distinguish between children who would likely benefit from school and those who would not. The test consisted of such items as tying shoe laces, naming the points of a compass, and discriminating between lengths of lines that were close, but not identical.

By administering the test to many children, he was able to determine the "mental age" for various levels of successful performance on the test. This mental age, when divided by chronological age and multiplied by 100 to remove the decimals, becomes the intelligence quotient (IQ).

In the United States, Lewis Terman, former teacher and principal, and in 1916 a professor at Stanford University, had Binet's test translated and adjusted to be appropriate for U.S. students. After revising the test, Terman renamed it the Stanford–Binet Test. He claimed it would reliably measure intelligence of children from ages 5 to 16. In addition, unlike Binet who created the test, Terman believed that what the test measured was a constant and was greatly influenced by heredity. The Stanford–Binet test was widely used in the early part of the twentieth century to help group the new influx of students from rural areas, immigrants from Europe, and those from urban areas when child labor laws were enacted and enforced. The Stanford–Binet was (and still is) individually administered by specially trained personnel. Group intelligence tests soon followed. The group tests, then and now, corresponded, at least roughly, to the Stanford–Binet. They were easier to administer—no special training needed —were relatively inexpensive, and made massive public school testing possible.

By the early 1920s, Terman and most school personnel firmly believed children should be grouped homogeneously, according to their intelligence levels. He specifically recommended five groups: gifted, bright, average, slow, and special. The students in the higher groups would be expected to be college-bound and have the appropriate curriculum for that destiny, while the others would pursue a vocational future or simply be graduated with a general diploma. Such ability grouping and tracking schemes are still commonplace today in many schools around the world.

The IQ test purported to measure general intelligence. Indeed, the "g" factor, as it was labeled, represented general intelligence. The notion that intelligence was unidimensional, represented by a simple ratio of mental age to chronological age, held sway for many generations. The stability of the IQ, that is, that it was primarily a function of heredity and not affected by environment, was the dominant thinking until the 1960s when J. McVicker Hunt wrote *Intelligence and Experience* (1961), wherein he argued quite successfully that intelligence should be viewed as the product of an interaction between an individual and environment.

Another challenge to Terman's notions came from Guilford, who claimed that as many as 150 separate elements of intelligence existed (Guilford, 1982). Through the use of factor analysis, Guilford built a three-dimensional model he called the "Structure of the Intellect (SOI)." Guilford constructed his SOI model to reflect five types of content, five different operations, and six kinds of intellectual products ($5 \times 5 \times 6 = 150$). Although there is a test to measure 26 separate factors, Eby and Smartny (1990) suggest the results of the test may be so peculiar to Guilford's definition of intelligence that they may not be of much practical help in programs based on other definitions.

Two other theories of intelligence were articulated in the 1980s: Gardner's and Sternberg's. Gardner's multiple intelligences (1993) include seven different kinds of intelligences, each with its own language, symbols, and processes. Linguistic intelligence includes oral and auditory functions and products. Musical intelligence is related to composing and performing music. Logical–mathematical intelligence involves understanding and handling chains of reasoning. Spatial intelligence requires visual skills associated with art and architecture. Bodily–kinesthetic intelligence is required for sports and performing arts. Intrapersonal intelligence means self-knowledge and understanding, and interpersonal intelligence is related to understanding others well enough to empathize or lead.

Gardner believes individuals have strengths and weaknesses among the various intelligences. No one instrument measures all seven of these, but not being able to measure all of them does not necessarily detract from the validity of the theory.

Sternberg (1985) developed a triarchic theory of intelligence. His three-part model includes "a contextual subtheory that relates intelligence to the external environment of the individual, a componential subtheory that relates intelligence to the internal environment of the individual, and an experiential subtheory that applies to both the internal and external environments" (Sternberg, 1985, pp. 318–319). Put more succinctly, the three subtheories correspond to analytical, creative, and practical abilities. Individuals are more or less adept at any of these processes with regard to their environment. One adapts, selects another, or shapes the environment to improve the overall fit with abilities, interests, and values. In the process, the individual capitalizes on strengths and compensates for weaknesses. No test currently exists that measures all three subtheories and even when one subtheory is tested, Sternberg advises, "any one instrument can work only for some of the people some of the time" (1985, p. 312).

Certainly, like Guilford before them, Gardner's and Sternberg's notions of intelligence are in contrast to Terman's one-dimensional belief. In addition, their multifaceted aspects are quite different from the typically unidimensional group intelligence tests that receive a great deal of use in public schools and, not infrequently, are used to identify gifted and talented children.

Gifted Education

Programs for gifted and talented students were limited to only a few before Terman conducted his ambitious survey of gifted children in 1921. Under the general title of *Genetic Studies of Genius,* Terman and various associates began publishing in 1925 results of his study of over 1,500 California boys and girls from the upper elementary grades who scored 140 or higher on an IQ test. There were five volumes in all; the fifth, subtitled *The Gifted Group at Mid-Life: Thirty-five Years' Follow-Up of the Superior Child,* was published in 1959.

Terman's conclusions about gifted children turned around any possible stereotypes of giftedness that existed prior to his massive study. As early as 1925, with the publication of volume I of his study, Terman "set the record straight" with regard to gifted children: Not only were they smarter, because of the high IQs, but they were bigger, stronger, and healthier. We will return to Terman later because we believe Terman's work represents the basic foundation for much of what modern day GT advocates promote.

Terman's preference for serving gifted children was acceleration through the grades, but the Great Depression made enrichment rather than acceleration the norm. Too few jobs awaited high school and college graduates during this period to warrant early graduation. Honors classes and special classes in foreign languages were the typical responses in secondary schools in big cities.

Little national interest for the gifted was evident until the then Soviet Union launched an earth orbiting satellite in 1957. The National Defense Education Act of 1958 promoted math and science study, but the interest waned somewhat when the U.S. launched its first satellite a few years later. In 1970 a big boost came to the gifted area with the Congressional mandate "Provisions Related to Gifted and Talented Children," that was attached to the Elementary and Secondary Educational Amendments of 1969 (Public Law 91-230). The mandate ordered the Commissioner of Education to examine programs for the gifted and to offer recommendations.

Marland's report to Congress in 1972 estimated that fewer than 4 percent of the children who should be receiving differentiated education actually were and that most of those who were receiving satisfactory service were concentrated in just 10 states. Marland articulated a definition of gifted and talented that is still used, at least in rhetoric, by most GT programs. It appears below under Identification and Selection Procedures.

By 1990 38 states reported serving more than 2 million K–12 gifted students. The Office of Educational Research and Improvement (Ross, 1993) claimed, "Programs for gifted and talented students exist in every state and in many school districts, but it is difficult to determine the exact number of students

served because not all states and localities collect this information" (p. 16).

The Jacob K. Javits Gifted and Talented Students Act of 1988 reestablished a federal influence in gifted and talented programs. This legislation provides monies for demonstration programs, a national research center (at the University of Connecticut), and other activities to focus attention on the needs of students who are identified as gifted and talented. Not surprisingly, given the dismal data on minority representativeness of virtually all programs into the 1990s, the Javits Act gives top priority for funding GT programs that will serve the economically disadvantaged, students who speak limited English, and those who have disabilities. It may be that the Javits Act represents tacit understanding of the inherently flawed nature of the original research of Terman and that is a response to the underrepresentation of most minorities in GT programs.

In returning to Terman, we note that a contemporary of his, Leta Hollingworth, a professor at Teachers College, Columbia University, wrote *Gifted Children: Their Nature and Nurture* in 1926. Many of her comparisons of gifted children with "the generality," or the general population, were based on Terman's study in California. Like Terman, she extolled the overall superior qualities of gifted children. Hollingworth taught a Teachers College course on the education of the gifted that contributed to the inspiration for Hunter College to establish a model school for the gifted in 1941. The school served high IQ children from the nursery school level through the sixth grade.

In addition to Terman's virtual lifelong study of over 1500 children through their adult years, the children of Hunter College Elementary School, a private, highly selective school, have likewise been studied for their adult achievements (Subotnik, Kassen, Summers, & Wasser, 1993). Thirty-five percent of the school enrollments from 1948 to 1960 (210 out of 600) responded to questionnaires on their life achievements.

The Hunter College Elementary School (HCES) study is important because it was aimed, like Terman's study, to detect adult life achievements of gifted children. Whereas Terman's study was (and still is by many) seen as an unbiased sampling of children, the HCES children were very consciously selected because of high IQ scores. The average IQ in both studies was over 150, and Terman reportedly considered the group a good comparison for his cohort of geniuses (Seagoe, 1975, in Subotnik et al., 1993).

Family backgrounds for the Terman group of 1500 and the HCES study were similar in that there was a preponderance of professional occupations for the fathers and the mothers of the children tested. The socioeconomic status then was much higher for these gifted children's families than their counterparts at the time. In the HCES case the higher socioeconomic status is no surprise. It is with the Terman study that the problem of selection becomes controversial.

Had Terman canvassed *all* the children of the Oakland and San Francisco Bay areas to find the 1,500 subjects, a daunting task to be sure, we could have more faith in his findings regarding characteristics of gifted children. He did not.

Terman concentrated on schools in "good" neighborhoods because the likelihood of finding brighter children in higher socioeconomic sections seemed greater. He used teacher nominations initially and found them quite accurate. (Hollingworth, in contrast, from her research in New York, found teachers that could nominate gifted students at a rate slightly above blind guessing (1926, p. 48).) The teachers in Terman's study were about 90 percent accurate (Terman & Oden, 1959, p. 2), indicating either the teachers on the West Coast were better selectors than those in the East, where Hollingworth worked, or Terman's teachers were choosing from among a more homogeneous group of students. We believe the latter. The preponderance of high socioeconomic status (SES) family backgrounds undoubtedly accounts for the underrepresentation of most minorities in both Terman's and in the HCES group as well.

At any rate, Terman's work is less credible because of his selection bias. Children from higher SES families tend to be bigger, stronger, and healthier than others. They also are more likely to perform better on IQ and achievement tests.

The real problem for the GT arena, however, is the lack of eminence found among Terman's 1500 and the HCES 210 subjects. If IQ scores were to be predictors of eminence, which many in the GT field believe they are, ample opportunity existed among these 1700 individuals to display it. They did not.

Although the subjects in both studies did achieve success and certainly seemed to be satisfied with their life accomplishments—high income, marital happiness, health and stability—none achieved eminence (Foster, 1986; Subotnik et al., 1993). Even with the powerful combination of high IQ and high socioeconomic status in both studies, the accomplishments were noteworthy only to the extent one might expect high SES children to obtain, irrespective of IQ score. The net effect of those studies may be the confirmation that privileged backgrounds contribute greatly to the likelihood of privileged adulthood. IQ scores well above the average seem not to make much difference when socioeconomic status is controlled. The most devastating cumulative finding, of course, is the lack of any outstanding accomplishment from those identified and studied over an unprecedented period of time.

One could conclude, therefore, that GT is something of an illusion or fabrication. Certainly, that is what Margolin (1994) and Sapon-Shevin (1994) conclude. Or, that promoting GT programs is a neoconservative reaction to too many funds being spent on students who need special help and that the country will not survive without more support for GT programs (Berliner & Biddle, 1995). The fact remains, however, that programs for the gifted and talented exist and show few, if any, signs of abating. As an administrator, you may well be expected to continue GT programs and that includes evaluating them. Even if you are philosophically opposed to GT programs, you are not likely to be able to simply close them down. A good deal of convincing will need to be done before that is about to happen.

CURRENT STATUS

Identification and Selection Procedures

To avoid the charge of overt prejudice in choosing children for GT programs, school personnel avail themselves of various instruments that purport to "objectively" measure intelligence or its potential. But tests that are objective are not possible. All tests are based on some values or experiences that may or may not be shared by all people (Sternberg, 1985). The critics of GT programs insist that performance on tests of intelligence and achievement used for identification are "strongly influenced by the child's socioeconomic status, racial and cultural background, and previous educational experience" (Sapon-Shevin, 1994, p. 32).

It seems safe, then, to conclude that whenever IQ, general intelligence, or achievement test scores are used as the primary screening device for identifying and selecting children for GT programs, there is a much greater likelihood of having larger disparities among racial and ethnic groups. Surveys suggest that most GT programs do indeed use such cut-off scores for identification and selection (Ross, 1993).

A nationwide examination of percentages of three ethnic minorities (Native American, Hispanic American, and African American) to the general school population compared with their respective percentages being served by GT programs showed a significant underrepresentation of these minorities in GT programs. Only about half of the overall percent were in GT programs. By comparison, Caucasians, who represented 67 percent of the student population made up 77 percent of those participating in GT programs in 1992 (Brown, 1995). In addition, a 1988 report found that only 9 percent of the nation's eighth graders who had been identified as GT were from families in the bottom quartile of family income, while 47 percent of the identified GT students were from families in the top quartile of family income (National Education Longitudinal Study, 1988).

Marland's definition (1972) of gifted and talented has been widely cited and represents a broad-based view of GT students:

Children capable of high performance include those with demonstrated achievement and/or potential ability in any of the following areas, singly or in combination:

1. General intellectual ability
2. Specific academic aptitude
3. Creative or productive thinking
4. Leadership ability
5. Visual and performing arts
6. Psychomotor ability

Marland went on to suggest that by utilizing these criteria schools would be serving a minimum of 3 to 5 percent of the school population.

Critics notwithstanding, identification and selection of GT students continue, because the programs continue. The variety of special programs for GT students are described below.

Enrichment in the Regular Classroom

Enrichment can take many forms. In essence, enrichment should be a qualitatively different set of experiences that is provided to the GT students in the classroom. Enrichment in the regular classroom is the easiest to provide but might be the most challenging to the regular classroom teacher.

Easy, because no special teachers, classrooms, or scheduling are required. Most challenging, because teachers may not be accustomed (or willing) to provide a wider variety of activities in their regular classrooms. Enrichment in the regular classroom simply means accommodating the wide range of abilities and interests that are present in any group of 20 some students. When some of these students have been identified as GT, their inclusion intensifies the need for a greater variety of classroom activities and teacher expectations.

Enrichment in the regular classroom is what the major critics of GT contend to be the most fair for everybody. Indeed, there is probably little, if any, justification for even identifying students as GT if they are accommodated within regular classrooms.

Examples of enrichment in the regular classroom at the elementary level include differentiated assignments in subject areas, for example, doing math problems in bases other than 10; writing different forms of poetry; and completing special homework assignments that extend or broaden the conventional topics usually encountered in regular classrooms. Expecting regular teachers to accommodate such varied abilities and interests may be unrealistic in most settings. (Certainly the GT literature suggests that without special training, most regular teachers would be at a loss in trying to respond to GT students.) Much of the GT interest and advancement, however, is predicated on how unrealistic it is to expect regular teachers to accommodate GT students, but we will return to the dilemma of the regular classroom teacher later. Suffice it here to say that enrichment is less likely to be achieved through regular, unassisted classrooms.

Consultant or Team-Teaching Model

Just as special education for children with disabilities seems to be moving toward inclusion, so it may make more sense for GT students to be served similarly with a consultant or team teacher working with the regular classroom teacher. If special training is required for teaching GT students—about half the states have such certification requirements (Gallagher, 1985) —then combining a specially trained teacher with the regular teacher should be an enormous aid in responding to the abilities and interests of all the children in the classroom.

Enrichment Pull-Out Programs

Pull-out programs entail GT students leaving the regular classroom for part or all of a day, one or two times a week, to meet with a resource teacher. Pull-out programs are more common at the elementary than the secondary level; at the latter, GT students would more likely be assigned to honors or advanced placement (AP) classes in lieu of regular classes.

Enrichment through pull-out permits a greater variety of activities because the class can be treated as a unit. All can go on field trips, engage in second language learning, or practice esoteric poetry writing. Actually the challenge to pull-out programs is the same that regular teachers have—meeting appropriately the wide variety of abilities and interests of students. GT students are not a homogeneous group. Whatever criteria were used for identification and selection should drive what the GT teacher has the children do. The child who shows great potential in math is going to need enrichment in math. Likewise, those who demonstrate achievement at the highest percentiles in reading/language arts, social studies, or science need enrichment activities that broaden or extend those particular abilities. That could be a tall order when only 20 students in a grade level have been identified and those 20 represent a wide range of subject area proficiencies. Making sound educational sense of such a situation will be addressed in the section on Contemporary Issues.

Acceleration

At the elementary school level, acceleration could mean early entry, for example, beginning first grade at 5 years of age, instead of the traditional entry at 6, or skipping grades, for example moving from third grade to fifth, and passing over the fourth grade. Acceleration makes sense when GT students are seen as being more like older students than their age-mates. Recall that the IQ is a comparison of chronological age to mental age and a typical definition of GT as having an IQ score of 130 or higher will mean a chronological age difference of about 2 to 3 years. The concern, of course, is that mental age alone does not account for all that any elementary child is. Therefore, parents and educators need to be concerned with the physical, social, and emotional needs of children who might be considered for acceleration. Incidentally, unlike retention in a grade, for which the evidence is overwhelmingly negative on student self-concept and performance, the research is equivocal on acceleration. (The exception to this is radical acceleration, which is discussed below.)

At the secondary school level, acceleration usually takes the form of advanced classes, honors classes, or some arrangement for advanced placement (AP classes) for college credit. Because of the larger number of students at the secondary level, creating special, advanced classes for GT students is easier than at the elementary level.

Radical acceleration, beginning at about age 11 or 12 for mathematically gifted children, has been successfully accomplished for over 20 years. Beginning at Johns Hopkins University in the early 1970s and currently at Iowa State University, the Study of Mathematically Precocious Youth (SMPY) has coordinated a program for young children who combine summer classes at the university with rapid acceleration through their secondary school. Typically SMPY participants complete high school requirements by age 14 or 15, a bachelor's degree by 16 or 17, and usually a doctorate by the time they are in their early 20s.

SMPY is probably the best known example of rapid acceleration and involves working closely with the student, the student's family, and the local school. Eligibility criteria are high, requiring being in the top 3 to 5 percentiles on standardized achievement tests and achieving equally high scores on the math battery of the SAT. After appropriate counseling with the student, family, and local district, the student has the opportunity to accelerate radically through school. All parties must be willing and able to have the student proceed.

Studies of students who have participated in SMPY suggest that the problems the students encounter are minor and temporary. The SMPY program is analogous to the talented gymnast or budding tennis star in at least two ways: The participant usually leaves home at an early age to receive the appropriate training, and there are not very many of them.

Curriculum Compacting

Because GT students are considered to be advanced for their age, it usually follows that they may know a lot about the material they will be encountering in any grade level before they begin that grade. Curriculum compacting is a means by which GT students can pass through the content without spending as much time as is usually allocated for it.

Whereas enrichment can be viewed as a horizontal exploration of content, that is, a branching out, curriculum compacting can be viewed as a vertical progression through the content in an accelerated manner. Compacting does not involve grade skipping, but does require working out arrangements with the teacher and student to ensure the student has mastered all of the material that has been compacted. An Individual Educational Program (IEP) form has been devised by Renzulli and Smith (1979) that can serve as a plan agreed to by teacher, parent, and child, much the same as the IEP serves the special education student.

Mastery Learning

Mastery learning is a common sense approach to accommodating students who have the ability to move quickly through material and is similar to, although less formal than, curriculum compacting. Subject areas that are inherently sequential, for example, mathematics and most sciences, are especially well suited for the application of mastery learning.

Just as in the case of curriculum compacting, the student must demonstrate mastery of the material before proceeding to new material. Mastery learning has the benefit of removing the lock-step, "we all proceed at the same pace," shackles that have characterized, often unfairly, regular classrooms.

Resource Rooms

A resource room is any room in which students can pursue various activities associated with learning more about a topic. Such a room is usually considered a supplement to the regular classroom and typically would be staffed by a teacher with special training.

Gallagher (1985) lists five major components of an ideal specialized training program for elementary or secondary certified teachers who would staff the resource room. The teacher should have the following:

1. Understanding [of] the development of gifted students and the major school adaptations made for them
2. Understanding [of] how children generate new knowledge, and the special capabilities of gifted students for such knowledge generation; the study of how children think productively and how teachers can enhance those characteristics
3. Knowledge in-depth in a given content field—a content specialty
4. The ability to understand other social, emotional, and educational needs of the gifted through special courses or experiences in measurement, counseling, curriculum development, etc.
5. A one-year internship working directly with gifted students. (pp. 388–389)

Revolving Door Identification Model

The Revolving Door Identification Model (RDIM) (Renzulli, Reis, & Smith, 1981) is associated with pull-out programs but, instead of the identified students remaining as an intact group for the entire school year, in the RDIM the students drop in and out, hence the revolving door label, according to interests. The talent pool of students eligible to participate in the RDIM can be as large as the top 25 percent, whereas most GT programs serve only students in the top 3 to 5 percent.

Enrichment Triad Model

The Enrichment Triad Model (Renzulli, 1977) consists of three types of activities. Type I activities are general exploratory experiences provided to all students, not just those in the talent pool. Activities could include any that acquaint or reacquaint students with topics, ideas or problems that could be pursued in-depth, either working alone or in small groups. Type II activities are process-oriented and are designed to equip the student with the skills necessary to pursue the area of interest. Type III activities involve the student as "an actual investigator of a real problem or topic by using appropriate methods of inquiry" (Renzulli, 1977, p. 29). As stated earlier, the resource room is often the setting in which Type II and III activities occur without interfering with regular classroom activities. Actually, according to Renzulli (1977), the resource room is not indispensable, especially for Type III activities, which could be carried out in the regular classroom, a library room, or even through distance education.

Distance Education

Any instruction that is transmitted through television, videotapes, or computer qualifies for the label *distance education* or *distance learning.* Whenever face-to-face instruction is unavailable or too costly, distance education, although rarely free of costs, may be the solution for students who need special training or other experiences, but live too far away to obtain them. Examples of distance education were reported by Schwartz (1994). In 1990–1991 the Satellite Educational Resources Consortium offered honors sections in world geography and advanced placement sections in economics, physics, and mathematics to a 23-state network.

Independent Study

Whenever students embark on an independent learning venture, for example, learning a language through

the use of audiotapes, reading all the works of a single author, or enrolling in a correspondence course, they are engaged in a form of independent study. Schwartz (1994) indicated Duke University's involvement with the Talent Identification Program resulted in a By-Mail Program for gifted middle school students. The program is especially convenient for rural students who would typically not have access to advanced courses. Enrollment includes assignment of a mentor either at Duke University or from the student's locality.

Gallagher (1985) warns that without a mentor or teacher to guide the student's inquiry, the independent study experience is likely to fail. He cites, for instance, three skills that cannot be assumed, but need to be taught: searching—finding appropriate materials, from libraries and other sources; assimilating—actually learning from the materials, from the lowest levels of the cognitive domain, knowledge and comprehension, to the highest, application, analysis, synthesis and evaluation; and reporting—developing or constructing a finished product or report that demonstrates the resolution or posing of a problem. (Note how these skills correspond to Renzulli's Enrichment Triad Model discussed earlier.)

Mentoring

An increasingly popular approach to responding to secondary level GT students is mentoring—"a procedure by which the gifted student leaves school for a period of time, perhaps two or three afternoons a week, and comes under the supervision of some specialist in the community who is an expert in the gifted student's particular area of interest" (Gallagher, 1985, p. 352). Mentoring is common in many adult occupations. Typically, the mentor is an older, more experienced professional who guides the neophyte into the profession, providing information and, occasionally, wisdom on how the system or organization works (O'Dell, 1990). Mentors for GT students would be expected to introduce the students to the area of work and to provide insights into their chosen field. The intention is that students would learn first hand within the "real world" what various occupational roles are available to them.

Ideally, the parents of the student would be consulted during the mentor selection process, would meet the mentor, and provide permission for the arrangement. Schwartz (1994) suggests mentoring as an especially important activity at the middle school level; a time when students are beginning to think seriously of long-term goals. She reported on the CHALLENGE program (Booth, 1980), wherein seventh and eighth graders spent a half day every other week with their mentors.

Sources for mentors could be professional associations, for example, the bar association; organizations, for example, civic and business clubs; or institutions, for example, hospitals, clinics, and universities. In some cases, GT secondary students could serve as mentors to younger GT students. Using students as mentors has the advantage of greater control for the kinds of experiences the mentee will have and because of the increased self-esteem of the mentor for having been chosen, provides a reciprocal benefit.

Extra-School Activities

In the vernacular, "extracurricular" means something outside the regular set of school activities. But if a program is planned for, anticipated, and thereby included in what the school intends for students, it is part of the curriculum, not extra to it. (The unintended experiences are truly extracurricular.) Extra-school does mean outside of the school day. After-school or Saturday programs can be opportunities to offer educational experiences that could not be available during the school day. Special courses offered by regular staff or volunteers can provide experiences for GT students that extend well beyond the regular school fare.

Several states and universities sponsor summer programs in math, the sciences, and the arts. Sometimes called the Governor's school, these state efforts are designed to attract bright youngsters who have interests in a variety of fields. Pennsylvania, Georgia, and North Carolina offer programs from 2 to 7 weeks in length, across many different areas of interest that typically appeal to students from grades 4 to 11.

Johns Hopkins and Iowa State University were discussed above for their roles in developing the SMPY program. In addition, the University of Pennsylvania, Yale, Vassar, Western Carolina, and Northwestern offer summer programs for GT students.

National level programs include Johns Hopkins Talent Search, Future Problem Solving, Odyssey of the Mind, and the Westinghouse Science Scholars Program. These national efforts are usually carried out through a school's GT program.

Magnet Schools

Two features of all magnet schools are that they specialize in a particular field or have a special emphasis (e.g., math and science, performing arts, or health care), and parents choose them. Typically, there are high admission standards so choice alone does not ensure admission. Students may have to audition, provide portfolios of previous work, or show high grades or test scores in the fields the magnet school emphasizes.

Originally established to counter white flight from inner cities, many magnet schools provide services to students of all races and are frequently housed within existing school structures. These "schools within schools" usually have enrollments of less than 300 and teachers, like parents, who have chosen to be there. More discussion of this topic is provided in Chapter 2, Alternative Educational Opportunities.

CONTEMPORARY ISSUES

Sources of Confusion

Some confusion in matters related to special programs for GT students resides in mistaking equality for equity. Equality means the same educational experiences for everybody. Equity means equal opportunity to achieve appropriately different educational experiences. All children can have an equal opportunity to take a test, but the test itself may be biased against certain racial or economic groups. Nearly as incriminating, the tests may not be valid for what the school is trying to promote.

The GT field is made up of proponents who claim the following:

1. Intelligence tests are not all that much biased.
2. Intelligence tests measure (or estimate) well what it is schools should promote.
3. Identification and selection should not be made on a single criterion, such as a test, anyway. Mul-

tiple criteria, for example, teacher recommendations, previous work, and task commitment should be considered for identification and selection purposes.

The overwhelming evidence of the underrepresentation of most minorities and low socioeconomic groups in GT programs makes number 1 appear questionable. The claims that tests predict well what schools promote is only partly right. IQ tests account for "between 5 percent and 25 percent of the variance in scholastic performance, rarely more. When more consequential kinds of criteria are used (success in real-world pursuits), the degree of relationship is even less" (Sternberg, 1985, p. 313). Claim number 3 requires more elaboration.

Ross (1993) indicates that a recent national survey showed that 73 percent of the school districts adopted Marland's definition for gifted and talented. (You will recall that Marland listed six different abilities in his definition.) But Ross goes on to report that "few said that they use it to identify and serve any area of giftedness other than high general intelligence as measured on IQ and achievement tests" (p. 16).

It would follow, then, to suggest that most special programs, if they use a single test score as a criterion, whatever form they take, are not true to a well-established, nationally recognized definition of gifted and talented. To that extent, they are lame and need to be dismantled.

But, some would argue, are there not some truly gifted (others might say severely gifted) individuals? Of course there are. We believe, however, that there are not very many of them.

That some children and adults exhibit extremely rare intellectual abilities cannot be denied. The idiot savant, for example, depicted in the motion picture *Rainman* (1991), can perform astounding tasks, such as knowing how many toothpicks there are in a spilled box or the day of the week for any date in history. Usually these individuals are institutionalized because they have great difficulty functioning within ordinary circumstances.

There remains, however, a relatively small number of children who not only meet the behavioral criteria for gifted, but exhibit rare ability in such subjects

as math and science. Fortunately there is at least one option for such children that has existed for more than 20 years, the aforementioned Study of Mathematically Precocious Youth (SMPY). Originally housed at Johns Hopkins University, and currently at Iowa State University, SMPY works with gifted children, their families, and the local school district to provide the opportunity for radical school acceleration through summer sessions at the University and adjusted progression through the child's local school system. The rationale for such radical acceleration through the grades and higher education is twofold: With appropriate planning, the student is capable of it and such precociousness normally peaks when these individuals are in their twenties. And lest administrators worry about such rapid acceleration, it is worth reminding them of observations of those responsible for such a program.

Julian Stanley, former director of SMPY when it was housed at Johns Hopkins, concluded, after reviewing over 270 cases, that the problems the young students encountered were minor and temporary (Stanley, 1980). More recently, the directors of SMPY at Iowa State University have echoed the same evaluation (Lubinski & Benbow, 1995). As we indicated earlier, such a rapid progression under expert tutelage is analogous to the accommodations made for specialized training for the budding gymnast or tennis star.

Two major issues surround most GT programs. The first is identification and selection into the program and the second is the nature of the program itself, that is, is it appropriate to the revealed gifts? The identification and selection issue revolves around the trait versus state consideration of human behavior; similar to the heredity versus environment argument on intelligence. If a trait definition of gifted is used, it is like the color of one's eyes. A child either has it or does not have it. A student is either gifted or not gifted. This view of GT has also been called elitist—referring to the fact that only a few, after all, are gifted.

The other kind of definition is more like a state. A child can behave in a gifted manner, given the appropriate set of circumstances. Renzulli, Reis, and Smith (1981) suggest three criteria for a behavioral definition: (1) above average intelligence; (2) a creative or imaginative approach to a task or problem;

and (3) persistence in working on a task or problem. This definition has been called behavioristic and egalitarian. The emphasis on behavior, as opposed to some mysterious potential (usually suggested by a high test score), is a movement toward opportunities for anyone to behave in a gifted manner. Renzulli and company, however, suggest that there be a talent pool from which the GT students are selected. The method for identification and selection for the talent pool can rest on a single criterion, for example, a test score, or several criteria, for example, test scores, teacher's recommendations, and self-selection. Even though this definition is driven by behavior—what a student does —it still limits, with few exceptions, the talent pool to 15 to 25 percent of the school population. If the talent pool were not limited and all students had an equal chance for inclusion, the labeling actually becomes a moot issue. If everyone can behave in a gifted manner, why bother with a special label?

The majority of programs for GT students, especially at the elementary level, are of the pull-out variety (Gallagher, 1985). In the course of a day or week, the GT students leave their regular class to attend the GT class. The class could range from 1 hour to several or in some cases, could be an entire day. What matters most, however, is that whatever is done with the GT students, it should be appropriate to whatever kinds of abilities the identification procedures revealed. For example, if a student appears to be gifted in mathematics, he or she should be engaging in higher-order mathematics. It is assumed that such advanced mathematics would only frustrate regular students. On the negative side, however, if GT mathematics students get to tour a computer assembly plant, one would be hard pressed not to argue that all students would benefit from such a field trip. Special programs for the GT students can be defended and make sense only when it is reasonable to assume regular students would not benefit from them as well.

Providing programs that reflect special needs is the matter of equity. Many times equity is confused with equality, which means presenting the same programs to everybody, irrespective of special needs or abilities. The controversy surrounding most programs that *are* appropriately different from the regular because they are tailored to special needs usually can be traced to the identification and selection criteria. If consensus can be achieved on defensible identification and selection criteria, and programs can be planned that appropriately challenge the students selected, (e.g., not just more field trips, from which all students would benefit), then GT programs can be defended. If either of the above conditions cannot be met, the GT program needs to be adjusted appropriately or abandoned.

Other Suggestions for Accommodating Advanced Students

If a student appears to be well above the norm, but not so advanced that special programs like SMPY seem warranted, other options are possible. If achievement in all subject areas is such that regular grade level work is no longer a challenge, then promotion to a higher grade probably is appropriate. School administrators typically are reluctant to have students skip grades or in some way progress through the system faster than the norm, but we see no well-founded rationale for such resistance.

If achievement is within one or two subject areas only, such as math or science, then having the student move up to that level of math and science makes good sense. The grade level school arrangement need not be so rigid and lock step that students of varying abilities cannot be accommodated. The consequence of such efforts may be early graduation or a senior year with few required courses remaining. So be it. Better that administrators can claim correspondence between students' needs and the response of the system than some perverted sense of uniformity regarding age-level grade assignments.

Behaviorist or egalitarian views of gifted are consistent with basic democratic values and notions of equal opportunity and therefore are easier to defend— especially in public schools—but are more difficult to implement when trying to identify students. School people, like most others, have a propensity to label and classify. If the definition and subsequent identification is temporary because it is circumstantial—if not downright fleeting—how can the school respond appropriately? Only if the teachers and administrators are very flexible about grouping students and scheduling classes, can the school respond appropriately when a behavioristic or egalitarian definition is the basis for identification. Incidentally, identifying a talent pool of the top 25 percent does not appear to us to be necessary; it may be deferring to the notion of democratic schools, but it retains enough elitism to make it anathema. In practice, we believe that students who behave in a gifted manner, that is, appear to be using above average intelligence with regard to a problem or topic (irrespective of test scores), are somewhat creative in their approach, and persist in their efforts, should be accommodated. Except for some bureaucratic reporting purposes, one can see that there is little need for labeling when actual behavior is the determining factor in the identification process. The primary problem with the behavioristic view is that as topics change, so may the behavior, creating classification or grouping schemes that are not very permanent or stable. The constant shifting and reassignments can be disconcerting to teachers, parents, and children. How disconcerting it is, compared with alternative solutions, can best be determined by those closest to the problem. Teachers, parents, and in some cases, students, should be consulted about possible solutions to problems of grouping and scheduling.

Earlier we noted that much of the impetus for GT programs resulted from the alleged inability of regular classroom teachers to accommodate these students. Trying to narrow the range of classroom abilities and interests in order to achieve the mythical homogeneous group has been tried before—and found wanting. Special education students used to be segregated. Special teachers and labs have been created and developed for learning disabled students, but, like other special education students, the learning disabled are more appropriately accommodated within the regular classroom, usually with the assistance of a teacher consultant or team teacher.

Advocating for special teachers or arrangements is rather common, but not always sound. Recently early childhood educators have used the strategy. How many transition grades between kindergarten and first were created because no one wanted to ask the first grade teachers to be more flexible and accommodating? In fairness to first grade teachers, however, it needs to be noted that frequently unrealistic expectations have been placed on them by administrators and second grade teachers. The point is that certain aspects of the system do work against intelligent responses to the wide variety of abilities and interests of all children. Sometimes those aspects can be identified and resisted. Assigning homework in each elementary grade because the grade above does it is one example of "the system" dictating what is done in any given grade. Only when all parties who are affected by such responses recognize the problems and endeavor to solve them is the likelihood of success increased. The impersonal "system" may seem to be unmanageable, but specific, incremental changes, beginning, for example, in the early grades, can be implemented and maintained when consensus is reached on the problem and possible solutions.

Few would argue that some regular classroom practices are archaic. As Sapon-Shevin (1994) asked when comparing lists of needs for low-achieving, at-risk students with those for the gifted and found that both groups need hands-on, participatory, enrichment activities, "then who are all the worksheets for?" (p. 23). We need not continue to indict regular classroom teachers or indirectly disparage them by lobbying for special teachers for these special children. As Berliner and Biddle (1995) remind us, in this country we are dedicated to educating all children and "if we are truly to improve American education . . . we must reform our public schools so that all those who labor in them are treated with compassion" (p. 349).

ILLUSTRATIVE PRACTICES AND ISSUES

Reis, S. M., & Renzulli, J. S. (1992). Using curriculum compacting to challenge the above average. *Educational Leadership, 52*(2), 51–57.

> Compacting is described as "organized common sense." It allows teachers to modify the curriculum for students who display strengths or interest in a content area. *Issues:* The authors challenge labeling by accommodating any student who displays exceptional interest in a content area.

Savitch, J., & Serling, L. (1995). Paving a path through untracked territory. *Educational Leadership, 52*(4), 72–74.

> An experiment combining "gifted" and mainstream students suggests that labels are misleading and unnecessary. *Issues:* Labeling, especially at early ages (6 and 7) serves few educational purposes.

SUMMARY

The field of gifted and talented is a quagmire for most elementary and secondary principals. One view suggests that it is based on a flawed legacy of intelligence testing that has promoted a hereditary, elitist view of intellectual superiority that has worked in the school tracking systems of Europe, but does not resonate with most people in the United States. The hard line for them is that having a group labeled as gifted automatically means having all others be non-gifted. The critics believe that such a condition is unacceptable in the public schools of a democracy.

Another view is that there are some (albeit a few) children who do demonstrate unusual gifts and talents. These students need to be accommodated through one or more of the forms described above. Exactly how that is accomplished, we believe, should be decided by those closest to the situation.

QUESTIONS FOR FURTHER CONSIDERATION

Research

1. Investigate further the concept of mentoring for gifted and talented children. Based upon your readings, develop a mentoring program for gifted and talented children. Include the types of activities that would be included in this program, the personnel needed to operate this program, and the costs that would be incurred.

Reflect

1. What are the social implications of acceleration? How can schools address these implications? As a school principal, how would you monitor children whose academic program is accelerated? What types of data would you want to collect to assist with this monitoring process?

2. Should enrichment activities be only for children labeled as gifted and talented? As you reflect, consider this statement: "if everyone can behave in a gifted manner, why bother with a special label?"

Respond/React

1. In a budget cutback, the superintendent wants each building in the district to utilize the resource center for both special education and gifted and talented children. Your task is to carry out the objectives of the district and superintendent. How will you implement this directive and maintain the integrity of the activities and support given to each one of these groups of children?

2. An irate parent complains to the districtwide gifted and talented coordinator that the processes and instruments used to identify and place students into the gifted and talented program in your building are biased. How would you determine whether this is true?

SUGGESTED READINGS

Gardner, H. (1993). *Multiple intelligences: The theory in practice.* New York: Basic Books.

Gould, S. J. (1981). *The mismeasure of man.* New York: Norton.

Sapon-Shevin, M. (1994). *Playing favorites: Gifted education and the disruption of community.* Albany, NY: State University of New York Press.

CHAPTER 9

GUIDANCE AND COUNSELING

Schools, from the very smallest to the largest, typically utilize the resources of a school guidance counselor. Throughout history, the school counselor has been referred to as guidance counselor, counselor, vocational counselor, and vocational guidance counselor. Confusing to be sure, but even more perplexing when one examines the historical trends in counseling (e.g., elementary school counselors did not even begin as a formal field until the early 1960s). The terms *guidance* and *counseling* currently are used interchangeably at the elementary, middle, and high school levels. Myrick (1987) concluded about guidance, "It is a term in education that has flip-flopped with the word 'counseling' for more than 50 years" (p. 3). What the school counselor was referred to throughout history is more easily understood by examining the trends in how school counselors were used to meet the needs of society while simultaneously meeting the needs of children.

Many practitioners believe that the guidance and counseling staff are the center of a school's student services program. School counselors find themselves involved in many activities, dependent on the grade and age level of students served by the school (e.g., primary, elementary, middle, secondary). The services provided by a school counselor look different at the elementary, middle, and high school levels. However, there are "constants" in the types of services that all school counselors provide, regardless of the grade and age level of students. For example, all school counselors conduct needs assessments of students. It is the results of the needs assessments that determine the specific services provided to students within the school community.

School counselors work with at-risk students to reduce drop-out rates; respond to teacher/administrator/ social worker referrals; provide personal counseling, guidance and career counseling, and crisis counseling; and work with students in both small and large groups. Often, the school counselor works with other support staff such as the school nurse, the social worker, teachers, administrators, and the school psychologist. If a school does not have a social worker, the school counselor also refers students and their families to outside agencies for assistance that the school cannot provide.

The work of guidance counselors has evolved over the years, and certain events in history have served as markers in the development of the role and function of the school guidance counselor.

HISTORY

1880s to 1920s

The earliest form of counseling may have taken place in the form of "chieftains and elders of ancient tribal societies . . ." (Gibson & Mitchell, 1995, p. 3). During the eighteenth and nineteenth centuries counseling was vocational in nature and sought to help youth discover appropriate vocational occupations. Paisley and Borders (1995) indicate that "Early programs were directive in nature and involved the provisions of guidance classes to promote character development, teach socially appropriate behaviors and assist with vocational planning" (p. 150).

The Industrial Revolution, in part, gave rise to the development of guidance programs in schools in the early 1900s. Rapid industrialization, however, had a negative impact on large, urban centers. Young children who lived in the slums of bigger cities were often working more hours than they attended school, even though compulsory education laws had been passed by this time.

Individuals both in the United States (e.g., Jesse B. Davis, George A. Merrill, and Frank Parsons) and in Europe (e.g., Francis Galton and Alfred Binet, both interested in psychological measurements) helped shape early vocational guidance programs.

The early field of psychology served as an impetus for the study of people and established the foothold for the development of testing instruments to measure the talents and abilities of young people. The field of psychology was established as a means to explore human motivation and behavior. The Industrial Revolution was reaching its peak and scientific, industrial, and budding international influences made it more difficult to find one's niche in the world of work.

Sir Francis Galton, a well-known English psychologist, studied people and their human abilities. According to Zunker (1994), "Francis Galton . . . published his first and second books devoted to the origins of human abilities in 1874 and 1883" (p. 4). Brewer (1942) reported that Galton believed "in the existence of native traits that could bring about success in one job and failure in another . . ." (p. 199). Galton believed that these native traits were tied to heredity and, in turn, heredity influenced what abilities a person possessed. The results of Galton's work were considered a breakthrough in that he was interested in studying individual differences in people as a means of determining what traits would make a person more suitable for varying types of trades or occupations.

In France, Alfred Binet is credited with being one of the first psychologist to develop tests "to single out individuals lacking in the general ability necessary to master the curriculum of the elementary schools" (Reed, 1944, p. 165). Later, in the United States, Terman in 1916 would expand the work of Binet by constructing an intelligence test, known then and today as the Stanford-Binet Test. A more complete overview of the intelligence testing movement and Terman's work appears in Chapter 8, Gifted and Talented.

Early Guidance Pioneers

Frank Parsons focused on social reform, and he was interested in occupational training and counseling. Baker (1992) reported that "Parsons established a Vocational Bureau in Boston in 1908, the purpose of which was to provide vocational guidance for out-of-school youths" (p. 2). Parson also was concerned with providing training to teachers who would guide students in finding their vocational niche, and he eventually developed a model for career counseling (Baker, 1992, p. 2–3). According to Parsons, there were three major goals of his model of career counseling "(1) self-analysis, (2) analysis of occupations, and (3) choosing a career using true reasoning" (Brown & Srebalus, 1988, p. 4).

From Parsons' work came what is known today as the trait-and-factor theory that "became the foundation of many vocational-counseling programs . . ." (Zunker, 1994, p. 25). Although developmental theories designed by such psychologists as Super (1976) and Ginzberg and colleagues (1985) have since emerged, the trait-and-factor theory developed by Parsons is still widely used today.

Sigmund Freud's work in psychoanalysis in the early 1900s increased interest in psychology in the United States. Closely related to the field of psychology was the work of G. Stanley Hall who was interested in the study of children and their needs. Miller (1961) indicated, however, that "Freudian ideas exerted relatively little influence on guidance practices in the secondary schools for the two or three decades following Parsons' death" (p. 167) in 1908.

Most guidance programs and efforts in the early 1900s were directed exclusively to secondary school students. Brown and Srebalus (1988) report, "There was no single starting point for the counseling profession, and a number of individuals made contributions to its inception" (p. 4). The literature is replete with information about three guidance counseling pioneers. These three individuals were Jesse B. Davis from Detroit, a teacher and then later principal; Eli Weaver from New York, a principal and then later an author who wrote the booklet *Choosing a Career;* and Anna Reed from Seattle, a teacher. Perhaps of most notable mention is Jesse Davis. According to Miller (1961), Davis "devoted most of his time to counseling. . . . And when he became principal of the Grand Rapids High School in 1907 he not only provided for counseling but introduced weekly periods in the English classes devoted to 'vocational and moral guidance' " (p. 150). Davis is often credited with developing the first formalized vocational guidance program. Gysbers and Henderson (1994) highlight by grade level, the guidance curriculum developed by Davis:

Seventh grade: Vocational ambition
Eighth grade: The value of education
Ninth grade: The elements of character that make
for success
Tenth grade: The world's work—a call to service
Eleventh grade: Choosing a vocation
Twelfth grade: Preparation for one's life work (p. 6)

The work of numerous people, the influences of psychology, and the emphasis on scientific measures in assessing a person's ability, aptitude, and interest created a movement beginning in or around 1913 that resulted in the development of the National Vocational Guidance Association, which published the *National Vocational Guidance Bulletin* and "began the unification and identification of what has become the counseling profession today" (Schmidt, 1993a, p. 9).

The Testing Movement and World War I

World War I (1914–1918) served as a major marker in the rise in vocational guidance and in the uses of testing and measurement. Binet's testing procedures and results had gained acceptance before the war, and his work served as a prototype for other psychologists who were called upon to develop testing procedures to handle the burgeoning number of men who were serving or about to serve in the military. The use of testing during the war occurred as a "response to the federal government's need to classify millions of young men eligible for the military . . ." (Baker, 1992, p. 3). As the need for testing increased, "several eminent psychologists produced a group-administered intelligence test . . . Army Alpha (paper and pencil administration) and Beta (performance administration), [that] popularized the idea of using group testing in education" (Baker, 1992, p. 3). In fact, the popularity that testing gained as a way to classify a large number of people in the army during the war had a profound effect on testing children in schools. "The possibilities of applying these and other psychometric techniques to pupil assessment resulted in the rapid development and expansion of standardized testing in education in the decade immediately following World War I" (Gibson & Mitchell, 1995, p. 9).

Perhaps due to the influences of World War I, the U.S. government passed the Smith-Hughes Act of 1917, which provided reimbursement for vocational–guidance resources at the secondary level. In 1918 the U.S. Office of Education (then referred to as the U.S. Bureau of Education) published the *Cardinal Principles of Secondary Education* (Herr, 1979). This document bolstered the role of the school guidance counselor and stressed the need for vocational guidance in secondary schools.

Although there was a need for the services that a vocational guidance counselor could provide to children in schools, "The growth of vocational guidance in schools, however, was an uphill battle" (Aubrey, 1977, p. 290). We believe Aubrey's use of the word battle accurately describes the evolution of the field of guidance and counseling during the nineteenth and early twentieth centuries.

Guidance Issues

Guidance practices were well established by the end of War World II. However, the development and identity of early vocational guidance programs in schools lacked a unifying philosophy. As Aubrey (1977) indicated:

> The early vocational guidance movement was largely devoid of philosophical or psychological underpinnings. The Parsonian model of vocational choice was grounded on simple logic and common sense and relied predominantly on observational data gathering skills . . . vocational guidance was not associated with the process of education nor was it viewed as a means of contributing to the development of the individual through a process extending over a number of years. (p. 290)

The use of psychometric measures was often at the end of the high school experience or a reaction to historical events (i.e., World War I draft, compulsory education, and the influx of immigrant children from differing social backgrounds). The role of testing in vocational guidance was not connected to planned curriculum for guidance as a means of assisting what Aubrey (1977) indicates "a primary interest in the individual and a preparation of that individual for a life in a fluid and ever changing environment" (p. 290).

According to Gysbers and Henderson (1994), the emphasis "on the social, industrial, and national-political aspects" was obscured by the

> attention . . . to the personal, educational, and statistically measurable aspects of individuals and as a result, guidance was more geared to meet the immediate needs of other agencies such as the federal government. (pp. 7–8)

It appears as if the school guidance counselor was typically a teacher who assumed the responsibility of "counseling" within the confines of the classroom. Although early attempts at developing a curriculum were the beginnings of a movement on behalf of children, they were overshadowed by the mental hygiene movement and the press for psychological measurements. Another factor that contributed to the rise in the scientific preoccupation with individuals was the child study movement initiated by G. Stanley Hall (Gysbers & Henderson, 1994).

In the mid-1920s, the elementary school guidance movement began and then ended quickly until the early 1960s. William Burnham, considered to be the "pioneer of what has become today the elementary school counselor . . . perceived the role of the human behavior specialist in the schools as extending beyond a focus on crisis, testing, and clinical diagnosis" (Faust, 1968a, pp. 11–12). Our discussion of the development of counseling for elementary schools will continue later. We only mention the elementary school counseling movement now to underscore the emphasis on the secondary student that existed from the 1900s to the 1960s.

The last issue from the early 1900s was that of clearly defining what was meant by the term *guidance.* To this day, professionals struggle with the exact meaning of the terms *guidance* and *counseling.* We believe Williamson's (1975) summation of the evolution of guidance and its current status is noteworthy here: "Historically, in the nineteenth century, *guidance* meant preparation for adulthood, including vocational choice, but it also meant religious and moral guidance. Then it came to mean only choice of work" (p. 85, emphasis in the original).

During the Depression, guidance programs in schools flourished and the trait and factor theory, associated with identifying individual strengths and weaknesses, became commonplace as a possible way of preparing the future work force. The uses, and possibly some abuses, in wide-scale testing continued throughout the 1930s and 1940s. The federal government supported the guidance movement of the 1930s by passing two major acts: the Wagner-Peyser Act of 1933 and the George-Deen Act of 1936. These Acts helped in establishing training centers for the large number of unemployed adults. Moreover, these acts had provisions for vocational education programs for high school students who would soon be entering the job market.

During the 1940s, a shift in guidance occurred once again with the emergence of new theories in "counseling." There were numerous individuals who made significant contributions to the field of counseling through the development of new counseling theories. One such individual was Carl Rogers, a noted psychologist who developed nondirective counseling approaches.

Carl Rogers's nondirective counseling approach began what is commonly referred to as the Rogerian era of counseling. "Carl R. Roger's book, *Counseling and Psychotherapy* (1942), triggered a revolution in all forms of counseling. His client-centered approach broadened the concept of counseling, emphasized the counseling relationship rather than diagnosis and information, and opened up therapeutic practice to those without medical or psychoanalytical training" (Tolbert, 1982, p. 111). Rogers's work had, according to Aubrey (1977), a "Steamroller impact" (p. 292). The "steamroller impact" that Aubrey referred to stemmed in part from the reactions of those who were more interested in the quantitative means of measuring a client's vocational interest against the notion that "the overnight replacement of testing by counseling . . . [so that] in a few years it would compete and contend with guidance in regard to the use of a counselor's time and the overall purpose of counseling and guidance" (p. 292).

Guidance in the 1950s: Developmental Guidance, Sputnik, and the National Defense Education Act of 1958

The field of guidance and counseling continued to undergo significant changes in the 1950s. For example,

Robert H. Mathewson, considered to be the founder of developmental guidance, "stressed development as the guiding concept in planning and implementing guidance programs in schools" (Beale, 1986, p. 16). With this view, school counselors began to concern themselves more with the social and emotional problems that affected children and their development in addition to providing vocational guidance. As such, counseling programs at the secondary level began to include "counseling" as a part of the curriculum. Both individual and small and large group counseling opportunities were made available to students. No longer was the counselor viewed primarily as the tester and interpreter of test results. This view would soon change with the launching of Sputnik in 1957.

Sputnik caused a wave of accountability efforts in education. The National Defense Educational Act (NDEA) was passed in 1958. This legislation, according to Tolbert (1982), "was designed to remedy shortcomings in our education system and to produce more scientific talent through testing and counseling. The goal was to catch up in science; guidance was to play a strategic role in achieving it" (pp. 111–112).

With the emphasis on producing more high-achieving students, counselors, who had increased their presence in high schools due to the provisions of the National Defense Education Act were called upon to work more with students. Realizing that students could benefit from the work of guidance counselors, lobbyists brought about legislation, geared at promoting guidance and counseling at the elementary level through the Elementary and Secondary Education Act of 1965.

It was during the 1960s that guidance programs at the elementary level began to flourish. Verne Faust authored two books in 1968: *The Counselor-Consultant in the Elementary School* and the *History of Elementary School Counseling: Overview and Critique.* Both of these books detail in-depth the history of counseling at the elementary level. The underpinnings of elementary school counseling can be traced back to the work of the child study movement in the early 1900s and the work of William Burnham in the 1920s who believed that "the learning climate" of the school and those employed by the school were of paramount importance (Faust, 1968b). Faust (1968a) reports that Burnham's

work, although both "primitive and modern," emphasized that "the child's first business is to grow and develop. Everything else can wait . . ." (p. 13). Burnham's work, as Faust (1968a) details, was a reaction to the mental hygiene movement or to the various issues surrounding children and their needs (social, emotional, and health).

Guidance in the Schools: 1970s, 1980s, 1990s

After the social unrest of the 1960s and as a way of helping students in developing their potential, school counselors began to modify the ways in which they counseled and advised students. Both individual and group counseling practices began to emerge. This shift was due, at least in part, to the realization that schools needed to offer less restrictive guidance and counseling and to develop programs that provide services to more students than those who were in trouble.

Guidance and counseling grew by defining more clearly what types of activities were appropriate at the elementary, middle, and high school levels. A commonality among elementary, middle, and high school counselors that began to emerge in the late 1960s and that has continued to the present day is the emphasis on group work rather than the traditional individual approach to counseling (see, for example, Gysbers & Henderson, 1994; Herr, 1979; Myrick, 1987; Schmidt, 1993a; and Tolbert, 1982). More developmental approaches to school counseling emerged (see, for example, Gysbers & Henderson, 1994; & Myrick, 1987).

As elementary and secondary school counselors were developing more responsive guidance and counseling programs (curriculum), we believe that junior high schools, more often now referred to as middle schools, also struggled with developing counseling programs that could meet the unique needs of children at this grade level.

Overall, the years between 1970 and 1990 have been ones marked by increased communication and collaboration between guidance counselors, teachers, and administrators. As dialogue between the guidance counselor and other school personnel increased, the counselor began to emerge more as a consultant who would work with teachers and administrators in identifying and meeting the needs of students and the overall school community. Schmidt's (1993a) discussion of the collaboration that emerged between counselors and teachers in the later 1960s and early 1970s is, in our opinion, comprehensive and points to a movement that has continued to present day.

CURRENT STATUS

School counselors are engaged in a variety of activities with children. They provide individual and group counseling. Guidance and counseling activities, regardless of the configuration (individual or group), can be classified as preventive (primary and secondary), personal (individual interviews to discuss personal adjustments), academic (course progress, testing, that is, American College Testing, Scholastic Aptitude Testing, and Armed Services Vocational Aptitude Battery), and vocational (long-term planning and career). Guidance and counseling services ideally are responsive to the needs of the school and the people—students, teachers, and parents—who comprise the community.

Guidance and Counseling Programs

Guidance programs that are comprehensive in nature are an integral part of the school's total educational program; moreover, the comprehensive program is based on individual, school, and community needs. The "glue" of any comprehensive guidance program is the counselor who works for the common good of students, staff, parents, and the community. The comprehensive counseling programs within the schools we have visited have certain attributes. These attributes include a clearly defined guidance curriculum, evidence of individual planning made by those closest to developing and implementing the guidance curriculum, responsive services such as small and large group programs centering around needs identified by the community, and finally, support for the school itself in meeting the needs of the organization. This last attribute is often referred to as system support.

Nejedlo (1992) offers the following three guidelines for school counseling programs, which we believe encompass the ways in which school guidance and counseling programs should be conceptualized:

1. School counseling programs are based on the identified needs of students.
2. School counseling programs are planned, comprehensive, outcome-based programs that focus on the developmental needs of all students.
3. School counseling programs are delivered by counselors in collaboration with other student service professionals and utilize students, teachers, administrators, and community members as resources. (p. 2)

Nejedlo's counseling program guidelines contain three major concepts—identified needs, developmental needs, and collaboration.

Identified Needs. School counseling programs can only serve the community if they are based on the needs of the organization and its people. Counselors need to be able to identify those needs. The identification process can only be achieved by working with students, parents, teachers, and administrators. Through collaboration at this stage of development can come programs that address the most pressing needs. Through the use of surveys, questionnaires, and focus group discussions can come a better understanding of what types of service will be of most value. Because teachers, school nurses, and other staff interact with large numbers of students on a daily basis, these individuals have a firsthand view of the most pressing needs and can give insight regarding the development of preventive services. Preventive counseling is aimed at providing a service "which seeks to prevent the occurrence of the disorder in the *first* place" (Gibson & Mitchell, 1995, p. 36, emphasis in the original). School counselors work with teachers and students in preventive ways that are proactive versus the reactive, crisis approach.

Developmental Needs. Throughout the early history of guidance, the focus of most programs centered upon vocational guidance at the secondary level. Although the child study movement began in the early 1900s, it was not until the 1960s that the recognition of the young child was realized enough for formalized programs of counseling to emerge at the elementary level. Wrenn (1968) in Faust (1968b) argued that elementary-aged children were much different than secondary school–age children; hence they dealt with different issues and concerns. The elementary child "was still dependent upon parents . . . was concerned more with peers of the same sex rather than those of the opposite sex . . . and was under little pressure to make vocational and curriculum choices" (pp. 3–4) whereas the adolescent was more concerned with "emancipation from parents, vocational interests . . ." and other issues (Wrenn, 1968 cited in Faust, 1968b, p. 3).

Likewise, middle school–age children and their unique needs came to the forefront in 1989 with the publication, *Turning Points*. "Teacher-based guidance programs—known under a variety of different names such as advisor/advisee, homebase, and even homeroom—are a part of the accepted canon of middle school education" (McEwin, Dickinson, & Jenkins, 1996, p. 75). Romano and Georgiady (1994) indicate that middle school–age children experience an "increased range and number of problems of a personal and social nature, along with academic difficulties . . ." (p. 234). Romano and Georgiady (1994) suggest that:

> guidance is not synonymous with counseling as it is applied to middle school aged children. Counseling is a component of guidance in much the same way that teaching is related to instruction. As with instruction, guidance should be viewed as an integral part of the middle school child's total learning experiences. (p. 235)

Many middle schools have in place an advisor/advisee program complete with a distinct curriculum for each grade level. As schools implement advisor/advisee programs, much planning and collaboration among teachers and support staff such as the guidance counselor, social worker, school nurse, and psychologist is warranted. Often, these support personnel will work alongside teachers developing curriculum, team teaching, and linking outside resources to assist with the advisor/advisee program. This type of assistance and collaboration does not, however, supplant direct counseling, social work, or psychological services.

Collaboration. The view of the counselor as collaborator aligns well with the discussion presented by Schmidt (1993a). Nejedlo's notion of comprehensive

has been underscored by both practitioners and theorists. Coy (1991) believes that

> A comprehensive developmental school counseling program does not just occur. Counselors, students, parents, staff, and administrators must be willing to give time and effort to achieve a workable program for their community. The program must be built on the developmental needs of the students in the school and the demand for the service. (p. 17)

Anderson and Creswell (1980) discussed the notion of collaboration among guidance specialists, health education specialists, and secondary school health educators. They reported a study conducted by Petersen who interviewed specialists in health and guidance and concluded that "school health personnel should participate actively as members of the school guidance team . . ." (p. 155). Although this study dealt with secondary school health personnel and issues, transferring these findings to the elementary and middle school levels seems reasonable to us.

Duncan (1989) underscores the importance of collaboration and visibility of the school counselor. He also describes the "unique position" of the school guidance counselor, "With a job description that is neither one of a classroom teacher nor school administrator, the counselor's role is frequently difficult to articulate accurately, particularly to some teachers who have few or infrequent direct interactions with the counselor" (Duncan, 1989, p. 192). To increase collaboration and to reduce isolation, Duncan (1989) suggests that the school guidance department develop a guidance committee comprised of teachers, administrators, and other support staff, including a counselor. This committee would be charged with helping the guidance counselor identify needs, develop plans for meeting identified needs, assess results of efforts, and assist counselors in developing a calendar of events such as testing, screening at-risk students, course selection, and other essential tasks that the guidance department typically coordinates (Duncan, 1989).

Developmental Guidance

A major method in guidance and counseling at the elementary, middle, and high school levels is developmental guidance. Developmental guidance is a departure from offering individual counseling by providing guidance and counseling opportunities to a wide range of students over a wide range of topics and subjects. Developmental guidance activities can occur in classrooms (e.g., homeroom), in small groups (students targeted as being at-risk), and with individuals. Developmental guidance looks at the developmental needs of students based upon grade and age level. Developmental guidance programs engage a variety of people in the process (e.g., counselors, teachers, administrators, social workers, and the school psychologist). A comparison of guidance approaches (Stanciak, 1995) is presented in Table 9.1.

Stanciak (1995) postulates that a developmental guidance program "is based on seven fundamental principles" (p. 63). The principles of developmental guidance, according to Stanciak include the following:

1. The program is for all students.
2. The program has an organized and sequenced curriculum.
3. The program is sequential and flexible.
4. The program is an integrated part of the total educational process.
5. The program involves all school personnel.
6. The program aims to help all students learn more efficiently and effectively.
7. The program includes counselors who can provide specialized services and interventions. (p. 63)

It appears that developmental guidance programs have attributes that help students develop self-knowledge and interpersonal skills; guide students in career planning and exploration; and provide multiple opportunities for educational and vocational development.

Developmental guidance is thought to be more effective than the traditional approach because of the more holistic view it takes by working with "all students." However, according to Myrick (1987), "Comprehensive developmental guidance and counseling programs have been relatively slow to make their appearance in school systems" (p. 2). Perhaps it is the intensive effort and emphasis on collaboration, coupled with relatively difficult ends to measure, that has slowed down the complete acceptance of developmental guidance. Baker (1996) offers a caveat to defining developmental guidance practices too narrowly, how-

TABLE 9.1   Comparison of Guidance Approaches

TRADITIONAL AND DEVELOPMENTAL COUNSELING PROGRAMS

Traditional	Developmental
Crisis counseling	Preventive
Information service	Guidance curriculum
Career information	Career planning
Scheduling	Program management
Reactive	Assertive
Clerical/task oriented	Goal-oriented
Unplanned	Planned daily activities
Unstructured	Accountable
Maintain status quo	Evaluates and changes

From "Reforming the High School Counselor's Role: A Look at Developmental Guidance," by L. A. Stanciak, 1995, *NASSP Bulletin, 79*(570), pp. 60–63. Reprinted with permission of NASSP. For more information concerning NASSP Services and/or programs, please call (703) 860-0200.

ever, "Much of what goes on when counselors engage in individual and small-group counseling and consultation *is* development enhancing" (Baker, 1996, p. 244, emphasis in the original). Perhaps developmental guidance suffers from the same definitional problems as did guidance and counseling.

Comprehensive School Guidance Programs

The Texas Education Agency has framed a statewide plan for the development of a comprehensive school guidance program. The Texas design has four major components:

- Guidance curriculum: The specific curriculum standards to be emphasized, the specific competencies to be developed, and the age-appropriate outcomes to be reached by students.
- Responsive services: The systematic and timely response to requests from students.
- Individual planning: The listing of activities that facilitate individual planning at priority grade levels.
- System support: The listing of activities and programs that best meet the school community's needs and use the counselor's professional skills.

Table 9.2 explicates the purposes of the guidance program, the areas addressed within each component, and the role of the counselor.

Standards

The American School Counselor Association (1995) has developed its current goals for school counselors based upon Goals 2000. *School Counseling 2000** asserts the "eight broad goals for American education by the year 2000 . . . [and] each national goal is tied to developmental school counseling programs" (1995, n.p.).

School Counseling 2000
GOAL I:

All children in America will start school ready to learn.

The SCHOOL COUNSELOR works directly with PARENTS and TEACHERS to:

- help create a positive school climate in which children can learn;
- assure a coordinated team effort to address needs of all students;
- enhance open communication to prepare children for the school environment;
- provide information and support regarding future educational development;
- identify those children who are developmentally disabled or disadvantaged and need access to pre-school programs; and
- work with preschool children as they make the transition into schools.

GOAL II:

The high school graduation rate will increase to at least 90 percent.

The SCHOOL COUNSELOR works directly with all STUDENTS, PARENTS, TEACHERS, COMMUNITY MEMBERS, and EMPLOYERS to:

*From *School Counseling 2000: Children Are Our Future,* by the American School Counselor Association, 1995, Alexandria, VA: American Counseling Association. © ACA. Reprinted with permission. No further reproduction authorized without written permission of the American Counseling Association.

- provide for the continual benefits of a comprehensive developmental school counseling program through life skills training;
- ensure access to the services of other professionals including school social workers, psychologists, and nurses;
- develop a comprehensive education/career plan for each student which targets high school completion and exploration of postsecondary opportunities; and
- establish school-to-work transition programs.

GOAL III:

Students will . . . demonstrate competency over challenging subject matter . . . and every school in America will ensure that all students learn to use their minds well, so they may be prepared for responsible citizenship, further learning, and productive employment in our Nation's modern economy.

The SCHOOL COUNSELOR works directly with STUDENTS through developmental counseling curriculum to acquire NEW BASIC SKILLS to:

- learn decision-making skills, how to manage time, and organize information;
- develop positive attitudes toward work and encourage work experience activities;
- acquire skills and make a smooth transition from school to work;
- develop skills for planning, monitoring, and managing personal, career, and lifestyle development; and
- develop transferable skills to facilitate change through out their life-time.

GOAL IV:

The Nation's teaching force will have access to programs for the continued improvement of their professional skills and to the opportunity to acquire the knowledge and skills needed to instruct and prepare all American students for the next century.

The SCHOOL COUNSELOR works directly with TEACHERS to:

- provide information about student needs;
- provide information to help identify children-at-risk or who are developmentally disadvantaged;

TABLE 9.2 Four Components of a Comprehensive School Guidance Program

Guidance Curriculum	Responsive Services	Individual Planning	System Support
Provides guidance content in a systematic way to all students.	Addresses the immediate concerns of students.	Assists students in monitoring and understanding their own development.	Includes program and staff support activities and services.
Purpose: Awareness, skill development, and application of skills needed in everyday life.	**Purpose:** Prevention, intervention	**Purpose:** Student planning and goal setting	**Purpose:** Program Delivery and Support

Areas Addressed:
• Self-esteem development
• Motivation to achieve
• Decision making, goal setting, planning, and problem-solving skills
• Interpersonal effectiveness
• Communication skills
• Cross-cultural effectiveness
• Responsible behavior
	Areas Addressed:
	• Academic concerns
	• School-related concerns
	  tardiness
	  absences and truancy
	  misbehavior
	  school avoidance
	  drop-out prevention
	• Relationship concerns
	• Physical/sexual/emotional abuse
	• Grief/loss death
	• Substance abuse
	• Family issues
	• Sexuality issues
	• Coping with stress
		Areas Addressed:
		• Educational
		  Acquisition of study skills
		  Awareness of educational opportunities
		  Appropriate course selection
		  Lifelong learning
		  Utilization of test scores
		• Career
		  Knowledge of career opportunities
		  Knowledge of vocational training
		  Need for positive work habits
		• Personal–social
		  Development of healthy self-concepts
		  Development of adaptive and adjustive social behavior
			Areas Addressed:
			• Guidance program development
			• Parent education
			• Teacher/administrator consultation
			• Staff development for educators
			• School improvement planning
			• Counselor's professional development
			• Research and publishing
			• Community outreach
			• Public relations

Counselor Role Guidance Consultation Program implementation and facilitation	**Counselor Role** Counseling Consultation Coordination Referral	**Counselor Role** Guidance Consultation Assessment	**Counselor Role** Program management Consultation

From Texas Education Agency. (1990). The Comprehensive Guidance Program for Texas Public Schools: A Guide for Program Development Pre-K–12th Grade (GE 31503). Austin, Texas: Author. Reprinted with permission.

- establish collaborative relationships among community mental health resources and agencies;
- develop partnerships with businesses which promote student school-to-work transition;
- develop classroom management skills which create a climate where students can learn;
- promote an understanding of continually emerging social problems and determine successful response strategies; and
- develop programs to integrate the learning of positive social behavior and emotional health into the academic curriculum.

GOAL V:

United States students will be first in the world in mathematics and science achievement.

The SCHOOL COUNSELOR works directly with STUDENTS to:

- emphasize the importance of math and science in the workplace for every student;
- encourage higher levels of math and science in preparation for pursuing postsecondary education;
- fully explore education career opportunities, particularly those based in math and science; and
- identify career opportunities for those who excel in mathematics and science.

GOAL VI:

Every adult American will be literate and will possess the knowledge and skills necessary to compete in a global economy and exercise the rights and responsibilities of citizenship.

The SCHOOL COUNSELOR works directly with students to:

- facilitate personal growth and development;
- understand the importance of physical, mental, and emotional health;
- develop excellent communication skills and cooperative work skills;
- learn how to develop interpersonal skill to relate well to others;
- ensure all students access to appropriate services and opportunities that promote maximum development; and
- encourage life-long learning.

GOAL VII:

Every school in America will be free of drugs, violence, and the unauthorized presence of firearms and alcohol and will offer a disciplined environment conducive to learning.

The SCHOOL COUNSELOR works directly with STUDENTS to:

- provide education and information in conjunction with social service agencies about personal safety and prevention of abuse;
- develop effective coping skills necessary to refuse participation in substance abuse and physical violence; and
- develop problem-solving and decision-making skills with focus on self-assertion and conflict resolution.

GOAL VIII

Every school will support partnerships that will increase parental involvement and participation in promoting the social, emotional, and academic growth of children.

The SCHOOL COUNSELOR works directly with PARENTS to:

- help parents enter into a partnership with the school to support the academic work of children at home and share educational decision making at school; and
- provide information on community resources; and help students as well as parents understand why it is so important that all students take rigorous courses.

The American 2000 Goals parallel the objectives developed by the American School Counselor Association (1995) and can serve as targets for school counselors, teachers, parents, and administrators in meeting the needs of students as they face "dramatic increases in substance abuse, suicide, child abuse, teen pregnancy, truancy, school drop out, and random acts of violence" (1995, n.p.).

In addition to the these standards, the American School Counselor Association has a clearly defined set of ethical standards for school counselors. These standards elaborate the responsibility of the school counselor to students, parents, colleagues and professional associates, the school and community, self, and the profession.

Education, Training, and Certification

School counselors need to have advanced training from an accredited college or university. Typically, the school counselor completes a master's degree in guidance and counseling that includes a field-based internship in a school setting. In addition to academic training and the internship, many states mandate the successful completion of a state exam.

CONTEMPORARY ISSUES

The field and practice of guidance and counseling has undergone three major phases throughout its history. These phases—trait and factor, mental hygiene, and developmental—have had certain emphases associated with them. For example, during the trait and factor period (approximately 1900–1920) school guidance counselors were more concerned with vocational guidance. During the mental hygiene period (1930–1960), school guidance counselors were concerned with social and emotional adjustment and preventing maladjustment. And finally, during the developmental period (1960 to present), school guidance counselors were and are concerned with developmental aspects of children while simultaneously providing vocational and career guidance, crisis counseling, preventive counseling, and myriad other activities to assist children in their development.

Throughout these periods, guidance counselors have struggled with identifying and establishing their role within schools (Schmidt, 1986b). On one hand, as part of the support staff, guidance counselors are responsible for assisting with screening suspected special education students, at-risk students, students who are more academically accelerated, and finding the best possible placements for these students. On the other hand, school guidance counselors are expected to arrange college visits, schedule schoolwide testing programs, assist with the development of the master schedule, coordinate course selection, and respond to crisis situations. All the while, the school guidance

counselor is on call to be available as a consultant to teachers, parents, and the school's administration.

Due to the myriad responsibilities that the school guidance counselor must fulfill, many find themselves in a state of overload. The school administrator relies heavily upon the school guidance counselor for assistance, and it is this reliance that can cause conflict for the school guidance counselor. Often the school guidance counselor is called upon to perform duties that conflict with the training and expertise that the counselor brings to the school. A representative example of this conflict at the middle and high school levels is the building of the master schedule. First, students need to be advised of the courses available after meeting general requirements. Throughout this process, guidance counselors either meet with students individually or in small or large groups to complete forms. Typically, then an administrator will meet with the guidance counselor to begin building the master schedule from these forms. When conflicts arise and student schedules must be changed, it is the school guidance counselor who must rework the student's schedule, which invariably requires contacting the student and/or possibly the student's parent(s). Although course selection and development of the master schedule is often a joint function of the school guidance counselor and administrator, time for counseling is reduced because of this quasi-administrative detail. It appears that a more balanced approach is needed.

Very much like the school social worker and nurse, the school guidance counselor is faced with counseling an increased number of students who are fragile, at-risk, and facing other issues that can put the counselor in a position to involve other outside agencies. For example, Davis (1995) indicated that there has been an increase in the number of school guidance counselors who find themselves having to provide testimony in the courtroom due to "custody hearings involving their students" (p. 12). In addition to custody hearings, there has been an increased number of court hearings surrounding physical and sexual abuse (Davis, 1995). School personnel in all states are bound by law to report suspected child abuse under the Child Abuse Prevention and Treatment Act of 1974.

Trust between the counselor and client is essential. In the school setting, like in any other local agency that provides counseling services, privacy rights can become an issue. McCarthy and Sorenson (1993) discuss at length legal duty and privacy rights for school counselors and for others such as the school psychologist and social worker. The right to privacy, confidentiality, and privileged information can become clouded for these professionals within the school because many school counselors, psychologists, and social workers utilize group methods (McCarthy & Sorenson, 1993). School guidance counselors can be confronted with the dilemma of confidentiality when a student discloses sensitive information, regardless if the information is revealed during an individual or group session. Issues surrounding confidentiality and liability will probably increase; therefore, the administrator needs to be in a position to guide the school counselor through these issues. With regard to confidentiality, McCarthy and Sorenson (1993) suggest, "It is important for counselors to realize that confidentiality is not absolute, and clients should be so advised" (p. 160).

Although both administrator and counselor preparation programs address school law and legal issues pertaining to the school setting, both the administrator and school counselor need to become familiar with the legal implications surrounding disclosure, confidentiality, duties to warn individuals of danger, and protected and privileged information. Updating information on these issues can be achieved through annual in-services and by reading professional journals.

With reform efforts and increased workloads and role demands, school counselors are involved in a wider range of counseling activities. With increased expectations and numbers of students receiving services, accountability becomes an essential component of the school's guidance and counseling program. Program evaluation has traditionally not been embraced by many school guidance counselors because many believe they "deal with 'intangibles' that can't be measured, research is antihumanistic, follow-up activities aren't feasible, replicability is difficult if not impossible, and costs are prohibitive" (Wheeler & Loesch, 1981, p. 573). This view obviously confuses program evaluation with research. Wheeler and Loesch (1981) offer a clear delineation between program evaluation and research:

Research is conducted to discover new knowledge, to advance current scientific knowledge, and to build or improve theory. By contrast, program evaluation seeks to provide meaningful information for immediate use in decision making. (p. 574)

Program evaluation needs to be based upon several factors:

- The goals and objectives of the program.
- The ability to involve those closest to the program in the evaluation process. This involvement would include counselors, teachers, students, administrators, and parents.
- The utilization of a variety of methods to collect information. Methods could include surveys, interviews, and case studies, for example. (Crabbs & Crabbs, 1977)

Hiebert (1994) believes that evaluating outcomes and reporting results have three strong functions:

1. They help to prepare strong accountability arguments to help avoid funding cuts.
2. They help identify and focus counselor-and-teacher energy on areas where improvements can be made.
3. Perhaps most importantly, they help to market and promote areas where success is being demonstrated. (p. 30)

For program evaluation to be effective, the school administrator needs to take the lead in the process. However, the principal cannot be the only one involved in the process. "For change to occur, a commitment to action must be made by both administrative and counselor leaders. . . . Counselors and their administrators must [make] a decision to study and improve the guidance program" (Texas Education Agency, 1990, p. 66).

The supervision of the school's guidance counselor is an issue that many principals continue to grapple with given that the work of a counselor is not always as open for viewing as the teacher whose classroom can be easily entered to make formal observations. On the one hand, most school counselors are employees of the school district and, as such, they are bound by contractual agreements to receive supervision and to be evaluated by the school principal. Counselors typically receive little direct supervision by the school principal because as VonVillas (1995) explains, administrators provide "loose supervision of guidance departments" (p. 81) since "counselors are generally located near the main office, they are often perceived as having administrative support for whatever they do" (p. 81). On the other hand, given the relationship that counselors establish with students, the sensitivity of what is discussed, and the child's right to privacy, not to mention issues such as confidentiality and disclosure, it is questionable whether an administrator should observe, for the purposes of offering supervision, the counselor work with a student. Observing counselors working individually with students is a case-sensitive issue, and the supervisor needs to determine with the assistance of the counselor whether this is a viable option. One supervisor we know observes counselors for a two-hour block of time. When a student enters the office, the counselor asks the student if he or she minds the principal being present during the session. If the student objects, the principal exits the session before it begins. This principal has worked out in advance a signal to leave so that if a student becomes nervous a smooth exit can occur.

There are other ways, however, of providing supervision for school counselors. Multiple opportunities exist for the principal to offer the counselor direct and specific feedback about his or her performance during large and small group counseling and classroom presentations. Supervisors also have opportunities to observe school guidance counselors while they carry out other related services such as participating in special education annual reviews and multidisciplinary conferences and while they provide consultation to teachers and other school personnel. Other areas in which the supervisor can assess the performance of the guidance counselor are technical aspects of their work through viewing artifacts such as IEPs, weekly summary logs, the master calendar of planned guidance activities, and course scheduling plans. Other opportunities to supervise the guidance counselor include the work done in developing disaster and crisis planning and the provision of counseling during these types of activities.

Ideally, counselors receive intensive feedback on their skill development during their practicum, which is typically the last phase of their formal college preparation. This type of feedback also is critical for counselors as they continue in their profession. Nejedlo (1988) indicates that counselors have the capacity to grow more professional and enhance their skills through supervision. "Counselors prefer supervisors who are actively empathetic, genuine, warm, flexible, and nonrestrictive. . . . The mark of a master supervisor is the ability to access levels of competency in the counseling process, and then to have the verbal acuity to communicate the extent to which the student is developing his/her level of skill development" (Nejedlo, 1988, p. 7). Although Nejedlo was referring to master's level students and their supervisory needs during the practicum, we believe that this type of ongoing dialogue is critical for the school guidance counselor's professional growth.

After supervision, then what? This question begs for discussion. Like teachers and other professionals within schools, guidance counselors need ongoing staff development opportunities that will assist them not only with their own professional and personal growth, but also with keeping current with the changing needs of students and innovations in the field of guidance and counseling. O'Rourke (1991) believes that the following social needs will continue to escalate:

1. Increased drug and alcohol abuse
2. Escalating juvenile delinquency and crime rates
3. Increased number of child abuse cases
4. Rising teen pregnancy and sexually transmitted disease rates
5. The changing family structure
6. The increasingly complex nature of career development
7. The threat of war
8. The increase of emotional problems in children
9. School vandalism and other school problems. (p. 44)

These issues, along with others yet to be determined, require both guidance counselors and principals to be prepared to meet the needs that these issues bring about. Through carefully planned staff development activities and opportunities, school counselors will be able to keep current with changes, trends, and practices that show promise in meeting the needs of the child, school, and community.

ILLUSTRATIVE PRACTICES AND ISSUES

Konet, R. J. (1991). Peer helpers in the middle school. *Middle School Journal, 23*(1), 13–15.

> Konet details the development of a peer helper program for the middle school level. Peer helpers are found from the ranks of the student body at the high school. High school students chosen as peer helpers receive training and then work with middle school–level students. Peer helpers are trained in conflict management, assist with transition activities between the middle and high school levels, help chaperone middle school–level activities, and welcome new students to the district. *Issues:* The recruitment and training of high school students to serve as peer helpers and confidentiality issues that surround a peer helper program are discussed.

SUMMARY

Since the 1960s, school guidance and counseling programs have developed as an organized way of meeting the wide range and increasing needs of students. The very core of guidance counseling programs include assisting students to better understand themselves and their immediate environment. To this end, guidance has become developmental and interactive in nature.

QUESTIONS FOR FURTHER CONSIDERATION

Research

1. Examine guidance and counseling program features for middle school students. How can these same features be adapted for the high school level? What types of staff development would a high school faculty need to implement these features? What types of administrative support would need to be provided?

2. Examine the books and articles of Nejedlo that deal with developmental guidance. What are the basic tenets of developmental guidance and how can these tenets be applied in the elementary, middle, and high school levels?

3. Shadow a guidance counselor for a day. What types of activities prevent the counselor from spending more time with children?

4. What does research indicate about the student–counselor ratio?

Reflect

1. The emphasis on success at the high school level almost precludes counselors from doing anything but career guidance. How can counselors both "guide" and "counsel" students?

2. The shift in the role and responsibility of school counselors has been dramatic in the past 10 years. What external factors have contributed to this shift?

3. In some settings, group counseling has become a replacement for individual counseling. What are the advantages and disadvantages of each?

Respond/React

1. School counselors should be supervised and evaluated in the very same way as teachers and other classified staff members. Is this statement a fair and accurate one? What steps would you take to supervise and evaluate a counselor? What types of activities would be different from those associated with supervising and evaluating

teachers? What are the ethical issues surrounding supervising counselors and the work they do?

2. Statement: School counselors are teachers. Is this statement an accurate one? Defend your response with supporting evidence.

SUGGESTED READINGS

Baker, S. B. (1992). *School counseling for the twenty-first century.* New York: Macmillan.

Brown, D., & Srebalus, D. J. (1988). *An introduction to the counseling profession.* Englewood Cliffs, NJ: Prentice-Hall.

Fischer, L., & Sorenson, G. P. (1991). *School law for counselors, psychologists, and social workers* (2nd ed.). White Plains, NY: Longman.

Gysbers, N. C., & Henderson, P. (1994). *Developing and managing your school guidance program* (2nd ed.). Alexandria, VA: American Counseling Association.

Myrick, R. D. (1987). *Developmental guidance and counseling: A practical approach.* Minneapolis, MN: Educational Media Corporation.

Schmidt, J. J. (1993). *Counseling in schools: Essential services and comprehensive programs.* Boston: Allyn and Bacon.

CHAPTER 10

PARENTAL INVOLVEMENT

Parents can be involved in school matters in myriad ways. Whether they should be, or the extent to which they should be, have been issues debated by administrators, teachers, parents, and policy makers in the recent past (Epstein, 1996; Henry, 1996). Before examining the substance of these debates, we will briefly trace the history and education of the family, its influence, and the influences on it—all factors that affect parental involvement.

HISTORY

Berger (1981) provides an excellent account of how the family was viewed vis-à-vis education throughout history. The following historical description is based on Berger's work, unless otherwise noted.

During prehistoric times, just as today, "the first teachers—the socializers—were parents and families" (p. 23). Throughout Greek and Roman eras there were some written references to children and families. Plato considered the family not sufficiently wise to educate the children for the idealized state he described in the *Republic*. Aristotle thought education was too important to be left to the parents, whereas the early Roman emperors considered the family the foundation of civil government. The Greeks envisioned a state responsibility for education, but in the Roman empire, the family was to be the educative influence.

As noted in Chapter 6 on Early Childhood Education, the discussion of education of the young during the Greek and Roman eras, and certainly before them, must be tempered with the knowledge that infanticide was practiced rather routinely. Indeed, there was only a beginning of interest in orphans in the first century A.D. And during the Middle Ages, from the fifth century to the fifteenth or sixteenth, the very concept of family was elusive. Families existed, to be

sure, but for the majority of people, that is, the poor, Aries observed:

> In the Middle Ages . . . and for a long time after that in the lower classes, children were mixed with adults . . . at about the age of seven. They immediately went straight into the great community of men, sharing in the work and play of their companions, old and young alike. (1962, p. 411)

Accounts of family life during the Middle Ages are sparse (Aries, 1962), but those that do exist are typically broken down by class.

The noblemen, the highest social class, arranged for their children to learn appropriate behaviors for that class, chivalry being an example. Commoners would keep their children until age 7, at which time the children would be apprenticed to a craft or trade worker. The serfs and peasants, the lowest social class, had virtually no privacy, hence no family life as we might know it in modern times.

Only in the sixteenth and seventeenth centuries were there the beginnings of a concern for childhood and, therefore, family life. Aries observed, "it was recognized that the child was not ready for life, and that he (sic) had to be subjected to a special treatment, a sort of quarantine, before he was allowed to join the adults" (1962, p. 412). By 1671 books were published that advised parents on how to raise and educate their children. And as a result of the Protestant Reformation in the sixteenth century, wherein everyone was to be responsible for reading the Bible, reading became a necessary skill—one that families felt obliged to teach their children.

During the eighteenth and nineteenth centuries, European influences from Calvin, Locke, Rousseau, Pestalozzi, and Froebel affected the way children were viewed and, consequently, how families behaved in regard to them. Calvin, one of the early leaders of the

Protestant Reformation, promoted the original sin doctrine as it applied to young children. Consistent with Calvinist ideas carried over by the Puritans, some of the earlier settlers in North America, was the assumption of the depraved nature of children and how they were to be reared to avoid spoiling them. Children were thought to have evil natures, and it was considered imperative that the families break the child's will. (Chapter 6, on Early Childhood Education, discusses John Wesley's similar beliefs.)

John Locke broke from the evil nature assumption in suggesting that children were born tabula rasa as a blank slate. Despite his neutral position regarding children's nature, he recommended that orphans and children of the poor be taken by the state at age 3 and placed in working schools until age 14, at which time they would be apprenticed to learn a craft or trade.

Rousseau's influence was in suggesting that a child's nature was not depraved, as so many of the Protestants believed, or just neutral, as Locke claimed, but good. It was the city and its evil influences that ruined children, according to Rousseau. Brought up in a more natural environment, Rousseau believed children would manifest their inherent goodness. (Rousseau did not practice what he preached, however. His own five children were sent to foundling homes shortly after they were born.)

Pestalozzi was influenced by Rousseau's romanticism about young children. Pestalozzi also was greatly affected by the devastating effects of poverty on children and established a school for the poor where he emphasized working with objects first, then ideas, then words—the object lesson. More importantly, for parents, Pestalozzi was the first modern theorist to stress the vital role parents play in raising their children. Berger considers Pestalozzi to be the "Father of Parent Education" (1981, p. 40).

Froebel, also influenced by Rousseau, and a follower of Pestalozzi, likewise believed the mother was an important asset in helping the child develop. Considered the "Father of the Kindergarten," Froebel too was convinced of the mother's importance. He wrote *Mother Play and Nursery Songs with Finger Plays.* Some of the finger plays such as, pat-a-cake, pat-a-cake, are still in use today.

By the end of the nineteenth century, the family unit idea had not changed—the upper classes always had it—but the poor were beginning to break from the traditions of the Middle Ages and enjoy, more or less, the privacy and cohesiveness of family life.

In the United States, family life was well established because of the influence of the Puritans and because many who could make the voyage were not from Europe's lower classes. The obvious exceptions, of course, were the slave families of the South who suffered displacement of husbands and wives and sons and daughters.

The three major regions—New England, Middle Colonies, and the South—shared certain common family values. The father ruled. Virtually all families in all regions were patriarchal. Children basically were to be seen and not heard. In the late eighteenth century *The School of Good Manners* was published. It contained no fewer than 163 rules for children.

By the end of the eighteenth century and for all of the nineteenth, the Industrial Revolution created many opportunities for the exploitation and abuse of children. Children as young as 7 and 8 would work upwards of 14 hours a day and, in some instances, actually slept in the shops where they worked; obviously, these children did not experience much of a family life.

During the nineteenth century the growing middle class began taking an interest in children, hitherto the exclusive interest of the upper class. As early as 1820, various mothers groups formed. These groups were usually called maternal associations; they consisted of "middle class members of Protestant–Calvinist religious groups" (Berger, 1981, p. 43). By the end of the 1800s, a number of other influences on childhood and the family had appeared.

The Society for the Study of Child Nature was founded in 1888. It was reflective of the new interest in child study by the likes of such famous psychologists as G. Stanley Hall. The society promoted child study and parent education. Various other womens groups, for example, the Women's Christian Temperance Union and the American Association of University Women, were committed to promoting the welfare of children and the education of parents.

The kindergarten movement that took place in the United States in the last few decades of the nineteenth century was fueled by the interest in Froebel's ideas of raising young children in wholesome, child-centered environments. The first public, English-speaking kindergarten had been opened in St. Louis by Susan Blow, the teacher, in 1873. By the turn of the century, many major cities had kindergartens; but interestingly, not just for the growing middle classes, but especially, though not exclusively, for settlement houses that served the new immigrants in large urban centers. Because of the influences of Pestalozzi and Froebel on the kindergarten movement, parents were always involved in some capacity with kindergartens.

The most important organization related directly to parental involvement in schools was established in 1897—The Congress of Parents and Teachers, originally named the National Congress of Mothers. This association was proactive in helping to pass child-labor laws and pure food and drug acts. It has been, and still is, an effective lobby for children, teachers, and parents and promotes parent education and involvement in schools.

In response to efforts to ameliorate the abject conditions of many of the children of the working poor, a White House Conference on Care of Dependent Children was held in 1909. By 1912, as a result of this conference, the Children's Bureau was created, thus establishing official national government concern for children. In 1914 *Infant Care* was published by the Children's Bureau. This booklet was the first in a series of government documents that provided information and advice on childrearing. Brim (1965) and Mead and Wolfenstein (1955) trace the specific patterns of child-rearing advice offered parents over time and note the shifting concerns on such issues as thumb sucking, masturbation, and scheduled feeding versus feeding on demand. Suffice it here to say that official publications, such as *Infant Care,* as well as the increasing number of articles appearing in the popular press, reflected, by and large, the predominant thinking of the time with regard to how children develop and what parents could and should do to nurture or control that development.

Berger (1981) documents the increasing response at the national level to the need for parent education:

> The Smith-Lever Act of 1914 provided 2000 County Home Demonstration agents. This county extension program included education in homemaking, improved nutrition, and child care. Later, the Smith-Hughes Act of 1917 established "homemaking" as a vocation and included a provision for education in child care and nutrition through extension classes, demonstrations, and institutions under the auspices of the Office of Education. (p. 50)

Concern for parent education, even at the national level, has been evident for the major part of the twentieth century.

As indicated in Chapter 6, the establishment of child development laboratory schools, usually within a university setting, promoted not just child study per se, but knowledge about and insight into optimal ways to help children develop. By the 1930s there continued to be a burgeoning interest in parent education.

Membership in the Parent–Teacher Association (PTA) "grew from 60,000 in 1915 . . . to nearly 1,500,000 in 1930" (Berger, 1981, p. 55). By 1935, 8,000,000 copies of *Infant Care* were distributed. But the real impact on parents by mid-century was from Dr. Benjamin Spock who wrote, *The Common Sense Book of Baby and Child Care,* first published in 1946.

Spock's book took something of a middle ground between issues like rigid feeding schedules versus feeding on demand. He anticipated typical questions about sleeping, clothing, toilet training, and illnesses. Spock indeed represented common sense, that is, he was not extreme in any advice he offered, and subsequent editions of his book made him a significant force in child care ideas throughout the 1950s and 1960s. In addition to Spock and other books on parenting from commercial publishers, the U.S. government continued studying children and parenting and advising parents through government publications. The PTA was often the conduit for such information and advice and delivered it via school-based functions.

The 1960s were tumultuous times. An unpopular war, an impatience for social, civil, and economic equality for minorities and women, and a rejection of the "melting pot" metaphor for all people who were not part of the dominant, white middle class led to a number of significant legal, social, and educational changes. The implications for parental involvement in schools were great.

In 1965 Head Start was established to break the "vicious cycle of poverty." Head Start was, and still is, a comprehensive approach to families. Originally serving 4 and 5 year olds (and later some 3 year olds), Head Start required parental involvement on advisory boards. In 1967 Project Follow Through was established to continue the Head Start efforts for children through third grade. Parental involvement was required for Project Follow Through as well.

The Elementary and Secondary Education Act (ESEA) was established in 1965. ESEA made federal funds available to public schools to help eliminate, or at least reduce, the educational disadvantages of children from low income families. The various titles of the legislation mandated parental involvement in helping to plan and evaluate the services provided children and families.

During the 1970s, schools continued with compensatory programs, but by the end of the decade, federal funding for some, for example, Follow Through, was greatly reduced. Many schools became caught up with competency-based instruction and other forms of bureaucratic accountability. By the 1980s, however, enough examples of parental involvement existed, or were then being launched, to warrant discussion of them in the professional literature. Indeed, the 1990s were a time when a rather coalesced knowledge base, drawing on the work done in the 1970s and 1980s, was articulated (Epstein, 1996). PTA membership by 1996 was 6.5 million, providing a more than adequate base for arrangements to include parents in schools. The next section will describe the knowledge base and illustrate aspects of it from various accounts of parental involvement experience.

CURRENT STATUS

> *Goals 2000: Educate America Act* has as goal number 8: By the year 2000, every school will promote partnerships that will increase parental involvement and participation in promoting the social, emotional, and academic growth of children. (National Education Goals Panel, 1995, p. 13)

Three specific objectives follow this general goal. One has to do with states developing policies to assist local schools to establish programs for increasing partnerships with parents. Another is that every school will engage parents and families to help with the children's academic work and to share in the educational decision making affecting children. The last objective is that "parents and families will help to ensure that schools are adequately supported and will hold schools and teachers to high standards of accountability" (National Education Goals Panel, 1995, p. 13).

The National Education Goals Panel (1995) found that about 90 percent of parents of children in grades 1 through 4 participate in parent–teacher conferences, but that only 60 percent of principals report that parents are involved in school-policy decision making. In general, parental involvement decreases as children proceed through the grades. "Parents' reports of their involvement in school activities show that involvement decreases from 74 percent in grades 3–5 to 62 percent in grades 6–8 and 53 percent in grades 9–12" (National Education Goals Panel, 1995, p. 71).

The National Education Goals Panel (1995, pp. 54–56) indicates that 77 percent of the teachers of eighth-grade public school students report that their students' parents attended parent–teacher conferences. Principals of eighth-grade public school students reported a 62 percent rate of involvement of parents in policy decisions. And 63 percent of the parents of children in grades 3 through 12 reported attending two or more school activities during the year. The general goal is to reach 100 percent by the year 2000. The figures above were collected in 1992 and 1993, hence, there may be time to reach the goal by the year 2000.

An argument could be made that parents should be involved in school matters because we live in an open society based on democratic principles. The Tenth Amendment of the U.S. Constitution essentially leaves to the states the conduct of formal education; and the states typically delegate the responsibility to local school districts, overseen by locally elected school boards. This arrangement can be cited as a rationale for parental involvement, that is, such involvement is simply an extension of the idea of local control. Another rationale, based on anecdotal accounts of involvement activities, was used by James Hymes, indomitable advocate for early childhood education. He promoted parental involvement as early as 1953. In a revised version of *Effective Home–School Relations* (Hymes, 1974), he listed four benefits of parental involvement:

1. Children's schools get more support. They begin to move toward the full backing that schools today need so desperately.
2. Children have more consistent guidance, in school and out. They are not pulled in competing directions, with each new yank-and-haul diluting all the previous efforts.
3. Children's learnings are constantly reinforced, wherever the children turn. In school and out, over and over, their understandings are strengthened by all whom they meet.
4. There is less danger of gaps in children's total education. The hazards of omissions and empty spots which can so easily occur when home and schools do not know what the other is doing and *not* doing. (p. 2, emphasis in the original)

The intent of improved home–school relations was to provide "richer, fuller, more nourishing lives for children" (Hymes, 1974, p. 2). In the 1990s the same kinds of arguments for parental involvement can be made, but now a wealth of empirical data supports them.

The National Education Goals Panel (1995) reviewed several summaries of parental involvement research and listed the following findings:

- Higher mathematics and reading scores
- Better report card grades, attendance, behavior, and attitudes in middle and high school
- Reduced likelihood that a student will repeat a grade or be in the lower half of his/her class
- Decreased likelihood that a student will be suspended or expelled from school
- Decreased likelihood that a child's parent will be contacted by the teacher about a classroom behavior problem
- Greater student participation in extra curricular school activities (p. 64)

In addition, the Panel found a great deal of evidence that parents, teachers, students, and business executives believe an increase in parental involvement in schools is needed.

School, Family, and Community Partnerships

Epstein (1996) suggests the term *parent involvement* placed the burden for involvement on parents and,

therefore, recommends the name *school, family, and community partnerships* to signify shared responsibilities for a variety of involvements. Once the concept is broadened and made to emphasize partnerships, more detailed analyses can be made.

Epstein and colleagues (1994) have devised an "overlapping spheres of influence" model that places family, school, and community as intersecting circles, with the child at the center. In addition, they have an internal model of family and school spheres, again, with the child in the center, being affected by interactions between each sphere. What is critical to understanding the model, however, is their reminder that:

> School and family partnerships do not "produce" successful students. Rather, the partnership activities that include teachers, parents, and students engage, guide, energize, and motivate students so that *they* produce their own success. (1994, p. 42, emphasis in the original)

Success, Epstein and colleagues go on to remind, includes more than just higher achievement test scores. Success means improvements in self-esteem, attitudes, independence, and other desired behaviors associated with successful students (1994).

Six Major Types of Involvement. Epstein (1996) has created six types of involvement that schools can initiate to improve the partnerships with families and communities.

> Type 1—Parenting: Assist families with parenting and child rearing skills, family support, understanding child and adolescent development, and setting home conditions to support learning at each age and grade level. (1996, p. 215)

Examples of Type 1 involvements could be workshops, study groups, and speakers that the school organizes, preferably with input from parents. Determining needs and interests of parents could be accomplished through surveys. Finding suitable times for such activities is important as well. Because of conflicting schedules or family responsibilities, many parents are not able to attend functions the school may plan, irrespective of their need for them. Epstein and colleagues (1994) suggest that schools anticipate these conflicts and make appropriate arrangements. For example, by using audio- or video-recording, the school could establish a resource for parents to use at their convenience.

A word of caution is needed here because all too often school personnel will proceed with education or training experiences for parents that are based on a deficit model of the families being served. Swap (1993) has observed, "we rarely question the effectiveness of our outreach strategies or seek advice from parents about the kind of information or support they would find helpful" (p. 34). Different values associated with parenting practices may not automatically warrant "correction" by the school. The inclusion of parents in the planning of parenting education and training is the best safeguard for avoiding the foisting of the school's values onto families with different values.

> Type 2—Communicating: Communicate with families about school programs and student progress with school-to-home and home-to-school communications. (1996, p. 215)

Examples of Type 2 involvements are report cards, announcements, permission slips, and other communications that the school finds it necessary to use to keep families apprised of how their children are doing and what the school is planning. The best written announcement or newsletter, however, may not be enough. Epstein and her colleagues (1994), for example, have found that in some instances as few as 33 percent of newsletters ever even made it home.

> Type 3—Volunteering: Improve recruitment, training, work, and schedules to involve families as volunteers and audiences at the school or in other locations to support students and school programs. (1996, p. 215)

At the beginning of each school year, surveys or questionnaires could be completed by parents on their interests, occupation, and willingness to participate as a volunteer in school. Volunteer work can take many forms.

Parents can be involved in classrooms or other educational settings in which the presence of another adult may make the difference between success and failure of an activity. Parents with interesting hobbies or special occupations may be willing to share their hobby or work experiences with children. Many of the responsibilities associated with after-school activities for example, athletic events and plays, can be fulfilled

by parents. The caution here, however, is not to expect parents to take on those responsibilities routinely abhorred by teachers, for example, recess or lunch duty, and expect them to maintain much interest in continuing their volunteering.

However long or varied the list of responsibilities school personnel can generate, chances are usually good that parents can be found who are willing and able to help with them. Finding and coordinating volunteers may be jobs in themselves with which volunteers could help.

> Type 4—Learning at Home: Involve families with their children in learning activities at home, including homework and other curricular-linked activities and decisions. (1996, p. 215)

Epstein and colleagues (1994) report that "research with thousands of parents has shown that parents want to motivate, encourage, monitor, keep track of, interact with, and talk about school work at home" (p. 47). Teachers need not worry so much that parents may not understand the lessons. Instead, teachers should build into their homework assignments opportunities (maybe requirements) for interaction with family members.

One method used to engage students with family members concerning homework at the middle school level is TIPS (Teachers Involve Parents in Schoolwork) (Epstein, Jackson, & Salinas, 1994). TIPS is used by teachers to improve the likelihood that students will complete homework assignments with greater understanding and, in the process, create a more informed link between the family and what the teacher is teaching.

> Type 5—Decision Making: Include families as participants in school decisions, governance, and advocacy activities through PTA, committees, councils, and other parent organizations. (1996, p. 216)

Many of the school reform efforts as well as various Title programs and state legislatures require parental involvement at the decision-making level. This type of involvement may be the most difficult to achieve.

Henry (1996) notes that schools, in their efforts to become more professional over the last 150 years, have often achieved that status by distancing themselves from the lay public. Expecting school personnel to form decision-making partnerships with parents is indeed a challenge. Perhaps requiring such partnerships by law is the only way they will occur. More about this type of partnership will be discussed under Contemporary Issues, below.

> Type 6—Collaborating with Community: Coordinate the work and resources of community businesses, agencies, colleges or universities, and other groups to strengthen school programs, family practices, and student learning and development. (1996, p. 216)

In addition to school–business foundations that typically generate funds to support a variety of teacher or school activities, many schools are requiring some form of community service from every student. Community agencies, profit and nonprofit alike, can benefit from such community service. Families also can be helped when social service agencies are included in the mix. All too often families may be unaware of available services within the community, and the school can be instrumental in linking families with appropriate agencies.

CONTEMPORARY ISSUES

Despite the great deal of progress made in the research literature on parental involvement in the 1980s and 1990s, more work and more discussion need to occur. Epstein (1996) has outlined a number of more specific kinds of questions that need to be examined in order to shore up or adjust various generalizations about parental involvement. A particularly important issue is the different kinds of families with which schools work.

Procidano and Fisher (1992) have provided an excellent treatment of the varieties of families, each one of which is potentially different in how it responds to or is affected by school partnerships. The types of families in contemporary America include, but are not limited to, those discussed by the contributors to Procidano and Fisher's book:

- Dual-wage
- Single-parent
- Stepfamilies
- Families of Hispanic origin
- African-American families

- Korean families
- Families in poverty
- Families facing death and serious illness
- Families with learning-disabled children
- Families of children with chronic illness
- Parents and children with psychological problems (pp. vii–viii)

The challenge to school practitioners is to realize that the variety of family types means generalizations about the "typical" family are suspect. For now, at least, it is safer to proceed on a family-by-family basis rather than to assume all families will respond in a like manner. Administrators need to know what kinds of families they are serving and what their particular concerns might be.

Overcoming Barriers to Parental Involvement

Henry (1996) believes the current dominant state of affairs in schools is administrators protecting teachers from parents and the community. And where schools do involve parents they "typically support families who most reflect the school's intentions and purposes" (Henry, 1996, p. 94). She encourages teachers "to learn not to hide behind bureaucratic norms and a traditional 'professional' cloak that distances them from families" (p. 84).

Citing Ballantine (1989), Henry (1996) notes that 85 percent of the nation's children are educated in 20 percent of the school districts. The likelihood of these schools being very homogeneous is remote.

> Today more than ever, educators must be committed to communicating with parents from an ever-increasing variety of cultural, ethnic, language and social class backgrounds, and orientations. The Eurocentric, middle class culture of the public school can no longer remain detached from its pluralistic clientele—expecting them to change while the school remains the same. (Henry, 1996, pp. 131–132)

Several changes need to occur, according to Henry (1996), for schools to establish partnerships with parents. Three of the changes are (1) exhibiting an ethic of care (as opposed to a concern for bureaucratic rules); (2) displaying a spirit of collaboration (as opposed to competition); and (3) showing a commitment to teaching and learning (as opposed to a division into management and teachers) (Henry, 1996).

In addition to the democratic reasons for involving parents in the public schools already alluded to, Henry (1996) argues for involvement for practical reasons:

> The intimate knowledge mothers and fathers gain in the course of rearing their children is valuable knowledge that is often neither respected nor utilized in the school setting. (p. 84)

It simply makes good sense, according to Henry, to use this knowledge to make better decisions about learning opportunities for children.

The challenge educators face in overcoming the barriers to any of the types of involvement is built into the system itself. Henry notes that as schools have become larger, more professional, and more bureaucratic, they can be characterized as gesellschaft in nature, that is, depersonalized and officious. The various legal mandates (e.g., Title programs) and national goals (e.g., Goals 2000) speak to partnerships with parents that are gemeinschaft in nature, meaning personalized and user-friendly. Henry (1996) considers it problematic to try to achieve gemeinschaft ends through gesellschaft means.

Swap (1993) reports that a number of studies indicate that teachers are not always strongly in favor of parental involvement. She notes that one possible explanation for this is that the National Council for Accreditation of Teacher Education (NCATE) did not include a standard for parental involvement (Ooms, 1989, in Swap, 1993). The 1995 edition of the *Standards, Procedures and Policies* (NCATE, 1995), however, does contain the following information on teacher preparation courses and what they should help develop understanding and use of:

- Collaboration with school colleagues, parents, and agencies in the larger community for supporting students' learning and well-being;

- Effective interactions with parents for supporting students' learning and well-being. (p. 18)

The *Approved Curriculum Guidelines* for educational leadership programs also include specific reference to collaborating with parents (NCATE, 1995).

PTA. This national organization, since its beginning in 1897, has always advocated for children. Currently present in many schools, the PTA has national and state organizations that can provide video-lending services, publications, newsletters, technical assistance, and leadership training opportunities to schools and their patrons.

The PTA represents an infrastructure that could facilitate the establishment of all types of partnerships. Ideally, members of the PTA meet to study problems, support teachers, volunteer in schools, provide workshops on parenting, and become informed and take action on issues regarding children and youth" (PTA brochure, n.d.). The PTA is "shedding the old, mistaken image of a cookie-baking, fund-raising women's group" (PTA brochure, n.d.).

ILLUSTRATIVE PRACTICES AND ISSUES

Chapman, W. (1995). The Illinois experience: State wants to improve schools through parent involvement. *Phi Delta Kappan, 72*(5), 355–358.

> Among the several partnerships schools that have formed in Illinois, the ones with families have the most impact on at-risk children. *Issues:* Partnerships cannot be formed unless there is mutual respect between parents and schools.

Thompson, S. (1996). How action research can put teachers and parents on the same team. *Educational Horizons, 74*(2), 70–76.

> Building collaborative partnerships between parents and teachers will ultimately help students. *Issues:* Sharing power between parents and teachers is an important accomplishment.

SUMMARY

For the majority of people, that is, all except the wealthy, childhood and family are relatively recent ideas. Family especially continues to evolve in its na-

ture and composition. Whereas childhood can be specified by chronological age, the family can, and does, take a variety of forms. The school's commitment to serving children necessarily affects the family. Partnerships with families increase the probability that the school's effort will be successful and, because of the partnerships, families can be more confident and supportive of the school's effort.

Parental involvement in schools has evolved into partnerships between and among schools, families, and the community. As a field of study, the area has grown significantly during the 1980s and 1990s. Generally speaking, all parties appear to benefit when such partnerships are formed, but the quality of the activities is an important factor.

"The American Family does not exist. Rather, we are creating many American families of diverse styles and shapes" (Footlick, 1990, in McCarthy, 1992, p. 3).

The tradition in schools has been to keep the lay public at a distance and when embraced, it is those who have similar values to the school who get the attention. Advocates for partnerships encourage schools to widen their reach to include all families to meet the spirit, as well as the letter, of partnership policies.

QUESTIONS FOR FURTHER CONSIDERATION

Research

1. Examine parental involvement trends in elementary, middle, and high schools. What does this research base tell you as far as developing parental involvement strategies for schools at each one of these grade levels?

2. The value and effectiveness of homework has been debated. What does the research indicate about homework and the relationship to parental involvement?

3. Extend the research presented in this chapter on Project Head Start. What is the "culture of poverty" that Head Start seeks to counteract?

Reflect

1. Examine the two seemingly contradictory ideas in this statement: We want parents to be 'involved' in schools, but then complain about them when they are involved. As a building principal, how would you reconcile these contradictory statements as you work with your teachers to develop better parental involvement?

2. If your school did not have a homework policy, how would you develop one? How would you involve staff, parents, and students in the development of this policy?

3. How do you get the parents of students who are experiencing failure in school involved? How would your strategies differ for these parents than for the parents of students who are on the honor roll?

4. What are the main features of parental involvement practices that are based on a deficit model?

Respond/React

1. Should parents be involved in developing school policies? Why or why not?

2. Many teachers believe that parent–teacher conferences should be only for the students who are having difficulties. A teacher in your building sends home a letter to the parents of students who have averages of "C" or better, indicating that they

should not attend the next parent–teacher night. As the principal, how would you respond to this?

SUGGESTED READINGS

Booth, A., & Dunn, J. F. (Eds.). (1996). *Family-school links: How do they affect educational outcomes?* Mahwah, NJ: Erlbaum.

Henry, M. E. (1996). *Parent–school collaboration: Feminist organizational structures and school leadership.* Albany, NY: State University of New York Press.

Kaplan, L. (Ed.). (1992). *Education and the family.* Boston: Allyn and Bacon.

CHAPTER 11

PHYSICAL EDUCATION

The third goal in *Goals 2000: Educate America Act* concerns student achievement and citizenship. One of the objectives within this goal is, "All students will have access to physical education and health education to ensure they are healthy and fit" (1994, p. 58). Physical education, like the fine arts, stakes at least part of its claim to legitimacy to its inclusion in *Goals 2000: Educate America Act.*

Whether it is a sports and games approach (Barney, 1979) or a concern with sport, play, dance, and exercise (Rivenes, 1978) or any physical "activity that serves as a medium through which a total learning experience takes place" (Seaton, 1992, p. 1), physical education has a presence in contemporary American education. Like fine arts education, physical education reflects the social interest in the subject; and whereas the fine arts combine a rational–creative duality, physical education has the more pronounced duality of mind and body. And, also like the fine arts, the origin of physical education can be traced to preliterate times and pagan ritual.

HISTORY

Preliterate, Greek, and Roman Eras

The daily rigors of survival in preliterate times sufficiently taxed the physical abilities of men and women, rendering a concern for anything resembling physical education unnecessary. The rituals, however, of paying homage to various and sundry gods did involve physical activity, such as dancing, and that activity took on a life of its own long after the ritual itself lost meaning. According to Rivenes, "all modern bat and ball games are descended from one common source, namely an ancient fertility rite observed by priest–

kings in ancient Egypt" (1978, p. 269). The origin of the very word *sport* reflects an important aspect of physical education.

Sport originally came from the verb "deporter—to carry away from or to be diverted. To disport thus meant 'to be at sport,' which was a way of saying that one was engaging in an activity that was not one's normal occupation or one of the chores of daily living" (Rivenes, 1978, p. 259). In time, the verb became a noun, and rather than describing the actual doing of something, the word sport became the name of the activity itself.

Informal sport existed by 800 B.C. in the manner of throwing, running, wrestling, boxing, and chariot races, but the first, formalized Olympic games of which there is a written record, were held in 776 B.C. (Hackensmith, 1966). The Greek era, from about the eighth century to the fourth, B.C., included sufficient growth of sports and interest in physical education to warrant the specialization and, in time, the professionalization of athletics.

Athletics has retained its original meaning. The Greek *anthos* means a struggle; and *athlon* means a prize. "Combined, they mean one who struggles or competes for a prize" (Rivenes, 1978, p. 259). By the fourth century B.C., Greek interest in physical education for all youth was waning because of the growth of the professional athlete and the increased interest in spectator sports (Hackensmith, 1966). Contests in the first Olympic games included running (barefoot and naked), long jumping, the discuss throw, the javelin throw, wrestling, and boxing. With the advent of the Roman influence, many of the sports took on a more brutal and sadistic nature. Because of the depravity of the "games" and the Christian influence that downplayed the importance of the body, the last of the original Olympics games was abolished by a zealous Christian emperor in 394 A.D. The Greek era, though relatively short-lived, was perhaps the best example of a society that valued equally the harmonious blending of the physical and intellectual (Rivenes, 1978).

The huge coliseums of the Roman era are ample testimony to the value placed on spectator sports. Whether watching gladiators or chariot races, the Romans provided sport of high entertainment value to satisfy the great masses of people who migrated to Rome. The ascendancy of spectator sports was promoted by the Romans, who seemed to be more interested in spectacles and entertainment than the personal development made possible through physical education.

During the Middle Ages, physical education was more closely related to self-preservation, at least for noblemen of the feudal society. Young squires learned the rudiments of knighthood that included horsemanship and the use of the lance and the shield. Endurance was developed by running, jumping, wrestling, and climbing ropes. The knight-to-be had to become proficient with the bow and arrow, battle ax, and spear. Once he passed all tests of proficiency and demonstrated valor, he was granted knighthood. Hackensmith notes (1966),

> The ideal knight was the embodiment of medieval virtue: pure in conduct, champion of those in distress, and defender of Christianity against unbelievers. Motivated by faith as well as by a lust for adventure and profit, knights by the thousands fought in the Crusades. (p. 72)

Among the nobles and the peasants there was still some interest and involvement in hunting, wrestling, foot races, and a variety of ball games, but essentially, physical education was ignored for about a millennium and a half. As Rivenes (1978) notes:

> [when] mind and body are in conflict with one another, the body is disparaged and neglected, so that physical education is nonexistent. (p. 277)

During the Middle Ages when there was nearly total domination by the Church, physical education was virtually nonexistent. And it was not much different in the North American colonies with their great Puritan influence.

Physical Education in the United States

The Renaissance, the Great Awakening, and the Enlightenment, all speak to the periods following the Middle Ages that led up to and included the founding of the American colonies in 1620. Public schools were still a long time coming, but the thoughts about schooling were influenced by various English and European philosophers and educators.

John Locke, English philosopher, advocated for "a sound mind in a sound body" (Rice et al., 1969, p. 56). Locke promoted physical education to harden and discipline the body. "(Locke) had much to say about hygiene but little about the value of play" (Rice et al., 1969, p. 57). As discussed in Chapter 6, Early Childhood Education, Locke was especially important to educators because he disabused them of the notion that children are born with a depraved or evil nature.

Rousseau, also discussed in Chapter 6, went further in promoting the natural goodness of children. According to Hackensmith (1966),

> the natural impulses of the child should be freed from the restriction and discipline of formalized education in favor of learning through play, games, manual arts, and direct acquaintance with nature. (p. 113)

Rousseau was consistent with Locke in that he believed a sound body makes a sound mind (Rice et al., 1969).

Pestalozzi, influenced by Locke and Rousseau, believed that "physical education should receive just as serious consideration in the school program as traditional subjects" (Hackensmith, 1966, p. 120). His concern for physical education for natural activities such as striking, carrying, thrusting, throwing, turning, running, jumping, and climbing were lost, however, by the major European interest in gymnastics as the sole activity of physical education. Indeed, the emphasis on gymnastics was to affect American physical education well into the twentieth century.

Despite the influence of Locke advocating for vigor and discipline of the body, the American colonists did not accept it. The Puritan attitudes were hostile to play, sports, and even exercise. In colonial New England, if you participated in sport or play on Sunday you were even subject to arrest (Seaton, 1992).

Church or no church, the young played games of football and cricket, and skating and sledding were common. Rice and colleagues write (1969):

> Practically all the colonies except the strongly church controlled ones of Massachusetts, New Hampshire, and Connecticut soon developed some forms of festivals, fairs, and pageants. (p. 140)

With increased immigration, the influence of the Puritans lessened considerably. There were even admonitions to attend to physical education.

Benjamin Franklin promoted physical education activities by the late 1700s and he is credited with writing the first detailed instructions for the teaching of swimming (Rice et al., 1969). By the early 1800s, George Barker Winship, a graduate of Harvard's medical school, became an advocate for what today we would call bodybuilding. He appealed to men who wanted bulging muscles and great strength; in effect, leading to the belief that great strength was the aim of health and well-being. Rice and colleagues note that "It has taken physical education almost a century to live down this concept" (1969, p. 150).

By the mid-1800s, the gymnasium in the United States was associated with prize fighters, weight lifters, and rowdies, but that soon changed because of the influence of Dio Lewis (Hackensmith, 1966). Lewis studied at Harvard medical school and began touring and lecturing on a new system of gymnastics. In 1860 he settled in Boston where he opened a teacher training school for gymnastics in 1861. Lewis did much to popularize physical education and convince the educators of the day for the need of it (Rice et al., 1969). Lewis published *The New Gymnastics for Men, Women and Children* in 1862, which included such suggestions as doing gymnastic exercises to music and replacing the dumbbell with the bean bag for women and children (Hackensmith, 1966). By the time Lewis's institute closed in 1868, more than 250 teachers of gymnastics had graduated. Lewis's work was especially important because it represented a U.S. venture and not just the adoption of the German or Swedish system of gymnastics.

The German system of gymnastics, also known as *heavy gymnastics,* was brought in by immigrants who settled in the Midwest. The system included free exercise with short and long wands, dumbbells, and rings; apparatus work with horizontal bar, parallel bars, and suspension rings; and marching, games, and play (Rice et al., 1969). By the end of the Civil War, the German system had a strong foothold in the larger cities of the Midwest. In contrast, the Swedish system, known as *light gymnastics,* was more of an influence in New England and the East. The Swedish system included the use of swinging ladders, the vaulting box, and, like the German system, some marching, rhythms, and games. "The system featured light exercise in calisthenic form for the development of flexibilities and grace of movement" (Barney, 1979, p. 196).

A third influence from abroad was the English emphasis on sports and games. The English system was based on "a philosophical view that sports participation by amateur athletes has inherent educational benefits" (Seaton, 1992, p. 3). According to Rivenes (1978), the "hard knocks" associated with sports activities, the "discipline of training," and "knowing one's capabilities under trying conditions" have all contributed to the "molding of character" rationale that has "been pervasive in Western culture from the late nineteenth century on, especially in North America" (Rivenes, 1978, p. 280).

The combination of influences from within, as well as from Europe and England, coupled with teacher training institutes for prospective gymnastics instructors, were sufficient to establish physical education as a part of most public schools by the turn of the century. California had passed the first state physical education law in 1866 and Ohio, North Dakota, and Wisconsin had similar laws by 1899 (Rice et al., 1969). "By the end of the century many schools were requiring at least five minutes of exercise of each pupil daily, or 20 minutes two or three times a week" (Rice et al., 1969, p. 208).

The progressive education movement in the early 1900s shifted the emphasis from learning for its own sake to learning for a kind of social utility. The concern was for learning physical skills as well as for acquiring strength and endurance, which would be useful in play and sports activities and in the ordinary tasks of life (Rice et al., 1968). Sufficient concern was raised about the social utility of gymnastics that by the 1940s only about 12 percent were giving gymnastics a place in their physical education programs (Rice et al., 1969). In the place of gymnastics and exercises, it was games and sports activities that constituted physical education (Jewett & Bain, 1985). In addition to the progressive education movement, several other factors affected physical education in the schools, in both its presence and its nature.

World War I required thousands of young men to have physical examinations to check their ability to serve in the military. About one third failed the physical, sending shock waves back to the schools (Rice et al., 1969). The net effect for the schools was more emphasis on physical education. Many stadiums, large gymnasiums, athletic fields, and swimming pools were added to existing facilities. (Curiously, a third of the draftees failed their physical examinations in World War II as well. However, it may have been the improved techniques of examination and diagnosis that increased the rejection rate (Rice et al., 1969).)

The National Education Association's Seven Cardinal Principles of 1918 included health, citizenship, and worthy use of leisure time, all of which could be accomplished through physical education. The worthy use of leisure, however, was probably the most obvious connection between the larger society and the schools. Making that connection was a basic tenet of Progressive Education and by the early 1900s, the social milieu was indeed changing.

The playground movement, begun in England in the nineteenth century, began making an impact in America in the early 1900s. In addition to informal recreation, sports at all levels of schooling and in the professional arena grew rapidly. Barney (1979) notes:

> Publicized by the nation's newspapers, magazines, and other literary works . . . aided in no small measure by the nation's swiftly growing transportation and communication system which provided the means to get to and from recreation and sporting sites as well as to learn the results of events in rapid order, and abetted by the continued efforts of sporting entrepreneurs to galvanize Americans toward embracing sport ardently, sport became a social factor fully as important in the lifestyle of Americans as its former antagonist and suppressant, religion. (p. 197)

The impact on high schools and interscholastic competition was felt by most schools. By 1925, for example, interscholastic high school associations existed in every state (Barney, 1979).

President Hoover, in 1930, held a White House conference on child health and protection. The conference concluded that for every child from birth through adolescence, there should be attention to health and "wholesome physical and mental recreation" (Rice et al., 1969, p. 293). The conference increased the support for physical education, and when the effects of the Depression were felt by all schools, physical education did not suffer as much as did music, art, and home economics (Rice et al., 1969). Indeed, by 1930 39 states had laws requiring physical education in the larger schools and permissive requirements in the smaller ones.

World War II revealed, again, the poor shape of draftees. About one third of the men were considered not fit physically and, of the women accepted in the military, many were found to be lacking in strength, endurance, and flexibility. A series of President's Councils on Fitness of Youth were held in the 1950s and 1960s and various conferences, commissions, and committees urged expansion of physical education programs. To improve overall fitness calisthenics was revived, and sports programs at all levels of school were expanded to include more students.

CURRENT STATUS

From the 1950s to the present, a number of changes have been initiated within physical education that are still not totally embraced by all physical educators (Steinhardt, 1992). Movement education, for example, has been suggested as a replacement name for physical education. Kinesiology, the science of human movement, is the "scholarly study of sport, play, dance, and exercise" (Rivenes, 1978, p. 8). Perhaps as an offshoot of the curriculum revisions of the 1960s, inspired primarily by the launching of Sputnik, physical educators were quick to define a discipline. "As a discipline, kinesiology is the body of knowledge on which the profession of physical education is based. The profession's responsibility is to improve conditions of society through some kind of service—to implement change" (Rivenes, 1978, p. 8). Barney (1979) views the advent of the science-based discipline (kinesiology) as contributing to the blend of the social themes to produce "an education of and through the physical" (p. 213). The advantage of a discipline-based approach to physical education is the same as that afforded the fine arts: Within formal education a discipline has more legitimacy than an activity. There are also disadvantages to such an approach. And they apply to the fine arts as much as they do to physical education.

When the discipline-based approach is embraced and time allotment remains constant, the particular activity, be it drawing, singing, or playing a game, receives less attention because more attention (time) has to be devoted to history, analysis, and theory. It may be that more time can be obtained, but that is not likely. The disadvantage is that less attention (time) will be placed on the activity aspect of the subject area, and it's the activity that accounts for much of its appeal. The question then becomes, will the subject area (one of the fine arts or a physical activity) suffer because of the lack of activity associated with it?

Title IX of the Education Amendments was approved by Congress in 1972. In part, Title IX said (U.S. Department of Health, Education, and Welfare, 1976):

> No person . . . shall, on the basis of sex, be excluded from participation in, be denied the benefits of, or be subjected to discrimination under any education program or activity receiving Federal financial assistance. (p. 1)

Regulations on compliance in physical education followed in 1976. Essentially, the regulations are the following (Jewitt & Bain, 1985):

- Physical education requirements must be the same for males and females.
- Physical education classes must be coeducational except for instruction dealing with human sexuality and for participation in contact sports (for these situations the separation is optional, not required). (p. 113)

"Title IX does not dictate program content. It requires only that activities offered be open equally to students of both sexes, and that procedures used for assignment of students to classes not discriminate on the basis of sex" (p. 113). Jewett and Bain (1985) and Hellison and Templin (1991) discuss in their texts some of the implications of Title IX, not the least of which is assessment. The reader should consult these texts for suggestions of alternative kinds of evaluation procedures.

Adapted physical education refers to programs that seek "active participation of all students who cannot safely or successfully take part in the unrestricted activities of the regular physical education program" (Willgoose, 1984, p. 297). Public Law 94-142 (1976) specifically states,

> The term "special education " means specially designed instruction, at no cost to parents or guardians, to meet the unique needs of a handicapped child, including classroom instruction, *instruction in physical education,* home instruction, and instruction in hospitals and institutions. (emphasis added)

Before children with special needs can be appropriately served, a needs assessment must occur. The difference between where a child currently is and what is realistic for him or her to achieve must be articulated.

Physical education teachers, working in concert with special education teachers, can plan appropriate activities for children requiring an adapted program. As discussed in Chapter 17, Special Education, an individualized educational program has to be developed for each child with special needs. Willgoose (1984) discusses a variety of techniques that can be used in adapted physical education programs.

With regard to the regular program, some compromises usually occur when making planning decisions about which approach to physical education will be used in classes with children. A teacher can (and should) be guided by some approach, whether it is called a philosophy, school of thought, or a method, but compromises among them will continue to be made. Jewett and Bain (1985) suggest there are three current subject matters and approaches to physical education. One is health-related fitness. Proponents seek the following:

- Aerobic fitness
- Muscular strength and endurance

- Flexibility
- Body composition (p. 36)

Another is play. The proponents see play "as an essential human activity or sport as a cultural universal" (p. 36). An abiding interest in play or sport would suggest that primary goals are as follows:

- To develop attitudes that will support voluntary participation in physical recreation activities and
- To achieve levels of skill development that will permit satisfying participation in appropriate lifetime sports. (p. 36)

The third subject matter content is human movement. Based on kinesiology, the human movement interest would promote at the elementary level:

- Body awareness
- Space awareness
- Effort and relationships through games, dance, and gymnastics activities (p. 36)

At the secondary level, emphasis would be on the physical movement "analysis of a sport, dance, or aquatics activity" (p. 37). Many physical education teachers probably would claim to promote a combination of any or all of the above. Certainly the national standards developed by the National Association for Sport and Physical Education (1995) attest to an eclectic approach, drawing from all three of the subject matters discussed above.

National Standards

The National Association for Sport and Physical Education (NASPE) is an association of the American Alliance for Health, Physical Education, Recreation, and Dance (AAHPERD). In the spring of 1992, a task force was appointed by NASPE to develop content standards and assessment guidelines for physical education.

The task force sought and achieved consensus from a wide range of expertise. Many members of NASPE and its organizations contributed to the process, including the Council on Physical Education for Children, Middle and Secondary School Physical Education Council, and the Curriculum and Instruction

Academy. Presentations by the task force were made at the 1993 and 1994 national AAHPERD conventions and also at each of the six district AAHPERD conventions and many state meetings. In addition, the process included "a review by selected leaders in the physical education profession, as well as consultation with educational representations from other subject areas (mathematics, arts, science) and educational organizations (Council of Chief State School Officers, Principal's Association, Association of Colleges of Teacher Education)" (NASPE, 1995, p. v.).

The rationale for the physical education standards is exactly the same as that used for the fine arts standards. "With the passage of *Goals 2000: Educate America Act* (1994), educational standards were written into federal law. Title II of the Act . . . establishes a National Education Standards Improvement Council, which has . . . the job of working with appropriate organizations to determine the criteria for certifying voluntary content standards . . ." (NASPE, 1995, p. vi). The objectives for the entire process include the following:

1. To ensure that the standards are internationally competitive,
2. To ensure they reflect the best knowledge about teaching and learning, and
3. To ensure they have been developed through a broad-based, open adoption process. (p. iv)

Like the fine arts standards, the physical education standards define what a student should know and be able to do.

The task force, hereafter referred to as NASPE, developed seven standards for content. These address the issue of "what students should know and be able to do." In addition, NASPE developed performance benchmarks to describe behavior that indicates progress toward a performance standard. Performance standards indicate levels of achievement that are expected within each content standard. The use of benchmarks is only the first step in the process of delineating specific levels of achievement.

The standards that follow are taken, with permission, from the NASPE (1995) document. All of the standards are included, but only sample, illustrative emphases and benchmarks will be included. One should examine the entire document not only for more detail on emphases and benchmarks, but also for explication of each content standard and teacher-friendly suggestions for assessment of each.

The NASPE document is configured by grade level: K, 2, 4, 6, 8, 10, and 12 for the convenience of administrators who routinely deal with grade-level concerns. We have changed the configuration to show more readily the progression of emphasis and benchmarks through the ascendancy of the grades.*

First, the seven content standards:

A physically educated person:

1. Demonstrates competency in many movement forms and proficiency in a few movement forms.
2. Applies movement concepts and principles to the learning and development of motor skills.
3. Exhibits a physically active lifestyle.
4. Achieves and maintains a health-enhancing level of physical fitness.
5. Demonstrates responsible personal and social behavior in physical activity settings.
6. Demonstrates understanding and respect for differences among people in physical activity settings.
7. Understands that physical activity provides opportunities for enjoyment, challenge, self-expression, and social interaction.

The content standard will be followed by one example of an emphasis and one benchmark. Again, the reader needs to consult the NASPE document to learn other emphases and benchmarks.

Content standard

1. Demonstrates competency in many movement forms and proficiency in a few movement forms.
   K-Emphasis: Demonstrate progress toward the mature form of selected manipulative, locomotor, and nonlocomotor skills.
   K-Benchmark: Travels in forward and sideways directions using a variety of locomotor (non-

*Reprinted from *Moving into the Future: National Standards for Physical Education* (1995) with permission from the National Association for Sport and Physical Education (NASPE).

locomotor) patterns and changes direction quickly in response to a signal.
2nd Emphasis: Demonstrate mature form in skipping, hopping, galloping, and sliding.
2nd Benchmark: Demonstrates skills of chasing, fleeing, and dodging to avoid others.
4th Emphasis: Demonstrate mature form in all locomotor patterns and selected manipulative and nonlocomotor skills.
4th Benchmark: Throws, catches, and kicks using mature form.
6th Emphasis: Demonstrate mature form for all basic manipulative, locomotor, and nonlocomotor skills.
8th Emphasis: Demonstrate competence in modified versions of a variety of movement forms.
8th Benchmark: Use basic offensive and defensive strategies in a modified version of a team sport and individual sport.
10th Emphasis: Demonstrate competence (basic skills, strategies, and rules) in an increasing number of more complex versions of at least three of the following different types of movement forms: aquatics, team sports, individual and dual sports, outdoor pursuits, self-defense, dance, and gymnastics.
10th Benchmark: Demonstrates a variety of proficient swimming strokes.
12th Emphasis: Demonstrate proficiency in a few movement forms.
12th Benchmark: Participates in a tennis match using all of the basic skills, rules, and strategies with some consistency.

Content standard

2. Applies movement concepts and principles to the learning and development of motor skills.
   K-Emphasis: Identify fundamental movement patterns (skip, strike).
   K-Benchmark: Walks, runs, hops, and skips, in forward and sideways directions, and changes direction quickly in response to a signal.
   2nd Emphasis: Identify the critical elements of basic movement patterns.
   2nd Benchmark: Identifies four characteristics of a mature throw.

4th Emphasis: Apply critical elements to improve personal performance in fundamental and selected specialized motor skills.

4th Benchmark: Transfers weight from feet to hands at fast and slow speeds using large extensions (e.g., mule kick, handstand, cartwheel).

6th Emphasis: Use information from a variety of sources of internal and external origin to improve performance.

6th Benchmark: Detects, analyzes, and corrects errors in personal movement patterns.

8th Emphasis: Understand and apply more advanced movement and game strategies.

8th Benchmark: Explains and demonstrates some game strategies involved in playing tennis doubles.

10th Emphasis: Use more specialized knowledge to develop movement competence or proficiency.

10th Benchmark: Performs a variety of dance forms (e.g., folk, country, social, and creative) with fluency and in time to accompaniment.

12th Emphasis: Know and understand pertinent scientifically based information regarding movement performance.

12th Benchmark: Explains the overload principle and designs a personal fitness program where this principle is in operation.

Content standard

3. Exhibits a physically active lifestyle.

K-Emphasis: Engage in moderate to vigorous physical activity.

K-Benchmark: Participates regularly in vigorous physical activity.

2nd Emphasis: Experience and express pleasure from participation in physical activity.

2nd Benchmark: Seeks participation in gross motor activity of a moderate to vigorous nature.

4th Emphasis: Select and participate regularly in physical activities for the purpose of improving skill and health.

4th Benchmark: Regularly participates in physical activity for the purpose of developing a healthy lifestyle.

6th Emphasis: Identify opportunities in the school and community for regular participation in physical activity.

6th Benchmark: Chooses to exercise at home for personal enjoyment and benefit.

8th Emphasis: Establish personal physical activity goals.

8th Benchmark: Participate in an individualized physical activity program designed with the help of the teacher.

10th Emphasis: Participate regularly in health-enhancing and personally rewarding physical activity outside the physical education class setting.

10th Benchmark: Participates in health-enhancing activities that can be pursued in the community.

12th Emphasis: Have the skills, knowledge, interest, and desire to independently maintain an active lifestyle throughout their life.

12th Benchmark: Participates regularly in physical activities that contribute to the attainment of and maintenance of personal physical activity goals.

Content standard

4. Achieves and maintains a health-enhancing level of physical fitness.

K-Emphasis: Sustain moderate to vigorous physical activity for short periods of time.

K-Benchmark: Sustain moderate to vigorous physical activity.

2nd Emphasis: Engage in sustained physical activity that causes an increased heart rate and heavy breathing.

2nd Benchmark: Sustains activity for longer periods of time while participating in chasing or fleeing.

4th Emphasis: Identify several activities related to each component of physical fitness.

4th Benchmark: Engages in appropriate activity that results in the development of muscular strength.

6th Emphasis: Participate in moderate to vigorous physical activity in a variety of settings.

6th Benchmark: Keeps a record of heart rate before, during, and after vigorous physical activity.

8th Emphasis: Participate in a variety of health-related fitness activities in both school and nonschool settings.

8th Benchmark: Maintains a record of moderate to vigorous physical activity.

10th Emphasis: Participate in a variety of health-enhancing physical activities in both school and nonschool settings.

10th Benchmark: Assesses personal fitness status in terms of cardiovascular endurance, muscular strength and endurance, flexibility, and body composition.

12th Emphasis: Participate regularly in health-enhancing fitness activities independent of teaching mandates.

12th Benchmark: Monitors exercise and other behaviors related to health-related fitness.

Content standard

5. Demonstrates responsible personal and social behavior in physical activity settings.

K-Emphasis: Apply, with teacher reinforcement, classroom rules and procedures and safe practices.

K-Benchmark: Knows the rules for participating in the gymnasium and on the playground.

2nd Emphasis: Apply rules, procedures, and safe practices with little or no reinforcement.

2nd Benchmark: Uses equipment and space safely and properly.

4th Emphasis: Follow, with few reminders, activity-specific rules, procedures, and etiquette.

4th Benchmark: When given the opportunity, arranges gymnastics equipment safely in a manner appropriate for the task.

6th Emphasis: Participate in establishing rules, procedures, and etiquette that are safe and effective for specific activity situations.

6th Benchmark: Makes responsible decisions about using time, applying rules, and following through with the decisions made.

8th Emphasis: Recognize the influence of peer pressure.

8th Benchmark: Identifies positive and negative peer influence.

10th Emphasis: Apply safe practices, rules, procedures, and etiquette in all physical activity settings.

10th Benchmark: Slides into a base in a manner that avoids injury to the defensive player.

12th Emphasis: Initiate independent and responsible personal behavior in physical activity settings.

12th Benchmark: Sets personal goals for activity and works toward their achievement.

Content standard

6. Demonstrates understanding and respect for differences among people in physical activity settings.

K-Emphasis: Recognize the joy of shared play.

K-Benchmark: Enjoys participation alone and with others.

2nd Emphasis: Play and cooperate with others regardless of personal differences (e.g., gender, ethnicity, disability).

2nd Benchmark: Appreciates the benefits that accompany cooperation and sharing.

4th Emphasis: Explore cultural/ethnic self-awareness through participation in physical activity.

4th Benchmark: Recognizes differences and similarities in others' physical activity.

6th Emphasis: Acknowledge differences in the behaviors of people of different gender, culture, ethnicity, and disability and seek to learn more about both similarities and differences.

6th Benchmark: Recognizes the role of games, sports, and dance in getting to know and understand others of like and different backgrounds.

8th Emphasis: Recognize the role of sport, games, and dance in modern culture.

8th Benchmark: Demonstrates an understanding of the ways sport and dance influence American culture.

10th Emphasis: Recognize the value of sport and physical activity in understanding multiculturalism.

10th Benchmark: Discusses the historical roles of games, sports, and dance in the cultural life of a population.

12th Emphasis: Recognize the influence of participation in physical activity on fostering appreciation of cultural, ethnic, gender, and physical diversity.

12th Benchmark: Identifies the effects of age, gender, race, ethnicity, socioeconomic status, and culture upon physical activity preferences and participation.

Content standard

7. Understands that physical activity provides opportunities for enjoyment, challenge, self-expression, and social interaction.

K-Emphasis: Engage in physical activities.

K-Benchmark: Enjoys participation alone and with others.

2nd Emphasis: Gain competence to provide increased enjoyment in movement.

2nd Benchmark: Appreciate the benefits that accompany cooperation and sharing.

4th Emphasis: Experience enjoyment while participating in physical activity.

4th Benchmark: Experience positive feelings as a result of involvement in physical activity.

6th Emphasis: Recognize physical activity as a positive opportunity for social and group interaction.

6th Benchmark: Recognizes the role of games, sports, and dance in getting to know and understand self and others.

8th Emphasis: Enjoy participation in physical activity.

8th Benchmark: Feels satisfaction when engaging in physical activity.

10th Emphasis: Enjoy participating in a variety of physical activities in competitive and recreational settings.

10th Benchmark: Identifies participation factors that contribute to enjoyment and self-expressions.

12th Emphasis: Enjoy regular participation in physical activity.

12th Benchmark: Derives genuine pleasure from participating in physical activity.

Reminder: The foregoing emphases and benchmarks are illustrative samples only. The NASPE (1995) document should be consulted for a complete listing.

Teacher Certification

Each state has its own specific requirements for certification of all variety of teachers. The National Council for Accreditation of Teacher Education (NCATE) examines teacher preparation programs regarding such issues as quality of faculty, coherence of curriculum, and professional standards of preparation. In 1960 the American Association of Health, Physical Education, and Recreation voted to put itself under NCATE jurisdiction and urged state departments of education, as well as local school boards, to hire only those physical education teachers who are graduates of NCATE-accredited institutions (Rice et al., 1969).

Because each state has its own specific requirements for certification, we can only note general requirements. Typically, a physical education teacher will have had course work in health education, sport, recreation, safety education, dance, first aid, kinesiology, physical education for special populations, social foundations of physical education, and assessment in physical education.

CONTEMPORARY ISSUES

One of the perennial issues that plagues physical education programs revolves around the intramural program and athletics. This issue is often most intense at the middle school level. The goal of intramural programs is to promote participation and enjoyment from the largest number of students. More often than not, athletic programs are very selective and are driven by a number of forces, not the least of which is the community, to win, win, win.

No easy solution exists for this issue—that is why it is a perennial one—but one possible partial remedy is to separate the intramural program and its director from the athletic program and its coaches. With such a separation, the school can maintain both programs and avoid instances of a conflict of interest in their physical education teachers and coaches.

No less than 79 issues in physical education have been compiled and addressed by Sandborn and Hartman (1982). There authors have divided the issues into 11 categories:

Philosophy and purposes
Sociopsychologic and biologic needs

Ethics
Fitness
Profession and/or discipline of physical
    education
Requirement of physical education
Relationship between physical education
    and leisure
Curriculum content
Methods
Students
Athletics (p. ix)

The unique contribution Sanborn and Hartman make is to present this wide variety of issues and then present opposing arguments for each of them, without taking sides themselves. The issues not discussed by them, except perhaps by implication, are the national standards and supervision of physical education teachers.

The national standards (NASPE, 1995) may cause some physical education teachers to think they have to abandon what they are currently doing in order to comply with them. It is clearly not the intention of NASPE to impose something on local educational efforts. It is, however, clear that the standards are broad enough that a variety of approaches could be used to work toward them. What appears to be operating is the somewhat guarded message within the NASPE document that standards are required if physical education, as a professional field, wants to be considered a legitimate part of the public education scene. This same message is contained in the fine arts standards document. (See Music Educators National Conference, 1994.)

The issue then is twofold. One is the acceptability of the standards. The process by which they were developed appears to have been quite open, providing many opportunities for dialogue and adjustment. Some people may not agree with that or simply did not have their points of view represented. Assuming the process was as open as NASPE claims, one then has to realize that consensus does not mean unanimity. The other aspect of the issue is appropriateness of the standards.

Physical education is not exclusively a psychomotor affair. The literature is replete with examples of affective concerns and goals for physical education students. Sportsmanship, sharing, and cooperating are examples of values physical educators seek to promote. In addition, the enjoyment of an activity or sport, sufficient to make it a lifelong activity, is an affective outcome physical education seeks to attain. It has been well documented that affective goals and objectives are not easily assessed. If only those aspects of the standards that are amendable to assessment are used, the data from national assessments may be both misleading and incomplete.

Physical education, although a part of every school's curriculum, is at times marginalized because it is staffed by itinerant teachers. The same concerns about itinerant teachers that were addressed in the fine arts chapter apply to physical education teachers who are assigned to more than one site.

ILLUSTRATIVE PRACTICE AND ISSUES

Siedentop, D., & Locke, L. (1997). Making a difference for physical education: What professors and practitioners must build together. *JOPERD, 68*(4), 25–33.

> The authors describe the challenges (and failures) of teacher preparation programs and how they could relate to the work of practitioners. *Issues:* The article raises the perennial issue of connections between professional preparation programs and practitioners.

Solomon, G. (1997). Fair play in the gymnasium: Improving social shifts among elementary school students. *JOPERD, 68*(5), 22–25.

> The author describes a program that improves communication skills and increases cooperation and sharing among elementary students. *Issues:* The question of moral education being addressed by the school is raised.

SUMMARY

Physical education is included in the schools in every one of the 50 states (Jensen, 1983). It was not always so. The history of physical education reveals a peak of equal emphasis toward the physical and intellectual during the Greek era (the sixth and fifth centuries

B.C.). Since then, the intellectual realm has been emphasized and the physical has had an uphill battle to maintain legitimacy.

Similar to the fine arts in that it is marginalized in the K–12 curriculum, physical education is even more plagued with various and sometimes conflicting views of what it should be. The national standards (NASPE, 1995), however, represent an attempt to accommodate the variety of view points within physical education and, perhaps more importantly, strengthen physical education's claim to legitimacy by their very presence.

QUESTIONS FOR FURTHER CONSIDERATION

Research

1. What kinds of evidence are available that support having physical education at the elementary and secondary levels?

2. How could any study of the effects of physical education rule out the influence of nonschool factors?

Reflect

1. What roles might a physical education teacher play in competitive sports at the secondary level?

2. Would intramural activities drain the talent pool for intermural activities? Why or why not?

Respond/React

1. In what ways could one argue for a greater need for physical education now than a decade ago?

2. Do professional sports have a positive or negative effect on physical education? Defend your answer.

SUGGESTED READINGS

Hellison, D. R., & Templin, T. J. (1991). *A reflective approach to teaching physical education.* Champaign, IL: Human Kinetics Books.

Jewett, A. E., & Bain, L. L. (1985). *The curriculum process in physical education.* Dubuque, IA: Wm. C. Brown.

Metzler, M. W. (1990). *Instructional supervision for physical education.* Champaign, IL: Human Kinetics Books.

National Association for Sport and Physical Education. (1995). *Moving into the future: National standards for physical education: A guide to content and assessment.* St. Louis, MO: Mosby.

Sanborn, M. A., & Hartman, B. G. (1982). *Issues in physical education* (3rd ed.). Philadelphia: Lea & Febiger.

Steinhardt, M. A. (1992). Physical education. In P. W. Jackson (Ed.), *Handbook of research on curriculum* (pp. 964–1001). New York: Macmillan.

CHAPTER 12

PREVENTION EDUCATION

Prevention is a multifaceted process that needs to involve the entire school community working toward the goal of promoting long-term well-being. The focus of prevention education should be to promote healthy choices, to reduce risk factors, and to develop protective factors that help guard against substance abuse, sexually transmitted diseases, teenage pregnancy, suicide, and school violence. Prevention education is concerned with promoting more healthy—physical and mental—lifestyles and assisting young people to develop the attitudes and habits necessary to sustain long-term health. Prevention education is proactive rather than reactive.

Prevention education is the responsibility of all educators, but school nurses, health teachers, social workers, psychologists, and counselors are more often involved in developing programs that target youth who are, for the most part, prone to conditions such as suicide, alcohol and substance abuse, eating disorders, sedentary lifestyles, sexually transmitted diseases, violence, and a plethora of other risky and dangerous habits and patterns of self-destruction. These students are at-risk. However, it is our belief that *all* students are, at times, at risk.

Klitzner, Fisher, Stewart, and Gilbert (1992) offer a continuum of care that includes the processes of "prevention, early intervention, treatment, and aftercare" (p. 3). Although this continuum represents a framework for addressing substance abuse, we believe the processes within it can be applied to the study of most youth morbidities (e.g., drug abuse and HIV/AIDS).

Prevention education has had a long history in schools, beginning with the initial work of school nurses and social workers. At the turn of this century, the very first school nurses provided instruction on health through a delivery method known as a demonstration project. Later, school nurses and social workers helped health teachers deliver large group demonstrations. Whereas early pioneers were concerned more with hygiene and screening children for communicable diseases, current school personnel deal with students who have more acute and catastrophic issues such as AIDS and chemical dependency.

HISTORY

The history of prevention education can be traced to the late 1800s and before; however, for our purposes, we fast forward to the 1980s as a beginning point. National reports and agendas of the 1980s and 1990s brought to the forefront the need for primary preventive health-related services and programs for school-aged children. About drug use/abuse prevention, Gonet (1994) writes,

> *Primary prevention* refers to the attempts to forestall or minimize the occurrence of substance use/abuse. This prevention includes education and activities that prevent the onset of drug use, abuse, and/or dependency, as well as reduce the risk that individuals will develop problems as a result of substance abuse. In the schools this effort needs to begin in the kindergarten and continue throughout high school. (p. 77, emphasis in the original)

Prevention educational initiatives were called for in such areas as health, nutrition, drug prevention, and prevention of sexually transmitted diseases. HIV and AIDS were beginning to emerge.

The report, *Turning Points: Preparing American Youth for the 21st Century* (1989), released by the Carnegie Corporation, detailed the need for both preventive and more proactive measures for dealing with at-risk health issues: drug abuse, mental health issues, nutrition, and the availability of health services. "Because of the direct link between the health of young adolescents and their success in school . . . middle grade schools must accept a significant responsibility . . . to ensure that needed health services are accessible to young adolescents and that schools become health-promoting environments" (p. 61). *Turning Points* sparked the need to examine the vulnerability of young adolescents: "Drug and alcohol use increasingly begins in the middle grades. . . . Mild to severe mental health problems are widespread among young adolescents . . . young adolescents often require expert counseling . . ." (p. 61).

A 1990 survey conducted by the U.S. Department of Education found that drug abuse among young people is often glamorized and that "Social influences play an important role in making drug use attractive to children" (1992, p. 7). There are myriad reasons why young people turn to drugs and alcohol. Regardless of the reasons, *The best way to fight drug use is to begin prevention efforts before children start using drugs. Prevention efforts that focus on young children are the most effective means to fight drug use*" (U.S. Department of Education, 1992, p. 7, emphasis in the original).

To combat the increase in sexually transmitted diseases (STDs) and HIV (human immunodeficiency virus) present in individuals who later develop AIDS (acquired immune deficiency syndrome), many schools have responded by adopting programs such as *Sex Respect*. Other school systems have designed their own curricula. Regardless of materials used, most states have required that prevention topics such as substance abuse and AIDS prevention be incorporated into the program of studies, usually as add-on topics in existing health courses.

In 1989, the Congress passed the Drug-Free Schools and Communities Act Amendments that mandates:

    (A) training and technical assistance concerning drug and violence prevention for local educational agencies and educational service agencies, including teachers, administrators, coaches and athletic directors, other staff, parents, students, community leaders, health service providers, local law enforcement officials, and judicial officials;

    (B) the development, identification, dissemination, and evaluation of the most readily available, accu-

rate, and up-to-date curriculum materials (including videotapes, software, and other technology-based learning resources) for consideration by local educational agencies;

    (C) making available to local educational agencies cost effective programs for youth violence and drug abuse prevention;

    (D) demonstration projects in drug and violence prevention;

    (E) training, technical assistance, and demonstration projects to address violence associated with prejudice and intolerance;

    (F) financial assistance to enhance resources available for drug and violence prevention in areas serving large numbers of economically disadvantaged children or sparsely populated areas, or to meet other special needs consistent with the purposes of this subpart; and

    (G) the evaluation of activities carried out within the State under this part. (Drug-Free Schools and Communities Act Amendments, 1989)

Moreover, Section 7116 of the Drug-Free Schools and Act includes, among other items, that "age-appropriate, developmentally based drug and alcohol education and prevention programs for students in all grades be provided" (20 U.S.C. 7101 et seq., West, 1996).

Healthy People 2000 (1990) is the health imperative of the 1990s that promotes the following goals:

- Increase the span of healthy life for Americans;
- Reduce health disparities among Americans;
- Achieve access to preventive services for all Americans. (p. 6)

The last goal includes, "Preventive services" in the areas of "counseling, screening, immunization . . ." with "Priority areas . . . HIV infection, sexually transmitted diseases, and infectious diseases" (*Healthy People 2000,* 1990, p. 7).

The *Goals 2000: Educate America Act* became a law in 1994. *Goals 2000* provides a framework for states and communities to develop and operationalize reform aimed at helping students reach academic, occupational, and health standards which are contained within each of the eight goals. Specifically, Goal 7 states,

By the year 2000, every school in America will be free of drugs, violence and the unauthorized presence of firearms and alcohol and will offer a disciplined environment conducive to learning.

Within this broad goal, several objectives are developed:

- Every school will implement a firm and fair policy on use, possession, and distribution of drugs and alcohol.
- Parents, businesses, governmental and community organizations will work together to ensure the rights of students to study in a safe and secure environment that is free of drugs and crime, and that schools provide a healthy environment and are a safe haven for all children.
- Every local educational agency will develop and implement a policy to ensure that all schools are free of violence and unauthorized presence of weapons.
- Every local educational agency will develop a sequential, comprehensive kindergarten through twelfth grade drug and alcohol prevention education program.
- Drug and alcohol curriculum should be taught as an integral part of sequential, comprehensive health education.
- Community-based teams should be organized to provide students and teachers with needed support.
- Every school should work to eliminate sexual harassment. (p. 135)

CURRENT STATUS

General Attributes of Prevention Programs

The attributes of effective and comprehensive prevention and health programs, reported by the Center for Disease Control, cited by Holtzman and colleagues (1992) indicate that prevention and health programs need to include the following:

1. A documented, planned, and sequential program of health education for students in grades kindergarten through 12;
2. A curriculum that addresses and integrates education about a range of categorical health problems and issues at developmentally appropriate ages;
3. Activities to help young people develop skills they will need to avoid:
   a. behaviors that result in unintentional and intentional injuries;

   b. drug and alcohol abuse;
   c. tobacco use;
   d. sexual behaviors that result in HIV infection, other sexually transmitted diseases, and unintended pregnancies;
   e. imprudent dietary patterns; and,
   f. inadequate physical activity;
4. Instruction provided for a prescribed amount of time at each grade level;
5. Management and coordination in each school by an educational professional trained to implement the program;
6. Instruction from teachers who have been trained to teach the subject;
7. Involvement of parents, health professionals, and other concerned community members; and
8. Periodic evaluation, updating, and improvement. (p. 422)

These attributes should be common across all areas (e.g., drug education and sex education). These attributes also are consistent with Lofquist's (1991) definition of prevention:

> prevention . . . emphasizes the idea of actively creating conditions which would preclude the occurrence of the symptoms one wishes to avoid. Thus the emphasis is on promoting the well-being of people through positive action that changes the conditions under which the behaviors to be prevented are most likely to occur. (p. 3)

Drug Prevention Programs

Dusenbury and Diaz (1995) report that "Historically, drug abuse prevention efforts can be grouped into five general approaches: (a) information dissemination approaches, including fear arousal and moralistic appeals; (b) affective education; (c) alternatives; (d) social influence approaches; and (e) broader competency enhancement that promotes the development of broader personal and social skills" (p. 239). Schinke and Cole (1995) report that the Institute for Prevention Research has been able to isolate skills interventions that complement prevention strategies through the development of, for example problem-solving skills, coping, communication skills, and decision making.

Gonet (1994) believes that "many of our early drug education programs were often ineffective, and in some cases the actual result was contradictory to the intended outcome" (p. 77). Early drug prevention programs were presented to students with the use of canned "kits" by adults who gave mixed messages, especially to nonusing students. "The message clearly implied that the nonusing student was different" (p. 78). Adolescents crave to be accepted, and for many, to be accepted, means "doing what the popular kids do." Gonet believes, moreover, that "the drug kit presenters went on to display a variety of drugs commonly abused, along with the methods by which they were ingested" (p. 78) which, in effect, hyped and made "drugs attractive to the nonuser and [taught] new drug-using behaviors to the user" (p. 78). Other early ineffective drug education and prevention techniques included, according to Gonet (1994): "Scare tactics . . . the 'one-shot program' . . . with no subsequent follow-up" (p. 79). Winters (1990) reports that:

> While some programs stress positive methods of prevention and intervention of drug abuse, others dwell too much on the negative aspects. Many children are exposed to drug use from a very early age, thus giving them attitudes regarding "getting high" before the subject is ever introduced to them at school. Others may have had pleasant experiences with drugs; therefore, being totally turned off by the teacher's depiction of drug taking as harmful and dangerous. (p. 22)

Gonet (1994) believes there are 10 components to drug prevention:

1. The curriculum should be comprehensive in scope.
2. At all levels a prevention-oriented curriculum should be offered in conjunction with instruction on health, science, driver education, and other relevant subject areas.
3. Prevention-oriented activities should be scheduled throughout the year, rather than in a short, concentrated unit. The "one-shot" approach should be avoided.
4. The curriculum should emphasize affective, as well as cognitive learning.
5. The curriculum should provide for the specialized needs of the local school community, including the need for cultural relevance.
6. Clearly stated objectives should be established for the total program at each level of instruction.
7. The curriculum should be developed through cooperative planning of school personnel, parents, and community representatives.
8. The social competencies model should be used at grade four and higher.
9. The curriculum should be sensitive and responsive to the special needs of children of chemically dependent families.
10. Provisions should be included for ongoing evaluation and program accountability. (p. 83–86)

Drug prevention programs such as Project DARE (Drug Abuse Resistance Education) have worked to develop strategies to make schools both drug and violence-free. DARE is an effort between schools and law enforcement agencies. Project DARE "is based on a curriculum designed to foster coping skills" (Kandall, 1996. p. 296). In a meta-analysis of eight Project DARE program evaluations, Ennett, Tobler, Ringwalt, and Flewelling's (1994) results indicate that Project DARE might be more effective with elementary and middle school children rather than high school–age children, "DARE's limited influence on adolescent drug use behavior contrasts with the program's popularity and prevalence" (p. 1399).

Another drug prevention program is Project Healthy Choices. "Project Healthy Choices was developed at the Bank Street College of Education" where "from 1990 to 1994 Project Healthy Choices offered a substance abuse and prevention program to young children in kindergarten through second grade. The program created a drug education curriculum for schools and families who wanted to educate children about the dangers of substance abuse before they were exposed to peer pressure" (Kandall, 1996, p. 296).

Lions-Quest (n.d.) is another widely used program at the middle school level. The goals of Lions-Quest are the following:

• To help young people develop positive social behaviors.

- To help young people acquire the social skills necessary to lead healthy and productive lives.
- To help young people develop strong commitments to peers, schools, and communities.
- To help young people develop strong commitments to themselves to live healthy, drug-free lives.
- To support parents, teachers, and others in finding constant renewal and energy needed in supporting young people. (p. 9)

HIV/AIDS and Sex Education Prevention.   Unks (1996) reports that "Although all humans are potentially at risk of becoming infected with the AIDS virus, teens, with their inexperience and lack of knowledge, are a particularly vulnerable group" (p. 205). Unks offers a possible reason for the lag in AIDS prevention programs being universally adopted across all schools across all states:

> The image of AIDS as an exclusively homosexual disease remains in the minds of many Americans, and it persists in some schools. When suggestions are made to establish HIV/AIDS education programs in schools or to increase funding or the time allotted for HIV/AIDS education, some parents and teachers conclude that what is being advocated is a program of instruction about homosexuality. . . . Unfortunately, as long as the homosexuality/AIDS linkage continues, schools will be very reluctant to say much of consequences about AIDS, and there will be little support for HIV/AIDS education. (p. 206)

Hagedorn (1993) reports, "Every student in both senior and junior high schools, each year, should receive a developmentally appropriate HIV prevention education program, with attention in the curriculum to gender, cultural, and relationship issues" (p. 359). Preventive HIV/AIDS programs designed to work with adolescents need to examine the risk taking and the typical sense of invulnerability that adolescents display. . . . Cognitive development also plays a role in teens' ability to make wise decisions on the road to independence. Teens in early adolescence (ages 12 to 14) are, in general, concrete thinkers; they have difficulty projecting themselves into the future" (National Commission on AIDS, 1994, p. 40).

However, AIDS education—according to Obeidallah and colleagues (1993)—needs to begin sooner than middle or high school. "Currently, the only available course of action to decrease AIDS-related morbidity and mortality is to modify risky behaviors or to prevent onset of these behaviors through developmentally appropriate AIDS education prior to adolescence" (p. 125). The findings of Obeidallah and colleagues indicate that AIDS/HIV education and prevention programs for elementary students need to take into account Piaget's stages of development, especially "preoperational, concrete operational, and formal operational thinking" (p. 127); otherwise, "AIDS education will be ineffective unless it corresponds to the conceptual level of the students' current knowledge and understanding of the meaning of commonly used terms" (p. 128).

For schools to develop HIV/AIDS prevention programs, those closest to the situation need, according to the National Commission on AIDS, to understand:

- The range of sexual and drug-taking activities in which young people engage
- Adolescent developmental issues and how to broaden adult/parental recognition of these issues
- The health and social service needs of adolescents
- The range of values and attitudes that individuals associate with drug-using and sexual behavior
- The combination of knowledge, attitudes, skills, and services necessary to influence behavior change
- The role of parents, schools, and other youth-serving organizations, as well as young people themselves, in prevention (p. 39)

Students want to be able to talk about issues surrounding sex with people who are "relaxed, nonjudgmental, knowledgeable, and available for discussion (Hagerdorn, 1993, p. 359). Molbert, Boyer, and Shafer (1993) believe that "Effective prevention of STDs requires that adolescents process complex information" (p. 258). Molbert and colleagues (1993) state "STD/HIV prevention programs should incorporate multiple communication strategies and be age-appropriate and sensitive to cultural issues" (p. 258).

Healthy People 2000 Goals.   The Healthy People 2000 Goals are divided across content areas (i.e., tobacco, alcohol and other drugs; violent and abusive behavior). Table 12.1 highlights the content areas and provides a sampling of the target goals for each.

CONTEMPORARY ISSUES

Prevention education, although commonly accepted and supported by school districts, parent groups, and the larger community can often be engulfed by controversies due to the very nature of the topics covered (sexually transmitted diseases and teenage pregnancy), and the teaching techniques employed (proper condom application), and the messages conveyed (abstinence and "safe sex"). Compounding these potential controversies, the belief of many parents is that topics of such a nature should be taught at home where the values of the family can guide the messages of prevention. Principals need to be able to guide the ongoing development of prevention programs in their schools as students will, due to myriad circumstances they encounter, continue to become even more at-risk.

Prevention can be likened to change—change in attitudes and beliefs—and as such, can cause some people to meet programs with mistrust—especially if the program is a new one or one that is undergoing modification. Controversy in sex education is an example. There are programs that prescribe abstinence through abstinence-based content and programs that only encourage abstinence, and that has caused a rift between people who believe the message is not strong enough versus those who believe encouragement *only* is needed.

Some schools try to eliminate this controversy and possible rift by providing parents with an opt in or opt out alternative. With this option parents have the right to have their child either receive or not to receive this education, which might be objectionable to the values promulgated by the family. Perhaps, however, children who are opted out by their parents might need preventive services the most.

Controversies can dampen preventive education programs and can upset the daily operations of the school. Communities become divided and the real issue, prevention, becomes clouded by ideology. As Rose (1996) states, "While rates of pregnancy, AIDS, and other sexually transmitted diseases remain alarmingly high among America's youth, opponents of sexuality education are trying to censor vital, life-saving information that has proven effective in dealing with these problems" (p. 78).

As health and well-being issues escalate in nature, controversy will continue to heighten as schools respond to the needs of students. Although many preventive topics are taught within the confines of health courses at the high school level, advisory periods at the middle school, and topically at the elementary level, schools work with other professionals to help shape both content and methodology of prevention education topics. Often, the school nurse, social worker, psychologist, and counselor are active in prevention education. Depending on the issues under consideration, parent advisory boards can and should be involved in assisting the school develop more comprehensive prevention programs—programs that are part of the curriculum and programs that evolve from support personnel (e.g., the nurse). On the one hand, parental involvement can encumber the process, but on the other hand, schools cannot assume the sole responsibility of providing prevention education programs. Parental involvement also can help promote prevention programs through the types of communication most parent groups have—informal and formal—within the larger community. When parents and the school can work together, the message of primary prevention is stronger.

Special care needs to be taken when hiring school nurses, social workers, and counselors—who also work in tandem with health teachers and outside agencies who provide prevention education services. Prevention programs need highly qualified instructors who are not only experts in their field, but who also have training to teach, instruct, and counsel students. Ongoing staff development is needed so that these individuals can keep up-to-date on their skills and knowledge about learning new strategies and techniques for prevention education.

Schools cannot possibly be expected to provide all that is needed in prevention education. Community resources can assist the school with prevention interventions. Many community-based groups can provide services to the school. Principals need to keep

TABLE 12.1   Healthy People 2000

CONTENT	GOAL NUMBER TARGET	GOAL
Tobacco	3.5	Reduce the initiation of cigarette and youth so that no more than 15 percent have become regular cigarette smokers by age 20. (p. 143)
	3.10	Establish tobacco-free environments and include tobacco use prevention in the curricula of all elementary, middle, and secondary schools, preferably as part of quality school health education. (p. 147)
	3.13	Enact and enforce in 50 states laws prohibiting the sale and distribution of tobacco products to youth younger than age 19. (p. 150)
	3.14	Increase to 50 the number of states with plans to reduce tobacco use, especially among youth. (p. 151)
Alcohol and Other Drugs	4.5	Increase by at least 1 year the average of first use of cigarettes, alcohol, and marijuana by adolescents aged 12 through 17. (p. 169)
	4.6	Reduce the proportion of young people who have used alcohol, marijuana, and cocaine in the past month . . . (p. 169)
	4.7	Reduce the proportion of high school seniors and college students engaging in recent occasions of heavy drinking of alcoholic beverages to no more than 28 percent of high school seniors and 32 percent of college students. (p. 170)
	4.11	Reduce to no more than 3 percent the proportion of male high school seniors who use anabolic steroids. (p. 172)
	4.13	Provide to children in all school districts and private schools, primary and secondary school educational programs on alcohol and other drugs, preferably as part of quality school health education. (p. 173)
Family Planning	5.1	Reduce pregnancies among girls aged 17 and younger to no more than 50 per 1,000 adolescents. (p. 189)
	5.4	Reduce the proportion of adolescents who have engaged in sexual intercourse to no more than 15 percent by age 15 and no more than 40 percent by age 17. (p. 193)
Mental Health and Mental Disorders	6.2	Reduce by 15 percent the incidence of injurious suicide attempts among adolescents aged 14 through 17. (p. 211)
Violent and Abusive Behavior	7.6	Reduce assault injuries among people aged 12 and older to no more than 10 per 1,000 people. (p. 233)
	7.9	Reduce by 20 percent the incidence of physical fighting among adolescents aged 14 through 17. (p. 235)
	7.10	Reduce by 20 percent the incidence of weapon-carrying by adolescents aged 14 through 17. (p. 236)
	7.16	Increase to at least 50 percent the proportion of elementary and secondary schools that teach nonviolent conflict resolution skills, preferably as part of quality school health education. (p. 239)

From *Healthy People 2000: National Health Promotion and Disease Prevention Objectives* (DHHS Publication No. PHS 91-50212), by the U.S. Department of Health and Human Services, 1990, Washington, DC: U.S. Government Printing Office.

current with what services and resources community agencies can provide to the school. The types of curriculum and the messages that these agencies provide to students need investigation. Many principals check with other local schools who have utilized an agency about the types of services, the reaction to these services, and the overall benefit derived from the services and resources of a community agency before committing. When agreeing to allow community agencies to provide preventive education services, many principals notify parents of the types of services, whether the service be a series of guest lectures or a long-term agreement between the school and the agency. It is assumed, however, that such agreements will be approved by the superintendent and board of education first.

Some schools use the resources of colleges and universities in providing prevention education services. For example, Molbert and colleagues (1993) report the process that the University of California, San Francisco, Medical Center used to develop a collaborative effort between the university and local school districts to provide STD/HIV prevention and intervention programs.

ILLUSTRATIVE PRACTICES AND ISSUES

Roth, J., & Hendrickson, J. M. (1991). Schools and youth organizations. *Phi Delta Kappan, 72*(8), 619–622.

Roth and Hendrickson identify "dysfunctional behaviors" that put students at risk, explore collaborative efforts between schools and other "outside" agencies, and highlight a program based on collaboration. Due to myriad reasons, Roth and Hendrickson believe ". . . that schools can succeed only partially—and occasionally by serendipity— . . ." (p. 621). They base this belief on the limitations of school systems and the lack of preparation and understanding of teachers in designing and delivering a preventive curriculum: This is why Roth and Hendrickson believe outside agencies need to collaborate. *Issues:* Identifying students at-risk is described. Development of an advisory board is explained. Interaction and support between and among schools and youth organizations are considered. The very structure of schools does not easily enable schools to undertake long-term issues of children.

Sagor, R. (1996). Building resiliency in students. *Educational Leadership, 54*(1), 38–43.

Sagor provides a discussion about resilience, including commonly accepted definitions. Also included are the attributes and/or experiences that promote resiliency— competence, belonging, and potency. Sagor presents a series of planned activities that schools can present to students. The inventory of resiliency-building practices includes the organizational/instructional practices and the traits reinforced in these practices. Sagor also provides another inventory that pictorializes a student's current condition, the strategic intervention needed to overcome the adverse condition, and a series of desired outcomes. With so many students being at risk for failure, Sagor offers a point of hope for teachers, schools, and students, "a lot of the techniques that build resiliency are most likely already part of many teacher's repertoires" (p. 42). *Issues:* How to measure the efficacy of resiliency strategies. How to provide a resiliency antibody to students. Why it is critical to provide resiliency strategies for youth. How can the school better incorporate resiliency strategies into the curricular/instructional program?

Weissberg, R. P., Shriver, T. P., Bose, S., & De Falco, K. (1997). Creating a district-wide social development project. *Educational Leadership, 54*(8), 37–39.

Weissberg et al. provide a description of a preventive education program—the New Haven, Connecticut, Social Development Project (SDP). The SDP began with district-level support for schools within the district. The types of district and building-level support are highlighted as well as the curriculum and goals of the SDP. The SDP "curriculum focused on self-monitoring, problem solving, conflict resolution, and communication skills" (p. 38). Weissberg et al. share the lessons they have learned implementing the SDP. *Issues:* The involvement of all stakeholders is central to the development of an SDP. Because schools are complex, a systems approach to prevention programs should be considered.

SUMMARY

The African proverb, "It takes an entire village to educate a child," ought to be remembered as schools provide preventive educational opportunities to students. With the increase in adolescent morbidities, schools are responding by developing more responsive programs and activities to meet the needs of students, but schools alone cannot achieve the lofty goals established by *Healthy People 2000*. Newer, more expansive prevention education efforts undertaken jointly by the school, the community, and parents might prove to be the way to reduce health risk factors. Time will tell.

QUESTIONS FOR FURTHER CONSIDERATION_____

Research

1. Given the information in this chapter, design a prevention education program for your school. Include (1) the rationale, goals, and objectives of the program; (2) the target audience (e.g., grade and student population); (3) essential features of the program; (4) the personnel and the types of training needed by them; (5) the type of administrative support needed; (6) the costs associated with the program and its delivery; and (7) the types of parental involvement needed.

2. Read the book *Full-Service Schools* by Joy Dryfoos. How do the full-service schools profiled in this book handle prevention education? Give examples of the approaches used.

Reflect

1. One of the distinguishing factors of youth is their idealism and sense of indestructibility. How should prevention programs be structured in light of this statement?

2. There are numerous preventive curricular programs and accompanying materials that schools can utilize. To what extent should schools use these "canned" materials?

3. Parents have the right to have their children opt out of many, if not all, prevention educational programs, regardless if these programs are part of the board of education approved curriculum. As a principal what is your role in working with parents who opt out their children? Do you have any other moral obligation to the child who has been forced by his or her parents to miss the activities of a particular program?

Respond/React

1. Some people think that sex education should be taught in the home; others believe that the school can teach sex education just as well. Should schools be responsible for teaching sex education? Defend your answer.

2. Research has indicated that many prevention education programs have a counter effect. That is, these programs in some ways promote the very behaviors they are trying to prevent. Can a prevention program reduce this phenomenon from occurring? How?

3. As the building principal you and the administrative team have just initiated a prevention program targeted at reducing drug abuse in freshmen. What school personnel would you use to implement such a program? What types of information would you need to communicate to the board of education? The community? Parents? Teachers?

SUGGESTED READINGS

Botvin, G. J., & Schinke, S. (1995). (Eds.). *Drug abuse prevention with multiethnic youth.* Thousand Oaks, CA: Sage.

Gonet, M. M. (1994). *Counseling the adolescent substance abuser: School-based intervention and prevention.* Thousand Oaks, CA: Sage.

Kandall, S. R. (1996). *Substance and shadow: Women and addiction in the United States.* Cambridge, MA: Harvard University Press.

CHAPTER 13

THE SCHOOL NURSE

There is a strong correlation between good health and academic achievement. Morgan's (1987) findings "indicate that the health status of the individual student may be an important factor in his/her ability to learn, in the development of classroom behaviors that enhance learning, and in the development of good social relationships with peers" (p. 43). Health care for children in schools is typically provided by a school nurse. It is interesting to note, however, that the role of the nurse has over the years expanded from being concerned with getting those students back to school who were once excluded for health reasons to working with community health agencies to develop school-based, full-service health clinics in the schools.

The health issues of the times, past and present, have shaped to a certain extent the role of the nurse, the types of training needed, and the types of outreach needed to promote and advocate for school-age children. As health issues have become more severe, the role of the school nurse has been elevated in status to match the critical nature of services that the school nurse finds himself or herself providing within schools. The school nurse faces many of the same health issues that plague other health care professionals—acute, technological care of persons with life-threatening diseases, HIV, and other sexually transmitted diseases.

As a health care professional, today's school nurse plays an integral part in helping school administrators create "healthy" environments through teaching, preventive counseling, and health awareness. It is our belief that the services provided by the school nurse should not be considered an add-on program of the school, but rather, an integral one.

HISTORY

School nursing falls within the rubric of community health nursing in that the school nurse, like other such types of nurses, works outside of the traditional hospital setting. The history of community health nursing started with the work of early pioneers such as Lillian Wald in the early 1900s. From the work of Wald, emerged the role of nurses in school settings.

Late in the 1800s physicians were the main health care providers in schools. Their purpose was "to detect communicable diseases among pupils and to exclude those infected from school" (Cromwell, 1963, p. 1). General health among young children at this time was abysmal, and it was not uncommon for high numbers of children to die from communicable diseases that included typhoid, scarlet fever, diphtheria, ringworm, and scabies. Communicable diseases worsened with the unsanitary living conditions associated with poverty. Antibiotics had not yet been discovered. Immunization of children would not become a reality until the 1920s.

In 1902 the New York City Schools began a health care program that emphasized preventive health counseling. This program began under the direction of Wald who worked to establish the Henry Street Settlement Visiting Nurse Service (Rosenberg, 1988). Wald's work was instrumental in getting schools to recognize the impact of health issues on school-aged children. At that time, children with diseases were excluded from schools and rarely returned (Wold, 1981). Wald's major goal was to get students back into school after health expulsions and to keep them there.

The first nurse to work in schools as a result of Wald's perseverance was Lina Rogers. Through Rogers' work, schools began to see a value in the role that the school nurse could play in promoting health and getting "pushed-out" children back to school.

The work of Wald and Rogers in the early 1900s caused school boards to rethink their uses of medical professionals in schools. Schools began to realize that health professionals could move beyond inspection for diseases. "This realization resulted in the incorporation of health education into the school curriculum" (Wold, 1981, p. 7). Health education, many believed, could help educate the general public. It was not until the late 1920s and early 1930s that the school nurse was viewed as a health educator, responsible for planning health education and seeking ways to prevent illness.

The work of school nurses also involved assuming an advocacy role for children. Many children, sons and daughters of immigrants, could begin working as early as the age of 14. Hawkins, Hayes, and Corlis (1994) reported that for children to go to work, they had to obtain a work permit. Children could not obtain a work permit until they had a physical exam, which was often performed by the school nurse, not by the school physician. School nurses, according to Hawkins and coworkers (1994), felt a tug between the professional responsibilities imposed upon by the school and the harsh realities of putting children at even greater risk of poor health due to the harsh working conditions found in factories. Thus, the school nurse became a social force in bringing attention to the health needs of poor children.

During the early 1900s, school nurses assumed more responsibilities. Struthers (1917, cited by Hawkins and coworkers, 1994) reported that "The school nurse [became] the principal's first assistant, the home health visitor, and the mother's friend and advisor, and in some communities she [was] the truant officer as well" (p. 418). Parsons and Felton (1992) report that "In the 1920s, school nurses began assuming responsibility for public health mandates" (p. 498). Anderson and Creswell (1980) report that the era from 1880 to 1920 included a child study movement, where "Educators studied the physical and psychological characteristics of child development as the basis for planning the school program. Before the end of this period, child study was an established basis for all school planning and activities" (p. 7). This emphasis on the study of the child led schools in the 1930s to develop physical education and other curriculum areas that would be taught cooperatively by the nurse and the teachers. In 1927 the American School Physicians Association was formed to help standardize the health care provided by physicians who were assigned to work in schools. Physicians assigned to work in school districts provided all screenings with the nurse acting as an assistant. This practice continued throughout the 1930s and 1940s.

The focus of nursing in schools was interrupted with World War I. Just before 1920, the army established its own school of nursing with the assistance of Annie Warburton Goodrich, a colleague of Wald at the Henry Street Settlement (Cookfair, 1991). With the national attention on war and the preparation of nurses, very few women were entering schools to tend to the health issues of children in schools. Cookfair (1991) reports that "In 1921, 500 nurses were graduated . . . and entered the Army Nurse Corps" (p. 13).

In 1930 President Hoover enacted the Children's Charter that explicitly put children and their health and safety in the forefront of the world. Essentially, Hoover's White House Conference of Child Health and Protection set the stage to strengthen the relationship of the school nurse to community health and education issues. Clemen-Stone, Eigsti, and McGuire (1991) discuss the 19 provisions called for by President Hoover. Perhaps of greatest impact on the role of the school nurse is Article Six:

> For every child from birth through adolescence, promotion of health, including health instruction and a health program, wholesome physical and mental recreation, with teachers and leaders adequately trained. (p. 515)

This provision, although focusing on health and welfare of children, addresses the adequacy of training for those professionals in schools—"teachers and leaders." The school nurse, during this period, was considered to be the lead teacher of health. Cookfair (1991) reports, "From the early development of the school nursing role during the 1920s and 1930s until the Second World War school nurses continued to develop their role in three areas: medical inspection, medical examination, and health education" (p. 221). According to Randall (1971), in the 1930s school nurses and physicians assigned to schools began to perform other duties: "Examinations were given for physical education, and screening athletes who wished to participate in competitive activities. Special examinations included boys and girls, faculty members, and anyone assigned to work as a food handler" (p. 125).

During the 1940s, the role of the school nurse changed because of the war. Many nurses were called to serve their country, therefore, in some schools health education was assumed by teachers and others who only could provide minimal health services. At the same time that the war created a nursing shortage, the issue of health in schools became critically important. Palmer (1944) reported in Wold (1981) that "the health of schoolchildren received increased emphasis during this time from educators and civilians for two reasons: (1) . . . large numbers of healthy young men were needed for the draft and (2) Selective Service data regarding prospective draftees revealed that approximately one fourth of the registrants were rejected because of physical defects" (p. 9). Even with a Depression, the government realized that health had to become a national priority and that children had to be more healthy to be ready to serve their country. School nurses, along with health and physical education teachers, became partners in providing services to schools.

In the 1950s the role of the school nurse remained the same as in the 1930s and 1940s. The nurse's duties in the 1950s, according to Portner (1996), were to teach personal hygiene and to teach health and physical education classes. "Their role . . . was to facilitate the delivery of health-care services, not to directly offer them" (Portner, 1996, p. 22). In 1953 the U.S. Department of Health, Education and Welfare was established to tackle health issues. Boards of education set out to hire more school nurses to provide for the health needs of students. However, during this time there was much debate about the role and function of the school nurse and this debate continues.

In the 1960s schools employed nurses in even higher numbers, although role confusion still existed (Wold, 1981). Cromwell's book, *The Nurse in the School Health Program* (1963), which served as a guide for school administrators to oversee the work of the school nurse, underscored even further the role confusion of the school nurse. School nurses were being supervised by nonmedical personnel—the school principal, the superintendent, and in some cases, the director of special programs or student services.

As the duties of the school nurse increased, health services in schools increased, partly due to the focus on health by the nation. "Between 1961 and 1968 Congress passed 138 laws influencing health care delivery" (Cookfair, 1991, p. 23), including Medicaid, and Head Start (p. 38). In 1965 President Johnson convened the White House Conference on Health. In the 1960s and 1970s a national health research agenda emerged as researchers began to examine the causes of chronic diseases, especially high blood pressure and high levels of cholesterol. Increased awareness of these chronic diseases brought health prevention programs to the schools. The Surgeon General began an anti-smoking campaign through his report on the ill-effects associated with cigarette smoking. Health programs and school nurses began to alert school children to the negative health effects of cigarette smoking.

The 1960s has often been characterized as a decade of storm and turbulence. Because this turbulence found its way into the schools, the school nurse faced increased numbers of students who were drinking and abusing drugs, sexually active students, increases in sexually transmitted diseases, and teenage pregnancy. Because student health issues began to escalate, numerous organizations began to question the qualifications that a nurse needed to practice in the schools.

During this time, the school nurse practitioner model emerged. According to Urbinati, Steele, Harter, and Harrell (1996): "In the 1960s, a new role was envisioned for nurses as primary health care providers. This new and expanded concept of advanced nursing practice was introduced as an effort to augment and improve health services to children who lacked primary care" (p. 6).

During the 1970s national health issues escalated even more and many initiatives emerged. In 1971 the President's Committee Report on Health Education raised several issues for schools to grapple with (e.g., alcohol and tobacco use, sexually transmitted diseases, and teen pregnancy) as they began to more formally plan and develop health programs in schools for all children. The Bureau of Health Education was established. Later, the U.S. Department of Health, Education, and Welfare created the Forward Plan. The Forward Plan provided a history of the government's role in preventing diseases and promoting health. As a result of the Forward Plan, three other significant acts were enacted: The Health Planning and Resources

Development Amendments of 1979, the Consumer Health Information and Health Promotion Act of 1996, and the Health Education Act of 1978.

In 1975, the passage of Public Law 94-142, Education for All Handicapped Children Act, which is discussed in great detail in Chapter 17, Special Education, created an even more expanded role for the nurse. The school nurse played (and still continues to do so) an important role on the special education team. The school nurse was expected to conduct health screenings to help identify and assess physical developmental disabilities. This practice presented a quandary in the 1970s because technically the school nurse could not diagnose physical impairments and thus had to uncover physical impairments by (1) examining prior health records; (2) conducting health histories from parents, guardians, and students; and (3) conducting screenings such as vision and hearing. From such, the school nurse assumed an advocacy posture for students and their special physical needs during initial health reviews both for regular and special education students. This advocacy position becomes even more imperative when conclusions can be drawn that a child is not receiving developmentally appropriate services. Then and today, an advocacy posture can potentially put a school nurse at odds with administrators of the school when the school does not have the necessary resources that, under the provisions of Public Law 94-142, must be provided. This situation, with the legislation surrounding the 1971 court ruling in the *Pennsylvania Association for Retarded Children (PARC) v. Pennsylvania* has been minimized in that schools cannot refuse to provide services under any circumstances, financial or otherwise, to students with special needs. Zanga and Oda (1991) note, "Furthermore, it is important to recognize that the instructional and administrative staff depend on the nurse to answer health-related questions and to assist them to recognize and refer students with potential problems that may affect learning as well as adapt teaching strategies for those students with special needs" (p. 440).

In 1978 Pubic Law 95-602, the Rehabilitation, Comprehensive Services, and Developmental Disabilities Amendments, provided specific definitions that school nurses had to be able to apply to children and their health needs when screening for disabilities.

PL 95-602 indicates that a "developmental disability means a severe, chronic disability of a person which is attributable to a mental or physical impairment or a combination of mental and physical impairments" (Programs for Individuals with Developmental Disabilities, 1978). It is clear that "mandates of the handicapped education laws . . . have placed increasingly younger children with increasingly more serious medical problems into the education 'mainstream'" (Zanga & Oda, 1991, p. 440–441).

In the 1980s, as a response to several factors—increases in teenage pregnancies, noninsured and underinsured children in schools, to name a few—school-based clinics began to find their ways into schools. Portner (1996) reported that "600 . . . school-based health centers are up and running nationwide, a staggering 1500 percent increase over the 40 such centers in operation in 1985" (p. 20). School-based health centers, often referred to as school-based clinics, could provide health services that were typically free of charge to children under the age of 18 whose families did not have medical insurance. School-based clinics enable students to have access through the schools to primary health care providers, school nurse practitioners, physician referral opportunities, and referrals to other necessary outside agencies that can facilitate meeting the physical and emotional needs of children.

The services that are offered through these school-based health centers and clinics range from immunizations, general medical evaluations, and physical examinations (yearly check-ups and sports physicals) to family planning counseling, contraceptive distribution, and the treatment of sexually transmitted diseases. Controversies have surrounded these services, that is, the distribution of contraceptives, examination of children and their treatment, and the duty and right of parents to be informed of such treatments.

As a precursor to the 1990s, the Carnegie Council Task Force on Education of Young Adolescents published *Turning Points: Preparing American Youth for the 21st Century* (1989). The substance of *Turning Points* contains concepts that, if implemented, could ensure student access to health services and establish the school as a health promoting environment (p. 61). The framers of *Turning Points* believed that schools should consider options such as school-based health clinics (located on school grounds), school-linked health centers (located off school grounds but joined functionally to the school and perhaps to other area schools), ties to community health centers, and arrangements with adolescent services in hospitals or health maintenance organizations (which might serve both adolescents in school and those who have dropped out). (p. 62)

From a national perspective two noteworthy initiatives, Healthy People 2000 and Goals 2000, have gained momentum in the 1990s. Healthy People 2000, the health imperative and disease prevention initiative for the 1990s had its genesis in 1979 with the publication, *Healthy People: The Surgeon General's Report on Health Promotion and Disease Prevention* (Healthy People 2000, 1990). One of the goals of Healthy People 2000 is for all people "to achieve access to preventative services for all Americans" (Public Health Service, 1991, p. 49). For schools and other social services that provide for the health of Americans, this goal can be accomplished under three interrelated priorities: health, health protection, and preventive services. Schools are a natural place to focus "on health protection, risk prevention, and equality in the health status" (National Center for Health Statistics, 1995, p. 3) of our youngest and perhaps most vulnerable audience—children.

The Goals 2000: Educate America Act of 1994 provides a framework for states and communities to develop and operationalize reform aimed at helping students reach academic, occupational, and health standards. The Goals 2000 Act contains eight goals, three of which link directly to health:

- By the year 2000, all children in America will start school ready to learn.
- By the year 2000, every school in the United States will be free of drugs, violence, and the unauthorized presence of firearms and alcohol and will offer a disciplined environment conducive to learning.
- By the year 2000, every school will promote partnerships that will increase parental involvement and participation in promoting the social, emotional, and academic growth of children.

These lofty goals point to a more comprehensive view of the role of the school nurse. It is clear that the services once rendered by the school nurse have been supplanted with more highly technical ones needing much more highly developed skills and training. To be sure, school nurses still provide health education and counseling to children and their families as well as make referrals to outside health care providers and other community-linked resources; however, the role and the ensuing responsibilities seem to be expanding as our nation becomes more "healthy smart."

An emerging concept of the 1990s is what Dryfoos (1994) refers to as the "full-service school." The full-service school concept that Dryfoos describes in her book, *Full-Service Schools: A Revolution in Health and Social Services for Children, Youth, and Families,* calls for schools to reorganize their structure so that a full complement of services can be offered to children and their families within the very structure of the school. Dryfoos advocates that full-service schools be developed to provide the immediate community with health care that is more responsive to the values that the school and its community embraces while meeting social, emotional, physical, and psychological needs. A full-service school, according to Dryfoos (1994), is one that can muster its resources to provide "more comprehensive, collaborative, unfragmented programs located in schools . . ." (p. 6).

CURRENT STATUS

It is essential that the administrator understand the role of the school nurse and the standards of preparation and certification at the state and national levels.

Common Themes in the Role of the School Nurse

Oda (1982) wrote about school nurses being able to "demonstrate their worth and effectiveness" (p. 359) within the overall context of the school. Certainly for as long as nurses have been in the schools, it is evident that they have responded to challenges by expanding their capacities to deal with the constantly changing special needs of the children who walk into their offices. Defining the role of the school nurse is difficult. The National Association of School Nurses (1993) states, "A licensed professional nurse . . . focuses on the health care needs of clients in the larger school community. . . . The school nurse may practice in school-based, school-linked, or collaborative school health programs" (p. 7). Bullough and Bullough (1990) define school nursing as "a specialty defined by the setting and age of the target population. The goal of school nursing is to develop and implement a school health program that prevents or corrects health problems interfering with learning. Another goal is to promote progressive self-care to achieve maximum wellness in each child" (p. 374).

Preparation and Training of the School Nurse

According to the National Association of School Nurses, as of 1993 23 of the 50 states require specialized training for school nurses. Requirements across states vary a great deal, however. Education and training requirements range from completing a registered nurse program of study with or without a bachelors degree to the completion of a masters degree, to specialized certification in a school nurse practitioner program to a doctorate in community health. Peters (1995) wrote, "the qualifications for school nursing practices vary considerably throughout the United States" (p. 380). A review of several states indicates that school nurses, in general, must have a bachelors degree and have completed an accredited registered nursing program. Many states, especially those states that require certification testing for teachers, administrators, and other school-related personnel, also have certification testing for the school nurse. Many colleges and universities offer specialized certification programs for nurses interested in working in schools. The nurse practitioner and adolescent health care specialist are examples of the extra and specialized training that nurses can bring to the school setting.

School Nurse Practitioners

In the 1960s the first nurse practitioner program emerged in Colorado. Since that time, with the emergence of school clinics, school health centers, and now with school-linked clinics, the school nurse practitioner provides services that can enhance health and increase the quality of services for many, especially for poverty struck and underinsured patients. A nurse practitioner typically is a registered nurse, with both a bachelor's and master's degree who has undergone post-master's course work. The average "extra" coursework can be up to 2 years of graduate work. Each college or university that offers this type of training and each state that recognizes, through its state board of nursing, has its own requirements and specifications. Nurse practitioners are able to provide services that in the past only physicians could perform. Nurse practitioners who work in schools combine their nursing skills with health counseling, health education, and anticipatory guidance (health prevention) with the skills of assessment and the management of illnesses and their causes. They are able to combine these practices because they have extra and intensive training in medical history–taking procedures, physical assessments, intervention strategies, and treatment skills. Although nurse practitioners, through their training and education, are able to assume much more responsibility with clients (in this context, we refer to the school), they typically work in collaboration with a physician.

In 1973 the American Nurses' Association and the American School Health Association jointly published *Recommendations on Educational Preparation and Definition of the Expanded Role and Functions of the School Nurse Practitioner.* This report was seminal in that the expanded role of the school nurse was beginning to gain credibility and acceptance within schools, communities, and perhaps, most importantly, within the medical field itself. For the first time in history, school nurse practitioners—by the nature of their training— were recognized as being able to, among other duties, "assess the factors that may operate to produce learning disorders, psychoeducational problems, perceptive-cognitive difficulties, and behavior problems, as well as those causing physical disease" (n.p.).

School Nursing Activities

Peters' (1995) describes the services offered through the school nurse's office. These services span broadly over three categories: (1) individual health services and population-focused health services; (2) health education; and (3) promotion of a healthy environment. Within each one of these categories is a multitude of tasks, functions, and activities that require specialized skills. For example, Withrow (1988) stated,

> The school nurse's functions include health assessment and management of the school population through observation, communication, and examination; monitoring the safety of the school environment; coordinating screening programs; and providing health education, case-finding, counseling, referral, and follow-up. Other functions include liaison, leadership, management, and program planning. (p. 781)

The work of school nurses does not always occur in the office, however. From a community health perspective, the school nurse provides children, their parents, teachers, and administrators with health information. The school nurse utilized in this capacity finds teachable moments for the members of the school community. The days of merely distributing health information pamphlets on selected topics are rare, although disseminating information to the schools and its community is not. Today, school nurses are, or have opportunities to become, instructional leaders in health information. Outreach efforts can include, for example, organizing health fairs during the day for students, and then in the evening for parents; teaching and/or team teaching during health classes; guest lecturing in classes; joining the work of teachers in preparing interdisciplinary units, including units on nutrition, within the context of other subject areas. Through creative utilization of the school nurse, schools can help members of their communities develop positive health attitudes and habits.

Throughout the history of nursing, the role of the nurse has changed. However, it appears that the basic or general functions of the nurse have remained constant, however. The American Academy of Pediatrics (1981) indicated that school nurses:

1. Serve as a health advocate for the pupils.
2. Assist parents in assuming greater responsibility for health maintenance of pupils and provide relevant health education, counseling, and guidance.
3. Conduct inservice training and serve as a resource person to teachers and administrators in implementing a comprehensive health instruction curriculum by providing current scientific information about disease prevention and health promotion.
4. Assess and arrange appropriate management and referrals for pupils with health problems who require further evaluation and care by their personal physician or others, and assist pupils in making decisions involving health care and services.
5. Help families who are without physician services find a primary care provider who will assume ongoing responsibility for health care.
6. Identify the health status of the child by securing and evaluating a thorough health and developmental history.
7. Collaborate with other health and educational professionals in the evaluation and management of children with physical, social, learning, and emotional problems.
8. Interpret the health and developmental assessment to parents, teachers, administrators, and other professionals directly concerned with the pupil. Provide guidance for adjustments and management of educational and health programs for pupils with special needs.
9. Initiate, perform, and assess developmental and screening tests. Refer, whenever necessary, through appropriate channels.
10. Conduct immunization programs to assure that every pupil's immunization status complies with the law and recommended medical practices.
11. Assess emotional disturbances and psychosocial–educational problems in childhood and adolescence. Plan for referral and management of these problems.
12. Provide emergency health services.
13. Advise and counsel pupils about acute and chronic health problems, and assume responsibility for intervention, management, or referral in consultation with the pupil's primary health care provider.
14. Make home visits, when indicated, for more effective identification and management of health problems.
15. Help provide anticipatory guidance and counseling to parents about childrearing and concerns such as developmental crises, common illnesses, accidents, dental health, and nutrition.
16. Utilize community resources in developing and coordinating health care plans which involve family, school, and community.

17. Evaluate school nursing practice and utilize consultation and continuing education for improvement.
18. Communicate with pupil's personal physician or other health care provider.
19. Maintain an accurate, complete, and well organized file of each pupil's cumulative health record.
20. Assist the physical education coaching and trainer staffs with training procedures, including rehabilitation. (pp. 12–13)

Standards for School Nurses and Services

The preface of the *Standards for School Nurse Services* (American Nurses' Association, 1970) underscores the importance of the school nurse within the overall school community. "The professional school nurse, in collaboration with other educators, utilizes the school health program to contribute significantly to the attainment of the full health and educational potential of each child" (p. 4). These early standards encompassed the school nurse's responsibility to the school staff, and also to health appraisal, health counseling, special education programs, communicable disease program, environmental health and accident prevention, health education, the school-community health program, school nursing service evaluation program as well as to the profession of nursing.

In 1983 the American Nurses' Association updated their standards by publishing the *Standards of School Nursing Practice*. The following table represents the standards:

Table 13.1 reflects a major shift in the professional role and responsibilities of the school nurse from the original standards published 13 years earlier. This shift is better understood by examining the knowledge bases

TABLE 13.1   Standards of School Nursing Practice, 1983

STANDARD	KNOWLEDGE BASE	GENERAL OBJECTIVE
1	Theory	The school nurse applies appropriate theory as the basis for decision making in nursing practice (p. 3).
2	Program Management	The school nurse establishes and maintains a comprehensive school health program (p. 4).
3	Nursing Process	The nursing process includes individualized health plans that are developed by the school nurse (p. 5).
4	Interdisciplinary Collaboration	The school nurse collaborates with other professionals in assessing, planning, implementing, and evaluating programs and other school health activities (p. 11).
5	Health Education	The nurse assists students, families, and groups to achieve optimal levels of wellness through health education (p. 12).
6	Professional Development	The school nurse participates in peer review and other means of evaluation to ensure quality of nursing care provided for students. The nurse assumes responsibility for continuing education and professional development and contributes to the professional growth of others (p. 13).
7	Community Health Systems	The school nurse participates with other key members of the community responsible for assessing, planning, implementing, and evaluating school health services and community services that include the broad continuum of promoting primary, secondary, and tertiary prevention (p. 14).
8	Research	The school nurse contributes to nursing and school health through innovations in theory and practice and participation in research (p. 15).

Adapted from *Standards of School Nursing Practice,* by the American Nurses' Association, 1983, Kansas City, MO: American Nurses' Association.

that have been added: theory, program management, interdisciplinary collaboration, community health systems, and research. These knowledge bases, coupled with the objectives, take into account the acceptance of the school nurse's role as school practitioner, the emergence of school-based clinics and health centers, and the comprehensive nature of the education and training that was required of a school nurse.

In 1993 the National Association of School Nurses, under the direction of Susan Tonskemper Proctor, Susan L. Lordi, and Donna Shipley Zaiger developed the document *School Nursing Practice:*

Roles and Standards in yet another attempt to make clearer to schools and their communities the "specialty standards of practice for the school nurse subsumed under the standards of clinical practice which apply to all nurses" (p. 1). Table 13.2 identifies these standards.

Table 13.2 reflects four major shifts in the knowledge and expectations held for school nurses in the 1990s. The addition of the knowledge areas—clients with special needs, collaboration within the school system, and collaboration with community health systems—underscores the primacy of the school nurse as a conduit for more encompassing and inclusive

TABLE 13.2   Standards of School Nursing Practice, 1993

STANDARD	KNOWLEDGE BASE	GENERAL OBJECTIVE
1	Clinical Knowledge	The school nurse utilizes a distinct clinical knowledge base for decision making in nursing practice (p. 20).
2	Nursing Process	The school nurse uses a systematic approach to problem solving in nursing practice (p. 24).
3	Clients with Special Needs	The school nurse contributes to the education of the client with special health needs by assessing the client, planning and providing appropriate nursing care, and evaluating the identified outcomes of care (p. 28).
4	Communication	The school nurse uses effective written, verbal, and nonverbal communication skills (p. 33).
5	Program Management	The school nurse establishes and maintains a comprehensive school health program (p. 36).
6	Collaboration within the School System	The school nurse collaborates with other school professionals, parents, and caregivers to meet the health, developmental, and educational needs of clients (p. 41).
7	Collaboration with Community Health Systems	The school nurse collaborates with members of the community in the delivery of health and social services and utilizes knowledge of community health systems and resources to function as a school–community liaison (p. 44).
8	Health Education	The school nurse assists students, families, and the school community to achieve optimal levels of wellness through appropriately designed and delivered health education (p. 48).
9	Research	The school nurse contributes to nursing and school health through innovations in practice and participation in research or research-related activities (p. 52).
10	Professional Development	The school nurse identifies, delineates, and clarifies the nursing role, promotes quality of care, pursues continued professional enhancement, and demonstrates professional conduct (p. 55).

Adapted from the publication *School Nursing Practice: Roles and Standards,* edited by S. T. Proctor, S. L. Lordi, and D. S. Zaiger, by the National Association of School Nurses, Inc. (1993). P.O. Box 1300. Scarborough, Maine 04070-1300. (207) 883-2117.

health services for children in schools. Of particular interest, we believe, are the two goals centering upon collaboration from both within and outside the school setting. We believe that more collaboration supports "more integration of education, health, and social services for children" (Center for the Future of Children, 1992, p. 7).

CONTEMPORARY ISSUES

This section provides some insights for school administrators on the contemporary issues that affect the services a school nurse can provide in the schools and offers suggestions for formats and structures in which these health services are being offered.

Primary, Secondary, and Tertiary Nursing Care in K–12 Schools

The overall goal of the school nurse appears to be to promote health and prevent illness (see, for example, Bullough & Bullough, 1990; Cookfair, 1991; Lloyd, Whiteoak, & Hodson, 1994). Cookfair (1991) believes that regardless of how the services of a school nurse are utilized, he or she basically oversees three types of nursing care: primary prevention, secondary prevention, and tertiary prevention. Primary prevention includes activities that include health promotion and disease prevention (Bullough & Bullough, 1990, p. 374). Secondary prevention is more concerned with early diagnosis of diseases "so that treatment can be prescribed to limit disability (Cookfair, 1991, p. 227). Tertiary prevention is concerned with "coordination and integration of health service resources within the school setting to support the child who is recovering from a major health problem or to enable the child who is chronically ill to remain well as long as possible" (Cookfair, 1991, pp. 232–233).

The range of services provided under the rubric of primary, secondary, and tertiary care by the nurse in schools is context-specific. Most school nurses take a proactive stance by working with teachers, parents, and students to promote health and well-being—the activities associated with this aspect of the role of the

school nurse fall under primary prevention. With the advent of school health clinics, school-linked health centers, and the other creative health-promoting structures that are emerging today in schools, more secondary preventive activities (e.g., diagnosis of specific diseases and handicapping conditions) are being undertaken by the school nurse. Along this same line of health practices and health care configurations in schools, school nurses (and school nurse practitioners), along with other school personnel (e.g., the school social worker), are working under the rubric of tertiary nursing care.

With the notion of primary, secondary, and tertiary prevention in mind, school nurses work with children who have more "acute and fragile health needs." Passarelli (1994) indicated that "school nurses currently provide health services for children and youth . . . with acute, chronic, episodic, and emergency health care needs and problems" (p. 141). In addition to the acute nature of more chronically ill children, the school nurse of the 1990s deals with such commonplace issues as teenage pregnancy, sexually transmitted diseases, HIV, drug and alcohol abuse, eating disorders, depression, and chronic and acute illnesses. Dryfoos (1994) referred to these issues as the "new morbidities" (p. 5). Gaining commonplace to be sure, but all the more complicated because more fragile children, needing highly technical assistance to cope with their medical issues, are in school. Because children are surviving catastrophic diseases and maladies, they are able to attend school with assistance from medical technology (e.g., portable oxygen). This trend will, according to the research of Iverson and Hays (1994), continue. These researchers conducted research in which they asked school nurses to predict the future needs and/or trends that will face schools and school nurses in the year 2005. Student health issues that the nurses sampled in this study believe they will see in the year 2005 include:

- More children with severe handicapping conditions in schools.
- More students with chronic diseases in [the] regular classroom.

- Students with more unique health needs due to artificial hearts, limbs, and transplants. (p. 23)

This same sample of school nurses also believed they would encounter the following expanded roles and expectations for their profession by the year 2005:

- School nurses will be doing more psychiatric mental health nursing.
- Increased equipment in schools: oxygen, nebulizers, Hinkman catheters, heparin locks.
- School-based clinics will provide primary care.
- School nurses will be responsible for the care of technology dependent students.
- School nursing practice will include more sports medicine activities. (p. 23)

From reviewing the work of Iverson and Hays (1994) and others, it is apparent that administrators need to hire highly qualified school nurses. As Bachman (1995) indicated, "there is a need for school nurses to have expanded knowledge and skills to meet the complex needs of children and families in school nursing practice" (p. 20). School nurse candidates who meet and/or exceed the standards posited by the National Association of School Nurses should actively be sought to work in school-based or linked health offices and centers within the school.

An issue that school administrators face is in determining the breadth and depth of health services that the school needs to provide to its students. The administrator needs to determine the current state of health in the school and the health care offerings being provided by the school. This can be achieved by reviewing with the school nurse the numbers of students and teachers served, types of services being offered, and then, together with the nurse, determining the types of services needed, but not provided because of certain limitations (e.g., budget and allocation of time, space, and authority). With this information, along with an understanding of the community, the school administrator will be in a better position to begin thinking about the possibilities. If the school nurse is the only health care provider in the building, there might be a need to increase personnel with the hiring of a health aide. In larger schools (elementary,

middle, and high), the nurse might be assisted by a health aide. Many districts who employ health aides mandate and provide training and inservice for these paraprofessionals. If the school has a health aide then the administrator, nurse, and school district need to have clearly defined "delegation of authority" procedures and guidelines. School nurses, can in effect, delegate some of their responsibilities to a health aide, but others cannot be delegated. Each state has its own guidelines that should be checked.

As the viability and need for more comprehensive health care in school continue to become commonplace and are addressed with the emergence of school health clinics, school-linked health clinics, and the popularity of "full-service schools," school administrators need to be able to coordinate within the structure of the school itself for these services so that they can become part of the organization. Some of the activities the school administrator may find himself or herself involved in as a result of expanding health care and practices being offered in the school include:

- Working with outside agencies in the coordination of health care activities (e.g., diagnostic services).
- Promoting health services that are offered in the school building with parents and the community.
- Establishing supervisory responsibility for the school nurse practitioner who might be employed by the school district but who also works within the school with outside agencies (local physicians and medical directors).
- Dealing with opposition of health care practices being offered in the school. Some controversies have been noted with the development and implementation of school-linked services. Some of the more frequent oppositions revolve around parent consent for the provision of health services, birth control, and treatment of sickness and illness. Procedures and policies need to be developed.

Through our research, we believe that more schools will continue to add on health clinics to meet the increasing needs of students and, in some cases, the families of students. The long-term impact of such health services within schools is still being weighed although many schools and districts report positive outcomes. "Although a fair amount of disagreement remains about the actual meaning of school-based clinics and their scope of services, the concept has 'caught on' and is being viewed as a desirable mechanism for delivering school health services" (Salmon, 1994, p. 138).

An area in which the school nurse is often overlooked for involvement is the wide-ranging health promotion activities within the school that can serve students, their parents, teachers, and community members. Nurses can and often do work in tandem with health teachers to provide information on topics of health. However, the school nurse also can provide instruction in nonhealth classrooms. For example, we know of a middle school where an eighth grade team does an interdisciplinary unit on the turn of the century arrival of immigrants to Ellis Island. This team utilizes the school nurse to present information about the health issues surrounding the immigrants during this time in history. Another school nurse we contacted has developed a schoolwide wellness fair. All teachers and students teach around wellness issues for a week and then the week's work of activities culminates with a health fair during the day for students and in the evening students return with their parents for a wellness fair geared for adults. This school nurse has been able to bring primary health and well-being to the forefront of the community by engaging local health care agencies in the evening health fair.

ILLUSTRATIVE PRACTICES AND ISSUES

Allensworth, D. D., & Bradley, B. (1996). Guidelines for adolescent preventive services: A role for the school nurse. *Journal of School Health, 66*(8), 281–285.

Allensworth and Bradley share the need for school nurses to be more actively and proactively involved in preventive education initiatives by utilizing the Guidelines for Adolescent Preventive Services (GAPS) that were developed by the American Medical Association. According to the authors, the GAPS can be used as a screening instrument to detect "behaviors that jeopardize health" (p. 281). This article details how the school nurse can initiate the GAPS program at the middle and high school levels. *Issues:* The scope of needed services has extended the means of most schools and districts. How can the school nurse find the time to thoroughly screen every student?

Bradley, B. J. (1997). The school nurse as health educator. *Journal of School Health, 67*(1), 3–8.

Bradley discusses critical issues such as student-to-nurse ratios, professional qualifications, and the standards associated with school nursing practice. Bradley also addressed how the school nurse can extend his or her opportunities in health classrooms. The school nurse can also promote "health" for the staff, act as an advocate for the health of the school within the community, and serve as a liaison with the community. *Issues:* The school nurse should be an active member within the school community, providing myriad services.

Harrison, B. S., Faircloth, J. W., & Yaryan, L. (1995). The impact of legislation and litigation on the role. *Nursing Outlook, 43,* 57–61.

Harrison and colleagues examine the role of the school nurse against the legal backdrop of Public Law 94-142 (and its amendments), Section 504 of the Rehabilitation Act of 1973. They discuss case law examples that have involved the work of the school nurse. Of special note is the treatment given to recent court cases related to "supportive services" and how the courts have viewed "reasonableness." Harrison and colleagues discuss implications for the nurse, who by definition and by law provides related health services to students with disabilities or other conditions provided for through Section 504. *Issues:* Training and inservice in the legal aspects of the role of the school nurse is requisite. School administrators need to ensure that school nurses are aware of legal issues.

Nelson, K. E. (1997). The needs of children and the role of school nurses. *Journal of School Health, 67*(5), 187–188.

Although Nelson does not illustrate a particular school nursing program in this article, she does explore the health needs of school-age children and then gives insights on how the school nurse can assist in meeting these needs. This article should be read by every school nurse, building-level administrator and districtwide health coordinator. *Issues:* As a unique member of the school community, the supervision, evaluation, and staff development for the school nurse should reflect the role he or she plays within the school community.

SUMMARY_____

We began this chapter by underscoring the correlation between health and academic achievement and by establishing the primacy of the school nurse in helping provide for the health of children. The role of the school nurse has evolved into a complex one due to the escalating health needs of students. Nursing and health care provided in schools have certainly changed since the turn of the century. We believe that this change will continue into the next century as schools address the health issues of children.

QUESTIONS FOR FURTHER CONSIDERATION_____

Research

1. Obtain a copy of the Occupational, Safety, Health Administration standards. How would you work with the school nurse to ensure that faculty and staff were properly educated about the hazards of blood-borne pathogens in the school setting?

2. Visit a clinic located in a school. Analyze the policies and procedures by which the clinic operates. Interview the principal to find out what types of support he or she had to obtain to open the school clinic. Develop your own questions, but include this question, "What stumbling blocks did you encounter (e.g., board of education, community, parents and staff)?" Report your findings in a report that includes recent research on school health clinics and the services that are typically offered.

3. Find a school that has a disaster plan in place. What duties are assumed by the nurse during the disaster plan? If your school does not have a disaster plan in place, begin to develop one. Who, beside the school nurse and principal, should be involved in the development of a disaster plan?

Reflect

1. How can the school nurse be utilized as a resource for prevention education? What types of administrative support are needed to ensure that the school nurse can become a more integral part of the school program?

2. As the building principal, how would you respond to the news that one of your students has tested positive for HIV? Does the district have a plan in place to cover the issues that surround HIV positive students? If your district does have a plan, examine this plan for (1) communication procedures and (2) the legal aspects surrounding services and other activities for the infected child. What types of information and training would be necessary for this child's teachers? What role would the nurse play in helping you work through these issues and procedures?

Respond/React

1. Should public funds be used for school-based health clinics? Defend your answer.

2. If the school nurse is out of the building, is it the principal's responsibility to administer medications, assess injuries, and otherwise perform the duties of the school nurse? Consult district policy to determine the answer to this question. If policy does not cover the answer to this question, consult the superintendent to determine the duty of the principal.

SUGGESTED READINGS_____

Behrman, R. E. (Ed.). (1992). *The future of children: School linked services. 2. (1).* Los Altos, CA: The Center for the Future of Children and The David and Lucille Packard Foundation.

Dryfoos, J. G. (1994). *Full-service schools: A revolution in health and social services for children, youth, and families.* San Francisco, CA: Jossey-Bass.

Wold, S. J. (1981) *School nursing: A framework for practice.* North Branch, MN: Sunrise River Press.

CHAPTER 14

THE SCHOOL PSYCHOLOGIST

School psychologists have, throughout history, been referred to as "clinical psychologists, psychometrists, psychoclinicists, Binet-testers, psychotechnicians, psychoeducational testers, and school psychologists" (Fagan, 1993, p. 4) These titles have resulted directly from the work of the school psychologist during specific historical periods. For an extended period of time, the school psychologist was referred to as a tester because most were more concerned with classifying children based upon measurements and observations. Lambert (1993) reports that "nearly all definitions of *school psychologist* reflect a consensus that the school psychologist is the cognitive, social and behavioral scientist in the school" (p. 163, emphasis in the original). School psychologists of today are still utilized in a testing and measurement capacity; however, due to the training these professionals have received and a few turning points in role clarification made since the 1950s, the role of the school psychologist now includes such activities as individual counseling, complementing the services of the school counselor, the social worker, and the nurse, and working with outside agencies.

All schools, regardless of size and grade-level configuration, employ or have access to a school psychologist. The enactment of special education and gifted and talented legislation mandates certain screenings for children that must be conducted by a licensed and/or certified psychologist or psychometrist. Smaller school districts typically share the services of a school psychologist or psychometrist with other schools within the district. Smaller, more rural districts often share the services of a single school psychologist and/or psychometrist among districts. Private schools (e.g., religious academies and private day schools) often contract the testing and other services of a licensed psychologist and/or psychometrist through local hospitals or mental health agencies.

HISTORY

The evolution of the school psychologist parallels that of the school nurse, social worker, and guidance counselor. Many of the historical trends that gave rise to development of these professionals also influenced the emergence of the psychologist in schools. However, the similarities in the development of these fields (e.g., school nurse, social worker, and guidance counselor) with that of the school psychologist need to be put into perspective. According to Bardon (1989), the emergence of the school psychologist's "development cannot easily be traced to significant and clear lines of theory or research, nor does it have national or international progenitors who are identified as its founders" (p. 2). The field of school psychology emerged from the larger, more generalized field of clinical psychology that was transported into schools.

Early Work

In the late 1800s and early 1900s compulsory school attendance laws, coupled with the high influx of immigrant children in U.S. schools, gave rise to the work of the school psychologist. Many of the immigrant children did not speak English well, and they were often classified as "dull." Schools did not readily know how to deal with the higher number of children who had special needs (Fagan & Wise, 1994). Because many of these same children came to school in poor health and suffered from physical ailments, they too were often referred, in addition to the school physician, to the school psychologist for examination. Fagan and Wise (1994) report that "it was widely regarded that defects in physical health could be symptomatic of defects in ability, school achievement, and behavior as well" (p. 25).

It was these "defects" that Fagan and Wise (1994) speak about that the first school psychologists dealt with as classrooms filled with students with special needs. Fagan and Wise "hypothesize that among the primary reasons for securing and employing school psychologists was the specific notion of having them help educators sort children reliably into segregated educational settings where exceptional children might be more successful . . . and where their absence would help the system itself function better for the masses of 'average' children" (p. 27). Phillips (1990) indicated, "School psychology was at first devoted almost entirely to the child study model, with its emphasis on individual differences among children, the causes of such differences, and their effects on children's learning and behavior" (p. 6).

The Child Study Movement

New knowledge about children and their needs began to emerge as a result of the combined work of social workers and psychologists. Two noteworthy people who emerged in the field of psychology and who had a lasting impact on the study of children were G. Stanley Hall and Lightner Witmer. Hall (1844–1924) was the first person to receive a Ph.D. in psychology, and he is "considered the father of American child study and developmental psychology . . ." (Fagan & Warden, 1996, p. 149). Later Hall would found what is now known as the American Psychological Association as well as several journals dealing with the field of psychology (Fagan & Warden, 1996). Witmer (1867–1956) studied psychology in Europe and founded the first psychological clinic in the United States, and "Witmer's major goals [were] to train psychologists to help educators solve children's learning problems" (Reynolds, Gutkin, Elliot, & Witt, 1984, p. 4).

The Testing Movement

Through the work of Hall and Witmer, school psychology gained acceptance in the United States, and testing was its main focus. Witmer opened a clinic at the University of Pennsylvania in 1896 where he studied children and their problems associated with school failure (Eiserer, 1963). Almost 10 years later in 1909,

"Dr. William Healy set up the first clinic for a juvenile court . . .", which would allow the psychologist to study and work with maladjusted youth (White & Harris, 1961, p. 2).

European psychologists Francis Galton and Alfred Binet, both interested in psychological measurements, also helped to shape the development of the testing movement in schools which, in turn, gave rise to the mental hygiene movement. The trait and factor influence that emerged during the early stages of psychological measurements would continue for the next 100 years.

In the 1880s Sir Francis Galton, a noted English psychologist, played an important role in the development of instruments to measure individual differences. Galton's "work on the heredity basis for intellectual superiority . . . played an instrumental role in stimulating thought and research about the psychology of individual differences" (Reynolds et al., 1984, p. 3). An expanded discussion of Galton's work with trait factors and the role of heredity can be found in Chapter 9, Guidance and Counseling.

In the 1890s James McKeen Cattell, a former student of Galton, established two research laboratories in the United States—first at the University of Pennsylvania and then a similar one at Columbia University (Kaufman, 1983). "Cattell elaborated upon and improved his mentor's methodology by emphasizing the vital notion that administration procedures must be standardized to obtain results that are strictly comparable from person to person and time to time" (Kaufman, 1983, p. 97). Cattell "coined the term 'mental tests' " (Kaufman, 1983, p. 97).

In France Alfred Binet is credited with being one of the first psychologists to develop tests to exclude children who lacked the ability to be successful in the elementary setting. In 1908, Binet, with the assistance of Henri Simon, developed the Binet-Simon scales of measurement. "The development of an individual intelligence test by Alfred Binet and Henri Simon . . . is commonly heralded as the beginning of the individual testing program which has characterized so much of the work of the school psychologist . . ." (White & Harris, 1961, p. 2). In the United States in 1916, Terman expanded the work of Binet by constructing the intelligence test, known then and today as the Stanford-

Binet Test. A more complete overview of the intelligence testing movement and Terman's work appears in Chapter 8, Gifted and Talented.

The first school psychologist was Arnold Gesell, appointed by the Connecticut State Board of Education in 1915 (Phillips, 1990). Gesell's work with children was limited because he was required to assess the need for the work that school psychologists could do. Gesell found his time split between examining the needs of the district, assessing students, and then making recommendations about what types of services children needed based upon his assessments. Although the number of school psychologists increased, their function remained focused upon testing and measurement.

The Testing Movement and the World Wars

World War I (1914–1918) served as another milestone in the development and widespread usage of testing instruments. Binet's testing procedures and results served as a prototype for the work of other psychologists who were called upon to develop testing procedures to classify men entering the military. During this time, large group administered tests referred to as Alpha and Beta tests were developed. Alpha tests were standardized paper and pencil tests whereas Beta tests were performance-driven to accommodate those soldiers who could not read well. Testing also was used for the same reasons during World War II. A more complete discussion of the testing movement is covered in Chapter 8, Guidance and Counseling. Eventually, the large-scale administration of testing that was used by the military would be duplicated within school settings. Psychologists, along with school counselors, were responsible for their administration, with the school psychologist primarily responsible for the interpretation of test results.

The Testing Movement Moves Forward

During the Depression, the trait-and-factor theory, associated with identifying individual strengths and weaknesses, became even more commonplace as a possible way of preparing the future workforce. Psychologists were concerned with developing alternative

instruments to measure intelligence. In 1939 David Wechsler introduced the Wechsler-Bellevue Scale, an IQ test that measured both verbal and performance abilities. From the "Wechsler scales . . . three IQs are yielded—a verbal IQ, a performance IQ, and full-scale IQ . . ." (Kaufman, 1983, p. 105). Binet's test, although widely used, was being overshadowed by more expansive measures and sources of intelligence. In the 1980s and 1990s, intelligence testing would come under the scrutiny of Howard Gardner and the multiple intelligences movement.

Another marker in the development of the school psychologist movement was the work of Gertrude H. Hildreth (1898–1984) who in 1930 wrote the first textbook on school psychology entitled *Psychological Service for School Problems* (Fagan & Warden, 1996). This book, according to Fagan and Wise (1994), "described the historical development of services" in addition to portraying "the school psychologist's role and function" (p. 38).

In 1940, Carl Rogers, a noted psychologist, introduced nondirective counseling, which emphasized the relationship between the "counselor" and the client. Rogers's theory competed with Freud's psychoanalytical theory, which emphasized "the importance of early years of life and had illuminating things to say about the motivation and personality of children" (Phillips, 1990, p. 8).

1950s to Present: Conferences That Set the Standards for School Psychologists

From the late 1800s through the 1950s, the field of school psychology experienced "growing pains" (Tindall, 1979). The larger field of psychology had within it the growing field of school psychology. The latter was a specialization. It was not until the early 1950s that school psychologists joined the larger field of psychology in a search for their professional identity and standards of preparation and training. Although schools used the services of psychologists, school psychologists were scarce, and the men and women serving in this field faced uncertainty about their role and identity both within the school setting and throughout the larger arena of clinical psychologists who were employed in different settings (e.g., hospitals and private practice). The work of psychologists was tied to clinicians outside of the school setting, and their work often overlapped that of school counselors. Tindall (1979) offered this insight:

> Historically, school psychology has been linked to guidance and to the counseling movement. As guidance evolved into the broader domain of counseling psychology, school psychologists and guidance counselors often found considerable overlap in roles. In training programs today there are varying amounts of duplication in the course work and practica for all three of the subprofessions of psychology that deal with mental health: clinical, counseling, and school psychology. (p. 11)

From the late 1940s until the 1980s, a series of conferences and symposia helped to better establish the role and function of the school psychologist, the needed training, and the critical issues that school psychologists needed to respond to in their work in schools.

Table 14.1 illustrates these conferences and symposia and also highlights the main topics addressed.

Recurring themes from these conferences include training (education, master's vs. doctorate and internship experiences); issues related to the professionalization of the status of the school psychologists in the eyes of the two premiere psychological associations—the American Psychological Association (APA, Division 16) and the National Association of School Psychologists (NASP); and role, function, and duty of the school psychologists and the means of better delivering services within schools.

CURRENT STATUS

Siegel and Cole (1990) believe that school psychologists encounter difficulties in schools because "there is little consensus regarding their role; traditionalists view them as technocrats whose purpose is to provide men-

TABLE 14.1   Milestone Conferences for School Psychologists

CONFERENCE TITLE	YEAR	MAIN TOPICS ADDRESSED
Boulder Conference	1949	Nonschool psychologist conference that sparked the interest of school psychologists.
Thayer Conference	1954	The current status of the school psychologist and future needs were examined. Education and training issues of school psychologists also were addressed.
Peabody Conference	1963	Internship and training issues were addressed.
Bethesda Conference	1964	This conference was a follow-up to the Peabody Conference.
Vail Conference	1972	Participants tried to delineate the differences between clinical psychologists and school psychologists.
Spring Hill National Symposium	1980	This conference was used to generate issues that school psychologists encounter. "The goal of the Spring Hill Symposium was to begin an intensive process of evaluating the status of school psychologists and attending to its future" (Reynolds et al., 1984, p. 13).
Olympia Conference	1981	The strategies used by school psychologists were examined.
National Conference on Internship Training in Psychology	1987	The internship experience as part of the overall training of school psychologists was examined.
Graduate Education in Psychology Conference	1987	Graduate training at the master's and doctorate level were examined.

From Bergman, 1985; Eiserer, 1963; Fagan & Wise, 1994; Phillips, 1990; Reynolds et al., 1984; White & Harris, 1961.

tal testing services to teachers, while a more encompassing perception views them as consultants who are able to draw on a wide body of knowledge for the benefit of students, parents, and educators" (p. 3). The school psychologist's role and function are, as White and Harris (1961) indicated, based upon "the dual influence of education and mental hygiene" (p. 3). Within the structure of a school, the school psychologist is involved in a variety of activities. These activities typically include assessing children through individual and group testing (e.g., intelligence and vocational) for inclusion in special educational programs (e.g., special education and gifted and talented programs), providing consultation services to teachers who work with targeted populations, and coordinating, when necessary, school-based services with that of outside agencies.

Common Functions of the School Psychologist

The professional conferences and symposia identified in Table 14.1 illustrate concerns and common themes in the development of a professional identity. Perhaps, however, these common themes have the functions of the school psychologist embedded within them.

As noted in the historical discussion, early psychologists, both within schools and in other settings, were preoccupied with testing and assessing students so they could be better served by the school. The practice of testing and measurement prevailed into the 1950s. After years of struggling with their professional role and identity, school psychologists of the 1960s began to include remediation as an extension of assessment and diagnosis. White and Harris (1961) provided a framework that depicted the role and function of the school psychologist in the 1960s. This framework included

1. Educational diagnosis
2. Educational remediation
3. Personality diagnosis
4. Personality remediation

Fagan and Wise (1994) identified the following roles and functions of the school psychologist:

1. Assessment of individual children
2. Planning and implementing interventions

3. Consultation
4. Interventions
5. Evaluation of interventions
6. Special education assessments
7. Research

To be sure, the roles, functions, and duties of the school psychologist have been enlarged to fit better with the current needs of students and schools. The role of the school psychologist, we believe, will continue to expand even more due to the ever-increasing needs of students and their families. We recommend that readers consult Fagan and Wise's (1994) book, *School Psychology: Past, Present, and Future,* for a full explanation of the commonly assumed roles, duties, and activities that keep school psychologists busy.

Special Education and the School Psychologist

Like the school nurse, social worker, and guidance counselor, the role of the school psychologist expanded due to the 1975 passage of PL 94-142, the Education for All Handicapped Children Act (EAHC). PL 94-142 and subsequent legislation are more fully detailed in Chapter 17, Special Education. Reynolds and coworkers (1984) believe that PL 94-142 had both a negative and positive impact on the work of the school psychologist and offer the following:

> On the positive side, the law increased the visibility of school psychologists, provided funds for more positions, and helped to differentiate school psychologists from pupil personnel specialists. On the negative side, the law was interpreted to effectively reinforce a testing role for school psychologists, a role that many school psychologists wanted to avoid or at least reduce. (p. 12)

The school psychologist plays an integral part in screening students who might qualify for services under the rubric of special education. Besides giving individual tests such as intelligence scales, the school psychologist is instrumental in developing the Individual Education Plan (IEP) for students who qualify for special education services. For those students whose scores do not render them eligible for special education services, the school psychologist often works with other support staff and personnel to develop accommodation plans under the provisions of Section 504, which is detailed in Chapter 17, Special Education.

School psychologists also help monitor and assess students once they are identified eligible to receive special education services. The ongoing involvement of the school psychologist during annual reviews and reevaluations of IEPs is highly desirable.

Consultation.   Bonney, Grosz, and Roark (1986) believe "the primary approach of consultation is to prevent problems rather than to treat them" (p. 12). School psychologists often act as consultants to teachers, staff, and administrators. The psychologist as consultant can be traced to the 1954 Thayer Conference and the subsequent report edited by Norma Cutts (1955). The conference proceedings addressed the consultant role of the school psychologist. The school psychologist:

Applies *principles of learning* in:

  a. Consulting with, organizing, or administering, special-education programs for the physically handicapped, the gifted, the retarded, and children with special learning disabilities.
  b. Helping to adapt the curriculum to the child's particular background.
  c. Consulting with teachers in order to help enrich the human relations aspects of their program. (p. 39, emphasis in the original)

There are many models of consultation. We are purposefully focusing on the instructional consultation model. Rosenfield (1987) indicates that "instructional consultation represents a joining of two major strands in the field of school psychology and educational consultation: the process of collaborative consultation and the knowledge domain of instructional psychology" (p. 3). In the instructional consultation model, the school psychologist can provide both indirect and direct types of consultation. Through direct consultation (often referred to as service), the school psychologist would be involved in a variety of activities such as "gathering data about the child directly through assessment, interviewing, or observation . . ." (Rosenfield, 1987, p. 11). Another example of direct services or consultation would be "providing psychotherapy to a child . . ." (Gutkin & Conoley, 1991, p. 205). It is not uncommon for the school psychologist to visit the classroom to observe the interaction between the student(s) and the teacher. It is essential for the school psychologist to be familiar with the classroom environment so that more appropriate suggestions and alternatives can be developed in subsequent discussions between the teacher and the school psychologist. On the other hand, with indirect service, according to Rosenfield (1987) the teacher or "the consultee works with the consultant, but remains responsible for most of the data gathering and intervention implementation" (p. 11). Hence, through indirect service, the school psychologist would meet with the teacher and ask the teacher to share what is occurring in the classroom, the successes or failures of the student in question, and the strategies employed to date.

Whether the school psychologist uses a direct, indirect, or even a combination of the two approaches, consultation is an important function of the school psychologist. Perhaps consultation can be better understood by examining the work of Dinkmeyer, Carlson, and Dinkmeyer (1994):

> *Consultation involves sharing information, ideas; coordinating, comparing observations; providing a sounding board; and developing tentative hypotheses for action.* The emphasis is on equal relationships developed through collaboration and joint planning. This is to be distinguished from the superior–inferior counseling relationships where the consultant is the only expert. The purpose is to develop tentative recommendations which fit the uniqueness of the child, the teacher, the parent, and the setting. (p. 16, emphasis in the original)

This view of consultation is interactive with both the teacher and the school psychologist on equal footing. Earlier consultative models were met with mistrust because often the school psychologist was perceived as being the "expert." Dinkmeyer, Carlson, and Dinkmeyer's (1994) discussion on equality and the relationship between the consultant and teacher hinge on four main points:

1. Information, observations, and concerns about a problem are *shared* between the consultant and the consultee.
2. *Tentative hypotheses* are developed to change the situation.

3. Joint *planning and collaboration* occur between the consultant and the consultee.
4. The hypotheses, or recommendations, *reflect* and *respect* the uniqueness of the child, the teacher, and the setting. (p. 16, emphasis in the original)

Likewise Anserello and Sweet (1990) identify the core elements of consultation as:

- Voluntary association
- Active participation
- Equal status
- Shared responsibility
- Right to accept/reject
- Confidentiality (pp. 181–182)

Other forms of consultation can include inservice efforts where the school psychologist along with teachers, other support staff, and administration explore areas that address existing needs. In their text, *School Psychology,* Bardon and Bennett (1974) give several examples of inservice programs that can be developed cooperatively between school personnel. Examples include teacher-selected topics such as child study groups, controversial issues (e.g., drug and sex education), and behavior modification (pp. 118–125).

Education and Certification of School Psychologists

From 1954 to 1987, proponents of the field of school psychology struggled with the education needed to be a school psychologist. As early as the 1960s and until the present day, there appears to be a wide range of differences needed in the training, education, and certification requirements of the school psychologist. Some people believe that the master's degree in school psychology is enough training for the school psychologist who conducts and then analyzes testing. Others believe that a doctorate in clinical psychology is needed, especially for school psychologists who want to conduct research and provide intensive counseling; and yet, others believe the education specialist is adequate training for the school psychologist (Fagan & Wise, 1994).

School psychologists need to have advanced training from an accredited college or university. Typically, the school psychologist completes a master's degree in psychology, which includes an internship usually spanning a semester with a specified number of contact hours. In addition to academic training and the internship, most states mandate the successful completion of a state exam covering the content areas of school psychology. Each state has its own certification and education requirements.

Standards of Practice for School Psychologists

There are two major professional organizations for school psychologists: the American Psychological Association (APA) founded in 1892 and the National Association of School Psychologists (NASP) founded in 1969. Both organizations have standards that have been refined to meet the needs of the field of school psychology. The 1992 National Association of School Psychologists' standards entitled, *Principles for Professional Ethics* from the *Professional Conduct Manual,* should be consulted as well as the Standards of Practice of the APA, which are not included in this text for no other reason than limitations of space.

CONTEMPORARY ISSUES

The school psychologist will, in our opinion, continue to be overidentified by others with testing. Although assessment is the main function of the school psychologist (Fagan & Wise, 1994), testing is but one aspect of formulating an assessment of children and their success in school. Assessments can include such qualitative measures as observations of students in classrooms, interviews with children and their family members, and consultation with teachers who work with children. These qualitative assessments are time-consuming, and many schools have large student-to-psychologist ratios. For example, in a study reported by Fagan and Schicke (1994), large school districts reported an average range of psychologist student ratios anywhere from "1: [to] 686 to 1: [to] 5,077 . . . [to an] overall district average ratio . . . 1: [to] 1,706" (p. 306).

Many school districts share a single school psychologist among several schools. To this extent, then, a school psychologist who travels from building to building develops an itinerant status, not really belonging to any one of the schools served. Fagan and Wise (1994) refer to the itinerant school psychologist as a "guest" very similar to Link's (1991) reference to the social workers contracted from outside of the school organization as " 'guest teachers' or 'guests' of another house" (p. 278).

It becomes difficult for the itinerant school psychologist to work effectively with a staff and be involved in the development of preventive and proactive services. Similar to the discussions of the marginalization of certain teachers—fine arts and physical education teachers—who often travel, perhaps such large psychologist-to-student ratios, coupled with the phenomenon of the itinerant status of many school psychologists, also marginalizes the school psychologist.

The supervision of the itinerant school psychologist can be problematic. Supervisory responsibility between building principals needs to be negotiated. Yearly activities such as annual reviews and testing will need to be scheduled well in advance due to the time limitations attached to some testing procedures, especially special education rules and regulations. Finally, many itinerant teachers believe that they are professionally isolated from the faculty because they travel. This is especially critical because one of the school psychologist's main duties is to provide consultation.

Issues relating to consultation will more than likely increase due to the inclusion movement in special education. With more special education students being placed in the least restrictive environment, regular education teachers will need assistance in the form of consultation from both special education specialists and school psychologists. Due to the myriad responsibilities that the school psychologist assumes, time becomes a factor in the availability of the school psychologist to provide either direct or indirect consultation. School psychologists often need time to interact with the people both within the school setting and other environments in which the child interacts (e.g., parents and other agencies).

Bradley-Johnson, Johnson, and Jacob-Timm (1995) are not optimistic, however, about the availability of the school psychologist to be involved in the inclusion movement because "school psychologists . . .

are too busy testing to be part of this process" (p. 191). Reschly (1988) cited in Bradley-Johnson and colleagues (1995) believes that the school psychologists of the 1990s and beyond will need to "make fuller use of the special knowledge and skills they have and to master new skills that will be valued in the schools" (p. 191). The tension between the availability of the school psychologist to conduct assessment and be simultaneously available for consultative work with teachers with more heterogeneous groupings of children will, we believe, continue to be an issue for school psychologists and administrators. The "ecological approach . . . considers multiple factors that affect learning and behavior, including classroom and instructional variables, characteristics of the student, and support from the home for school achievement" (Bradley-Johnson et al., 1995, p. 192). The ecological approach is quite different from the "clinical" model that the field of psychology evolved from throughout the course of most of the twentieth century. With the shift from the historical 'search for pathology' within the child . . . to an ecological model of assessment . . . to develop remedial strategies . . ." (Bradley-Johnson et al., 1995, p. 192), school psychologists will need to continue to redefine their role within the school community.

Regarding both consultation practices and the work load of school psychologists, Fish and Massey's (1991) study on systems approaches in school psychology practice is worth exploring. "Systems approaches promote ecologically sound views of children by recognizing that the contexts in which they exist are critical to understanding their behavior" (p. 361). Fish and Massey's study indicates that more time is needed for the school psychologist to work with the school, family, and community to improve "interactions to facilitate services to children" (p. 365). The context of the school, the characteristics of the students, teachers, and the ways in which these interact with one another need constant attention by both the school psychologist and the school principal. A natural complement to the systems approach might be the indirect service model of consultation. Gutkin and Conoley (1990) make the case for the need of indirect service— "indirect service is the logical alternative if we hope to serve more than a small minority of individuals who need service" (p. 208). This is consistent with what Fish and Massey (1991) found in their study. However, Gutkin and Conoley (1990) provide a solid discussion of why indirect service has not, in the past, been widely implemented:

> The dominant practice, training, and research activities of school psychologists are based on direct service foci, such as identifying and treating pathology, gleaned from medicine and traditional clinical psychology. Many of the problems facing school psychologists are actually the result of trying to solve indirect service delivery problems with direct service methodologies. (p. 209)

School psychologists have the capacity to work with teachers as consultants, allowing them to work with larger numbers of students in preventive ways during homeroom (secondary level) and advisory periods (elementary and middle school levels). The needs of students are increasing (e.g., drug use, health issues, pressures from peers, and dysfunctional families), and the school psychologist needs to be seen as a resource person who can work with teachers to develop strategies to deal with prevention. "Indirect service is the logical alternative if we hope to serve more than a small minority of individuals who need service" (Gutkin & Conoley, 1990, p. 208).

With the possibilities of the school psychologist being used in more comprehensive ways than mere testing, several practices will need to be reevaluated in the school. The practice of referral for testing needs to be addressed. Typically, students who have problems in the classroom, both behavioral and academic, are referred to either the school counselor or the school psychologist for testing. It is not uncommon that once a student is referred for testing by either a teacher (or possibly a team of teachers) or a counselor, the school psychologist is expected to begin the process of testing the student for a learning and/or a behavioral disorder. Our experience is that not many school psychologists or counselors would refute the contention that most children referred and then tested do not qualify for special education services. This process of referral and then testing is time-consuming because the student is in a state of limbo, not "legally" eligible for "special" services, but experiencing difficulties in the classroom and perhaps falling further behind in his or her studies.

Alternative methods of identifying students for possible testing are becoming a priority. Some schools have developed a model with which the school psychologist works with the teacher or team of teachers who have referred a student for testing; the objective being getting teachers to develop alternative strategies, such as modification of assignments, that fit more with the student's learning style. After multiple strategies have been attempted and then modified, the school psychologist can then visit the classroom to gain insight about the student in the learning environment. Feedback can then be given to the teacher who can further modify practices. Through this type of interaction, the psychologist will have a more complete profile of the student and be in a better position to determine if testing is the answer. This up-front work can be beneficial, especially if the student is tested and does qualify for special education services. All parties will have an idea of what alternative strategies have been most successful.

SUMMARY

The school psychologist is an integral member of the school community who can, if afforded the opportunity, break from the traditional role of tester that has historically permeated the practice of this profession. The role and function of the school psychologist, like most other support professionals (e.g., school social worker, counselor, and nurse), depends upon how the principal employs the talent and training that the school psychologist brings to the school.

School psychologists can provide both indirect and direct services. Indirect services are provided through consultation (e.g., classroom observations, development of student plans of remediation, faculty and staff inservice, and group therapy). Direct services are provided primarily through counseling and testing with individuals on a one-to-one basis.

School psychologists also can help develop preventive programs for certain conditions that put students more at risk for drug abuse, sexually transmitted diseases, and other destructive behaviors. As the needs of students increase and as schools move toward meeting these needs, the services that the school psychologist can provide will become invaluable in creating more responsive schools.

QUESTIONS FOR FURTHER CONSIDERATION

Research

1. Tracking and ability grouping are two common practices that still exist. What does research say about how widespread these practices are?

2. It is not uncommon for a school to have a building Student Assistance Team (SAT) that includes the school psychologist, nurse, social worker, guidance counselor(s), administrator(s), and special education teachers. Examine, by reading journal articles and books, the function of such a team. What services would each one of these professionals perform as a part of the SAT?

Reflect

1. After reading this chapter, refer to Chapter 9, Guidance and Counseling. How is the work of the school guidance counselor similar to and different from the school psychologist?

2. As an administrator, how can you use the expertise of the school psychologist and social worker to improve the climate of the school setting?

3. What types of large group instruction should the school psychologist be encouraged to do at the elementary, middle, and high school levels?

Respond/React

1. Historically, the school psychologist's role has been that of a tester. Although schools have used the talents of the school psychologist beyond the realm of testing, a majority of the work that needs to get done for special education, for example, requires extensive testing. As an administrator, how could you develop, collaboratively with the school psychologist, procedures to reduce the amount of screening and testing that needs to be done?

2. Should the school psychologist be supervised and evaluated by the central administration or by the building principal?

SUGGESTED READINGS

Dinkmeyer, D., Jr., Carlson, J., & Dinkmeyer, D. (1994). *Consultation: School mental health professionals as consultants.* Muncie, IN: Accelerated Development.

Fagan, T. K., & Wise, P. S. (1994). *School psychology: Past, present, and future.* White Plains, NY: Longman.

CHAPTER 15

THE SCHOOL SOCIAL WORKER

School social workers help children adjust and function within the school setting. They are engaged in a wide range of activities—individual and group counseling, development of special education social histories, coordination of community social services on behalf of the school, and development of special activities such as forming 'help' groups for children who are dealing with death and bereavement, violence and abuse, and promiscuity, pregnancy, and sexually transmitted diseases—while simultaneously working with parents, teachers, school guidance counselors, administrators, the school psychologist, and nurse, to name just a few. Moreover, school social workers act as advocates for children and their families.

The school social worker is also a key person in the development and management of crisis procedures (e.g., suicide, death, and catastrophe), the reporting of suspected child abuse, and coordinating activities that work in tandem with the student services' team—student assistance programs, pupil personnel, and a variety of other activities that help guide and nurture children in their social development, adjustment, and general well-being. If it appears that school social workers deal with just about every aspect of children and their social development and well-being in schools—they do. The National Association of Social Workers' position is that "School social workers are the *link between home, school, and community*" (emphasis in the original; n.d.)

There were numerous factors that gave rise to the emergence of the school social worker.

HISTORY

Just as the school nurse emerged in the early 1900s so too did the first wave of school social workers. The school social worker movement began as a way to provide care for the underprivileged and poverty stricken who lived in settlement houses. Freeman (1995) indicates that "initial services were provided not in schools, but in private agencies and civic organizations in the community" (p. 2087). According to Costin (1969), "The early twentieth century was a fertile period for the development of school social work," (p. 440) and that social work emerged as a result of the following:

1. Passage of compulsory school attendance laws
2. New knowledge about individual differences among children and their capacity to respond to improved conditions
3. Realization of the strategic place of school and education in the lives of children and youth, coupled with concern for the relevancy of education to the child's present and future (p. 440)

The very first social workers were referred to as "visiting teachers" (Allen-Meyers, 1991) and "friendly visitors" (Haynes & Holmes, 1994). McCullagh (1994) reported that "the visiting teacher or home and school visitor movement combined the professions of social work and education to forge a new school profession" (p. 34). Pioneer visiting teachers were, according to Allen-Meares, Washington, and Welsh (1996) instrumental in "bringing about more harmony between school and home, to make the child's education more effective" (p. 24). Although these visiting teachers worked in settlement houses and in private practices to assist doctors (both medical and psychological) with family histories, the very first school social workers did not appear as employees of the school system until 1913 in New York (Allen-Meares et al., 1996).

School social workers helped in the schools to address issues that they had never before faced. During the early 1900s, school enrollments swelled as a result of compulsory school attendance legislation and heavy immigration. With compulsory education legislation, *all* children had to attend school, regardless of their academic ability level and social status. Many immigrant children and their parents did not speak English, and these same parents did not understand the concept of formalized education. The visiting teacher was able to provide a link between the child, the parent, and the school, helping both the child and parent understand the importance of a formal education.

Jane Fullerton Culbert (1880–1962) played a pivotal role in the development of school social work practices. As McCullagh (1994) writes,

> Culbert was instrumental in the creation and development of the National Association for Visiting Teachers and Home School Visitors, and exercised primary responsibility for visiting teacher demonstration programs . . . under the auspices of the National Committee on Visiting Teachers . . . promoted the expansion of school social work throughout the United States. (p. 34)

Early visiting teachers employed by schools dealt not with issues of children and their success in school, but rather with the external forces that prevented children from being productive in school, namely, with "the exploitation of students through child labor" (Freeman, 1995, p. 2087). Like the school nurse, the visiting teacher became a crusader to keep children from working in the harsh conditions of the unsupervised factories that could hire children for low wages.

President Roosevelt's national conference in 1909 brought to the forefront the problems of children. With mounting enthusiasm, schools began to realize the value of social workers in helping them address the problems of children. Jane Addams, noted social worker and founder of the Hull House in Chicago, attended this conference to speak about "the best care to be given [to] dependent children" (Lundblad, 1995, p. 664). Addams's work with immigrant children who were working long and excessive hours in factories pointed to the need to get children in school.

A milestone in the field of social work in general occurred in 1917 when Mary Richard, a pioneer social worker, wrote the first textbook, *Social Diagnosis.* According to Zastrow (1996):

> The book focussed on how the worker should intervene with individuals. The process is still used today and involves study (collecting information), diagnosis (stating what is wrong), prognosis (stating the prospect of improvement), and treatment planning (stating what should be done to help clients improve). This text was important because it formulated a common body of knowledge for casework. (p. 46)

With the work of Richard and her book *Social Diagnosis,* (in print until 1963), in the 1920s schools began to employ the visiting teacher to study the problems of children in schools and those phenomena outside of school that interfered with school success. However, a marked shift in school social work occurred during this time period through the work of Sigmund Freud, begun in the late 1800s. According to Haynes and Holmes (1994) "Freud's theories of personality development gained popularity in the United States and diverted attention from social conditions to the diagnosis and treatment of [an] individual's psychiatric ills instead" (p. 66).

According to DeWeaver and Rose (1987), "School social work grew rapidly in the 1920s, with the main focus being on the liaison's role" (p. 47). One of the major issues visiting teachers dealt with during this period of time was working with juvenile delinquents (Hancock, 1982). Delinquents were classified and characterized by schools as maladjusted. School social workers were enlisted to help schools address the problems and maladjustments that the juvenile delinquent brought to the school. Truancy, failure, and drop-out prevention absorbed much of the social worker's time and energy.

Although the school social worker continued to combat juvenile delinquency and other maladjustments of school-age children, in the 1930s and 1940s the number of school social workers declined as a result of the Great Depression. However, the work of those school social workers who remained employed by schools and districts centered on assisting children in dealing with poverty and the conditions of the Depression.

In 1935 the federal government passed the Social Security Act, which made provisions for child health care and aid to crippled children. These provisions gave rise to the new ways in which social workers worked in schools. The social worker often worked closely with the school nurse and others to find assistance for and counsel children whose disabilities fell within the range of the provisions outlined by the Social Security Act. These activities were consistent with the liaison role that the school social worker assumed. The school social worker provided these services through "The social casework tradition of direct practice . . . for the next two decades" (DeWeaver & Rose, 1987, p. 47). The social casework method has been defined by Skidmore, Thackery, and Farley (1997) as "a method of helping people solve problems. It is individualized, scientific, and artistic" (p. 61).

Another group of students that the school social worker assisted were those labeled as *maladjusted,* or who were later referred to as *mentally retarded* but who are now referred to as children with special needs. Special education and the role of the school social worker will be more fully discussed later in this chapter.

In the 1940s school social workers began to shift the ways in which they worked with children, their families, and within the school system. Up until this time, school social workers were concerned with the changes needed to bring about improvements surrounding the external forces that caused children to experience failure in schools. The term *social casework* and its processes emerged. Social casework was viewed as a clinical model by which individual assistance was provided to students who were identified by teachers and administrators and then referred to the school social worker.

In the 1950s social casework was replaced with case management, defined now by the National Association of Social Workers (1992) as the "Organizing, coordinating, and sustaining activities designed to optimize the functioning of children and/or families" (p. 21). Brown (1992) believes, "Case management is appropriate to any population with multiple needs such as children and the elderly" (p. 60). The years between 1940 and 1950 marked an increase in school social workers. "Public school boards began to assume greater responsibility for financing their own social workers to address the needs of students and their families during and shortly after World War II" (Winters & Easton, 1983, cited by Torres, 1996, p. 8). Moving

away from dealing almost exclusively with social ills and conditions of society, the school social worker began to focus on critical issues of children in schools. In 1955 the National Association of Social Workers was formed. By the late 1970s this association established a branch for school social workers.

During the 1950s the school social worker's responsibilities included an increase in attention to special needs students. DeWeaver and Rose (1987) reported that "in 1950 parents of mentally retarded children formally organized into an advocate organization then known as the National Association for Retarded Children" (p. 49). With the parents of disabled (mentally and physically) children growing into a force demanding more educational opportunities for their children in regular schools, the school social worker's role increased as an advocate for these children and their acceptance in schools, as a provider of what is now referred to as *related services,* and as liaison between regular and special education teachers.

Because the types of services school-age children needed in the 1960s increased due to the turbulent tenor of the times, school social workers experienced issues new to the field. Cook (1984), reflecting back upon an article she wrote in 1966, indicated:

> In 1966 the new social workers were extremely isolated. Most school pupils had no knowledge about social workers. Parents frequently identified social workers with "welfare workers" who were too often approached in a guarded or suspicious manner. School personnel—teachers, administrators, special services staff, and board members—often felt ambivalent about the uncertain role of these intruders from outside the bailiwick of education. (pp. 4–5)

Although the use of social workers in the 1960s increased in many districts, a large percentage of school systems across the United States did not employ social workers. Frequently, children who needed the services of the social worker were referred to outside agencies. Other school districts contracted the services of social workers from outside agencies who provided a single social worker who would deliver services across many schools within the district. Although the term *visiting teacher* had become obsolete by this time, a new term emerged to describe the phenomenon of contracted social worker services in schools, *guest teachers.* Link (1991) refers to social workers "employed by non-social work organizations such as schools . . . 'guests' of another house" (p. 278).

It was during the late 1960s and 1970s that the role of the social worker became recognized in a significant way by schools and their communities. It was also during this time that school officials began to ponder how the talents of social workers within their communities could be used more creatively. This issue is a fundamental one, and administrators continue to question the best way to employ the school social worker.

By virtue of the training these professionals receive, they could assist school counselors in providing both individual and group counseling, establishing relationships with the parents of the students who were experiencing the most severe difficulties in schools, and helping administrators build bridges with parents and the community agencies that could offer complementary services to their children and them. Fisher (1988) indicated that the era of the 1960s helped the field of school social workers expand its services beyond merely working with juvenile delinquents and the maladjusted. "By the middle and end of the 1960s, society had refocused, and the center of attention in social work shifted to broad societal issues such as race relations, poverty, and the war in Vietnam" (Fisher, 1988, p. 16). This shift caused many to struggle with clinical, direct services versus the use of group work, for example. Fisher (1988) provided a sound discussion on yet another struggle of the changes in social work. Tensions surrounded the use of direct, one-on-one services for students in schools instead of more far-reaching approaches such as small group therapy. Costin's (1969) seminal national study cited in Fisher (1988) revealed

> that school social work was sadly out of step . . . social workers in schools were still trying to solve problems one student at a time and called for the introduction of systems theories and group work to enable school social workers to have larger impacts upon the school community (p. 16–17).

Social workers, by the very nature of their training and disposition, historically and currently, serve as advocates for children. With the passage of Public Law 94-142 (Education for All Handicapped Children Act) in 1975, the school social worker's role increased. In short, Public Law 94-142 and its subsequent amendments in IDEA (Individuals with Disabilities Education Act) required school social workers to conduct social histories of children and their families as they helped screen students who might be eligible to receive special education services. Moreover, school social workers often were instrumental in providing "other related services" for students who were identified as learning disabled. A detailed description of the provisions of Public Law 94-142 are offered in Chapter 17, Special Education. The increase in work with special education services, some concluded, however, left the social worker with little time to perform other services.

The social conditions of the 1990s have brought about an acute need for social workers in schools. Children are more fragile. Schools and society have witnessed increases in drop-out rates, teenage pregnancies, child abuse, poverty, suicide, drug abuse, sexually transmitted diseases, learning disabilities, gang violence, and homeless and run-away children (see, for example, Dryfoos, 1994). Consider the following: "An estimated 500,00 to 1.5 million young people run away or are forced out of their homes annually. An estimated 200,000 are homeless and living on the streets" (Reingold & Frank, 1993, p. 29). Teachers and school administrators cannot possibly handle these problems alone. They depend on support staff who have specialized training such as the school social worker, the school nurse, the school psychologist, and the school guidance counselor to help students cope with their problems.

A precursor to the 1990s were the reform-minded publications of the 1980s (e.g., *A Nation At-Risk* (1983) and *Turning Points* (1989)). Two such initiatives discussed in Chapter 13 (School Nurse) are The Goals 2000 and Healthy People 2000. The Goals 2000: Educate America Act became a law in 1994. Goals 2000 provides a framework for states and communities to develop and operationalize reform aimed at helping students reach academic, occupational, and health standards. The Goals 2000 Act contains eight goals, all of which have implication for the school social worker. Table 15.1 portrays the Goals 2000.

The school social worker has the potential to play a significant role in delivering services to children, their families, and school personnel. The history of school social work has evolved from concerned with the outside societal factors that negatively affect children and their ability to cope in school to looking at those factors both in and out of the school system that negatively affect learning.

A second milestone in the history of social work in schools has been the processes and procedures that social workers use as they work with students and their families. In the early periods social workers employed clinical, one-on-one interventions and counseling methods with students. Later, ecological and/or systems approaches and group activities became the means to have more 'teachable' moments with a larger number of students.

CURRENT STATUS

The modern day social worker provides direct one-on-one and group counseling services for children and

TABLE 15.1 Goals 2000: The National Education Goals

GOAL	DOMAIN	IMPERATIVE
1	Readiness to Learn	By the year 2000, all children in America will start school ready to learn.
2	School Completion	By the year 2000, the high school graduation rate will increase to at least 90 percent.
3	Student Achievement and Citizenship	By the year 2000, all students will leave grades 4, 8, and 12 having demonstrated competency over challenging subject matter in English, mathematics, science, foreign language, civics and government, economics, arts, history, and geography, and every school in America will ensure that all students learn to use their minds well so they may be prepared for responsible citizenship, further learning, and productive employment in our nations's modern economy.
4	Teacher Education and Professional Development	By the year 2000, the nation's teaching force will have access to programs for the continued improvement of their professional skills and the opportunity to acquire the knowledge and skills needed to instruct and prepare all American students for the next century.
5	Mathematics and Science	By the year 2000, U.S. students will be first in the world in mathematics and science achievement.
6	Adult Literacy and Lifelong Learning	By the year 2000, every adult American will be literate and will possess the knowledge and skills necessary to compete in the global economy and exercise the rights and responsibilities of citizenship.
7	Safe, Disciplined, and Alcohol- and Drug-Free Schools	By the year 2000, every school in the United States will be free of drugs, violence, and the unauthorized presence of firearms and alcohol and will offer a disciplined environment conducive to learning.
8	Parental Participation	By the year 2000, every school will promote partnerships that will increase parental involvement and participation in promoting the social, emotional, and academic growth of children.

Adapted from *The National Education Goals Report: Building a Nation of Learners*. (1995). (pp. 10–13). Washington, DC: National Educational Goals Panel.

their families. Glass and Nemeth (1996) indicated, "School social workers counsel students individually and in groups, provide crisis intervention, make referrals to community agencies, hospitals and local mental health clinics, train students in conflict management and help kids with their social skills and behavior" (p. 10). The work of school social workers is concerned with intervention strategies that reduce impediments to learning and that help children adapt to change. The work of the school social worker is in alignment with the overall purpose of social work. According to Skidmore and colleagues (1997):

> The purpose of social work is to prevent or cure the breakdown of a healthy relationship between an individual and his or her family or other associates. It helps people to identify and resolve problems in their relationships or, at least, to minimize their effects. In addition, social work seeks to strengthen the maximum potential in individuals, groups, and communities. (pp. 63–64)

Role of the School Social Worker and Common Duties

With this view, then, social workers can provide services such as the following (Link, 1991):

- Alerting schools to special needs that exist within the context of the school and the community.
- Promoting parental involvement and participation in activities for both students and parents.
- Ensuring parent and student rights in relation to special education (e.g., testing, screening, right of rebuttal, and placement).
- Negotiating home, school, and community cooperation, collaboration, and interagency collaboration and services between school, home, and agency.
- Working with teachers, support staff, and others with an eye toward identifying the social context of problems that children are encountering (p. 279).

School social workers are concerned with providing both restorative and preventive services to children, their families, and the school organization itself. Restorative services are concerned with assisting children and families to cope with issues that are affecting them. Restorative services could include, for example, counseling to deal with physical and sexual abuse; assisting runaway children in moving back home; and intervening during crises such as was witnessed with the Oklahoma City bombing (April 19, 1995) and the TWA Flight 800 tragedy (July 16, 1996). Restorative services then are those activities that assist with getting things back to their natural or acceptable state. Preventive services are more proactive in nature and could include, for example, activities that promote, support, and reinforce healthy lifestyles among students and their families.

During both restorative and preventive activities, the school social worker is in a constant state of (1) identifying issues, (2) intervening with assistance, (3) assessing the nature and/or severity of the issue and its potential consequences on the child, family, and school, (4) referring to outside agencies when necessary, (5) coordinating efforts between and among the child, the resources of the school, family, and other outside agencies, if necessary, (6) supporting strategies utilized, steps taken, and directions needed to provide assistance, (7) following through with ongoing assessment and evaluation, and (8) modifying services based upon the results of assessment and evaluation.

Allen-Meares (1991) portrayed highlights of the varying tasks that school social workers typically perform in urban schools. We believe that many of these tasks are performed by urban, suburban, and rural school social workers in both private and public schools. With permission, we have reproduced Allen-Meares' table (see Table 15.2) that originally appeared in the text, *School Social Work: Practice and Research Perspectives,* edited by Constable, Flynn, and McDonald (1991). Furthermore, we believe that this table can assist administrators in defining not the end, but the range of possibilities of services that school social workers can provide within the context of a school. As Allen-Meares offered the caveat that no listing could possibly capture all of the tasks and work that school social workers can provide, we too offer the same advice to the school administrator who employs a school social worker in his or her building. It is merely a beginning point.

TABLE 15.2 Some Pupil Groups and Social Work Tasks

	EXAMPLES OF SCHOOL SOCIAL WORKERS' TASKS	
School Population	*Remedial*	*Preventive*
A. Handicapped Pupils (The Education for All Handicapped Children Act—1975 [P.L. 94-142])	1. Assist in the development of community-based referral procedures to locate children needing service 2. Make home visits and provide information about the social development and adaptive behavior of the pupil 3. Assist in the formulation and monitoring of Individual Educational Programs (IEPs) 4. Facilitate the involvement of parents/guardians in the special education program and IEP development 5. Inform parents of their rights and the school's due process procedure 6. Implement and define support services for pupils (e.g., develop social skills to facilitate mainstreaming work with members of the multidisciplinary team to develop new instructional options; this could be remedial and preventive)	1. Work with community agencies and health providers to stress the importance of prenatal care 2. Work with handicapped pupils targeted to increase their social skills and to ensure a positive outcome 3. Work with secondary handicapped pupils on vocational skills and social skills to ensure employment 4. Work with community businesses and employers to encourage hiring special populations 5. Work with the regular and special educational staff to maximize equal educational opportunities once pupils are mainstreamed
B. Racial/Ethnic/Language-Minority Pupils (Emergency School Aid Act—P.L. 92-318 and Bilingual Education)	1. Work with educational staff to develop culturally and racially sensitive curricula 2. Work with the parents of pupils to ascertain their views of the school system and to interpret these views to school staff 3. Work with parents in groups to explain the requirements of the educational system and how to make use of its opportunities 4. Work with the educational staff and community groups to develop avenues of communication essential for two-way communication 5. Develop schoolwide advisory committees of significant school and community groups to facilitate desegregation	1. Work with the community to gain support for educational plans and programs to facilitate integration and curricula and modifications sensitive to cultural diversity 2. Organize consciousness-raising groups for the educational staff prior to the implementation of a desegregation plan 3. Provide testimony at public hearings to support the funding and expansion of programs that target these pupils 4. Develop human relations activities for the entire pupil population to promote amicable relationships and an environment hospitable to diversity 5. Eliminate barriers by working with the educational staff to remove school practices and policies that exclude a particular population (e.g., the provision of extra busing services so pupils who are bused to school can participate in extracurricular after-school programs)
C. Sexually Active and Pregnant Adolescents (Title IX)	1. Refer these youth to family planning agencies and health providers 2. Develop in-school programs for pregnant adolescents so they can continue their education with minimal interruptions	1. Develop in-school sex education programs 2. Work with teacher and parent groups to facilitate their awareness of sexual development and to discuss how to communicate appropriate information to pupils

(continued)

177

TABLE 15.2   Continued

School Population	EXAMPLES OF SCHOOL SOCIAL WORKERS' TASKS	
	Remedial	*Preventive*
	3. Develop with necessary community support services (e.g., child care, special tutoring, financial resources, family planning, health services) required to help the pupils attend school	3. Work within the community to develop parent–pupil programs that emphasize decision making and problem solving to prevent pregnancy
D. Abused and Neglected Pupils (Child Abuse Prevention and Treatment Act)	1. Contact the child welfare agency responsible for investigating abuse and neglect	1. Provide and develop inservice training for the educational staff and community groups on identification and legal responsibilities for reporting abuse and neglect
	2. Provide emotional support to pupils who are victims of abuse and neglect through the provision of casework, short-term family intervention, group work, and crisis intervention	2. Establish parent education programs across the school district/unit and community to teach techniques of discipline and parent effectiveness
	3. Work with relevant agencies (child welfare and the police department) as a part of follow-up services to enhance pupil's social functioning and schooling	3. Establish within the school a procedure for reporting abuse and neglect
	4. Work with teachers in their classrooms to provide materials on how pupils can protect themselves from sexual abuse (this task could be considered both remedial and preventive)	
E. Truants	1. Contact home and assess conditions that prevent pupils from attending (e.g., is the pupil kept at home to babysit younger siblings?)	1. Refer families to appropriate social services
	2. Consult with teachers and assess classroom conditions/expectations and the pupil's readiness for learning to identify those factors that alienate pupils	2. Identify, in collaboration with the educational staff and administration, school practices that alienate pupils
	3. Assess with the assistance of the school staff whether the pupil needs remedial educational services	3. Organize groups of pupils and teach social skills to enhance functioning with peers and adults, emphasizing how to ask for help and to constructively convey dissatisfaction
	4. Assess by observing the pupil's functioning in the classroom and informal situations whether he/she has appropriate social skills for peer interactions	4. Develop with the school's staff educational alternatives to accommodate unique needs of a diverse student population
	5. Work in collaboration with the school staff to develop modified educational schedules that facilitate reentry into the educational system once the pupil has missed considerable time	5. Develop awareness of cultural/ethnic differences among pupils to minimize isolation

From Allen-Meares, P. (1991). The contribution of social workers to schooling. In R. Constable, J. P. Flynn, & S. McDonald (Eds.), *School Social Work: Practice and Research Perspectives* (2nd ed.). Chicago: Lyceum Books. Reprinted with permission.

SCHOOL SOCIAL WORK
METHODS AND APPROACHES

Up to the 1970s, according to Freeman (1994), "school social workers shifted gradually from a focus on the intrapsychic problems of individual children to an ecological perspective for helping change students' environments" (p. 204). In other words, social work services before this shift were typically considered "clinical" in nature. Because many social workers were influenced by Freud's personality traits and characteristics theories, clinical practice, that is, one-on-one-counseling, was the dominant method.

Ecological and Systems Approaches

Germain (1982) described the ecological movement in social work as a means to "interface" the social worker with the world of the client. The ecological approach, according to Clancy (1995), "focuses on the social ecology of the school community" (p. 40). This means then, that the "school social workers's practice is not focussed on individual 'problem' pupils but on the range of social interplays that occur among systems within the school environment. The student's immediate ecological environment consists of microsystems, such as the family, the classroom, the neighborhood, and the playground, and mesosystems, comprising the interrelationships between two or more of the microsystems" (Clancy, 1995, p. 41).

People within systems interact with one another. The school social worker is trained to recognize patterns of interaction, both positive and negative, between the student and his or her social environments, which can include, for example, the school and home; and the school, the home, and the community (e.g., church, youth group, and sports team). A systems theory and approach provides, according to Haynes and Holmes (1994), a "conceptual framework for social workers" (p. 236). This conceptual framework was built upon concepts from the fields of biology, medicine, and other sciences. Haynes and Holmes (1996) discuss systems theory in detail. They indicate that a systems approach is important because it tells us the following:

1. People and their environment are in constant interaction with one another.

2. Searching for cause–effect explanations *only* in people or *only* in their environment is seeing just part of the big picture.

3. Our attention must be directed toward the dynamic totality of what we see. (pp. 236–237, emphasis in the original)

Group Work

Another method of social work services delivery in schools is group work and counseling. Group methods are a popular method of delivery because group formation enables the social worker and others to work with students who have the same problems. During group work, these problems can be addressed to a larger number of students than did the typical one-on-one services of the past. With the increase of responsibility and services that are placed upon the social worker, group work is more efficient. In addition, group members can support each other. In group work, the social worker acts as a facilitator, leading participants to explore their problems and develop plans for solving them, while also providing support. Group topics within a school are limitless in range and typically represent issues encountered within the home and school. For example, one school we contacted had groups addressing the loss (death) of a parent, study skills, homeless and runaway children, and assertiveness. This school social worker indicated that he gets his ideas for groups from working with the guidance and counseling department, the school nurse, and the administrative team. He also indicated that groups typically last an entire semester; however, some groups can last an entire year.

Special Education and the Social Worker

School social workers play a pivotal role in the screening of children who are suspected of having a learning disability by conducting social histories of children and their families. Moreover, social workers provide direct services to children who have learning and/or other handicapping conditions as specified on Individual Educational Programs (IEPs).

Section 504 of the Rehabilitation Act of 1973 was designed to eliminate discrimination on the basis of disability in programs and activities receiving federal financial assistance. The Rehabilitation Act is more fully discussed in Chapter 17, Special Education. School social workers are often called upon to help the school develop modifications to assist students in the instructional setting. Often students need a modification due to a handicapping condition, learning or health-related. These students need to receive the modification without experiencing an adverse effect on their ability to derive educational benefit. An example of an accommodation might include an extended passing period for a paraplegic student or an extended time period for tests and modified assignments for a student with an attention deficit disorder. All special education eligible students are protected under Section 504 provisions. However, not all Section 504 students are classified as special education. Section 504 provided the means for more children to derive services that are not necessarily accounted for through IDEA.

Standards

The National Association of Social Workers (NASW) has developed standards that guide the preparation, certification, and work of school social workers. In 1978 the association adopted its first set of national standards. These standards have shifted over time to reflect the increased professional knowledge base about the work, function, and role of the professional school social worker. In 1992, under the direction of the Educational Commission Task Force, the association updated their standards. These standards, fall under three larger, umbrella standards:

  I. Competence and professional practice
  II. Professional preparation and development
  III. Administrative structure and support

    Note that the standards of administrative structure and support can give insight to administrators as they work with the school social worker to ensure success for students. The following association standards are applied to the school social worker:*

Standard I: **Competence and Professional Practice**

Standard 1: A school social worker shall demonstrate commitment to the values and ethics of the social work profession and shall use NASW's professional standards and Code of Ethics as a guide to ethical decision making.

Standard 2: As leaders or members of interdisciplinary teams, school social workers shall work collaboratively to mobilize the resources of the local education agencies and the community to meet the needs of children and families.

Standard 3: School social workers shall develop and provide training and education programs that address the goals and mission of the educational institution.

Standard 4: School social workers shall organize their time, energies, and work loads to fulfill their responsibilities and complete assignments with due consideration of the priorities among their various responsibilities.

Standard 5: School social workers shall maintain accurate data that are relevant to the planning, management, and evaluation of the school social work program.

Standard 6: School social workers shall be responsible for identifying individual children and target populations in need of services. They shall do so through a process of needs assessment that includes planned consultation with personnel of the local education agency, community representatives, and children and their families.

Standard 7: School social workers shall know how to use objective measures and shall integrate them into their evaluation and subsequent development of reports, when appropriate.

Standard 8: Following an assessment, the school social worker shall develop and implement a plan of intervention or, when the most suitable intervention is not available, shall develop an alternative plan that will enhance children's ability to benefit from their educational experience.

Standard 9: School social workers, as systems change agents, shall identify areas of need that are not being addressed by the local education agency and community and shall work to create those services.

Standard 10: School social workers shall provide consultation to personnel of the local education agency, members of the school boards, and representatives of the community to promote understanding and the effective utilization of school social work services.

Standard 11: School social workers shall ensure that children and their families are provided services within the context of multicultural understanding and sensitivities that enhance the families' support of the children's learning experiences.

Standard 12: School social work services shall be extended to children in ways that build on the children's individual strengths and that offer them maximum opportunity to participate in the planning and direction of their own learning experiences.

Standard 13: School social workers shall empower children and their families to gain access to and effectively use formal and informal community resources.

Standard 14: School social workers shall maintain adequate safeguards for the privacy and confidentiality of information.

Standard 15: School social workers shall be trained in and use mediation and conflict-resolution strategies to resolve children's educational problems.

Standard 16: School social workers shall advocate for children and their families in a variety of situations.

Standard II: Professional Preparation and Development

Standard 17: School social workers shall possess knowledge and understanding that are basic to the social work profession and specialized knowledge and understanding of the local education agency, of the process of education, and of relevant legislation and due process.

Standard 18: School social workers shall develop skills for effective service to children, families, personnel of the local education agency, and the community.

Standard 19: School social workers shall meet the standards for practice set by NASW, as well as the standards established by the states.

Standard 20: School social workers shall assume responsibility for their own continued professional development.

Standard 21: School social workers shall contribute to the development of the profession by educating and supervising social work interns.

Standard III: Administrative Structure and Support

Standard 22: School social work services should be provided by credentialed school social workers who are employees of the local education agency as part of integrated services to children.

Standard 23: Social workers in schools should be designated "school social workers."

Standard 24: The administrative structure of the local education agency should show clear lines of support and accountability for the school social work program.

Standard 25: The administrative structure established by the local education agency should provide for appropriate school social work supervision.

Standard 26: The local education agency should employ school social workers with the highest level of qualification for entry-level practitioners.

Standard 27: A local education agency's classification and salary schedule should provide for school social workers' positions and salaries at a level appropriate to their education, experience, and responsibilities. Classifications and salaries should be formulated by procedures that are consistent with those of similarly qualified professional personnel of the local education agency.

Standard 28: The local education agency should provide a work setting that permits social workers to use their competencies effectively.

Standard 29: The local education agency should provide opportunities for social work staff to engage in a program of social work in-service training and staff development.

Standard 30: The goals, objectives, and tasks of a school social work program should be clearly and directly related to the mission of the local education agency, the educational process, and the use of educational opportunities by children.

Standard 31: All school social work programs, new or long standing, should be evaluated on an ongoing basis to determine their relevance, effectiveness, efficiency, and contributions to the process of educating children.

Standard 32: Each state department of education should employ a state school social work consultant who is a credentialed and experienced MSW school social worker.

Although lengthy, these standards, established in 1992, can serve as guideposts for school administrators as they work with the school social worker. We believe that the school administrator should consult the *NASW Standards for School Social Work Services* (1992) in its entirety to gain further perspective and explication of the philosophical underpinnings and activities surrounding the utilization of the school social worker. This publication also provides two appendices that cover recommendations on school social workers and student population ratios and a listing of the knowledge, skills, and ability areas that school social workers need to have mastery over to be successful in the school setting.

Preparation, Training, and Certification

Most school social workers have a master's degree in social work (M.S.W.), although some may possess a bachelor's degree (B.S.W.). Although preparation programs vary, those accredited by the NASW have commonalities such as components in individual, group, and family counseling; intervention strategies; and requirements in psychology, sociology, anthropology, and health. The M.S.W. typically takes 2 years to complete and includes a sustained internship, spanning up to 900 hours of a clinical internship. The NASW establishes standards for school social workers. Although each state varies its requirements for school social workers, most states require passing a state exam to qualify to practice social work in a school setting. The NASW reported that as of 1995, 31 states had established school social work certification (Hare, 1995). Certain distinctions need to be made when discussing licensure and certification of the school social worker. Hare (1995) indicated, "School social work 'certification' differs from the general social work 'license' granted by state social work licensing

boards . . . 'Licensure' refers to general social work licensing, 'certification,' . . . refers to school social work certification" (p. 1). The NASW periodically publishes a report entitled, *School Social Work Certification Requirements from State Departments of Education: What You Need to Know to Apply for a School Social Work Position* (1995).

CONTEMPORARY ISSUES

Tom Cardellichio, principal of Bell Middle School, Chappaqua, New York, was quoted as saying,

> A school social worker is a great asset in keeping alienated and troubled students engaged in the life of the school, and in keeping lines of communication open between those children and the adults in the school. The school social worker also benefits children and parents by communicating with them during family crises which interfere with school work. (NASW and NASW's School Social Work Section, n.d.)

Allen-Meares (1990) challenged the status quo in the use of school social workers with the following message:

> The school social worker has the opportunity to be creative, to develop new ways to approach problems, to work with a variety of pupil groups and their families, to draw the community into the school as a support system, to use every conceivable social work approach to prevent and remediate problems that hinder learning, to collaborate with different professionals, and to advocate for policies and practices that promote learning and equality. (p. 4)

Although optimistic, Allen-Meares's message is often overshadowed by the lack of full understanding of the "best" way to utilize the school social worker. Often, school administrators employ support personnel such as the social worker to "fix and patch" students— after the fact. This view is reactive versus proactive. Link (1991) indicated that "guidelines for school social workers in the United States refer to promoting individual students, facilitating change, and taking risks. These objectives often are not shared by school boards" (p. 279). From these views, it then appears that schools and their boards need to better understand the complex services that social workers can provide to schools and their communities.

The underlying issues, as we see them, involve school administrators understanding the characteristics of the students, their parents, and then knowing the school's personnel. But this understanding is not enough, especially if you believe that the person and the environment interact, and that it is from this interaction of the individual with the environment that a better understanding of individual and collective needs can be identified and then met. These beliefs stem from the ecological or systems approach to social work practice.

Another contemporary issue that schools face regarding social worker services is that of "turf wars." Turf war issues evolve from not clearly defining what the social worker will accomplish and what role the social worker will assume within the school's structure. Social workers can do much more than work with children in crisis. Social workers can work with all children—from high achievers to special education children. A major role of the social worker is to help children adjust to their environment and overcome the obstacles that children can face along the way to achieving success in school—and possibly in life. Social workers also work with the parents of children who are experiencing difficulties. Within this role, the social worker often becomes the liaison and advocate of the child. Turf issues arise when the boundaries of the social worker's role are not clearly understood by other support staff, especially the school counselor and the nurse. This problem has the potential to derail the working relationships among members of the support staff team. As schools become more inclined to work with outside agencies or to move to what Dryfoos (1994) refers to as "full service" schools, the likelihood of turf issues intensifies.

As the social worker examines the environments that the child interacts within and works with the varying people within these environments, the social worker is in a prime position to see possible shortcomings. If the social worker is able to identify shortcomings of, for example, policies and procedures of the school environment, then the social worker has a duty to bring these shortcomings to the attention of

the principal. Thus, the social worker is probably in a good position to make recommendations for change to the system itself. This type of intervention could verge on another turf—the principal's bailiwick of policies and procedures.

Utilization of the social worker's services can be problematic, depending on the circumstances of the school and the district in other ways as well. Although the national agendas found within Goals 2000 and Healthy People 2000 call for more social services to children and their families, fiscal realities can interfere with the provision of these necessary services. Some school districts can only afford to staff several schools with a single social worker who travels from one building to another, splitting time among these buildings. In this type of scenario, the social worker does not have the time to establish long-term relationships with each school and the people who make up its community. We suspect that under these conditions, the bulk of the social worker's time is spent meeting requirements of IEPs by providing "related" services, assisting with the screening of suspected special education children, and providing "quick-fix" services to the children in the most acute phases of crisis. This also could be the case with the social worker split among several rural communities with inordinate amounts of time being spent traveling from one site to another.

Another common scenario is the social worker who provides services in large, urban schools. Many geographical areas are experiencing significant increases in enrollment; hence, these schools are becoming "big and impersonal," with some children perhaps slipping through the cracks and not receiving the services they need. In larger schools, it becomes more difficult to identify the neediest students. Moreover, it is likely that there will be a larger number of students who require assistance. With increased numbers of students, mandated special education services, and a host of other activities, the social worker's time becomes splintered among all the all too many people and services that are necessary for the well-being of all the students.

Although there are no universal answers to these quandaries, principals can take proactive steps with regard to the utilization of the social worker. The following, although not definitive answers, are suggestions that we believe are useful. We encourage principals to do the following:

1. Work with the social worker, agree on the role of the social worker in your building. Include other members of the support staff (e.g., school counselor, psychologist, nurse, teachers). This shared work can assist in the formation of the student support team. Role expectation and duty become clear, and "turf" issues lessen.

2. Develop a description of the services the social worker is available to offer to students, parents, and teachers and make this description available to parents and teachers.

3. Allow the types of services that are most important to the school and its community (e.g., clinical, one-on-one, group-oriented) to continually change as needs of the school community change. This can be achieved by periodically assessing existing services and their overall effect on community members who utilize the social worker.

4. Coordinate with other building principals who share a social worker between schools within the same district so that the expectations in one building do not conflict with those in another building.

Because of time constraints and difficulties in scheduling common free time with teachers, it is often difficult for teachers and social workers to find the time to communicate about students and their needs. As a result, teachers often need to meet with the social worker before school, during lunch periods, and after school. If a common time can be found for teachers and support staff to meet, more interaction can occur between the teachers and the social worker. Social workers need to be part of the system whereby they can meet and work collaboratively with teachers. A powerful partnership between teachers and the social worker can be more beneficial to the system than a reactive "patch and fix" one. To achieve more harmony between teachers and the social worker, principals need to adjust schedules to build in common times for communication.

Principals also need to support ways in which the social worker can have access to parents and the home environment. This access becomes problematic because many children come from two-parent working homes or possibly single-parent working homes. So-

cial workers often need to do home visitations in the late afternoons and evenings, well after the school day has concluded. But, increased outreach to parents can take many shapes. For example, some schools offer evening group sessions for parents of children who have been identified with similar problems.

With more emphasis on dealing with multiple issues that negatively affect the lives of children (e.g., medical, social, and psychological) and the emergence of more comprehensive services being offered in the schools (e.g., school-linked and -based health clinics and services), the school social worker frequently functions as a case manager where "Professional assistance is required in linking these clients with agencies in the community which can address their identified needs. Without this specialized assistance, these clients will not receive necessary services [and] may further deteriorate . . ." (Brown, 1992, p. 61). Although there is an increase in the number of schools that are moving to become more fully inclusive (see Dryfoos, 1994, for example), many schools do not have the much needed resources to meet the needs of their children. Therefore, school social workers spend countless hours "connecting" social services from outside of the school to meet the needs of children and their families.

ILLUSTRATIVE PRACTICES AND ISSUES

Marsiglia, F. F., & Johnson, M. J. (1997). Social work with groups and the performing arts in the schools. *Social Work in Education, 19*(1), 53–59.

Marsiglia and Johnson describe a unique model that joins social work with groups and the performing arts and is, according to the authors, a "culturally grounded approach to social work with group aims to create environments in which the whole child is acknowledged, supported, and empowered" (p. 53). Creative dramatics (e.g., modern dance) are used to help form groups by helping group members break down barriers in communicating with one another. The model designed by Marsiglia and Johnson was piloted in a middle school. The stages of the program are discussed in great detail. The discussion and implications section details the benefits and future directions for research. *Issues:* Integration and multidisciplinary aspects of planning a SWGPA type program are discussed. The involvement of support staff (e.g., social worker and counselors) with classroom teachers to identify students is examined.

SUMMARY

We began this chapter with an exploration of the history of the school social worker. It is interesting to note that the first wave of school social workers in the early-1900s school had a concern for providing services that could enhance the child's possibility for success in school. Costin (1969) is quoted as saying that the school social worker has a "Realization of the strategic place of school and education in the lives of children and youth, coupled with concern for the relevancy of education to the child's present and future" (p. 440). We found it interesting that the central aim of the school social worker has not changed very much since the early 1900s.

School social workers can enhance the overall functioning of children in the school environment. The role of the social worker can be cast as a change agent, a link, and a conduit for networking with others both within and outside of the school system to provide for the needs of children. As children become more "needy," the work of school social workers will continue to increase. With these increases there will be a need for a variety of services that can be provided by, for example, one-on-one counseling and group work. The method of service is not the central issue. Rather, the issue is to empower the school social worker to provide a variety of services that best meet the identified and emerging needs of students. This aim can only be achieved if the school principal works in tandem with the school social worker in identifying new directions.

QUESTIONS FOR FURTHER CONSIDERATION

Research

1. Conflict resolution and mediation programs in schools have emerged at a rapid rate. Examine the various conflict resolution–remediation program designs and develop a program for your building. Highlight: (1) goals and objectives, (2) personnel to be involved, (3) the use of peer mediation as part of the program design, (4) the type of administrative support needed for the program to be successful, (5) the types of training needed for the personnel involved, and (6) the integration of the program into the school system itself (e.g., what are the limitations and potential areas that need direct intervention by the administrator?).

2. Examine the needs of your school system. Develop a community resource packet for parents. What items and agencies would need to be included in this packet and why? What issues surround using these community-based resources? Does distributing the packet to parents constitute the making of a recommendation?

3. Consult school-district policy surrounding the reporting of suspected child abuse. Discuss with a social worker what procedures for reporting suspected child abuse exist. Who would be involved in the process? What are the legal implications of not reporting child abuse in your state?

Reflect

1. Currently, what external forces prevent children from being productive in school? How does the principal work with the school social worker to address these external forces that seep into the school?

2. What internal forces found in your school cause children to be unsuccessful? As a building-level administrator, how can you utilize the services of the school social worker to address these issues?

3. From a systems perspective, how can the school social worker assist the school administrator making changes within the school?

4. Many social workers have itinerant assignments. With this in mind, what types of activities and programs can the school social worker develop with a limited amount of time in a single building?

Respond/React

1. Has the perception of what is meant by "delinquent" changed over time? Compare and contrast these ideas (past and present). What trends do you predict for the future?

2. The work of the school social worker often extends the boundaries of the school day in location and in time. Should the school social worker be allowed to develop his or her own work schedule? What problems could this "flex scheduling" have on the daily operations of the school?

3. The school social worker can be involved in a variety ways within the school. Should the school social worker be involved in classroom instruction? Elaborate.

SUGGESTED READINGS

Allen-Meares, P., Washington, R. O., & Welsh, B. L. (1996). *Social work services in schools* (2nd ed.). Boston: Allyn and Bacon.

Allen-Meyers, P. (1991). The contribution of social workers to schooling. In R. Constable, J. P. Flynn, & S. McDonald (Eds.), *School social work: Practice and research perspectives* (2nd ed., pp. 5–16). Chicago: Lyceum Books.

Clark, J. P. (1992). (Ed.). *Best practices in the supervision of school social work programs.* Des Moines, IO: Iowa Department of Education, Bureau of Special Education.

Dryfoos, J. G. (1994). *Full-service schools: A revolution in health and social services for children, youth, and families.* San Francisco: Jossey-Bass.

Freeman, E M., & Pennekamp, M. (1988). *Social work practice: Toward a child, family, school, community perspective.* Springfield, IL: Charles A. Thomas.

Specht, H., & Courtney, M. E. (1994). *Unfaithful angels: How social work has abolished its mission.* New York: The Free Press.

Winters, W. G., & Easton, F. (1983). *The practice of social work in schools: An ecological perspective.* New York: The Free Press.

Zastrow, C. (1996). *Introduction to social work and social welfare* (6th ed.). Pacific Grove, CA: Brooks/Cole.

CHAPTER 16

SCHOOL-TO-WORK

The School-to-Work Opportunities Act of 1994 is a federal initiative to provide money to states and local education agencies (LEAs) to address the following problems:

- Three-fourths of high school students in the United States enter the workforce without baccalaureate degrees, and many do not possess the academic and entry-level occupational skills necessary to succeed in the changing United States workplace.
- A substantial number of youths in the United States, especially disadvantaged students, students of diverse racial, ethnic, and cultural backgrounds, and students with disabilities, do not complete high school. (p. 4)

In addition to the above two problems, the School-to-Work Opportunities Act lists eight others. In short, the other eight are:

- An intolerably high unemployment rate among the youth and an increasing disparity in earnings between high school graduates and those with additional education.
- New technologies in the workplace that are shrinking the demand for and undermining the earning power of unskilled labor.
- The lack of a comprehensive and coherent system to make an effective transition from school to career-oriented work or to further education and training.
- Students can learn higher levels of both academic and occupational standards within a context than in the abstract.
- While many students have part-time jobs, there is infrequent linkage between such jobs and career planning or exploration, or the school-based learning, of such students.

- Work-based learning combined with school-based learning can be an effective approach.
- Federal resources currently fund a variety of categorical, work-related education and training programs that are not administered as a coherent whole.
- In 1992 about 11 percent of the age group 16 to 24 had not completed high school and were not enrolled in any kind of school, indicating that this group is particularly unprepared for the twenty-first century.

Given the above problems, the Act is intended to provide resources to states and local education agencies to begin addressing them.

The purposes of the Act include facilitating education reform, especially within the context of *Goals 2000: Educate America Act* (1994) and "offer(ing) opportunities for all students to participate in performance-based education and training programs that will enable the students to earn portable credentials, prepare (them) for first jobs in high-skill, high-wage careers; and increase their opportunities for further education, including education in a 4-year college or university" (School-to-Work Opportunities Act of 1994, p. 5). Other purposes include involving employers (both private and public) as partners with all levels of schooling, including postsecondary, as well as labor organizations, community organization, parents, and students. The intent is to establish a network or system of entities, the thrust of which is to improve school-based education, by making it more relevant to work or career. It is hoped that this concerted effort will help establish work-based learning experiences that will help students explore work and career opportunities.

The School-to-Work Opportunity Act is to be administered jointly by the Secretary of Labor and the Secretary of Education. That the Secretary of Labor is involved and by virtue of the very title of the Act, one could assume school-to-work is somehow related to vocational education. Despite some of the wording of the Act regarding "all students" and the "creation of a universal . . . system," and the rhetoric of some school-to-work advocates, the Act appears to us to be targeting "the forgotten half," namely, those students who are neither in a vocational track nor in the highest college preparation track yet aspire to "go to college," only to either never begin or drop-out after a semester or two and end up in low-paying jobs for which they have been poorly prepared. Focusing on this group of students is not bad, but it can be confusing to the administrator if he or she is targeting a group of students different from what other partners in the system are targeting.

School-to-work is simply too recent to have any kind of history. Because of its connection to vocational education, however, a brief look at its history will provide some context for understanding better the school-to-work possibilities.

HISTORY

An excellent account of the history of vocational education is provided by Copa and Bentley (1992). The brief account that follows is based on their account, unless otherwise indicated.

The Smith-Hughes Act of 1917, also known as the National Vocational Education Act, established vocational education as a part of the high school curriculum. The subfields of vocational education are agriculture, business, career, health occupations, home economics, industrial education, and marketing education. Each of these subfields existed in some form or other during the nineteenth century, but the Smith-Hughes Act of 1917 can be viewed as the official beginning of vocational education.

Agricultural Education

When the percentage of families living on farms was greater than it is currently, agricultural education was a high priority in secondary education. "In the 1990s only three percent of the American people are farmers" (p. 913). One of the adjustments that occurred was

embodied in the Vocational Education Act of 1963. With its passage, "the agricultural curriculum was to give attention to preparing students for both farm *and* off-farm agricultural occupations" (p. 893, emphasis in the original).

An upshot of the 1963 Vocational Education Act was a broadening of goals for agricultural education to explore related career opportunities in agriculture and develop abilities in human relations and effective leadership appropriate to agricultural occupations. In addition, the areas for possible instruction in agriculture were expanded to include agricultural production, supplies, mechanics, and products as well as ornamental horticulture and forestry.

Business Education

Originally called commercial education, business education was well established in private schools in the nineteenth century, but did not have much of a presence in public schools until the 1920s and 1930s when the public high school was trying to accommodate a wider cross section of students. The core of business education subjects included bookkeeping, commercial arithmetic, business writing, shorthand, and typing.

Early leaders in business education were mindful of adjusting the curriculum to reflect changes in the business world. By the 1950s economic literacy was added to the curriculum, and the dual intent of teaching about business as well as for business occupations was established. Currently there is consumer economics as well as economic education, and shorthand has been replaced with data processing.

Career Education

Frank Parsons, discussed in Chapter 9, Guidance and Counseling, was responsible for introducing career education into the public schools. In 1909 his book, *Choosing a Vocation,* was published and set the stage for teachers and counselors to begin helping students choose an occupation. By the 1970s career education took on a somewhat different meaning.

The idea that career education was for everybody, as the advocates of the 1970s insisted, meant career information and exploration were moving beyond the confines of vocational education. With federal funding in the 1970s and the establishment of an office of career education, a great deal of activity on career development occurred, even at the elementary school level. And just as quickly as it surfaced in 1971, its funding was withdrawn in 1981. "In summary, the career education movement of the 1970s is too close to the present moment to assess with precision" (p. 926).

Health Occupations Education

"The development of health occupations education is closely related to the history of the education of working class women in the United States" (pp. 903–904). Training in practical nursing was common in the nineteenth century, but the Smith-Hughes Act of 1917 provided a great impetus for the public schools to take it over. The George-Barden Act of 1946, and its amended version in 1956, that established state-level leadership for practical nursing, served to establish health occupations education as a separate entity from the more generic industrial education.

In the 1970s and 1980s health occupations education was provided another boost by the U.S. Department of Education establishing the position of a secondary and postsecondary Health Occupation Education Program Specialist. Health occupations education (HOE) has grown to include several areas in the public schools:

1. Health careers orientation programs, provided at grades K through 8
2. Health career exploratory programs, provided at grades 9 and 10, in which students are exposed to health options in cluster groupings and given the opportunity to participate in hands-on, related activities
3. Health occupations programs provided at grades 10, 11, and 12, in which students are provided skill development in two or more health occupations
4. Health occupations programs provided at grades 11 and 12, in which students are offered training in a single health occupation, with nursing-related programs the most prevalent (p. 925)

Home Economics

Informal education of young girls in household responsibilities was a staple of early American development. The heightened immigration, especially of poverty-stricken families in the nineteenth century, helped to formalize the teaching of primarily female roles to more than just middle class girls. "By the 1890s, domestic science, as it was then called, had been introduced into many U.S. public schools" (p. 897). The science aspect was legitimate in that early advocates applied scientific knowledge to the understanding of food, clothing, and shelter. With the passage of the Smith-Hughes Act of 1917, most of the seventh and eighth grade girls were required to take home economics.

By the 1930s, the home economics curriculum expanded to include "the family and its relationships; the house, its equipment and management; family economics; food and nutrition; textiles and clothing" (p. 898). By 1963 the name of the field was temporarily changed to consumer and homemaking education, reflecting an even more encompassing curriculum, for example, the needs of minorities, the cognitive aspects of child development, the concern for the environment, and the concern for the disenfranchised. The original name persists in the 1990s, and there is still debate about the various purposes home economics should pursue.

Industrial Education

Within all of vocational education, industrial education comes the closest to representing a general education interest over a relatively narrow vocational interest. Although rooted in the nineteenth century, along with most of the other vocational education subfields, industrial education was seen as more of a source or springboard for general education than as a funnel for specific occupations.

The Smith-Hughes Act of 1917 served to separate industrial education from vocational industrial education. The former received no funding, but the latter did. Influenced by the progressive education movement, industrial education, also known as industrial arts education, was promoted as relevant to all levels of schooling. Only during World Wars I and II however, did students in industrial arts do similar work as those in vocational industrial education, in that both groups made articles in school for the direct benefit to the war efforts. Previously, industrial arts students seldom engaged in any kind of practical activities.

Philosophical differences kept industrial arts education separate from vocational industrial education, and it was not until 1972, when Congress began funding industrial arts education, that the differences became less marked. By the 1980s industrial arts education became known as industrial technology. Technology was viewed "as an integral part of human adaptive systems" (p. 919). Six classes of inputs into the system (people, knowledge, materials, energy, capital, and finance) are affected by various processes (the actions and practices applied to the inputs) that produce outputs in "the form of products, services, or desired conditions of the environment" (p. 919). The level of abstraction inherent in this example of industrial technology curriculum reveals the original purpose of being applicable to all levels of schooling and not just an eleventh- and twelfth-grade preparation for an occupation.

Marketing Education

Originally known as distributive education, marketing education separated itself from business education in 1936 through funding from the George-Deen Act, an extension of the Smith-Hughes Act of 1917. Distributive education started with an adult, postsecondary school emphasis, but by the 1940s and 1950s was part of most secondary school programs. DECA (Distributive Education Clubs of America) was founded in 1948 with the purposes of "developing leadership, vocational understanding, civic consciousness, and social intelligence" (p. 902).

Distributive education made great use of a work experience component in its program. Although still school-based, the work experience made instruction more relevant to the context of work, whether it was an entry-level job, a career-sustaining job, a specialization, or an entrepreneurial job.

By 1963 the four areas of subject matter for marketing education were "social skills, basic skills, product or service technology, and marketing skills" (p. 920).

In 1978 the U.S. Office of Education added economic concepts of private enterprise as a fifth area of subject matter. One of the exemplary state curriculum guides for marketing education is by the Wisconsin Department of Public Instruction, published in 1987. It contains "a conceptual framework for marketing education made up of 'foundations' and 'functions' that address marketing education at various career levels" (p. 923).

General Vocational Education

Vocational education has always meant teaching people so they learn to work. The variety of forms this teaching has taken is great. From Ben Franklin's academy in 1751 through lyceums on the frontier, to the manual training in public schools reflecting the influence of Pestalozzi, vocational education has been about teaching young people to work, more than anything else. Certainly there was (and still is) an interest in general vocational education. Historically, industrial arts and career education have come the closest to demonstrating relevance to general education. The distinction between general and specific vocational education is readily apparent when lists of topics or areas or skills are made. General vocational education includes technology education, consumer education, family life education, career education, and economic education.

More specific vocational education includes secretarial education, sales education, agribusiness education, health occupations education, and transportation occupations education. The traditional categories of vocational education discussed above can have both kinds of content. The variety of subfields (e.g., health education and marketing education) and the different levels of abstraction of topics within the subfields should remind the reader of Gardner's (1993) multiple intelligences, "some of which are directly (and perhaps uniquely) addressed by vocational education in the K–12 curriculum" (p. 933).

CURRENT STATUS

School-to-work emerges out of the above context as an effort, it seems to us, to capitalize on several features of vocational education that have withstood the test of time. One feature is the partnership/cooperative arrangement between school and other sites. The School-to-Work Opportunities Act (1994) states,

> [Another purpose of this act is] to promote the formation of local partnerships that are dedicated to linking the worlds of school and work among secondary schools and postsecondary educational institutions, private and public employers, labor organization, government, community-based organizations, parents, students, state educational agencies, local educational agencies, and training and human service agencies; (p. 5)

In addition to the partnerships common to most vocational education programs, the recognition of an emphasis on learning at sites other than the school is another feature of the Act:

> [Another purpose is] to utilize workplaces as active learning environments in the educational process by making employers joint partners with educators in providing opportunities for all students to participate in high-quality, work-based learning experiences; (p. 5)

And lest anyone be concerned that the Act is not for all students, even the traditional college-bound, another purpose is:

> to help all students attain high academic and occupational standards; and to improve the knowledge and skills of youths by integrating academic and occupational learning, integrating school-based and work-based learning and building effective linkages between secondary and postsecondary education; (p. 6)

Finally, "all students" is made even more explicit:

> The term "all students" means both male and female students from a broad range of backgrounds and circumstances, including disadvantaged students, students with diverse racial, ethnic, or cultural backgrounds, American Indians, Alaska Natives, Native Hawaiians, students with disabilities, students with limited English proficiency, migrant children, school dropouts, and academically talented students; (p. 6)

All of the above, and more, that only a read of the Act will reveal, is intended to result in the award of:

1) a high school diploma or its equivalent, such as—
   a) a general equivalency diploma (GED); or
   b) an alternative diploma or certificate for students with disabilities for whom such alternative diploma or certificate is appropriate;

2) a certificate or diploma recognizing successful completion of 1 or 2 years of postsecondary education (if appropriate); and
3) a skill certificate; and (or)
   May lead to further education and training, such as entry into a registered apprenticeship program, or *may lead to admission to a 2- or 4-year college or university.* (p. 8 emphasis added)

The intent seems clear: The schools will establish partnerships with a variety of local and state entities, involve the students in work-based as well as school-based learning, and include all students.

Reminiscent of career education of the 1970s, the STW Act says a proposal shall include:

> career awareness and career exploration and counseling (beginning at the earliest possible age, but not later than the 7th grade) in order to help students who may be interested to identify, and select or reconsider, their interests, goals, and career majors, including those options that may not be traditional for their gender, race, or ethnicity; (p. 12)

Selection of a "career major" should occur not later than the beginning of the eleventh grade. A career major is "a coherent sequence of courses or field of study that prepares a student for a first job and that—

1) integrates academic and occupational learning, integrates school-based and work-based learning, establishes linkages between secondary schools and post secondary educational institutions;
2) prepares the student for employment in a broad occupational cluster or industry sector;
3) typically includes at least 2 years of secondary education and at least 1 or 2 years of postsecondary education;
4) provides the students, to the extent practicable, with strong experience in and understanding of all aspects of the industry the students are planning to enter. (pp. 7–8)

The specific requirements for the work-based learning component are:

1) work experience;
2) a planned program of job training and work experiences (including training related to preemployment and employment skills to be mastered at progressively higher levels) that are coordinated

with learning in the school-based learning component . . . and are relevant to the career majors of students . . . ;

3) workplace mentoring;
4) instruction in workplace competencies, including instruction and activity related to developing positive work attitudes, and employability and participative skills; and
5) broad instruction, to the extent practicable in all aspects of the industry. (p. 13)

It is permissible, according to the Act, to have "such activities as paid work experience, job shadowing, school sponsored enterprises, or on-the-job training" (p. 13).

The proposal embedded in the School-to-Work Opportunities Act of 1994 seems to us to address what Gray (1996) calls the "one-way-to-win mentality" and that is the mistaken (according to Gray) belief that a baccalaureate degree is the only way to be successful. This belief helps to explain why enrollment in the high-school vocational education track is less than 20 percent nationally (Gray, 1996). Gray sums up the situation this way:

> According to conventional wisdom, the fact that two thirds of all high school graduates go on to higher education directly after high school is cause for pride and celebration; the idea that there may be victims in the process is unheard of. Yet the euphoria over baccalaureate education seems misplaced when the data suggest that, at best, only half of those who matriculate ever graduate and that, of those who earn a bachelor's degree, at least one third will end up underemployed. (p. 531)

The tragedy, according to Gray, is that parents, teachers, and counselors continue to misadvise adolescents about getting a bachelor's degree. Citing researchers from the U.S. Department of Labor, Gray (1996) claims "lifetime earnings of individuals who work in such occupations as precision metals, the crafts, specialized repair, and other nonprofessional technical occupations will exceed the earnings of all college graduates save for those who are successful in finding work in the professional or managerial ranks" (p. 532).

The solution Gray proposes is multifaceted, involving changing the way guidance is offered, changing the "general" college-prep curriculum, and

changing the culture, at least of the high school, where the college-bound students are considered the elite. According to Gray (1996), the alternatives to the four-year degree:

> lie in the numerous high-skills/high-wage occupations where jobs are going unfilled. An associate's degree or a certificate program in a technical field related to nonprofessional, high-skills/high-wage work is the best way for many high school graduates—especially those graduating in the middle of their high school class—to prepare for a career. (p. 532)

The School-to-Work Opportunities Act of 1994, though never specifically referred to by Gray, seems to be on target in addressing these alternatives.

Undoubtedly, the publication in 1983 of the National Commission on Excellence in Education's *A Nation At Risk* contributed to strengthening the link between public schools and the nation's economy, providing a backdrop, if not a galvanizing effect, for the creation of the School-to-Work Opportunities Act. Knowing some aspects of the background and context out of which the Act emerged may be helpful, but no adequate evaluation of it can occur for many more years since its implementation. Some preliminary activity has occurred in some schools and reports of this activity, as well as conceptual assessments and speculations, can be reported.

Goldberger and Kazis (1996) report on their experiences working with Jobs for the Future, a Boston-based agency that assists schools in making the transition from traditional practices to those that seem to hold greater promise for larger numbers of students—especially those students that the traditional high schools serve poorly. The authors substitute school-to-career for school-to-work because the latter has negative connotations resulting, they think, from the belief that school-to-work implies a one-time transition to an entry-level job. School-to-career, by contrast, suggests a broader view of work and a variety of pathways.

Essentially, Goldberger and Kazis (1996) believe the school-to-career movement "is motivated by two related, but distinct goals for young people:

1. Improved educational performance and advancement

2. Improved employment and career prospects (p. 548)

Achieving the two goals requires establishing and maintaining "a delicate balancing act" (p. 548). School people must see the advantages in terms of number of students affected and ways in which teaching and learning are improved. At the same time, those at the work sites must be convinced there are enough students involved to be prepared, including screened, for their potential pool of employees. Goldberger and Kazis go on to critique three approaches that in their view, fail to achieve what the School-to-Work Opportunity Act proposes and then describe their version of what a successful school-to-career initiative would be like.

The first approach Goldberger and Kazis review is the maintaining of rigid college preparation and technical training tracks. They believe these divisions foreclose options for most students in that high-stakes decisions are made at a relatively tender age. Also, this separation exacerbates the "class" system in high schools and tends to make more remote the possibility that academic subjects will ever be associated with the world of work. And it is this infusion, association, or contextualization of academic concepts with work that can make some subjects more appealing to a greater number of students.

The second approach that is found wanting is that which has a job-specific vocational education program. The authors note that only about one out of four participants in such specific training finds employment in the field for which he or she was trained. They advocate for "more generic academic and technical learning" (p. 549). Specialized training, they believe, should be provided at the postsecondary level.

The third approach is one that begins at the eleventh grade when students are old enough to enter the paid labor market. Goldberger and Kazis believe that too many students have dropped out of school by then and therefore are missed entirely. In addition, they encourage beginning as early as middle school to achieve two important goals—to make academic classes more relevant to students, thereby improving their achievement within them and to introduce students to the variety of career options by having ex-

ploratory experiences within a number of careers before their last 2 years of high school.

Goldberger and Kazis (1996) advocate four design principles for successful school-to-career programs:

1. High schools should be organized around non-tracked, thematic programs of study designed to prepare all students for entry into both higher education and high-skill employment through intellectually rigorous practical education.
2. Selection of a career-focused program of study in high school should be based on general interests and should not be a high-stakes career decision.
3. Work-based learning should be an integral part of the core curriculum for all students, because it yields benefits that school-based education alone cannot provide.
4. The integration of secondary and postsecondary learning environments is critical to the development of rigorous programs of career-related education. (1996, p. 550)

All of the above principles are consistent with the School-to-Work Opportunities Act of 1994. In addition, the authors claim that their principles are consistent with the 1994 recommendations of the National Assessment of Vocational Education. Goldberger and Kazis go further, however, in that they advocate changing the quality of teaching and learning in all high schools.

Thematic programs of study would be "at the heart" of their proposal. Examples could be health care, finance, and industrial and engineering systems. Such themes permit, indeed, require, an interdisciplinary approach. Teams of teachers could work together in clusters or schools-within-schools configurations. "Broad educational goals rather than training requirements for specific careers would drive program design. However, employers would be involved in designing curriculum and in setting expectations for what students should know and be able to demonstrate upon graduation from high school" (Goldberger & Kazis, 1996, p. 550).

Choice of a theme or occupational cluster would be based on interest and not be a high-stakes decision. Whatever career cluster would be chosen would have room for such activities as a student newspaper or an arts component. Management or business interests too could be pursued within a variety of clusters. And students could opt out of a particular choice without penalty. Teachers and counselors would be helping students explore the various facets of a career and in making decisions about new ones. Goldberger and Kazis mention such career academies in California, Philadelphia, Portland, Oregon, Boston, and Cambridge.

The greatest challenge may be the identification of appropriate worksites. A community would have to enlist private and public employers who would be willing to be partners with schools in providing work-based learning sites. Although exploration of worksites would begin as early as the middle school, Goldberger and Kazis recommend waiting until the eleventh and twelfth grades before students spend very much time at worksites.

Integrating high schools and postsecondary learning environments has two effects. One is to make the transition from high school to a training facility easier. Vocational technical schools, for example, would be important partners in helping to provide a seamless transition from high school to advanced technical training. The other effect involves colleges and universities and their admissions requirements. Adjustments in admissions requirements could be worked out in a partnership arrangement with certain colleges and universities. The authors indicate that some dialogue has already been initiated about such adjustments in Wisconsin and Oregon.

Many questions remain unanswered, but Goldberger and Kazis's article addresses the major ones. Similarly, Grubb (1996) examines the School-to-Work Opportunities Act and offers his assessment of its potential.

Grubb (1996) targets the release of *A Nation at Risk* in 1983 as the impetus for using an economic rationale for school reform. He considers school-to-work the "new vocationalism" that is made up of several strands. One strand included increasing standards for graduation from high school that had the effect of reducing enrollment in vocational education.

Another strand involved improving the teaching of "work place basics" through experiential learning and contextualized teaching. The third strand was to broaden conventional (read specialized) vocational education and connect it better to academic content. Tech-prep programs that are linked to broader conceptions of occupations and include an articulation with postsecondary schools are examples of this third strand.

The fourth strand Grubb discusses was embodied in the School-to-Work-Opportunities Act of 1994. This strand incorporates "school-based learning (in which academic and vocational education would be integrated within 'career majors' and linked to at least one year of postsecondary education); a work-based component; and 'connecting activities' to make school-based learning consistent with work-based learning" (1996, p. 538).

In Grubb's conception of the four strands, including the Act, there could continue to be a separation between academic and vocational tracks. The fifth strand Grubb discusses has much greater potential for school reform and can be manifested in programs similar to those described by Goldberger and Kazis (1996).

Career academies can be viewed as schools-within-schools. Typically, according to Grubb, "four teachers collaborate: one each in math, English, science, and the occupational area that defines the academy (health, electronics, finance, tourism, and so on)" (p. 539). Students take all four subjects from these same teachers for 2 or 3 years. (Other subjects are taken in the "regular" high school.) Opportunities for working on projects that are interdisciplinary are greater with this arrangement. Establishing partnerships with worksites is more manageable because of the smaller numbers of teachers and students involved. Finally, a sense of community among teachers and students is more likely to be achieved because of the prolonged association. This last point makes cooperative learning experiences more likely to be successful and instills a sense of identity so often missing in large high schools.

Clusters are like academies for all students. "Clusters are usually broad occupational or industry-based groupings that reflect local labor markets and structure the curriculum of the remaining two or three years of high school accordingly" (p. 539). As with the career academies, the cluster provides a focus for students and usually has a required sequence of courses. Also like academies, clusters promote a sense of community and identity.

Occupational high schools and magnet schools are similar to academies, but schoolwide and usually dedicated to one occupational cluster. Established examples are Aviation High School, the High School of Fashion Industries, and the Murry Bergstraum High School for Business Careers in New York. Magnet schools, designed for desegregation, often have an occupational cluster as their focus.

Grubb, like Goldberger and Kazis, sees the potential for school reform in the school-to-work movement and is cautiously optimistic "that the schools can avoid the prospect of 'reforming again and again and again'" (p. 544).

CONTEMPORARY ISSUES

Unlike some other chapters, this one deals with a contemporary topic—one that has only recently emerged and around which only a few practices have begun or speculation ensued. It would be premature to discuss issues other than those presented or implied in the previous section, and then we run the risk of redundancy. One issue bears mentioning here, however, because of its relevance to change.

The degree to which students, teachers, and administrators, as well as parents and other school-linked partners, can feel a sense of ownership in whatever form the school-to-work initiative takes, is likely to be the degree to which the change will be successful. Federal monies can attract some interest—usually from administrators before teachers—but if a majority of the participants, and preferably nearly all of them, are not in favor of changing toward a school-to-work model, there can be little optimism for the change, if it occurs at all, to be successful and sustained. "Top-down" decisions are the bane of teachers and unless there is some version of a "grass roots" movement for the reforms associated with school-to-work, it will likely be one of those reforms that is experienced again and again and again.

ILLUSTRATIVE PRACTICES AND ISSUES

Bluestein, D., Phillips, S., Jobin-Davis, K., Finkelberg, S., & Roarke, A. (1997). A theory-building investigation of the school-to-work transition. *The Counseling Psychologist, 25*(3), 364–402.

> A research project attempts to build a theory base to understand better the transition of school-to-work. *Issues:* The article raises important concerns that need to be considered in school-based school-to-work programs.

SUMMARY

The School-to-Work Opportunities Act of 1994 is enabling legislation for states to establish a system of school-linked partnerships among employers, postsecondary education, and a host of other entities, all of whom would assist in increasing the relevance of a high school education to a majority of its students. The Act is a kind of "new vocationalism" that seeks to broaden vocational education and all of its subfields.

This Act is seen by some as a vehicle for reforming secondary education. At the very least vocational education would be infused with more academic subject matter and connections with postsecondary education would be improved. The Act has the potential for making traditional academic subjects more contextualized (in terms of the working world) and by requiring work-based learning would improve vocational learning and thereby enhance the quality of the prospective employee pool.

Although it is way too early to determine how well the initiative will work or what the nature of its impact will be on schools and communities, the prospects for success warrant a cautious optimism.

QUESTIONS FOR FURTHER CONSIDERATION

Research

1. School-to-work initiatives have shifted to be inclusive of all students, regardless of ability level. Explore the reasons why many college-bound students are reluctant to be involved in these programs.

2. Utilizing the information presented in this chapter and from independent reading, determine the most important features of a school-to-work program?

Reflect

1. If you are a principal in a unified district that includes elementary, middle, and high schools, how could elementary and middle-level experiences lead into a school-to-work program, which is typically associated exclusively with the high school level? How would you begin the articulation needed among grade levels to ensure that once students entered high school they would be more ready to begin a school-to-work experience?

2. School-to-work programs are interdisciplinary in nature. How would you, for example, include such areas as math, science, and physical education in such a program?

3. What types of human and fiscal resources are need to maintain a school-to-work program? What role does the community play in this kind of initiative?

Respond/React

1. Statement: Only "slow" students need school-to-work opportunities. Is this an accurate statement? Elaborate.

2. School-to-work programs, like other curricular programs, need to be continuously monitored and evaluated so that they may be more responsive to the needs of the school and community. How should the external school community be involved in these evaluations?

SUGGESTED READINGS

Copa, G. H., & Bentley, C. B. (1992). Vocational education. In P. W. Jackson (Ed.), *Handbook of research on education* (pp. 891–944). New York: Macmillan.

Goldberger, S., & Kazis, R. Revitalizing high schools: What the school-to-career movement can contribute. *Phi Delta Kappan, 77,* 547–554.

Gray, K. (1996). The baccalaureate games: Is it right for all teens? *Phi Delta Kappan, 77,* 528–534.

Grubb, W. N. (1966). The new vocationalism: What it is, what it could be. *Phi Delta Kappan, 77,* 535–546.

CHAPTER 17

SPECIAL EDUCATION

Special education programs, procedures, and services are a part of every school system—urban, suburban, rural—and are found in just about every type of school system—private, public, parochial. Although each system provides its own rendition of programs to meet the needs of special students, this was not, however, always the case. The development of special education programs and services has not been an easy road to travel for students, parents, and school officials. The road has been rocky with many sharp turns and detours.

This chapter addresses special education from the late 1950s to the present day, offering an overview of the court cases, legislation, and movements brought about by an increasing awareness of special needs students and the decisions that schools have had to make as a result of changed attitudes about such students. From knowing and understanding the past can come a better conceptual framework for supervising and administering current and special education programs of the future.

HISTORY

A comprehensive history of special education can be found in the book, *Special Education Policies: Their History, Implementation, and Finance* (1983), edited by Chambers and Hartman. One of the book's contributors, Lazerson (1983), chronicles the emergence of special education in the early 1900s. Lazerson details the "tensions between humanitarian and controlling aims between concern to enhance the lives of the handicapped and to protect "normals" from the handicapped" (p. 21). This tension between "humanitarian" and "controlling" aims is consistent with the development of the field of special education, as Lazerson further accounts, "Special education received its impetus from the enforcement of compulsory attendance legislation, the retardation studies which showed large num-

bers of children overage for their classes, and the association of retardation with the foreign-born, truants, and the mentally deficient" (p. 20). This discussion could be extended with the inclusion of Terman's intelligence studies and the impact of large numbers of children in the 1920s and 1930s, who because of low IQ scores, were classified as slow or special. A discussion of intelligence and the IQ movement is provided in detail in Chapter 8, Gifted and Talented. Tweedie (1983) indicates, "The severely handicapped were viewed as something less than human creatures, to be treated as decently as limited charity would allow, not as persons with rights" (p. 48). During the early 1900s, however, special education was the responsibility of parents and institutions, not public schools.

The 1950s were relatively quiet and uneventful on special education legislation and litigation. The Grants for Teaching in the Education of Handicapped Children Act (1958, repealed 1970), Public Law 85-926, was the first national commitment to provide resources for children with disabilities by providing funding to colleges and universities to train individuals who wanted to teach children classified as mentally retarded. Public Law 85-926 acknowledged the increasing numbers of students who needed to be educated by properly trained individuals.

In the 1960s, however, the amount of legislation on special education and the unique needs of children with disabilities began to rise. The 1958 Act opened the door for the Mental Retardation Facilities and Community Mental Health Centers Construction Act (1963), Public Law 88-164. This act extended coverage of the previous legislation by including those children who were categorized as deaf, speech-impaired, crippled, and those who had other health impairments. The Facilities and Community Mental Health Centers Construction Act also extended funding to include training for others who worked in school settings (e.g., college and university professors and K–12 school administrators). These two acts widened a once narrow categorization of children who could benefit from special education services, and, moreover, acknowledged the need to improve the training and professional preparation of school personnel who would be working with handicapped children.

The 1960s, considered by most to be a decade of storm, stress, and unrest, was also a time of harsh criticism of special education practices in the United States. Dunn (1968) argued, "A better education than special class placement [is] needed for socioculturally deprived children with mild learning problems who have been labeled educable mentally retarded" (p. 5). Dunn's premise was that too many children were inappropriately being placed in special education programs that were, in this period of history, designed to work almost exclusively with the mentally retarded. Dunn spoke critically of the large numbers of children placed in special education classes who were from minority and/or poverty backgrounds. The prevailing practice of the time was to remove slow learners from regular education classes, thus segregating them from the regular education context of the neighborhood school. Dunn, like others, was concerned about the impact that labeling of children as "special" had on them and their subsequent growth as productive students. Labeling continues to be a perennial problem, although there have been strides at eliminating the stigmatization of receiving special services. Dunn warned schools, parents, and lobbyists about the damages that can occur from such seemingly benign labeling of students, "Our past and present diagnostic procedures . . . have probably been doing more harm than good in that they have resulted in disability labels and in that they have grouped children homogeneously in schools on the basis of these labels" (p. 8). Dunn's words also point to another perennial problem that we still grapple with—diagnosing accurately the specific needs of students. During this time frame, individuals began to challenge the practice of placing mildly handicapped individuals in special classes. Professional organizations at this turning point in special education also helped further the cause of examining such placements. Two influential organizations, the Council for Exceptional Children and the Association for Retarded

Children, both played an active role in elevating the issues of special education to a national level.

Three federal acts in the 1960s had a profound effect on special education: the Civil Rights Act of 1964, the Elementary and Secondary Education Act of 1965, and the Handicapped Children's Early Education Assistance Act of 1968. These legislative acts brought national attention to several inadequacies in the education of children with emotional, physical, and other handicapping conditions. In addition to heightening the public's awareness, of an often forgotten population, many of these acts served as lightening rods to litigation. For example, the Civil Rights Act of 1964 dealt with such issues as equal rights and desegregation. This Act made it possible to address inadequacies not only in education, but also in employment and housing practices. The Civil Rights Act, like the Brown decision (*Brown v. State Board of Education of Topeka, 1954*) a decade earlier, held the mirror to practices in education. The *Brown* case was landmark in as far as the Supreme Court ruled on behalf of Brown's plight to secure an equal education by declaring "separate but equal" was untenable. This ruling essentially reversed the "separate but equal" doctrine and established the principle that social segregation denies the constitutional rights associated with equality of education. This ruling, along with others, would help further the cause of creating legislation to protect the rights of special needs children in schools.

Key Litigation Surrounding Special Education Leads to Legislation

The decade of the 1970s brought great attention to the realm of special education with the landmark Education for All Handicapped Children Act (1975). The Act was a culmination of legislation that began in the late 1950s and has continued to be elaborated and refined.

With the foundation for educational services being secured, the legislation and litigation surrounding special education in the 1970s continued with a renewed furor as lobbyists, parent activist groups, and formal and informal organizations banded together to push for more appropriate services and treatment for children with handicapping conditions. It is interesting to note that "between 1970 and 1975, Congress passed

50 pieces of legislation on the handicapped" (Lazerson, 1983, p. 42). Regarding litigation, Tweedie (1983) noted that by "1973, 27 right-to-education lawsuits in 21 states were pending or recently completed" (p. 53). With this legislation and the increased litigation for the protection of special needs children, this period was a time of inclusion, shutting the door on exclusionary practices of the previous two decades. Tweedie (1983) states that "the history of special education has been a tale of exclusion—the exclusion of the handicapped from school and the exclusion of their representatives from participating in education policymaking" (p. 48). Categories of exceptionality were expanded with the Developmental Disabilities Services and Facilities Construction Amendments of 1970 in that funds were earmarked to promote and support programs for developmentally disabled people who had such handicapping conditions as mental retardation, cerebral palsy, and epilepsy. Section 504 of the Rehabilitation Act of 1973 stated:

> No otherwise qualified handicapped individual in the United States . . . shall, solely by reason of his handicap, be excluded from the participation in, be denied the benefits of, or be subject to discrimination under any program or activity receiving Federal assistance.

The Rehabilitation Act had specific language addressing areas previously not covered by any other legislative statute. For example, the Rehabilitation Act stipulates that all handicapped individuals, regardless of their age, were to be covered. Moreover, stipulations were included for handicapped individuals to participate and/or receive beneficial services equal to those provided to other nonhandicapped individuals. The Rehabilitation Act also states explicitly that the exclusion of handicapped children from school programs constitutes a violation of their civil rights. Perhaps, however, the milestone for special education was the provision provided under the rubric of Section 504 when in 1990, the Act was amended by the Individuals with Disabilities Education Act (1990) (IDEA). Children in regular education programs who had a disability, but who otherwise did not qualify for special education, could be accommodated.

Litigation surrounding the denial of services to the handicapped began to rise in the 1970s. For example, plaintiffs in the *Pennsylvania Association for Retarded Children* (PARC) v. *Pennsylvania,* (1972) alleged that state statutes were unconstitutional under the Equal Protection Clause of the Fourteenth Amendment. The *PARC* court held that Pennsylvania could not exclude special education children from the public schools and that mentally retarded children were entitled to homebound tutoring and similar services. The court also found that statutory language excluding mentally retarded children less than 6 years old was improper. Regarding procedures and policies, the *PARC* case brought about change in that the school district had to (1) identify handicapped children, (2) provide a suitable education, (3) integrate them with children in regular education classes when possible, and (4) provide due process hearings to resolve parental concerns and complaints. Essentially, the stage was set for securing more formidably the rights of special needs students—"the parties recognized that a child could neither be denied admission to a public school nor be subjected to a change in educational status unless formal due process was provided" (Thomas & Russo, 1995, p. 7).

In 1972 another case, *Mills v. Board of Education of the District of Columbia,* further paved the way for providing special education services for children with handicapping conditions. In its finding, the *Mills* court held that the board of education had to provide an education for the plaintiffs and any other children similarly situated by accepting and then providing a comprehensive plan of services for physically and mentally impaired children between the ages of 3 and 21. Another requirement emerging from this landmark case was the duty of the district to hire special education teachers to comply with the court order. The court also underscored the importance of due process that must be given by the district when making decisions that had an effect on the educational program of special needs children. The *Mills* case also declared that a district could not claim insufficient finances as a reason for its failure to provide services to the handicapped.

According to Safford and Safford (1996), the *PARC* and *Mills* cases "established precedent for Free Appropriate Public Education (FAPE), the cornerstone of Public Law 94-142, and *zero inclusion*" (p. 290, emphasis in the original). Persistent tension surrounded the issues of these two court cases. These tensions typically put parents at odds with the school systems. On the one hand, many students who needed services were not receiving them because programs were not clearly defined, nor were the exact needs of students known because identification and screening standards were not sophisticated in nature or a part of the school's program. This limitation in screening and identification procedures often resulted in misplacements. On the other hand, many students who were identified as having special needs were denied services because the primary services provided by schools were, for the most part, geared for the mentally retarded and not for the wide variety and range of the other needs of children with learning disabilities. The eligibility of students to receive services and to attend school became rallying points. We believe that schools have dramatically changed as a result of the decisions of these two significant court cases.

These court cases paved the way for the emergence of the passage of the Rehabilitation Act (1973). This act made clear the fundamental right of every U.S. citizen not to be denied access to programs that were supported by federal funds. The Rehabilitation Act was a springboard to the passage of the Education of All Handicapped Children Act.

The Education of All Handicapped Children Act

The passage of the Education of All Handicapped Children Act (EAHCA) (1975) opened the doors for students with special needs. Chambers and Hartman (1983) indicate the effect of this "was to raise the expectations of parents of handicapped children, special education advocacy groups, and others concerned with the welfare of handicapped children" (p. 3). Moreover, Ferguson (1987) believes that EAHCA "attempts widespread, emancipatory reform in special education. The law mandates inclusion of a variety of previously unserved and undeserved students, including severely handicapped students" (p. 95). The Act was "emancipatory" because the provisions of the act were intended to do away with what Ferguson (1987) claims as "Dispropriate segregation of minority students into special education classes, together with continued exclusion of large numbers of handicapped students . . ." (p. 95).

The due process clause of EAHCA "gives parents the capacity to challenge either denial of services or misclassification, by using the due process hearings as an enforcement or political strategy" (Tweedie, 1983, p. 66).

David and Green (1983) provide an excellent discussion of the provisions of EAHCA that encompasses accessibility of services; identification, evaluation, and prescriptive services to be provided; the development of an IEP (individual educational program); placement of handicapped children in a least restrictive environment (LRE); involvement of parents and others in the processes of identification, evaluation, and prescription of services; and notification of parents before initiating testing and other screenings. Later, we will discuss each one of these areas in terms of administrative responsibility in supervising special education programs because the legislative wording mandates certain procedures and practices to be in operation.

Subsequent Amendments to The Education of All Handicapped Children Act

Changes and modifications to Public Law 94-142 were made in the 1980s and 1990s. In 1986, EAHCA was amended to "provide funding incentives for states that would make a free appropriate public education available for all eligible preschool children with disabilities ages three through five. Provisions were also included to help states develop early intervention programs for infants and toddlers with disabilities" (National Information Center for Children and Youth with Disabilities, 1993, p. 1). In 1990 the Act was amended by Public Law 101-476 and is now referred to as the Individuals with Disabilities Education Act (IDEA). In 1992 the IDEA was amended by Public Law 102-119.

This history of special education has been brief, but it does capture, we believe, the major legislative and judicial milestones. Throughout this overview of special education, several themes have emerged that reveal the tenor of the times as people struggled with providing education to children in a least restrictive environment. Several concepts have emerged and signify philosophical and ideological beliefs about children and the meeting of their needs. To understand these concepts, we will first identify them and then explain what types of services and activities were and, in some cases still are, typically associated with them in schools. It is hoped from these descriptions and elaborations that we will be able to underscore some of the perennial issues that school administrators face as they supervise the coordination of special education programs and services within their buildings.

Tensions Continue

With the enactment of EAHCA and subsequent legislation (e.g., IDEA, 1990), special and regular educators began developing programs that would better help meet the needs of special students. These efforts have come in waves. The first wave of programs and services to meet the needs of special children were the pull-out programs. Typically, students who were identified as having a special need, whether a learning disability, a physical impairment, an emotional disorder, or a giftedness, were pulled out of the regular classroom to receive services. Depending on the degree of the condition, some students were excluded from the regular classroom and placed in what is still referred to as a self-contained classroom environment. Pull-out programs were questioned as to their overall effectiveness in meeting the needs of special students. Meyers, Gelzheiser, and Yelich (1991) indicate that "Pull-out programs have limitations: segregating students unnecessarily, reducing time on task, minimizing classroom teacher responsibility for instruction and fragmenting the curriculum" (p. 7). Moreover, they report "collaboration between classroom and pull-out teachers is inadequate" (p. 7). One of the tenets of developing educational opportunities for special needs students is the importance of communication and interaction among regular and special education teachers, administrators, parents, students, and the larger community served by the school system. More inclusive services soon began to emerge for special needs students. This trend, which continues today, has come in the form of mainstreaming, the Regular Education Initiative (REI), integration, and inclusion—all of which are or were ways of applying the standard of providing students with an education in a least restrictive environment. We believe that there have been tensions surrounding these ways of providing a more inclusive education for special needs students. Moreover, we believe that these tensions are healthy and well worth the experience as schools continue to experiment with ways and methods of embracing all students within the purview of the school and its community, regardless of their exceptionality.

CURRENT STATUS

We will begin by exploring what is meant by the term *least restrictive environment*. Next, we will explore in detail the Regular Education Initiative as well as mainstreaming and inclusion.

Least Restrictive Environment

Perhaps some scholars will disagree with us because we are linking inclusive services and initiatives under the umbrella of least restrictive environment, but the intent of this section is to illustrate some of the major movements in special education as educators grapple with implementing and embracing environments that are inclusive rather than exclusive. The debates, some grounded in research and some in opinion, are all worthy of consideration.

Regular Education Initiative. EAHCA played a significant part in the emergence of the regular education initiative (REI) and inclusion movements that surfaced in the 1970s, 1980s, and 1990s. REI, an initiative that encouraged the placement of handicapped students in the least restrictive environment, was a development that affected both special and regular education students, teachers, and schools. The REI movement grew from issues highlighted in a 1986 speech given by Madeleine Will, then Assistant U.S. Education Secretary. From a historical, philosophical, and moral perspective, Will (1986) believed that "the language and terminology we use in describing our education system is full of the language of separation, of fragmentation, of removal. To the extent that our language reflects the reality of our system as many diverse parts never or rarely connected as a whole, it reflects a flawed vision of education for our children" (p. 412). Will's description of this language mirrored educational services and practices, specifically those services provided for special education students. Will's plea was made before special and regular education teachers and special education administrators from all over the world in this keynote speech at the Wingspread Conference Center in Racine, Wisconsin. Will challenged those closest to these students—teachers and administrators—to rise above the empty rhetoric of providing services, programs, and opportunities in a least restrictive environment by creating interrelated services for special needs students, building by building, district by district, state by state, through creating a vision for inclusion and acceptance. "One thing that can be accomplished is reform at the building level. Building-level administrators often cannot mold all the resources in their building to produce effective programs. Special programs can prevent this. Building-level administrators must be empowered to assemble appropriate professional and other resources for delivering effective, coordinated, comprehensive services for all students based on individual educational needs rather than eligibility for special programs" (Will, 1986, p. 413). These words shook the consciences of the educators who viewed special needs students as separate. Will's message was clear, special needs students and programs need interdisciplinary efforts, referred to in special education as multidisciplinary approaches. This is consistent with Fuchs and Fuchs (1994) portrayal of REI supporters' desire to "merge special and general education into one inclusive system" (p. 297). We will return to this discussion later in this section to highlight the tensions between this initial attempt to merge special and regular education.

There were two underlying issues that fueled the REI movement. The first issue was the labeling of students by a dysfunctional characteristic, usually a learning disability—speech/language impairment, mental handicap, or emotional disturbance. The second issue was the eventual separation of such students from regular education programming so they could receive special education services via pull-out arrangements.

Both issues were the end result of the implementation of EAHCA. This federal law required districts to identify and label students with special needs and to provide services to them. Under this federal mandate of providing a free, appropriate, public education, a preponderance of pull-out special education programs

emerged where resource programs proliferated with the passage of the law in 1975. These procedures, in a sense, created a more restrictive environment.

Those concerned about the labeling and the exclusion of students from the mainstream (regular education classroom) found a platform as early as 1969. Glasser (1969, cited in Gardner, 1977) stated, "We must and we can find ways to help them gain enough from regular schools and regular classes so that they need not be removed from them for individual and group treatment by specialists. The specialist in the schools—counselors, psychologists, remedial instructors—should help the teacher in the classroom cope with the problems she has, both disciplinary and educational. They should examine in what ways classroom education can be improved and they should implement their ideas in the regular classes in *cooperation* with the classroom teacher" (p. 71, emphasis in the original).

The intent of REI was to address these concerns by increasing handicapped student participation in the regular education classroom. In a 1990 paper, Will challenged states to serve students with learning problems by beginning to "search for ways to serve as many of these children as possible in the regular classroom by encouraging special education and other special programs to form a partnership with regular education" (Illinois State Board of Education, 1990). After Will's emotional plea, schools and districts began to develop their own forms of REI. For example, the principles of the REI in Illinois included the following:

- The goal of education is to enable all students to become productive adult citizens.
- Students are most likely to achieve this goal of education fully by learning in the company of their peers.
- How students achieve the goal of education will vary depending on their strengths and needs. Schools have a responsibility to accommodate these strengths and needs.
- However, schools also have unique characteristics; therefore, strategies for accommodating student needs will vary from school to school.
- Personalized instruction for students should take into account the goals of education. This means

that social and behavioral skills as well as academic skills should be priorities.

- No single group of school professionals can be expected to possess the entire body of knowledge and skills needed to educate students.
- Professionals, when they collaborate, are better able to address student needs.
- When schools function successfully, expectations are explicit and appropriate; professionals and parents communicate clearly with students and each other; and differences are celebrated, not tolerated nor diminished (n.p.).

The advocates and supporters of the REI had opponents, however. Some who opposed REI believed it was a political strategy (see, for example, Braaten, Kauffman, Braaten, Polsgrove, & Nelson, 1988; Kauffman, 1989). Kauffman (1989) believed the REI was a political subterfuge "of the Reagan-Bush attempts to reduce federal expenditures for education, which have resulted in declining federal support for programs designed to ensure equity in induction of the disadvantaged and handicapped" (p. 256). Others believed the REI would deter schools from addressing the real concerns of schools (see for example, Fuchs & Fuchs, 1994). Kauffman (1989) cautioned the larger special education community to be careful implementing REI and believed that the REI "rests on illogical premises, ignores the issues of specificity in proposed reforms, and reflects a cavalier attitude toward experimentation and research" (Kauffman, 1989, p. 256).

Mainstreaming. The term *mainstreaming* is used universally to denote the placement of exceptional children in the regular classroom. Section 14 12 (5) (B) of IDEA mandates that states provide procedures to ensure that children with disabilities are educated "to the maximum extent of appropriateness" with nondisabled children in regular classes. This is a critical foundation of mainstreaming. An early definition of mainstreaming was offered by Hasazi, Rice, and York (1979), "The practice of providing educational programs for handicapped students in environments that maximize contact with non-handicapped peers . . ." (p. 6). Mainstreaming, according to Bowd (1991), "exists as long as students' 'needs' are met in an 'appropriate' place-

ment judged by the professional to be 'least restrictive' " (p. 14). From a connotative and past practice perspective, mainstreaming is probably met with disdain by many special and regular educators (both teachers and administrators) who truly believe in inclusiveness. Mainstreaming generally meant that students were both in and out of special and regular education classrooms. This might have been appropriate in some cases; it all depended on the particular needs of the child. Rogers (1993) asserts that, "Mainstreaming proponents generally assume that a student must 'earn' his or her opportunity to be mainstreamed through the ability to 'keep up' with the work assigned by the teacher to the other students in the class" (p. 1). This assumes, we believe, rightfully so, that a student who is mainstreamed will be judged against the work of the other nonspecial needs students in the classroom.

Inclusion. We believe that inclusion is more than a process of having special needs students in regular classrooms. To us, inclusion is a mind-set, it is a way of approaching special needs students with dignity for the talents they bring with them. We also believe that the pain, strife, and struggles of early attempts to develop inclusive classrooms (e.g., mainstreaming and REI) have enabled most educators to now provide what we refer to as "meaningful and substantive" educational opportunities in a least restrictive environment—classrooms, period. This might appear to be overly optimistic, perhaps simplistic; however, with the advent of embracing democratic ideals, celebrating cultural diversity, and practicing more authentic forms of assessment and instruction (e.g., constructivist), schools can, if properly staffed, supervised, and trained, become "communities" (Stainbach & Stainbach, 1992, p. xv). They further state that "Inclusion means welcoming everyone—all students, all citizens—back into our schools and communities" (Stainbach & Stainbach, p. xv). As a point of departure to the exploration of inclusion, we will refer to Stainbach and Stainbach (1992), as their thoughts capture a different, more informed view of what inclusion is really about: "we must return to the 'basics': the ABCs—acceptance, belonging, and community; and the new three Rs—reading, writing, and relationships" (p. xvi).

Roach, Ascroft, and Stamp (1995) assert that inclusion, "At its core [inclusion] means that students attend their home school along with their age and grade peers" (p. 7). Moreover, they indicate that "Inclusion is not just a place or a method of delivering instruction. It is a philosophy of supporting children in their learning that undergirds the entire system. Inclusion is a part of the very culture of a school or school district and defines how students, teachers, administrators, and others view the potential of children. Inclusion is truly grounded in the phrase, 'all children can learn' (p. 7).

CONTEMPORARY ISSUES

Special education in today's schools is "bigger than life" in that "one in ten students in public education" (Terman, Larner, Stevenson, & Behrman, 1996, p. 21) qualify for and receive services under the rubric of special education. Overseeing special education in a K–12 setting is not an easy prospect for administrators due to the large number of students in any given population who qualify for services, the expenses involved in providing a "free and appropriate public education," and the types of support and development efforts needed to provide educationally sound services to the students who qualify for special services. Besides the technical information (e.g., "rules and regulations" and legal aspects), there are emotional issues that surround special education (e.g., helping parents cope with their child's disability and instituting changes within special education services). Another issue that administrators face is hiring qualified teachers. Now with more schools restructuring to work more inclusively with students with special learning needs, administrators not only have to hire special education teachers who have certain academic qualifications, but also, administrators are now faced with hiring regular education teachers who are willing and able to work with special needs students in the regular classroom environment.

In our brief overview of the development of special education as we know it today, we underscored the importance of understanding the statutes, legislation, and legal decisions that need to be translated to and operationalized within the school setting. It is these pieces of legislation and legal opinions that serve as the basis by which special education can be evaluated within any building, regardless of the context (e.g., overall population, geographic setting (urban, suburban, rural), and level (elementary, middle, high school). A caveat is offered here, however. School administrators need to remember that special education programs and services are in a constant state of flux. This flux is caused by constant changes in school demographics that often can signal increases in the numbers of special needs students. This section of the chapter will guide the administrator of special education in understanding more specific rules and regulations, safeguards, and procedural aspects that, in part, shape any given special education program, regardless of the contextual aspects of the school.

IDEA Revisited

IDEA includes four overarching provisions or "procedural safeguards": (1) Free and appropriate public education, including related services that can range from transportation to speech therapy and from homebound instruction to health screening. Within Section 300.1 of the Code of Federal Regulations, language indicates that related services will be provided to meet the unique needs of students who have been identified as eligible for services. (2) Due process procedures for parents, guardians, and children. (3) Least restrictive setting. (4) Individualized educational program (Assistance to States for the Education of Children with Disabilities, 1992).

A "free and appropriate public education" is guaranteed for all children with disabilities. Under this provision, children are entitled to an education provided at public expense, under public supervision and direction, without charge (Individuals with Disabilities Education Act, 1990). The quality of education received by a special education child must meet the standards of the state educational agency. Moreover, the school and its district agency must include all levels of schooling—preschool, elementary, secondary (PK–12).

The most noteworthy premise of IDEA is the mandated legislation of a free and appropriate public education. It is from this premise that the legislation calls for certain components to be in place in schools.

Many educators refer to these components as the "rules and regulations" of special education. The most basic of these rules and regulations, mandated by state and federal law include the following:

1. Least restrictive environment (LRE)
2. Individualized educational program (IEP)
3. Due process procedures for parents and/or legal guardians

Least Restrictive Environment

School administrators who supervise special education programs are responsible for ensuring that children identified as handicapped or otherwise learning disabled receive a free and appropriate public education in a least restrictive environment. The intent of IDEA is for children with disabilities to be educated with nondisabled children when and where possible. There are advocates and opponents to inclusive practices. Terman and colleagues (1996) believe, like many, that "Regular education, if appropriately modified, could assume more of the responsibility of providing education to students with learning disabilities, mild mental retardation, or orthopedic impairments . . ." (p. 17). Although the intent of IDEA is for full-services for learning disabled children, there are, however, exceptions. IDEA states specifically that "special classes, separate schooling, or other removal of children with disabilities from the regular educational environment occurs only when the nature or severity of the handicap is such that education in regular classes with the use of supplementary aids and services cannot be achieved satisfactorily" (Individuals with Disabilities Education Act, 1990).

To comply with this legislation, schools need to provide a continuum of services to ensure success of learning for physically and emotionally disabled children in the regular "mainstream" classroom and other aspects of the educational program. Schools are required to provide the necessary supplementary resources; for example, specialized resource room tutoring and special education aides who are trained to work in tandem with both special and regular education teachers. Inclusion of learning disabled children in other aspects of the educational program is critical

to consider as well. Learning disabled children cannot be shut out of extracurricular activities and programs that are a part of the overall school program. We advise school administrators to consult with their district special education coordinator, legal counsel, and others when questions arise to handicapped and/or learning disabled children participating in other school programs such as clubs and activities and sports. These types of programs and their activities are considered by most, at least from a philosophical grounding, to be a part of and extension to the school day and its program.

Placement of students with learning and/or handicapping conditions typically follows a continuum that can span from the least restrictive to the most restrictive environment. Least restrictive environments are ones in which handicapped children are in regular education classrooms all day with appropriate support services. This practice is referred to as full inclusion and defined by the National Information Center for Children and Youth with Disabilities (NICHY, 1995) as a setting in which "students with disabilities . . . receive their entire education within the general education setting" (p. 2). Moving along the continuum are variations with children spending a half of their day in regular education classrooms and the other half of their day being pulled out into specialized classrooms (e.g., resource room). The NICHY (1995) refers to this as "partial inclusion." "Partial inclusion would refer to the practice of educating students with disabilities in general education classrooms for some portion of their school day, while they spend the other portion of the day receiving instruction in a special education classroom or resource room outside of the mainstream" (NICHY, 1995, p. 2). Children with even more severe or profound learning disabilities spend as much as three-fourths of their day in a special education classroom (e.g., resource room) and the remaining one fourth of their day in a regular education classroom. At the extreme end of the continuum, children with the most severe learning disabilities (e.g., emotional, severe mental retardation) spend all of their time in special education classrooms, special schools (e.g., schools for the deaf, blind, severely mentally retarded), alternative schools and residential settings (severely emotionally disturbed children), and/or services are provided in the home by district and/or state home-bound programs (severely and chronically physically sick and/or emotionally disturbed children (school phobia)).

We believe that when considering placement of children and the idea of least restrictive environment school administrators and personnel need to ask the critical question, "What types of supports and aids are available within the school system to ensure success?" The answer to this question begs for further inquiry from those who identify and place eligible students in special education programs and from the providers of special education services in buildings. The reader is reminded of the ruling in the PARC case. Essentially, no school or agency can claim they do not have the finances available to provide services to disabled students.

With this legal and legislative foundation for the establishment of least restrictive environments, school administrators and regular and special education personnel need to examine the existing process in place and begin to develop a mind-set for inclusion. The National Information Center for Children and Youth with Disabilities has offered a series of recommendations for schools as they seek to provide more inclusive schools and programs for children with disabilities. These recommendations are our departure as we discuss the roles and responsibilities of the building administrators in providing a solid beginning point to develop schools that can meet the needs of children with disabilities. Rude and Anderson (1992) indicated that "The attitude of the administrator was cited as the most influential factor for the success of an inclusion program" (p. 33). Moreover, Rude and Anderson's work supports the premise that "administrators at inclusive schools cultivated a school climate that signified that all students belonged at the school site, and that all teachers would teach all students" (p. 33). Hence, we believe that schools need to be guided with appropriate administrative support for inclusion by:

- Establishing a philosophy that embraces inclusion. This philosophy needs to become part of the overall school philosophy and not an add-on to the special education department's purpose, objectives, and goals.

- Developing plans for inclusion. One of the most fundamental errors, we believe, that schools make is that only special education teachers are involved in the planning for inclusion. Because learning disabled children will be in the mainstream, these very same children need to be involved in the planning, developing, and implementing of inclusion and inclusionary practices.

- Providing staff development and training for both regular and special education teachers, support staff, and others who work in the school setting. As the National Information Center for Children and Youth with Disabilities (1995) indicated, "It is unrealistic and unfair to expect general education teachers to creatively and productively educate and include students with disabilities in their classrooms in the absence of adequate training" (p. 6).

Of course, these suggestions for practice will make little impact, we believe, unless schools and their staff involve parents, community members, and the students themselves in the process of developing inclusive environments. Administrators need to take the lead in these areas by:

- Assessing periodically, the beliefs and attitudes of teachers and support staff who work with disabled children. Administrators need to ask if negative perceptions cloud expectations of disabled children versus the beliefs and expectations held for nondisabled children. There have been numerous studies that identify the beliefs of teachers—both regular and special education teachers—who work with disabled children. As early as 1977, Gillung and Rucker studied the expectation levels of teachers who taught special education children. Gillung and Rucker's (1977) results pointed to a lowered set of expectations of children by both special and regular education teachers.

- Opening lines of communication by providing cooperative planning time between special and regular education teachers. The National Information Center for Children and Youth with Disabilities (1995) indicates that collaboration is a critical component for inclusion to be effectively implemented. Moreover, "collaboration needs to occur all along the path of inclusion: during the initial planning stages, during implementation, between home and school, between all members of the student's individual planning team, between general and special educators during the course of the school day, between teachers and administrators, and between students" (NICHY, 1995, p. 7).

There can be unexpected benefits and outcomes to developing "inclusive" environments within schools. Our experiences in elementary, middle, and high schools have given us several insights worth highlighting. We believe schools that embrace the philosophical underpinnings of inclusion and that "less restrictiveness is best" reap the following:

- Students of all ability levels learn how to interact with one another. Tolerance for individual differences gives rise to students accepting, respecting, and embracing individual differences in one another.
- Students not eligible for special education services but who have learning needs can benefit from paraprofessionals in the classroom. Special education teachers, teacher aides, and others can give assistance to both regular and special education students. Better teacher-child ratios can help promote these types of unexpected but welcome benefits.
- Reciprocal learning can occur as a result of sharing instructional methods, classroom management strategies, and other strategies between special and regular education teachers. In special education, teachers often refer to "best practice" strategies to meet individual needs. In our view, we believe that best practice is best practice, regardless of the types of students in a classroom. Increased interaction, opportunities for dialogue, and exchanges of instructional and other classroom strategies can pave the way for an overall stronger instructional program from all teachers.

Individualized Educational Program

Beginning first with EAHCA (1975) and then being expanded upon with its amendment in 1990 the law requires that every child with a confirmed learning disability must have on file an individualized educational program (IEP), or what most practitioners call a "plan." The IEP is an integral part of a child's special services for it is the plan that identifies in specific terms what services are to be provided, the length of these services, and the arena in which these services will be provided (e.g., regular education class, resource room). More importantly, however, the IEP specifies the child's current performance level, the educational goals and objectives needed to be worked toward, and the special education programs and services to be provided to meet these goals and objectives.

The mandate for the IEP ensures, according to the National Information Center for Children and Youth with Disabilities (1994), that parents and school personnel jointly make decisions about the educational program for the child, and the IEP document itself serves as an official record of the decisions made on the child's program of study. The IEP also is a document of function because it indicates related services to be provided. These services can include but are not limited to the following (Assistance to States for the Education of Children with Disabilities, 1992):

- Audiology
- Psychological services
- Physical therapy
- Occupational therapy
- Medical services for diagnostic or evaluation purposes only
- School health services
- Recreation, including therapeutic recreation
- Counseling services, including rehabilitation counseling
- Early identification and assessment of disabilities in children
- Social work services in schools
- Transportation
- Speech pathology
- Parent counseling and training

The IEP also ensures that educational goals and objectives indicated in prior IEPs are being met. The IEP also is a way for state agencies to ensure that schools and districts are in compliance with the mandates (processes and procedures) of IDEA. Existing IEPs must be reviewed annually. Goals are then assessed, modifications for the next school year are made, and parents can bring issues on their child's education to the forefront. This process is referred to as an annual review. During this annual review, several people are in attendance. Most commonly, the following people attend the annual review:

- Parent and/or legal guardian, child, and any other person the parent wishes to attend
- Special education teacher, regular education teacher(s)
- School and/or district psychologist
- School and/or district social worker
- School and/or district nurse
- School and/or district guidance counselor
- Representatives from outside agencies as needed and appropriate

These people represent an umbrella program for every school and/or district: the student services team. Others refer to this team as the multidisciplinary team because these people represent and advocate for their disciplines (e.g., health, social, psychological) when the services inherent within them would benefit the child's likelihood to be successful in school. IDEA language does not necessitate that every one of these people attend. In our earlier discussions, we spoke of inclusive schools, schools where all share in the responsibility and obligation of educating disabled children. Open and active participation of a variety of people in developing the educational program for students with disabilities is one such way to begin creating an awareness. In other chapters, we have discussed the role that each one of these individuals plays in the provision of services in both special and regular education programs within the school. For example, the nurse evaluates health by conducting specific screenings (hearing, vision), conducting health histories, and coordinating with physicians (medications).

Typically, children with learning disabilities are reevaluated every 3 years. This reevaluation includes appropriate retesting to determine a child's continued need for special education and related services. It is critical that timelines are followed in meeting this 3-year rule for completing a reevaluation. Because a variety of people are involved in reevaluating students and their needs (e.g., school nurse, social worker, psychologist), it is advisable to begin the reevaluation process at least 60 days before the end of the 3-year period. Provisions also must be in place for parents to be notified of the reevaluation and sign off on permission forms before any evaluation (even reevaluation) can be initiated. There are specific timelines for notice and the right to respond to the proposed evaluation. Later we will discuss the importance of notification and due process.

The law of special education is quite specific on when an IEP must be in place. The law states that an IEP must be in effect before special education and related services are provided to a child; and the IEP must be implemented as soon as possible following the meeting (Assistance to States for the Education of Children with Disabilities, 1992). The law is equally specific about when delays in service may occur; however, unnecessary delays in the provision of special education and/or related services are a violation of IDEA.

Building administrators are encouraged to be familiar with the development of IEPs. State agencies conduct yearly audits to ensure that paperwork is filed for each child receiving special education and/or related services. Administrators need to make provisions for the filing of IEPs in each child's file. Many administrators appoint a member of the multidisciplinary team to assume the responsibility of ensuring compliance measures with regard to IEPs. It appears logical that the school social worker or psychologist fulfills this responsibility because either one of these individuals would be involved in the development of all IEPs regardless of the child's disability. Often this person would be called the case manager. A caveat is offered here, however. A supervisor cannot give up his or her responsibility for IEP compliance by assigning responsibility to others to manage and oversee IEP development. A principal we are familiar with has developed a tracking system for IEP management using a computer spread sheet.

We have purposefully spent time discussing the development and implementation of the IEP because the IEP is the only record that is recognized as being a legal document of the child's special education program of studies. This document can be amended, if, for example, a child is being continually suspended. The IEP might need to be amended to include alternative placement in lieu of suspension. There are laws and procedures that must guide the administrator when dealing with the suspension and/or expulsion of a special education student. We suggest that the administrator become familiar with the rules and procedures involved in this aspect of supervising special education. State and federal legislation should be used as a guide. Moreover, supervisors are encouraged to consult with district level administration (e.g., director of special programs, special education, or student services) and district legal counsel. The complexities of building an IEP abound especially when special education students receive their education away from the "neighborhood" school.

Due Process Procedures for Parents and/or Legal Guardians

Due process under IDEA includes specific rights for parents of special education children. Generally speaking, safeguards must be provided for in the areas of notice, consent, evaluation procedures, provisions for independent educational evaluation, access to school records, hearings, and in the development of the IEP. Parents have a right and the authority to be actively involved in the process of developing their child's program of study and the processes and procedures leading to determination that their child does, indeed, have a learning disability. Under the Assistance to States for the Education of Children with Disabilities Act (1990) parents are afforded such involvement in the development of their child's IEP. These safeguards include the following:

- Notification: Parents must be notified that the annual review is going to occur and then be modified for the next academic year.
- Parents also must be notified of the purpose of the meeting, who will be in attendance, the time and location of the meeting, and then be given notice that they may request others to be present.

If the parent will not or cannot attend, schools must offer other alternatives such as a teleconference.

It is the principal's responsibility to document a parent's inability or unwillingness to attend and what steps were taken to involve the parents (e.g., telephone calls, letters, visits to home or work). The Assistance to States for the Education of Children with Disabilities Act (1992) also stipulates that it is the school's responsibility to provide to parents such services as interpreters (for non-English speaking and/or deaf parents and/or guardians).

If an administrator believes that a reevaluation is needed during the course of the year, that services provided under the current IEP need to be changed, or that an alternative placement will better serve the child in attaining educational objectives, due process also must be provided before these changes in program, services, or placement can be initiated by the school. If a child presently not being served by special education is referred for consideration in special education, the parent and/or legal guardian must also be notified, and "written consent must be obtained before any testing and/or assessments can be made (The Assistance to States for the Education of Children with Disabilities Act, 1992). Notice must be given of each evaluation instrument, procedure, test, record, or report the agency (school) used as a basis for any intended changes in the educational program of the child. The Assistance to States for the Education of Children with Disabilities Act (1992) also states that notice must be given to parents that informs them that their child is going to be identified, evaluated, or placed in a special education program. Due process provides for parents to agree to or deny consent at any stage of the process of testing, identification, development of the IEP, evaluation, and reevaluation.

Records of all school children are sacred and contain sensitive material such as IQ scores, health records, and other educational evaluations. IDEA provides for "an opportunity for parents and guardians of a handicapped child to examine all relevant records with respect to the identification, evaluation, and educational placement of the child" (Individuals with Disabilities Education Act, 1990).

Parents also have other due process rights in that they may disagree with such information on evaluation results and placement recommendations made during initial assessments, annual reviews, and reevaluations.

If agreement between the parent and school cannot be achieved, parents have the right to challenge the results and consult with other professionals who may be able to shed more light on this information. More often than not, disputes can be resolved through discussion with the multidisciplinary team. The role of the principal should center around coming to an agreeable settlement between the school and parent—all working to better serve the child's educational needs. If agreement cannot be reached, then the parents have the right to ask for a formal appeal. The school needs to outline the steps involved in a formal appeal, called a due process hearing. Under no circumstances, however, can the time period of the dispute be used to deny students their right to a free and appropriate education.

Here, too, principals and supervisors need to be familiar with the official rules and regulations so that the best interest of the learning disabled child may be served. Each district has its own procedures for operationalizing the provisions of IDEA and the development of the IEP and its many parts; however, the specified rules and regulations need to be carried out to the letter of the law.

ILLUSTRATIVE PRACTICES AND ISSUES

Logan, K. R., Diaz, E., Piperno, M., Rankin, D., MacFarlano, A. D., & Bargamian, K. (1995). How inclusion built a community of learners. *Educational Leadership, 52*(4), 42–44.

> Logan and colleagues describe the benefits of full inclusion for students with severe disabilities. The major benefits of inclusion for *all* students were numerous. However, the Gwinnett Public Schools reported in this case study that students and teachers were able to foster "authentic learning" by helping to "find a deeper purpose as they learned to read, write, and solve problems" (p. 42). *Issues:* While implementing full inclusion it is important to (1) keep the parents and community involved and appraised of efforts, and (2) provide planning time for school personnel.

Marston, D. (1996). A comparison of inclusion only, pull-out only, and combined service models for students with mild disabilities. *The Journal of Special Education, 30*(2), 121–132.

> Marston chronicles how his district collected data to measure the efficacy of teachers and students in full-inclusion, pull-out and combined models. *Issues:* The importance of research on the effects of various instructional models is critical to making decisions about service models.

Sheppo, K. G., Hartsfield, S. J., Ruff, S., Jones, C. A., & Holinga, M. (1995). How an urban school promotes inclusion. *Educational Leadership, 52*(4), 82–84.

> Sheppo and colleagues detail an inclusion effort utilizing science and technology. According to the authors, Project LINCOL'N (Living in the New Computer Oriented Learning 'Nvironment) has its primary goal "to enable all students, including those with disabilities, to engage in authentic learning in a problem-solving environment" (p. 82). *Issues:* The development of integrated curriculum, utilizing existing and emerging technologies, can enhance learning in the mainstream for both special and regular education students.

Staub, D., & Peck, C. A. (1995). What are the outcomes for nondisabled students? *Educational Leadership, 52*(4), 36–39.

> Straub and Peck highlight concerns parents of nondisabled children raise about special education children being included in the mainstream. The authors identify the potential benefits of inclusion for nondisabled children. They believe nondisabled children can lose their fear of human differences, grow socially, increase their self-esteem, develop caring friendships, and grow morally and ethically (pp. 37–38). *Issues:* Will inclusion reduce academic progress for both disabled and nondisabled students? Will inclusion reduce teacher time with nondisabled students?

Villa, R. A., & Thousand, J. S. (1992). How one district integrated special and general education. *Educational Leadership, 50*(2), 39–41.

> Villa and Thousand account how the Winooski, Vermont, School District eliminated labeling students (gifted and special education) by providing educational opportunities for all students. The district was able to restructure their instructional programs and personnel by (1) redefining roles eliminating "categorical" labels on job descriptions and integrating support personnel (e.g., counselors, social workers, and special education teachers) into the school community, and (2) including students in making critical decisions. *Issues:* For systems to change, change must be embraced by all stakeholders.

SUMMARY

The supervision of special education services in the K–12 school arena requires a constantly updated knowledge of key legislation and emerging practices. Perennial issues such as inclusion, classification of students and their disabilities, and the provisions for the development of emerging program offerings requires the school administrator to keep current with the field and other related school and community services, programs, and personnel (e.g., health issues and the school nurse, the school psychologist, and counselors who comprise the guidance and counseling pro-

gram). The administrator not only has to be an advocate for the rights of children, but also must be an advocate for more inclusive school practices which include, for example, the provisions of a free and appropriate education for all children. In this sense, the administrator has to be able to lead his or her school in a direction that provides fair and equitable educational practices for both special and regular education students, that allows teachers to work with one another in new and expansive ways, and that provides the types of support necessary to achieve these goals.

QUESTIONS FOR FURTHER CONSIDERATION

Research

1. Inclusion is a controversial issue. From the information presented in this chapter and independent readings, identify the major strengths for including all children in regular classrooms. What types of support are needed for regular education teachers in order to practice inclusion?

2. Consult the "Rules and Regulations" for special education in your state. What are the guidelines for suspending a special education student?

3. Very often teacher aides are used in regular classrooms with special education students. Develop a training program for regular and special education teachers so that teacher aides can be better utilized to help students. Also develop a policy and the procedures needed to enact the policy for the supervision and evaluation of special education aides. Who should be involved in the supervision and evaluation of teacher aides? What are the limits of the law on their supervision and evaluation?

Reflect

1. What types of sensitivity training do regular education teachers need to better implement inclusion initiatives? What role does the principal play in providing the needed resources to implement inclusion? What types of staff development activities are needed to promote inclusion in the school?

2. Conduct an audit on the special needs students in your building. Examine what types of activities and sports these children are involved in. If the number of students who are involved in sports and extracurricular activities is low, what can an administrator do to determine the reasons? How can an administrator ensure that special needs students are more involved in the activities of the school?

Respond/React

1. Are there instances where inclusion "just can't work?" What typically surrounds these instances?

2. Should there be a limit to the "modifications" we make for children? Has the pendulum swung too far or are we where we should be?

3. Some principals believe that special education children should not be required to take standardized tests (often required by the state). Should principals keep special needs students out of the building on schoolwide testing days? What are the moral and ethical issues that surround this issue?

SUGGESTED READINGS

Chambers J. G., & Hartman, W. T. (1983). *Special education policies: Their history, implementation, and finance.* Philadelphia: Temple University Press.

Stainbach, S., & Stainbach, W. (Eds.). (1992). *Curriculum considerations in inclusive classrooms: Facilitating learning for all students.* Baltimore: Paul H. Brookes.

Epilogue

The variety of special programs in regular schools reflects the evolving nature of elementary and secondary education in this country. Only 100 years ago, schools served a very small percentage of students for a rather narrow function—to prepare them for college. The child study and Progressive Education movements, combined with the great influx of immigrants, all occurring within a decade or two of the turn of the century, contributed greatly to the expansion of the purposes for elementary and secondary education.

As the purposes of education began to include more than academic preparation, schools expanded their menu of services to accommodate the broad range of individual interests and abilities. The shift to making schooling more student-centered—not to the exclusion of other interests or concerns but in addition to them—took place within a few decades after the turn of the century and is still occurring. The special programs described in Chapters 1 through 17 began as add-ons to the earlier and more narrow versions of schooling. It could be argued that some of these programs, such as Activities, Early Childhood Education, Fine Arts, Guidance and Counseling, Physical Education, and Special Education, have become sufficiently ensconced in regular schools that referring to them as special no longer makes sense. The other special programs may appear to be still seen as extra—for now. The lists of what is special and what is regular have changed over time and will, undoubtedly, continue to change.

Whatever programs have become a part of the regular school will depend on local conditions of the specific school and district. National concerns also will affect schools and districts as can be seen by the effects of legislation, such as the Smith-Hughes Act of 1917, that was the impetus for vocational education, which, in turn, has given rise to school-to-work programs. The Great Depression not only kept children in school longer—there were no jobs to be had—but also provided some employment opportunities to artists in the schools. Likewise World War II had important effects on schools. Women working in defense-related industries meant government-sponsored day care, at least during the war years. Subsequently, the G. I. Bill was a major explanation for increased schooling at all levels, meaning more exposure to the special programs in addition to regular ones.

A host of other national issues had effects on schools, and they have been discussed throughout all of the chapters. Professional associations have had effects on schooling as have the counselors, nurses, psychologists, and social workers who have actively discussed their respective roles in the schools. Overall, these "outsiders" have made inroads and in some instances at least have become established fixtures in the regular programs. The likelihood is that more of them, not fewer, will continue to become a regular aspect of schooling.

The evolution of schooling has not been smooth and without tumultuous times. For example, the 1980s and 1990s were filled with concerns about the alleged crisis in education. The 1983 publication of *A Nation at Risk* started the furor and thankfully the 1995 release of *The Manufactured Crisis* counterbalanced the shift to another back-to-basics movement. In addition, many of the recent school reform efforts have been predicated on the crisis mentality and as has often been the case in the past, many of these efforts will dissipate, and schools will emerge, once again, looking and functioning pretty much the way they were before the "crisis"—with one important exception and that is more attention to individual children.

MULTIDISCIPLINARY APPROACH

When schools attend to the individual needs and interests of children, it is often through a multidisciplinary approach. In addition to regular programs, all those that are called special can be used to improve and enhance whatever services are provided to children and their families. That we treated the special programs separately here in no way suggests they cannot be merged or coordinated in a manner that best serves the school's clients.

The Illustrative Practices and Issues at the end of each chapter reinforces the notion that children rarely have isolated needs. The involvement of children in special programs is always as a complement to the regular or other special programs, and more often than not involves teachers or other professionals with a variety of training and special skills backgrounds.

No formula exists for determining which disciplines ought to be brought to bear in assisting children and their families. The IEP model is as good as any in identifying appropriate professionals who can help resolve the problems children experience at school and, in some cases, beyond school. As in the instance of appropriate pacing for above average children, the operating principle should be organized common sense.

ACCOUNTABILITY AND EVALUATION

Professional accountability is inherent to the role of the professional educator. The vast majority of professionals associated with schools have a moral purpose (helping children and their families) with a sufficiently strong moral compass (doing the right thing). It is bureaucratic accountability that often is the only measure of motive. And many times bureaucratic accountability involves some sort of formal evaluation or assessment.

It was no surprise to us that most of the Illustrative Practices referenced at the end of chapters contained little or no attention to evaluation or assessment. Formal evaluation has been the bane of educators and others in the helping professions for at least two reasons.

The first reason evaluation is often overlooked is because the sheer press of the moment to respond to a human need often displaces the detached and dispassionate attitude necessary for evaluation. Time is often a luxury for school personnel and those who are responding responsibly rarely have the time to plan for evaluative schemes and collect relevant data.

The second reason formal evaluation is often overlooked is the inadequacy of measuring devices. Rarely, if ever, does a child show improvement in only some narrow category for which there is an adequate assessment instrument. Usually the whole child is affected, positively or negatively, and conventional measures are simply not up to the task of assessing holistic effects or detecting subtle but important changes in disposition and attitude.

By no means are we suggesting that evaluation be omitted for any of the above reasons. We only wish that those who request or require evaluation would be more sympathetic to practitioners who often have many other issues with which to contend. When evaluation is required and inescapable, we offer the following suggestions:

1. Consider the context of the school, that is, choose methods of data collection that are reasonable extension of what students, teachers, and parents would anticipate.

2. Collect qualitative data, that is, listen to participants and record (or take notes of) what they say. Describe in narrative form how attitudes and values may have changed. Use personal testimonials that are reflective of the changes for which the program could reasonably be responsible. Personal stories have a powerful impact.

3. Collect quantitative data as simply as possible, that is, sophisticated pencil and paper tests requiring high inference should be used only when other sources of quantitative data are unavailable. Simple frequency counts of referrals, playground or lunchroom altercations, and other indicators of dysfunction can be tabulated over time to see if trends appear. Simple attendance counts often indicate the popularity, if not the success, of special programs, especially for various activities after school hours or for fine arts productions.

The intents of any program evaluation should be refinement and development regardless of the types of data used. To fully achieve these intents from the onset, those closest to the program itself need to be involved in the process of program evaluation and refinement. Involvement of stakeholders in the processes of evaluation will reduce anxiety and provide a sense of ownership. A by-product of program evaluation is decision making which will be much more sound if they are made by examining results and including those who provide special services within the school and community.

SUPERVISION OF SPECIAL PROGRAM PERSONNEL

More often than not, special program personnel are full-time, certified personnel, who are bound by school and district policies. Supervision and evaluation are policy-bound for all school personnel, regardless of the services they provide. Unfortunately, special program personnel (e.g., social worker, guidance counselor, psychologist, and nurse) are often supervised and then evaluated using the same forms and processes as the classroom teacher. This type of supervision and evaluation perpetuates superficiality and, moreover, provides very little incentive for professional growth. To provide more effective and developmentally appropriate supervision for special program personnel, the principal is encouraged to examine their particular job description and standards of practice (e.g., National Association of School Social Workers). From examining these standards against the services provided and directly observing the work of special programs personnel, the principal will be in a better position to assess more accurately the work and performance of special programs personnel.

STAFF DEVELOPMENT AND SPECIAL PROGRAMS

As special programs become less "special" through interdisciplinary efforts between all personnel, staff development opportunities become even more important to the overall development of both the organization and the people who comprise the school community. When the regular education initiative (REI) began in the 1980s, one of the difficulties that many schools encountered was a lack of staff development for both regular and special education teachers. The lack of staff development created barriers between regular education teachers and special education teachers who were not trained to work in collaboration with special education personnel (teachers, speech pathologists, and aides). These barriers could have been minimized with a proactive staff development program that emphasized collaborative and inclusive working environments and the intents of REI (now referred to as inclusion).

The principal should be informed with the needs of his or her school in order to better examine the work of special programs personnel so that opportunities are provided for the entire community to work more collaboratively. One of the traditional shortcomings of staff development has been in its delivery and conception. Typically, school personnel have little regard for staff development because activities are presented in a lockstep fashion that resembles a "one size fits all" approach. These same activities and program initiatives are developed as a one-time "shot in the arm" approach with little follow-up supervision by the school administrator. The effect of this approach is minimal. With special services becoming less special and more universal for all students, staff development, likewise, will need to be more inclusive of the various needs of the faculty so that they can better meet the unique and emerging needs of all students.

Whether one is concerned with activities programs, early childhood education, parental involvement, or any of the so-called special programs, the rallying cry for all of them has been to provide more and better services and opportunities to children. However the services and opportunities are coordinated and provided, what remains important is that they indeed are delivered. If that means that something called Student Assistance Teams or Student Services Teams need to be assembled and coordinated by school administrators, so be it. How such teams collaborate and cooperate will be a function of how the local school or district views these special programs. Knowing more about each of the special programs is a necessary prerequisite to their effective utilization in the provision of service and opportunities for students. We hope we have provided the prerequisite.

Acceleration the more rapidly than usual progression through curricular content within a grade or through the grades by skipping one or more.

Accommodation the altering of cognitive structures necessary for understanding new information, within Piaget's view of intellectual development.

"ACT" (Education for All Handicapped Children Act, PL 94-142) established in 1975 outlines the rulings and rights of handicapped and/or disabled children. The Act was later amended by IDEA.

Action(s) (theatre) the core of a theatre piece; the sense of forward movement created by the sense of time and/or the physical and psychological motivations of characters.

Adapted physical education a program that seeks active participation of all students who cannot safely or successfully take part in the regular activities of physical education.

Advanced placement (AP) classes at the high school level that teach college-level material. General course descriptions are available from the College Board for high school teachers interested in such classes.

Alignment (dance) the relationship of the skeleton to the line of gravity and the base of support.

Alla breve (music) the meter signature cent indicating the equivalent of 2/2 time.

American with Disabilities Act (ADA) federal legislation prohibiting the denial of disabled students from fully benefiting from programs and services.

Assessing to analyze and determine the nature and quality of achievement through means appropriate to the subject.

Assimilation the taking in and processing of information, within Piaget's view of intellectual development.

Assimilationists those who believe the mission of public schools is to promote a common language and common national identity by having non-English–speaking immigrants and Native Americans discard their language and cultural roots and adopt the majority culture and its language.

Axial movement(s) (dance) any movement that is anchored to one spot by a body part and using only the available space in any direction without losing the initial body contact. Movement is organized around the axis of the body rather than designed for travel from one location to another; also known as nonlocomotor movement.

BD refers to students who have behavioral disorders.

Behaviorists believe in stimulus-response and operant conditioning wherein the environment, in terms of stimuli and reinforcements, is all important.

Bilingual education the use of two languages for the purpose of instruction.

Career academies secondary school cooperative ventures typically including a math, English, and science teacher along with a teacher representing a career area, such as health, electronics, or tourism, all of whom work with a group of students over a 2-year period, integrating, whenever possible, the teachers' respective fields of study.

Career cluster a secondary school organizational arrangement whereby a career such as health care or finance would be the center of an interdisciplinary approach, involving traditional subjects as they applied to the particular career area.

Case management the coordination and management of the services that a person is receiving. For example, a special education student might be receiving social work, health, adaptive physical education, psychological services, modification of academic work, and alternative placement in an outside setting for specialized training. The social worker, who coordinates these services, is considered to function as a case manager. The case management approach is an efficient way to coordinate a multitude of services.

Charter schools alternative schools that combine underlying aspects of public schooling with the freedom of the private sector to craft their own curriculum, administer their own budget, and make their own decisions. Because charter schools have autonomy, two rarely will be the same. Although not always, many charter schools are designed to serve at-risk students.

Child development associate (CDA) a mid-level professional in early childhood education with a minimum of 480 hours of work with children and 120 clock hours of formal training in early childhood education. The CDA credential is earned when a team of professionals finds teaching performance satisfactory.

Child development laboratory a setting, usually within a university, that provides educational services to preschool-age children, promotes the study of child development, and serves as a training site for prospective early childhood teachers.

Children's theatre a formal theatre production intended for audiences of children. Performers could be children or adults, or both, and amateurs or professionals.

Choreographic (dance) describes a dance sequence that has been created with specific intent.

Classical (dance) dance that has been developed into highly stylized structures within a culture. Generally developed within the court or circle of power in a society.

Classroom dramatizations the act of creating character, dialogue, action, and environment for the purpose of exploration, experimentation, and study in a setting in which there is no formal audience observation except for that of fellow students and teachers.

Constructed meanings (drama/theatre) the personal understanding of dramatic/artistic intentions and actions and their social and personal significance, selected and organized from the aural, oral, and visual symbols of a dramatic production.

Constructivists believe knowledge is constructed by the individual through interaction with others and the environment.

Consultant teacher one who has special training in the area of special needs children and works with regular classroom teachers in planning appropriate teaching/ learning strategies.

Creative drama(tics) a student-centered process in which students interpret and improvise. Lines are not written down or memorized, and it is not intended for an audience.

Curriculum compacting the collapsing of time for sequenced material, permitting students to master or demonstrate mastery in a much shorter time than usual.

Developmentally appropriate practice (DAP) an early childhood term that means knowledge of child development is evident in the early childhood setting and activities in which the children engage.

Developmental guidance a philosophical approach that stresses approaches that are more responsive to the social and emotional needs of children.

Discuss to engage in oral, written, or any other appropriate form of presentation.

Distance education the provision of educational content to settings in which the teacher is not physically present.

Distance learning receiving educational content without the actual presence of a teacher.

Dramatic play (drama) the natural role-taking and playing in which young children engage to make sense of their world.

Elements (dance) the use of the body moving in space and time with force/energy.

Elevation (dance) the body's propulsion into the air away from the floor, such as in a leap, hop, or jump.

Enrichment the provision of additional educational experiences that typically broaden the area of study.

Enrichment triad model an instructional routine that has three parts: an introduction, skills training, and an individual or small group activity.

Environment (drama/theatre) physical surroundings that establish place, time, and atmosphere/mood, and the physical conditions that reflect and affect the emotions, thoughts, and actions of characters.

Equal Access Act was signed into law in 1984 and withstood a constitutional challenge in 1990. Essentially the Act requires that if a public school provides access to a noncurricular club such as a chess club, it must provide similar access to other noncurricular clubs.

Equilibration the sharpening of mental structures between assimilation and accommodation, within Piaget's view of intellectual development.

ESL (English as a Second Language) pull-out programs that are a part of bilingual education programs at the secondary school level. ESL programs are predicated on proficiency in the native language.

Expression (drama/theatre) expressive expression, with appropriate dynamics, phrasing, style, and interpretation and appropriate variations in dynamics and tempo.

Extracurricular activities typically refer to those activities that are not part of the regular school day but, because the school sponsors them, if in no other way than providing space, they technically are part of the more broadly conceived curriculum.

FAPE an acronym that stands for a free and appropriate public education. A free and appropriate education, required by IDEA legislation, guarantees that all students between the ages of 3 through 21 receive an appropriate public education at the expense of taxpayers.

Folk dances usually created and performed by a specific group within a culture. Generally these dances originated outside the courts or circle of power of a society.

Formal production (drama/theatre) the staging of a dramatic work for presentation for an audience.

Fretted (music) instruments with frets (strips of material across the fingerboard allowing the strings to be stopped at predetermined locations), such as the guitar, ukulele, and sitar.

Genre (music)   a type or category of music (e.g., sonata, opera, oratorio, art song, gospel, suite, jazz, madrigal, march, work song, lullaby, barbershop, Dixieland).

Group intelligence tests   pencil and paper, multiple choice, timed tests that can be administered without special training. Most such tests correlate, at least roughly, to the Stanford-Binet, an individually administered test.

Group work   concerned with organizing people who are experiencing "like" difficulties into a common support system—the group.

Head Start   a federally funded early childhood program that serves children from low-income families.

Heterogenous grouping   allows students who function at different academic levels to be grouped together. The inclusion movement has had an impact on this educational practice.

Homogeneous grouping   includes children who function at the same ability levels (e.g., honors, learning disabled) with one another.

IDEA or the Individuals with Disabilities Education Act   formerly the Education for the Handicapped Act. IDEA is a federal law that mandates a free and appropriate education for children with disabilities. IDEA has been amended in 1986 and again in 1990.

IEP or Individual Educational Program   the annual document that must be written to document the program of study for children classified as having special needs. Before a child can receive special education services, an IEP must be developed by the multidisciplinary team of individuals within the school, or other associated agencies that represent, for example, health, speech pathology, and psychological services.

Improvisation (dance)   movement that is created spontaneously, ranging from free-form to highly structured environments, but always with an element of chance.

Improvisation (theatre)   the spontaneous use of movement and speech to create a character or object in a particular situation. Provides the dancer with the opportunity to bring together elements quickly and requires focus and concentration. Improvisation is instant and simultaneous choreography and performance.

Inclusion   the practice of providing a child with disabilities with his or her education within the general education classroom, with the supports and accommodations needed by that student.

Individuals with Disabilities Act (IDEA)   a reauthorization of the Education of All Handicapped Children Act (PL 94-142). This federal legislation mandates that all handicapped children receive a free appropriate public education in the least restrictive educational environment based on documented individual educational plans.

Informal production (drama/theatre)   the exploration of all aspects of a dramatic work (such as visual, oral, aural) in a setting in which experimentation is emphasized. Similar to classroom dramatizations with classmates and teachers as the usual audience.

Initiation (dance)   the point at which a movement is said to originate. This particularly refers to specific body parts and is generally said to be either distal (from the limbs or head) or central (from the torso).

Instructional unit   a state mechanism for financing special education by which a specified amount of money is distributed to local districts based on the number of special education classrooms (often referred to as teacher units).

Intelligence quotient (IQ)   the mental age, as determined by a score on an intelligence test, divided by the chronological age, and multiplied by 100 to remove the decimal points.

Interactionists   early childhood educators who believe development is affected by children interacting with their environment.

Kinesiology   the science of human movement. More specifically it is the scholarly study of sport, play, dance, and exercise.

LD   an acronym for learning disability.

LEP   stands for children with limited English proficiency.

LRE   an acronym that stands for the least restrictive environment, which was mandated with the passage of PL 94-142 in 1975 and later reinforced with the passage of IDEA. IDEA requires that special education students be placed in a learning environment that offers open opportunity for learning.

Magnet schools   designed to attract students of different races by appealing to special interests like business, performing arts, and other occupational clusters.

Mainstreaming   where students with disabilities are placed in the general education setting where students without disabilities receive their education. At the onset of the mainstreaming movement, special needs students typically spent a portion of their day in the special education classroom (resource room) and the other portion of their day, depending on the severity of the disability, in regular education classrooms.

Mastery learning   the demonstration of adequate comprehension of a subject that permits continuation in that subject. It is similar to, but less formal than, *curriculum compacting*.

Maturationists early childhood educators who believe development is from within and unaffected by environment.

Medically fragile children come to school with a host of potentially difficult medical conditions that necessitate more acute types of treatment and management of health issues by school nurses.

Mental age the score derived from an intelligence test that corresponds with the average age of children who score the same.

Mentoring the pairing up of an inexperienced person with an experienced one with the expectation that the latter will provide insights and guidance to the former.

Movement education based on body and space awareness at the elementary level and analysis of a sport, dance, or other physical activity at the secondary level.

Multidisciplinary team a group of professionals who provide special services to children with learning disabilities. These individuals include, minimally, a special education teacher, school nurse, psychologist, social worker, guidance counselor, parent, and student. Other individuals from within and outside the school setting might also comprise the multidisciplinary team. The people who comprise the multidisciplinary team often are members of the school or district's Student Assistance Team.

Multiple intelligences (MI) articulated by Gardner (1993) and include linguistic, musical, logical mathematical, spatial, bodily-kinesthetics, intrapersonal, and interpersonal. Naturalistic was added in 1997.

Nurse practitioners registered nurses who have additional education and training beyond the masters degree and who can provide services that in the past only physicians could perform. School nurse practitioners combine their nursing skills with health counseling, health education, and anticipatory guidance (health prevention) with the skills of assessment and the management of illnesses and their causes.

Nursery schools typically serve children 2, 3, and 4 years of age, 2 or 3 days a week, for a few hours per day.

Occupational high schools relatively narrowly focused schools that prepare students for careers in such areas as business, aviation, and the fashion industry.

Pluralists those who believe that the public schools should promote a common language and common national identity by progressing through phases beginning with a native identity, continuing through a bicultural identity, and arriving at an American identity with a positive experience with the host culture for non-English–speaking immigrants and Native Americans.

Prevention education concerned with promoting more healthy—physical and mental—lifestyles and assisting young people in developing the attitudes and habits necessary to sustain long-term health. The focus of prevention education is to promote healthy choices, to reduce risk factors, and to develop protective factors that help guard against substance abuse, sexually transmitted diseases, teenage pregnancy, suicide, and violence.

Primary prevention includes activities that include health promotion and disease prevention.

Project method developed by William Kilpatrick. The project method relies upon students constructing knowledge through projects based upon a person's experience. The project method is thought to be the first foothold in combining community service as part of a formalized curriculum in schools.

Psychometrist is primarily concerned with testing and the interpretation of results. A school psychologist can function as a psychometrist, merely testing and interpreting results without providing direct services to children and their families. A school psychometrist, on the other hand, rarely, if ever, provides direct services to children other than testing and interpreting results.

Pull-out programs programs that pull special education children out from regular education classes. Pull-out programs are offered, more than likely, in a resource room where a child with special needs can receive more intensive services than would be available in a regular education classroom.

Reader's theatre a dramatic technique for the teaching of reading. Typically, it is a minimally staged interpretation of dramatic literature.

Readiness most often associated with a *maturationist* view of child development, wherein development is entirely from within.

REI an acronym that refers to the regular education initiative, which includes special needs students in a regular education setting. The REI movement began in the 1980s as a way to include special education students in regular education classrooms. The REI movement provided a segue to the inclusion movement of the 1990s.

Resource room a room, outside the regular classroom, in which special services are provided for students.

Revolving door identification model (RDIM) developed by Renzulli, Reis, and Smith (1981) for gifted and talented students to move in and out of special accommodations, depending on their interests.

School-based (health) clinics have emerged as one way for schools to assume a more proactive role in promoting health and wellness. School-based health clinics offer, for example, more comprehensive medical diagnosis and treatment to children in the school setting by nurse practitioners and attending physicians.

School health demonstrations   provide the opportunity for school nurses to reach a larger number of students and school personnel. Topics are determined through examining the needs of the community and by working with other support staff (e.g., school counselor, social worker, psychologist, and administration).

School of the 21st Century   a school-based/school-linked family support system designed to promote children's optimal development by providing high-quality child day care and support services to children from birth through age 12.

Secondary prevention   more concerned with early diagnosis of diseases so that treatment can be prescribed to limit disability.

Section 504 of the Rehabilitation Act of 1973   federal legislation specifying that no handicapped individual may be excluded from or denied the benefits of any program or activity receiving federal assistance.

Service learning   a method, a tool, and a process by which service and learning are blended within the curricular offerings of the school.

Social casework   concerned with direct, one-on-one services provided to students. Varying methods of problem-solving and coping strategies, coupled with forms of psychotherapy, are used. Social casework was eventually replaced, for the most part, with case management. The major component of this method is the individual interview.

Social history   a chronicling of lifetime events that a person has experienced. Information is collected from both the student and parents or guardian. Under the provisions of PL 94-142, students suspected of having a learning disability are required to have a social history as part of the screening process in determining eligibility for special education services. Once a child is identified as being eligible for special education services, a reevaluation is required every 3 years (or possibly sooner) thereafter. The social history also is a part of the reevaluation process.

Staves (music)   plural of staff (the five parallel lines on which music is written).

Structures (visual arts)   a means of organizing the components of a work into a cohesive and meaningful whole, such as sensory qualities, organizational principles, expressive features, and functions of art.

TBE (transitional bilingual education)   intended to move LEP (Limited English Proficiency) students into mainstream classes within 2 or 3 years by teaching reading and writing and other subject matter in the student's native language and teaching English for only a small portion of the school day.

Team teacher   one who works with the regular classroom teacher in planning special accommodations for children with special needs.

Tech prep   a cooperative effort between high schools and community colleges to facilitate the articulation of technical preparation programs.

Technical accuracy and skills (music)   the ability to perform with appropriate timbre, intonation, and diction and to play or sing the correct pitches and rhythms.

Technologies (visual arts)   complex machines used in the study and creating of art, such as lathes, presses, computers, lasers, and video equipment.

Tension (drama/theatre)   the atmosphere created by unresolved, disquieting, or inharmonious situations.

Tertiary prevention   concerned with the coordination and integration of health service resources within the school setting to support the child who is recovering from a major health problem or to enable the child who is chronically ill to remain well as long as possible.

Threshold hypothesis   bilingual education means one needs to be sufficiently competent in one's native language before competence can be achieved in a second language.

Timbre (music)   the character or quality of a sound that distinguishes one instrument, voice, or other sound source from another.

Title IX   approved by Congress in 1972, says, in part, No person shall, on the basis of sex, be excluded from participation in, be denied benefits of, or be subjected to discrimination under any education program or activity receiving federal financial assistance.

Title IX of the Education Amendments of 1972   prohibits sexual discrimination (in terms of provision of programs and services) by entities receiving federal financial support.

Title I of The Improving America's Schools Act of 1994   a reauthorization of the Elementary and Secondary Education Act of 1965, Title I is a federal statute providing a compensatory funding system operated by the U.S. Department of Education.

Traditional (drama/theatre)   forms that use time-honored theatrical practices.

REFERENCES

Allen-Meares, P. (1990). Social work in education: An expansion of mission. *Social Work in Education, 13*(1), 3–5.

Allen-Meares, P. (1991). The contribution of social workers to schooling. In R. Constable, J. P. Flynn, & S. McDonald (Eds.), *School social work: Practice and research perspectives* (2nd ed., pp. 5–16). Chicago: Lyceum Books.

Allen-Meares, P., Washington, R. O., & Welsh, B. L. (1996). *Social work services in schools* (2nd ed.). Boston: Allyn and Bacon.

Allensworth, D. D., & Bradley, B. (1996). Guidelines for adolescent preventive services: A role for the school nurse. *Journal of School Health, 66*(8), 761–764.

Alliance for Service Learning in Education Reform. (1993). Standards of quality for school-based service-learning. *Equity & Excellence in Education, 26*(2), 71–73.

Alliance for Service Learning in Education Reform. (1995). *Standards of quality for school-based and community-based service learning.* Alexandria, VA: Close Up Foundation.

American Academy of Pediatrics. (1981). *School health: A guide for health professionals.* Evanston, IL: American Academy of Pediatrics Committee on School Health.

American Nurses' Association. (1973). *Recommendations on educational preparation and definition of the expanded role and functions of the school nurse practitioner.* Kansas City, MO: Author.

American Nurses' Association. (1983). *Standards of school nursing practice.* Kansas City, MO: Author.

American School Counselor Association. (1995). *School counseling 2000: Children are our future.* Alexandria, VA: Author.

Americans with Disabilities Act, 42 U.S.C. § 12101 *et seq.*

Anderson, C. L., & Creswell, W. H. (1980). *School heath practice* (7th ed.). St. Louis, MO: C. V. Mosby.

Anderson, V., Kinsley, C., Negroni, P., & Price. C. (1991). Community service learning and school improvement in Springfield, Massachusetts. *Phi Delta Kappan, 72*(10), 761–764.

Anserello, C., & Sweet, T. (1990). Integrating consultation into school psychological services. In E. Cole and J. A. (Eds.), *Effective consultation in school psychology* (pp. 173–199). Toronto, Ontario: Hogrefe & Huber.

Apple, M. W., & Beane, J. A. (Eds.). (1995). *Democratic schools.* Alexandria, VA: Association for Supervision and Curriculum Development.

Aries, P. (1962). *Centuries of childhood: A social history of family life.* (R. Baldick, Trans.). New York: Vintage Books.

Ascher, C. (1982). Alternative schools—Some answers and questions. *The Urban Review, 14*(1), 65–69.

Assistance to States for the Education of Children with Disabilities, 34 C.F.R. § 300 *et seq.* (1992).

Aubrey, R. F. (1977). Historical development of guidance and counseling implications for the future. *Personnel and Guidance Journal, 55,* 288–295.

Ausubel, D. (1964). Adults versus children in second language learning, *American Journal of Education, 48,* 420–424.

Bachman, J. (1995). A need for school nurse education. *Journal of School Nursing, 11*(3), 20–24.

Baker, S. (1996). Take care not to define developmental guidance too narrowly. *The School Counselor, 43,* 243–244.

Baker, S. B. (1992). *School counseling for the twenty-first century.* New York: Macmillan.

Ballantine, J. (Ed.). (1989). *Schools and society: A unified reader.* Mountain View, CA: Mayfield.

Barbour, N. H., & Seefeldt, C. (1993). *Developmental continuity across preschool and primary grades.* Wheaton, MD: Association for Childhood Education International.

Bardon, J. I. (1989). The school psychologist as an applied educational psychologist. In R. C. D'Amato & R. S. Dean (Eds.), *The school psychologist in nontraditional settings: Integrating clients, services, and settings* (pp. 1–32). Hillsdale, NJ: Erlbaum.

Bardon, J. I., & Bennett, V. C. (1974). *School psychology.* Englewood Cliffs, NJ: Prentice-Hall.

Barik, H., & Swain, M. (1975). Three-year evaluation of a large scale early grade French Immersion program: The Ottawa study. *Language Learning, 25,* 1–30.

Barney, R. K. (1979). Physical education and sport in North America. In E. F. Zeigler. *History of physical education and sport* (pp. 171–227). Englewood Cliffs, NJ: Prentice-Hall.

Beale, A. V. (1986). Trivial pursuit: The history of guidance. *The School Counselor, 34*(1), 14–17.

Behrman, R. E. (Ed.). (1992). *The future of children: School linked services, 2*(1). Los Altos, CA: The Center for the Future of Children and The David and Lucille Packard Foundation.

Bennett, W. (1984). *To reclaim a legacy: A report on the humanities in higher education.* Washington, DC: National Endowment for the Humanities.

Berger, E. H. (1981). *Parents as partners in education: The school and home working together.* St. Louis, MO: C. V. Mosby.

Bergman, J. R. (1985). *School psychology in contemporary society: An introduction.* Columbus, OH: Charles E. Merrill.

Berk, L. E. (1992). The extracurriculum. In P. W. Jackson (Ed.), *Handbook of research on curriculum* (pp. 1002–1043). New York: Macmillan.

Berliner, D. C., & Biddle, B. J. (1995). *The manufactured crisis: Myths, fraud and the attack on America's public schools.* Reading, MA: Addison-Wesley.

Bhaerman, R., Cordell, K., & Gomez, B. (1995). *Service-learning as a component of systemic reform in rural schools and communities.* Philadelphia: Research for Better Schools.

Bittner, M. (1994). The constitutionality of public school community service programs. *The Clearinghouse, 68*(2), 115–118.

Bloom, B. S. (1964). *Stability and change in human characteristics.* New York: John Wiley & Sons.

Bluestein, D. L., Phillips, S. D., Jobin-Davis, K., Finkelberg, S. L., & Roarke, A. E. (1997). A theory-building investigation of the school-to-work transition. *The Counseling Psychologist, 25*(3), 364–402.

Blumenfeld, S. L. (1996). *The whole language/OBE fraud.* Boise, ID: The Paradigm Company.

Bonney, M., Grosz, R., & Roark, A. E. (1986). *Social psychological foundations for school services.* New York: Human Sciences Press.

Booth, A., & Dunn, J. F. (Eds.). (1996). *Family-school links: How do they affect educational outcomes?* Mahwah, NJ: Erlbaum.

Booth, L. (1980). Motivating gifted students through a shared-governance apprentice/mentor program. *Roeper Review, 3*(1), 11–13.

Bowd, A. D. (1991). Promoting regular classroom integration: The limitations of least restrictive environment. *Case in Point, VI*(1), 14–18.

Boyer, E. J. (1983). *High school: A report on secondary education in America.* New York: Harper & Row.

Braaten, S., Kauffman, J. M., Braaten, B., Polsgrove, L., & Nelson, C. M. (1988). The regular education initiative: Patent medicine for behavioral disorders. *Exceptional Children, 55*(1), 21–27.

Bradley, B. J. (1997). The school nurse as health educator. *Journal of School Health, 67*(1), 3–8.

Bradley-Johnson, S., Johnson, C. M., & Jacob-Timm, S. (1995). Where will—and where should—changes in education leave school psychology? *Journal of School Psychology, 33*(3), 187–200.

Bredekamp, S. (Ed.). (1987). *Developmentally appropriate practice in early childhood programs serving children from birth through age 8.* Washington, DC: National Association for the Education of Young Children.

Bredekamp, S., & Glowacki, S. (1996). The first decade of NAEYC accreditation: Growth and impact on the field. In S. Bredekamp & B. A. Willer (Eds.), *NAEYC accreditation: A decade of learning and the years ahead* (pp. 1–10). Washington, DC: National Association for the Education of Young Children.

Brewer, J. M. (1942). *History of vocational guidance: Origins and early development.* New York: Harper & Brothers.

Brim, O. (1965). *Education for child rearing.* New York: Free Press.

Brockett, O. G. (1995). *History of the theatre* (7th ed.). Boston: Allyn and Bacon.

Brown, C. (1995). *The underrepresentation of minority group students among those identified for gifted educational programming as an equal protection issue under the fourteenth amendment.* Unpublished doctoral dissertation, University of Oklahoma, Norman.

Brown, D., & Srebalus, D. J. (1988). *An introduction to the counseling profession.* Englewood Cliffs, NJ: Prentice-Hall.

Brown, J. A. (1992). *A handbook of social work practice.* Springfield, IL: Charles A. Thomas.

Brown v. Board of Education of Topeka, 347 U.S. 483 (1954).

Bruck, M., Lambert, W., & Tucker, G. (1977). Cognitive consequences of bilingual schooling: The St. Lambert project through grade six. *Linguistics, 13–32.*

Bullough, B., & Bullough, V. (1990). *Nursing in the community.* St. Louis, MO: C. V. Mosby.

Butts, R. F., & Cremin, L. A. (1953). *History of education in American culture.* New York: Henry Holt.

Campbell, P. S., & Scott-Kassner, C. (1995). *Music in childhood: From preschool through the elementary grades.* New York: Shirmer Books.

Carnegie Council Task Force on Education of Young Adolescents. (1989). *Turning points: Preparing American youth for the 21st century.* Washington, DC: Carnegie Corporation of New York.

Castellanos, D. (1983). *The best of two worlds: Bilingual bicultural education in the United States* (p. 17).

Chalker, C. S. (1996). *Effective alternative education programs: Best practices from planning through evaluating.* Lancaster, PA: Technomic.

Chambers J. G., & Hartman, W. T. (1983). Special education policies. In J. G. Chambers & W. T. Hartman (Eds.), *Special education policies: Their history, implementation, and finance* (pp. 3–12). Philadelphia: Temple University Press.

Chapman, W. (1991). The Illinois Experience: State grants to improve schools through parent involvement. *Phi Delta Kappan, 72*(5), 355–358.

Checkoway, B. (1996). Combining service and learning on campus and in the community. *Phi Delta Kappan, 77*(9), 600–606.

Child Abuse Prevention and Treatment Act (CAPTA) of 1974, Pub. L. No. 93-247, 88 Stat. 4.

Children's Defense Fund. (1996). *The state of America's children: Yearbook.* Washington, DC: Children's Defense Fund.

Civil Rights Act of 1964, Pub. L. No. 88-352, 78 Stat. 241.

Clancy, J. (1995). Ecological school social work: The reality and the vision. *Social Work in Education, 17*(1), 40–47.

Clemen-Stone, S., Eigsti, D. G., & McGuire, S. L. (1991). *Comprehensive family and community health nursing.* St. Louis, MO: Mosby-Yearbook.

Cleverly, J., & Phillips, D. C. (1986). *Visions of childhood: Influential models from Locke to Spock.* New York: Teachers College Press.

Clinton, W. J. (1993). *Inaugural address.* January 20, 1993.

Coggin, P. A. (1956). *The uses of drama.* New York: George Braziller.

Community Intervention. (1996). *It's easier to fix the problem when someone hands you the tools.* [Brochure]. Minneapolis, MN: Author.

Connell, W. F. (1980). *A history of education in the twentieth century world.* New York: Teachers College Press.

Conrad, D., & Hedin, D. (1991). School-based community service: What we know from research and theory. *Phi Delta Kappan, 72*(10), 743–749.

Consortium of National Arts Education Associations. (1994). *What every young American should know and be able to do in the arts.* Reston, VA: Music Educators National Conference.

Constable, R. T., Flynn, J. P., & McDonald, S. (Eds.). (1991). *School social work: Practice and research perspectives.* Chicago: Lyceum Books.

Contreras, R. A., & Valverde, L. A. (1994). The impact of *Brown* on the education of Latinos. *Journal of Negro Education, 63*(3), 470–479.

Consortium of National Arts Education Associations. (1994). *What every young American should know and be able to do in the arts.* Reston, VA: Music Educators National Conference.

Cook, L. (1984). The many roles of the school social worker revisited. *The School Social Work Journal, 9*(1), 4–8.

Cookfair, J. M. (1991). *Nursing processes and the practice of the community.* St. Louis, MO: Mosby-Yearbook.

Cooper, J. M., & Eisenhart, C. E. (1990). The influence of recent educational reforms on early childhood education programs. In P. Spodek & O. N. Saracho (Eds.), *Early childhood teacher preparation* (pp. 176–191). New York: Teachers College Press.

Copa, G. H., & Bentley, C. B. (1992). Vocational education. In P. W. Jackson (Ed.), *Handbook of research on education* (pp. 891–944). New York: Macmillan.

Costin, L. B. (1969). A historical review of school social work. *Social Casework, 50,* 439–453.

Cousins, N. (1979). *Anatomy of an illness as perceived by the patient: Reflections on healing and regeneration.* New York: Bantam Books.

Coy, D. R. (1991). The role of the counselor in today's school. *NASSP Bulletin, 75*(534), 15–19.

Crabbs, S. K., & Crabbs, M. A. (1977). Accountability: Who does what to whom, when, where, and how? *The School Counselor, 25*(2), 104–109.

Crawford, J. (1995). *Bilingual education: History, politics, theory and practice.* Reading, MA: Addison-Wesley.

Cromwell, G. E. (1963). *The nurse in the school health program.* Philadelphia: W. B. Saunders.

Cummins, J. (1978). Educational implications of mother tongue maintenance in minority language groups. *Canadian Modern Language Review, 34,* 395–416.

Cummins, J. (1981). The role of primary language development in promoting educational success for language minority students. In Office of Bilingual Bi-cultural Education, California State Department of Education, *Schooling and language minority students: A theoretical framework* (pp. 3–50). Los Angeles: California State University, Evaluation, Dissemination, and Assessment Center.

Cummins, J. (1985). The construct of language proficiency in bilingual education. In J. E. Alatis (Ed.), *Perspectives on bilingualism and bilingual education* (pp. 209–231). Washington, DC: Georgetown University Press.

Curiel, H., Rosenthal, J. A., & Richek, H. G. (1986). Impacts of bilingual education on secondary school grades, attendance, retention and drop-out. *Hispanic Journal of Behavioral Science, 8*(4), 357–367.

Cutts, N. E. (Ed.). (1955). *School psychologists at mid-century.* Washington, DC: American Psychological Association.

David, J. L., & Greene, D. (1983). Organizational barriers to full implementation of PL 94–142. In J. G. Chambers & W. T. Hartman (Eds.), *Special education policies: Their history, implementation, and finance* (pp. 115–135). Philadelphia: Temple University Press.

Davis, S. (1994). How the gateway program helps troubled teens. *Educational Leadership, 52*(1), 17–19.

Davis, T. (1995). Elementary and middle level counselors' courtroom hearing experiences. *NASSP Bulletin, 79*(570), 10–15.

Developmental Disabilities Services and Facilities Construction Amendments of 1970, Pub. L. No. 91-517, 84 Stat. 1316.

DeWeaver, K. L., & Rose, S. R. (1987). School social work with developmentally disabled pupils: Past, present, and future. *School Social Work Journal, XI,* 47–58.

Dewey, J. (1916). *Democracy in Education.* New York: Macmillian.

Dewey, J. (1936). *Experience and Education.* London: Collier Books.

DiBlasio, M. K. (1989). The landscape of educational research and Getty initiatives. In D. B. Pankratz & K. V. Malcahy (Eds.), *The challenge to reform arts education* (pp. 43–57). New York: American Council for the Arts.

Dinkmeyer, D., Jr., Carlson, J., & Dinkmeyer, D. (1994). *Consultation: School mental health professionals as consultants.* Muncie, IN: Accelerated Development.

Donegan, C. (1996). Debate over bilingualism. *CQ Researcher, 6*(3), 51–58.

Dorrell, L. D. (1996a). *Ensuring tomorrow: Breaking the cycle of dependency.* Columbia, MO: Missouri State Teachers Association.

Dorrell, L. D. (1996b). *Why students fail.* Paper presented at the annual national Dropout Prevention Conference, Tampa Bay, FL.

Drug-Free Schools and Communities Act, 20 U.S.C. § 7101 *et seq.* (West 1996).

Drug-Free Schools and Communities Act Amendments of 1989, Pub. L. No. 101-226, 1033 Stat. 1928.

Dryfoos, J. G. (1994). *Full-service schools: A revolution in health and social services for children, youth, and families.* San Francisco: Jossey-Bass.

Duckenfield, M., & Wright, J. (Eds.). (1995). *Pocket guide to service learning.* Clemson, SC: National Dropout Prevention Center.

Duke, D. L. (1978). *The retransformation of the school: The emergence of contemporary alternative schools in the United States.* Chicago: Nelson-Hall.

Duncan, J. A. (1989). The school guidance committee: The counselor's support group. *The School Counselor, 36*(3), 192–197.

Dunn, L., & Kontos, S. (1997). What have we learned about developmentally appropriate practice? *Young Children, 52*(5), 6–13.

Dunn, L. M. (1968). Special education for the mildly retarded —Is it too much or is it justifiable? *Exceptional Children, 35,* 5–22.

Dusenbury, L., & Diaz, T. (1995). Developing interventions for multiethnic populations: A case study with homeless youth. In G. J. Botvin, S. Schinke, & M. A. Orlandi (Eds.), *Drug abuse prevention with multiethnic youth* (pp. 233–254). Thousand Oaks, CA: Sage.

Eberly, D. J. (1993). National youth service: A developing institution. *NASSP Bulletin, 77*(550), 50–57.

Education for All Handicapped Children Act of 1975 (EAHCA), Pub. L. No. 94-142, 89 Stat. 773.

Education of the Handicapped Act Amendments of 1990, Pub. L. No. 101-476, 104 Stat. 1103.

Efland, A. (1990). *A history of art education: Intellectual and social currents in teaching and visual arts.* New York: Teachers College Press.

Eiserer, P. E. (1963). *The school psychologist.* Washington, DC: The Center for Applied Research.

Elementary and Secondary Education Act of 1965, Pub. L. No. 89-10, 79 Stat. 27.

Elementary and Secondary Education Act Amendments of 1969, Pub. L. No. 91-230, 84 Stat. 121–154.

Ennett, S. T., Tobler, N. S., Ringwalt, C. L., & Flewelling, R. L. (1994). How effective is drug abuse resistance education? A meta-analysis of Project DARE outcome evaluations. *American Journal of Public Health, 84*(9), 1394–1401.

Epstein, J. (1996). Perspectives and previews on research and policy for school, family, and community partnerships. In A. Booth & J. F. Dunn (Eds.), *Family-school links: How do they affect educational outcomes?* (pp. 209–246). Mahwah, NJ: Erlbaum.

Epstein, J. L., Jackson, V., & Salinas, K. C. (1994). *Manual for teachers: Teachers involve parents in schoolwork (TIPS) language arts, science/health, and math interactive homework in the middle grades* (Rev. ed.). Baltimore: Center on Families, Communities, Schools and Children's Learning, Johns Hopkins University.

Equal Access Act of 1984, Pub. L. No. 98-377, 98 Stat. 1302.

Erikson, E. (1963). *Childhood and society* (2nd ed.). New York: W. W. Norton & Co.

Ervin-Tripp, S. (1974). Is second language learning like the first? *Tesol Quarterly, 8,* 111–127.

Escamilla, K., & Medina, M. (1993). English and Spanish acquisition by limited-language proficient Mexican-Americans in a three year maintenance bilingual program. *Hispanic Journal of Behavioral Sciences, 15,* 108–120.

ESL Information Packet. (1988). Rosslyn, VA: National Clearinghouse for Bilingual Education.

Fagan, T. K. (1993). Separate but equal: School psychology's search for organizational identity. *Journal of School Psychology, 31,* 3–90.

Fagan, T. K., & Schicke, M. C. (1994). The service ratio in large school districts: Historical and contemporary perspectives. *Journal of School Psychology, 32*(3), 305–312.

Fagan, T. K., & Warden, P. G. (1996). (Eds.). *Historical encyclopedia of school psychology.* Westport, CT: Greenwood Press.

Fagan, T. K., & Wise, P. S. (1994). *School psychology: Past, present, and future.* White Plains, NY: Longman.

Farrington v. Tokushige, 1927: 273 U.S. 284, 47 S. Ct. 406.

Faust, V. (1968a). *History of elementary school counseling: Overview and critique.* Boston: Houghton Mifflin.

Faust, V. (1968b). *The counselor–consultant in the elementary school.* Boston: Houghton Mifflin.

Ferguson, D. L. (1987). *Curriculum decision making for students with severe handicaps: Policy and practice.* New York: Teachers College Press.

Fertman, C. I. (1994). *Service learning for all students.* Bloomington, IN: Phi Delta Kappa Educational Foundation.

Fish, M. C., & Massey, R. (1991). Systems in school psychology practice: A preliminary investigation. *The Journal of School Psychology, 29,* 361–366.

Fisher, R. A. (1988). Clinical aspects of school social work. *School Social Work Journal, 13,* 13–22.

Foster, C. R. (1982). Defusing the issues in bilingualism and bilingual education. *Phi Delta Kappan, 63*(5), 342–344.

Foster, W. (1986). Giftedness: The mistaken metaphor. In C. J. Maker (Ed.), *Critical issues in gifted education: Defensible programs for the gifted* (pp. 5–30). Rockville, MD: Aspen Publishers.

Fowler, C. (1988). *Can we rescue the arts for America's children? Coming to our senses 10 years later.* New York: American Council for the Arts.

Fowler, C. (1994a). *Discipline-based music education: A conceptual framework for the teaching of music.* Chattanooga, TN: University of Tennessee at Chattanooga.

Fowler, C. (1994b). Strong arts, strong schools. *Educational Leadership, 52*(3), 4–8.

Fowler, R. C., & Corley, K. K. (1996). Linking families, building families. *Educational Leadership, 52*(7), 24–26.

Freeman, E. (1994). School social work report card: Beyond the challenge of survival. *Social Work in Education, 16*(4), 203–206.

Freeman, E. M. (1995). School social work overview. In R. L. Edwards & J. G. Hopps (Eds.), *Encyclopedia of Social Work.* (19th ed., pp. 2087–2099). Washington, DC: National Association of Social Workers Press.

Fuchs, D., & Fuchs, L. S. (1994). Inclusive schools movement and the radicalization of special education reform. *Exceptional Children, 60*(4), 294–309.

Fuller, G. C., & Sabatino, D. A. (1996). Who attends alternative high schools? *The High School Journal, 79*(4), 293–297.

Funk, G., & Brown, D. (1996). A storefront school: A grassroots approach to educational reform. *Educational Horizons, 74*(2), 89–95.

Furth, H. G. (1969). *Piaget and knowledge: Theoretical foundations.* Englewood Cliffs, NJ: Prentice-Hall.

Gaddy, B. B., Hall, T. W., & Marzano, R. J. (1996). *School wars: Resolving our conflicts over religion and values.* San Francisco: Jossey-Bass.

Gallagher, J. J. (1985). *Teaching the gifted child* (3rd ed.). Boston: Allyn and Bacon.

Gardner, H. (1993). *Multiple intelligences: The theory in practice.* New York: Basic Books.

Gardner, W. I. (1977). *Learning and behavior characteristics of exceptional children and youth: A humanistic behavioral approach.* Boston: Allyn and Bacon.

Germain, C. B. (1982). An ecological perspective on social work in the schools. In R. Constable & J. P. Flynn (Eds.), *School social work: Practice and research perspectives* (pp. 3–12). Homewood, IL: The Dorsey Press.

Gibson, R. L., & Mitchell, M. H. (1995). *Introduction to counseling and guidance* (4th ed.). Englewood Cliffs, NJ: Prentice-Hall.

Gillung, T. B., & Rucker, C. N. (1977). Labels and teacher expectation. *Exceptional Children, 43*(7), 464–465.

Ginzberg, E. E., Davis, E., & Ostow, M. (1985). *Local health policy in action: The municipal health program.* Totowa, NJ: Roman & Allan Held.

Glass, R. S., & Nemeth, P. (1996, March). Unsung heroes. *American Teacher,* 10–11.

Goals 2000: A world-class education for every child. (1994). Washington, DC: U.S. Department of Education.

Gold, M., & Mann, D. (1982). Alternative schools for troublesome secondary students. *The Urban Review, 14*(4), 305–316.

Goldberger, S., & Kazis, R. (1996). Revitalizing high schools: What the school-to-career movement can contribute. *Phi Delta Kappan, 77*(8), 547–554.

Gonet, M. M. (1994). *Counseling the adolescent substance abuser: School-based intervention and prevention.* Thousand Oaks, CA: Sage.

Goodlad, J. J. (1984). *A place called school: Prospects for the future.* New York: McGraw-Hill.

Grants for Teaching in the Education of Handicapped Children Act, 20 U.S.C. § 611 *et seq.* (1958) (repealed 1970).

Gray, J. A. (1989). *Dance instruction: Science applied to the art of movement.* Champaign, IL: Human Kinetics Books.

Gray, K. (1996). The baccalaureate games: Is it right for all teens? *Phi Delta Kappan, 77*(8), 528–534.

Gray, S. W. (1963). *The psychologist in the schools.* New York: Holt, Rinehart and Winston.

Grubb, W. N. (1996). The new vocationalism: What it is, what it could be. *Phi Delta Kappan, 77*(8), 535–546.

Guilford, J. P. (1982). Cognitive psychology's ambiguities: Some suggested remedies. *Psychological Review, 89,* 48–59.

Gutkin, T. B., & Conoley, J. C. (1990). Reconceptualizing school psychology from a service delivery perspective: Implications for practice, training, and research. *Journal of School Psychology, 28,* 203–223.

Gysbers, N. C., & Henderson, P. (1994). *Developing and managing your school guidance program* (2nd ed.). Alexandria, VA: The American Counseling Association.

Hackensmith, C. W. (1966). *History of physical education.* New York: Harper & Row.

Hagedorn, S. (1993). Student views of the school nurse's role in a secondary school condom availability program. *Journal of School Health, 63*(8), 358–360.

Hancock, B. L. (1982). *School social work.* Englewood Cliffs, NJ: Prentice-Hall.

Handicapped Children's Early Education Assistance Act of 1968, Pub. L. No. 90-538, 82 Stat. 901.

Hare, I. (Ed.). (1995). *School social work certification requirements from state departments of education: What you need to know to apply for a school social work position.* Washington, DC: National Association of Social Workers.

Harrison, C. H. (1987). *Student service: The new Carnegie unit.* Princeton, NJ: The Carnegie Foundation for the Advancement of Teaching.

Hasazi, S. E., Rice, P. D., & York, R. (1979). *Mainstreaming: Merging regular and special education.* Bloomington, IN: Phi Delta Kappa Educational Foundation.

Hastings, C. (1992). Ending ability grouping is a moral imperative. *Educational Leadership, 50*(2), 14.

Hawkins, J. W., Hayes, E. R., & Corliss, P. (1994). School nursing in America—1902–1994: A return to public health nursing. *Public Health Nursing, 11*(6), 416–425.

Haynes, K. S., & Holmes, K. A. (1994). *Invitation to social work.* White Plains, NY: Longman.

Hazelwood School District v. Kuhlmeier, 1988: 484 U.S. 260, 108 S. Ct. 562.

Health Education Act of 1978, Pub. L. No. 89-10, 92 Stat. 2221.

Health Planning and Resources Development Amendments of 1979, Pub. L. No. 96-79, 93 Stat. 592.

Hedin, D., & Conrad, D. (1987). Service: A pathway to knowledge. *Community Educational Journal, 15*(1), 10–14.

Hellison, D. R., & Templin, T. J. (1991). *A reflective approach to teaching physical education.* Champaign, IL: Human Kinetics Books.

Henry, M. E. (1996). *Parent–school collaboration: Feminist organizational structures and school leadership.* Albany, NY: State University of New York Press.

Hepworth, D. H., & Larsen, J. (1987). Interviewing. In A. Minihan (Ed.), *Encyclopedia of Social Work* (18th ed., Vol. 1, pp. 996–1008). Silver Springs, MD: National Association of Social Workers.

Herr, E. L. (1979). *Guidance and counseling in the schools: Perspectives on the past, present, and future.* Falls Church, VA: American Personnel and Guidance Association.

Herrnstein, R., & Murray, C. (1994). *The bell curve: Intelligence and class structure in American life.* New York: Free Press.

Hiebert, B. (1994). *Moving to the future: Outcome-based comprehensive guidance and counseling in Alberta schools.* Edmonton, Alberta: Alberta Department of Education, Special Education Branch.

Hildreth, G. H. (1930). *Psychological service for school problems.* New York: World Book.

Hirsch, E. D. (1987). *Cultural literacy: What every American needs to know* (Rev. ed.). Boston: Houghton Mifflin.

Hofferth, S. L., Brayfield, A. A., Deich, S., & Holcomb, P. (1991). *National child care survey, 1990.* A National Association for the Education of Young Children (NAEYC) study. Washington, DC: Urban Institute Press.

Holland, A., & Andre, T. (1987). Participation in extracurricular activities in secondary school: What is known, what needs to be known? *Review of Educational Research, 57*(4), 437–466.

Hollingworth, L. S. (1926). *Gifted children: Their nature and nurture.* New York: Macmillan.

Holt, J. (1964). *How children fail.* New York: Dell.

Holtzman, D., Greene, B. Z., Ingraham, G. C., Daily, L. A., Demchuk, D. G., & Kolbe, L. J. (1992). HIV education and health education in the United States: A national survey of local school district policies and practices. *Journal of School Health, 62*(9), 421–427.

Honnet, E. P., & Poulsen, S. J. (1989). *Principles of good practice for combining service and learning: A Wingspread special report.* Racine, WI: The Johnson Foundation.

Hunt, J. M. (1961). *Intelligence and experience.* New York: Ronald Press.

Hymes, J. L., Jr. (1974). *Effective home-school relations* (Rev. ed.) Sierra Madre, CA: Southern California Association for the Education of Young Children.

Hymes, J. L., Jr. (1991). *Early childhood education: Twenty years in review.* Washington, DC: National Association for the Education of Young Children.

Illinois State Board of Education. (1990, August). Department of Special Education, Administration Bulletin.

Improving America's Schools Act of 1994, Pub. L. No. 103-382, 108 Stat. 3518.

Individuals with Disabilities Education Act of 1990, 20 U.S.C.A. § 1400 *et seq.* (1990).

Individuals with Disabilities Education Act Amendments of 1991, 20 U.S.C. 1400 *et seq.* (1991).

Iverson, C. J., & Hays, B. J. (1994). School nursing in the 21st century: Prediction and readiness. *The Journal of School Nursing, 10*(4), 19–24.

Jacob K. Javits Gifted and Talented Students Education Act of 1988, Pub. L. No. 100-297, Title I, 1001, 102 Stat. 237.

Jensen, A. R. (1969). How much can we boost IQ and scholastic achievement? *Harvard Educational Review, 39,* 1–123.

Jewett, A. E., & Bain, L. L. (1985). *The curriculum process in physical education.* Dubuque, IA: Wm. C. Brown.

Kamii, C., & Ewing, J. K. (1996). Basing teaching on Piagets' constructionism. *Childhood Education:* 1996 Annual Theme, pp. 260–264.

Kandall, S. R. (1996). *Substance and shadow: Women and addiction in the United States.* Cambridge, MA: Harvard University Press.

Kaplan, L. (Ed.). (1992). *Education and the family.* Boston: Allyn and Bacon.

Kauffman, J. M. (1989). The regular education initiative as Reagan–Bush education policy: A trickle-down theory of education of the hard-to-teach. *The Journal of Special Education, 23*(3), 256–278.

Kaufman, A. S. (1983). Intelligence: Old concepts—New perspectives. In G. W. Hynd (Ed.), *The school psychologist: An introduction* (pp. 95–117). Syracuse, NY: Syracuse University Press.

Keene, J. A. (1982). *A history of music education in the United States.* Hanover, NH: University Press of New England.

Kellmayer, J. (1995). *How to establish an alternative school.* Thousand Oaks, CA: Corwin Press.

Kelly, D. M. (1993). *Last chance high school: How girls and boys drop in and out of alternative schools.* New Haven, CT: Yale University Press.

Kessler, S., & Swadener, B. B. (Eds.). (1992). *Reconceptualizing the early childhood curriculum.* New York: Teachers College Press.

Kinsley, C. (1994). Service-learning: An educational process for teaching and learning. In P. Toole, K. Corak, & R. Warnes (Eds.), *Peer Consultant Initiative Handbook* (pp. 1–76). The National Youth Leadership Council and The National Service-Learning Cooperative/Clearinghouse.

Kinsley, C., & McPherson, K. (1995). Introduction: Changing perceptions to integrate community service learning into education. In C. Kinsley & K. McPherson (Eds.), *Enriching the curriculum through service learning* (pp. 1–15). Alexandria, VA: Association for Supervision and Curriculum Development.

Klitzner, M., Fisher, D., Stewart, K., & Gilbert, S. (1992). *Substance abuse: Early intervention for adolescents.* Princeton, NJ: The Robert Wood Johnson Foundation in collaboration with The Pacific Institute for Research and Evaluation.

Klonsky, M., & Ford, P. (1994). One urban solution: Small schools. *Educational Leadership, 51*(8), 64–67.

Knauft, E. B. (1992). *America's teenagers as volunteers.* Washington, DC: Metropolitan Life Foundation.

Knutson, G. G. (1996). Alternative high schools: Models for the future? *The High School Journal, 79*(2), 119–124.

Kohl, H. R. (1969). *The open classroom: A practical guide to a new way of teaching.* New York: Vintage Books.

Konet, R. J. (1991). Peer helpers in the middle school. *Middle School Journal, 23*(1), 13–15.

Kozol, J. (1982). *Alternative schools: A guide for educators and parents.* New York: The Continuum Publishing Company.

Kraus, R., Hilsendager, S. C., & Dixon, B. (1991). *History of the dance in art and education* (3rd ed.). Englewood Cliffs, NJ: Prentice-Hall.

Lambert, N. M. (1993). Historical perspective of school psychology as a scientist–practitioner specialization in school psychology. *Journal of School Psychology, 31,* 163–193.

Lambert, W., & Tucker, G. (1972). *Bilingual education of children: The St. Lambert experience.* Rowley, MA: Newbury House.

Landis, B. (1972). Realization in movement as a way of comprehending music. In B. Landis & P. Carder (Eds.), *The eclectic curriculum in American music education: Contributions of Dalcroze, Kodaly, and Orff* (pp. 178–190). Washington, DC: Music Educators National Conference.

Landis, B., & Carder, P. (1972). *The eclectic curriculum in American music education: Contributions of Dalcroze, Kodaly, and Orff.* Washington, DC: Music Educators National Conference.

Landy, R. J. (1982). *Handbook of educational drama and theatre.* Westport, CT: Greenwood Press.

Langenbach, M., & Neskora, T. W. (1977). *Day care: Curriculum considerations.* Columbus, OH: Charles E. Merrill.

Lanham Public War Housing Act (Defense Housing Insurance Act), Jan. 21, 1942, ch. 14, 56, Stat. 11.

Lau v. Nichols, 1974: 414 U.S. 563, 94 S. Ct. 786.

Lazerson, M. (1983). The origins of special education. In J. G. Chambers & W. T. Hartman (Eds.), *Special education policies: Their history, implementation, and finance* (pp. 15–47). Philadelphia: Temple University Press.

Learn and Serve America. (n.d.). *Learn and Serve America.* Author.

Leeper, S. H., Witherspoon, R. L., & Day, B. (1984). *Good schools for young children: A guide for working with three, four, and five year old children.* New York: Macmillan.

Lehman, P., & Sinatra, R. (1988). Assessing arts curricula in the schools: Their role, content and purpose. In J. T. McLaughlin (Ed.), *Toward a new era in arts education: Interlochen symposium* (pp. 53–79). New York: American Council for the Arts.

Leonhard, C. (1991). *The status of arts education in American public schools.* Urbana, IL: Council for Research in Music Education.

Leyba, C. F. (1978). *Longitudinal study, Title VII bilingual programs, Santa Fe, New Mexico.* Los Angeles, CA: California State University, National Dissemination and Assessment Center.

Link, M. (1991). Social work services to schools in the Midwestern United States and in London: A comparative study on the nature of guest status. *Social Work in Education, 13*(5), 278–294.

Lions-Quest. (n.d.). *Skills for adolescence: Skills for growing. Combination workshop guidebook.* Granville, OH: Quest International. Author.

Lloyd, L., Whiteoak, H., & Hodson, C. (1994). Setting standards for a school nursing service. *Health Visitor, 67*(12), 436–437.

Lofquist, W. A. (1991). *Discovering the meaning of prevention: A practical approach to positive change.* Tucson, AZ: AYD Publications.

Logan, K. R., Diaz, E., Piperno, M., Rankin, D., MacFarland, A. D., & Bargamian, K. (1995). How inclusion built a community of learners. *Educational Leadership, 52*(4), 42–44.

Lowenfeld, V. (1947). *Creative and mental growth.* New York: Macmillan.

Lubeck, S. (1994). The politics of developmentally appropriate practice: Exploring issues of culture, class, and curriculum. In B. L. Mallory & R. S. New (Eds.), *Diversity and developmentally appropriate practices: Challenges for early childhood educators* (pp. 17–43). New York: Teachers College Press.

Lubinski, D., & Benbow, C. P. (1995). Optimal development of talent: Respond educationally to individual differences in personality. *The Educational Forum, 59*(4), 381–392.

Lundblad, K. S. (1995). Jane Addams and social reform: A role model for the 1990s. *Social Work, 40*(5), 661–669.

Mallory, B. L., & New, R. S. (Eds.). (1994). *Diversity and developmentally appropriate practices: Challenges for early childhood education.* New York: Teachers College Press.

Mallory, B. L. (1994). Inclusive policy, practice, and theory for young children with developmental differences. In B. L. Mallory & R. S. New (Eds.), *Diversity and developmentally appropriate practices: Challenges for early childhood education* (pp. 44–62). New York: Teachers College Press.

Margolin, L. (1994). *Goodness personified: The emergence of gifted children.* New York: Walter de Gruyter.

Mark, M. L., & Gary, C. L. (1992). *A history of American music education.* New York: Schirmer Books.

Marland, S. (1972). *Education of the gifted and talented: Report to Congress.* Washington, DC: U.S. Government Printing Office.

Marsiglia, F. F., & Johnson, M. W. (1997). Social work with groups and the performing arts in the schools. *Social Work in Education, 19*(1), 53–59.

Marston, D. (1996). A comparison of inclusion only, pull-out only, and combined service models for students with mild disabilities. *The Journal of Special Education, 30*(2), 121–132.

Martin, K. A., & Ross, J. (1988). Developing professionals for arts education. In J. T. McLaughlin (Ed.), *Toward a new era in arts education: Interlochen symposium* (pp. 30–42). New York: American Council for the Arts.

Maxim, G. (1985). *The very young: Guiding children from infancy through the early years* (2nd ed.). Belmont, CA: Wadsworth.

McBride, B. A., & Lee, J. (1995). University-based child development laboratory schools. In S. Reifel (Ed.), *Advances in early education and day care* (pp. 95–121). Greenwich, CT: JAI Press.

McCarthy, A. R. (1992). The American family. In L. Kaplan (Ed.), *Education and the Family* (pp. 3–26). Boston: Allyn and Bacon.

McCarthy, M. M., & Sorenson, G. P. (1993). School counselors and consultants: Legal duties and liabilities. *Journal of Counseling and Development, 72,* 159–167.

McCaslin, N. (1987). *Creative drama in the primary grades.* New York: Longman.

McCullagh, J. G. (1994). Jane Fullerton Culbert (1880–1962): Visiting teacher leader. *School Social Work Journal, 19,* 34–49.

McEwin, C. K., Dickinson, T. S., & Jenkins, D. M. (1996). *America's middle schools: Practices and progress—A 25 year perspective.* Columbus, OH: National Middle School Association.

McLaughlin, J. T. (Ed.). (1988). *Toward a new era in arts education: Interlochen symposium.* New York: American Council for the Arts.

Mead, M., & Wolfenstein, M. (1955). *Childhood in contemporary cultures.* Chicago: University of Chicago Press.

Medina, M., Jr. (1993). Spanish achievement in a maintenance bilingual education program: Language proficiency, grade, and gender. *Bilingual Research Journal, 17,* 57–81.

Medina, M., Jr., & Escamilla, K. (1992a). Evaluation of transitional and maintenance bilingual programs. *Urban Education, 27*(3), 263–290.

Medina, M., Jr., & Escamilla, K. (1992b). English acquisition by fluent- and limited-Spanish proficient Mexican-Americans in a 3-year maintenance bilingual program. *Hispanic Journal of Behavioral Sciences, 14*(3), 252–267.

Medina, M., Jr., & Escamilla, K. (1994). Language acquisition and gender for limited-language-proficient Mexican-Americans in a maintenance bilingual program. *Hispanic Journal of Behavioral Sciences, 16*(4), 422–437.

Meier, D. W. (1996). The big benefits of smallness. *Educational Leadership, 54*(1), 12–15.

Meixner, C. (1994). Teaching with love at Oasis High. *Educational Leadership, 52*(1), 32.

Mental Retardation Facilities and Community Mental Health Centers Construction Act, 42 U.S.C. § 6000 *et seq.* (1963).

Meyer v. Nebraska, 1923: 262 U.S. 390, 43 S. Ct. 625.

Meyers, J., Gelzheiser, L. M., & Yelich, G. (1991). Do pull-in programs foster teacher collaboration? *Remedial and Special Education, 12*(2), 7–15.

Miller, C. H. (1961). *Foundations of guidance.* New York: Harper & Brothers.

Mills v. Board of Education for the District of Columbia, 348 F. Supp. 866 (D.C. 1972).

Molbert, W., Boyer, C. B., & Shafer, M-A. B. (1993). Implementing a school-based STD/HIV prevention intervention: Collaboration between a university medical center and an urban school district. *Journal of School Health, 63*(6), 258–261.

Morgan, P. (1987). Relationship of health status to learning. *School Nurse, 3*(3), 38–43.

Morris, C. (1992). Mandated volunteerism: Is it right? Do we want it? *Updating School Board Policies, 23*(7), 1–4.

Morrissey, P. A. (1993, November/December). The ADA & vocational education: What schools must do to guarantee the rights of disabled people. *Vocational Education Journal, 68*(3), 22–24.

Mursell. (1927). *Principles of music education.* New York: Macmillan.

Myrick, R. D. (1987). *Developmental guidance and counseling: A practical approach.* Minneapolis, MN: Educational Media Corporation.

National and Community Service Act of 1990, Pub. L. No. 101-610, 104 Stat. 3127.

National Association for Bilingual Education. (1996). Bilingual education: Separating fact from fiction. *NABE News, 19*(5), 11.

National Association for Sport and Physical Education. (1995). *Moving into the future: National standards for physical education: A guide to content and assessment.* St. Louis, MO: C. V. Mosby.

National Association of School Nurses, Inc. (1993). *School nursing practice: Roles and Standards.* Scarborough, ME: Author.

National Association of School Psychologists. (1992). *Professional conduct manual.* Silver Spring, MD: Author.

National Association of Social Workers. (n.d.). *Position Statement.* Washington, DC: Author.

National Association of Social Workers. (1992a). *NASW standards for school social work services.* Washington, DC: Author.

National Association of Social Workers. (1992b). *School of Social Work Certification Requirements from State Departments of Education: What you need to know to apply for a school social work position.* Washington: DC: Author.

National Association of Social Workers. (1995). *School social work certification requirements from state departments of education: What you need to know to apply for a school social work position.* Washington, DC: Author.

National Association of Social Workers. (n.d.). *School social workers: Enhancing school success for all students* [Brochure]. Washington, DC: Author.

The National Campaign to Prevent Teen Pregnancy. (1996). [Brochure]. Washington, DC: Author.

National Center for Education Statistics. (1996). Projections of education statistics to 2006 (25th ed.). (NCES 96-661). Washington, DC: U.S. Department of Education, Office of Educational Research & Improvement.

National Center for Health Statistics. (1995). The health of the nation. Highlights of the healthy people 2000 goals. 1995 Report on Progress. Washington, DC: U.S. Department of Health and Human Services.

National Commission on AIDS. (1994). Preventing HIV/AIDS in adolescents. *Journal of School Health, 64*(1), 39–51.

National Consumer Health Information and Health Promotion Act of 1976, Pub. L. No. 94-317, 90 Stat. 695.

National Council for Accreditation of Teacher Education. (1995). *Standards, procedures, and policies for the accreditation of professional education units.* Washington, DC: Author.

National Defense Authorization Act for Fiscal Year 1997, Pub. L. No. 104-201, 110 Stat. 2422.

National Defense Education Act of 1958, Pub. L. No. 85-864, 72 Stat. 1580.

National Dropout Prevention Center. (1995). *Pocket guide to service learning.* Clemson, SC: Author.

National Education Association. (1918). Cardinal principles of secondary education. Report of the Commission on the Reorganization of Secondary Education. Washington, DC: Bureau of Education Bulletin.

National Educational Goals Panel. (1995). *The national educational goals report: Building a nation of learners.* Washington, DC: National Educational Goals Panel.

National Information Center for Children and Youth with Disabilities. (1993). Part I: Background information on the IDEA. Washington, DC: *NICHY News Digest, 3*(2), 1–15. Author.

National Information Center for Children and Youth with Disabilities. (1994). Individualized education programs. Washington, DC: NICHY Briefing Paper. *LG2 Update,* 1–24. Author.

National Information Center for Children and Youth with Disabilities. (1995). Planning for inclusion. Washington, DC: *NICHY News Digest, 5*(1), 1–31. Author.

National Service Trust Program Act of 1993, 42 U.S.C.A. § 12571 *et seq.*

Nebgen, M. K., & McPherson, K. (1990). Enriching learning through service: A tale of three districts. *Educational Leadership, 48*(3), 90–92.

Neill, A. S. (1960). *Summerhill.* New York: Simon & Schuster.

Nejedlo, R. (1992, September). *Valuing pluralism: Community building for the 21st century.* Paper presented at the American Counselors Education Society Convention, San Antonio, TX.

Nejedlo, R. J. (1988). Approaches to supervision: Expectations for master's students' skill development, and criteria for evaluation. *Illinois Association for Counseling Development Quarterly, 8*(111), 5–10.

Nelson, K. E. (1997). The needs of children and the role of the school nurse. *Journal of School Health, 67*(5), 187–188.

New, R. S. (1994). Culture, child development, and developmentally appropriate practices. In B. L. Mallory & R. S. New (Eds), *Diversity and developmentally appropriate practices: Challenges for early childhood education* (pp. 65–83). New York: Teachers College Press.

Obeidallah, D., Turner, P., Iannotti, R. J., O'Brien, R. W., Haynie, D., & Galper, D. (1993). Investigating children's knowledge and understanding of AIDS. *Journal of School Health, 63*(3), 125–129.

Oda, D. (1982). School health services: Growth potential for nursing. In L. H. Aiken (Ed.), *Nursing in the 1980s: Crisis, opportunity, challenges* (pp. 359–379). Philadelphia: J. B. Lippincott.

O'Dell, S. J. (1990). Support for new teachers. In T. M. Bey and T. C. Holmes (Eds.), *Mentoring: Developing successful new teachers* (pp. 3–24). Reston, VA: Association for Teacher Educators.

Ooms, T. (1992). *Family-school partnership: A critical component of school reform.* Washington, DC: Family Impact Seminar, The American Association for Marriage and Family Therapy. Background briefing report for seminar held in February 1992.

Ornstein, A. C., & Hunkins, F. P. *Curriculum: Foundations, principles, and issues.* Englewood Cliffs, NJ: Prentice-Hall.

O'Rourke, K. (1991). A report of the ASCA counselor certification survey. *NASSP Bulletin, 75*(534), 43–48.

Osborn, D. K. (1991). *Early childhood education in historical perspective* (3rd ed.). Athens, GA: Daye Press.

Oxley, D. (1994). Organizing schools into small units: Alternatives to homogeneous grouping. *Phi Delta Kappan, 75*(7), 521–526.

Padilla, R. V. (1984). Federal policy shifts in bilingual education: Consequences for local implementation and national evaluation. *Professional Papers.* Los Alamitos, CA: National Center for Bilingual Research.

Paisley, P. O., & Borders, L. D. (1995). School counseling: An evolving specialty. *Journal of Counseling & Development, 74,* 150–153.

Pankratz, D. B. (1989). Arts education research: Issues, constraints, and opportunities. In D. B. Pankratz & K. V. Mulcahy (Eds.), *The challenge to reform arts education* (pp. 1–28). New York: American Council for the Arts.

Pankratz, D. B., & Mulcahy, K. V. (Eds.). (1989). *The challenge to reform arts education.* New York: American Council for the Arts.

Parc v. Pennsylvania, 1972: 343 F. Supp. 279.

Parsons, F. (1909). *Choosing a vocation.* Boston: Houghton Mifflin.

Parsons, M. A., & Felton, G. M. (1992). Role performance and job satisfaction of school nurses. *Western Journal of Nursing Research, 14*(4), 498–511.

Passarelli, C. (1994). School nursing: Trends for the future. *Journal of School Health, 64*(4), 141–147.

Patchen, J. (1994). Introduction. In Fuller, C. (Ed.), *Discipline-based music education: A conceptual framework for the teaching of music* (pp. vi–xi). Chattanooga, TN: University of Tennessee at Chattanooga.

Pennsylvania Association for Retarded Children (PARC) v. Pennsylvania, 343 F. Supp. 279 (Pa. 1972).

Peters, R. M. (1995). Teaching population-focused practice to baccalaureate nursing students: A clinical model. *Journal of Nursing Education, 34*(8), 378–383.

Phillips, B. N. (1990). *School psychology at a turning point: Ensuring a bright future for the profession.* San Francisco: Jossey-Bass.

Phillips, J. L. (1969). *The origins of intellect: Piaget's theory.* San Francisco: W. H. Freeman.

Points of Light Foundation. (1995). *Everyone wins when youth serve: Building agency/school partnerships for service learning.* Washington, DC: Points of Light Foundation.

Portner, J. (1996, May 15). Nurse's orders. *Education Week, 15*(34), 20–28.

Posner, J. K., & Vandell, D. L. (1994). Low-income children's after-school care: Are there beneficial effects of after-school programs? *Child Development, 65,* 440–456.

Postman, N., & Weingartner, C. (1973). *The school book.* New York: Delacorte Press.

Powell, D. R. (1994). Parents, pluralism, and the NAEYC statement on developmentally appropriate practices. In B. L. Mallory & R. S. New (Eds.), *Diversity and developmentally appropriate practices* (pp. 166–182). New York: Teachers College Press.

Powell, D. R., & Dunn, L. (1990). Non-baccalaureate teacher education in early childhood education. In B. S. Spodek & O. A. Saracho (Eds.), *Early childhood teacher preparation* (pp. 44–66). New York: Teachers College Press.

Powers, S., & Rossman, M. (1984). Evidence of the impact of bilingual education: A meta analysis. *Journal of Instructional Psychology, 11*(2), 75–78.

Pratt, D. (1980). *Curriculum: Design and development.* New York: Harcourt Brace & Jovanovich.

Procidano, M. E., & Fisher, C. B. (1992). *Contemporary families: A handbook for school professionals.* New York: Teachers College Press.

Proctor, S. T., Lordi, S. L., & Zaiger, D. S. (Eds.). (1993). *School nursing practice: Roles and standards.* Scarborough, Maine: National Association of School Nurses.

Programs for Individuals with Developmental Disabilities, 42 U.S.C.A. § 6001 (1978).

Public Health Service. (1991). *Healthy people 2000: National health promotion and disease prevention objectives.* Washington, DC: Government Printing Office.

Public Law 101-610. (1990). National and Community Service Act of 1990. Washington, DC: Author.

Ramirez, A., & Politzer, R. (1978). Comprehension and production in English as a Second Language by elementary school children and adolescents. In E. M. Hatch (Ed.), *Second language acquisition: A book of readings* (pp. 202–228). Rowley, MA: Newbury House.

Randall, H. B. (1971). School health in the seventies: A decade against disease. *The Journal of School Health, 41*(3), 125–129.

Raywid, M. A. (1994). Alternative schools: The state of the art. *Educational Leadership, 52*(1), 26–31.

Reed, A. Y. (1944). *Guidance and personnel services in education.* Ithaca, NY: Cornell University Press.

Rehabilitation Act of 1973, 42 U.S.C. § 504 (1973).

Rehabilitation, Comprehensive Services, and Developmental Disabilities Amendments Act of 1978, Pub. L. No. 95-602, 92 Stat. 2955.

Reingold, J. R., & Frank, B. R. *Targeting youth: The sourcebook for federal policies and programs.* Flint, MI: Charles Stewart Mott Foundation.

Reis, S. M., & Renzulli, J. S. (1992). Using curriculum compacting to challenge the above average. *Educational Leadership, 52*(2), 51–57.

Renzulli, J. S. (1977). *The enrichment triad model: A guide for developing defensible programs for the gifted and talented.* Mansfield Center, CT: Creative Learning Press.

Renzulli, J. S., Reis, S. M., & Smith, L. H. (1981). *The revolving door identification model.* Mansfield Center, CT: Creative Learning Press.

Renzulli, J. S., & Smith, L. H. (1979). *A guidebook for developing individualized educational programs for gifted and talented students.* Mansfield Center, CT: Creative Learning Press.

Reynolds, C. R., Gutkin, T. B., Elliott, S. N., & Witt, J. C. (1984). *School psychology: Essentials of theory and practice.* New York: John Wiley.

Rice, E. A., Hutchinson, J. L., & Lee, M. (1969). *A brief history of physical education* (5th ed.). New York: The Ronald Press.

Richmond, M. E. (1917). *Social diagnosis.* New York: Russell Sage Foundation.

Riley, R. R. (1995, February 1). The State of American Education: Second Annual Address at Thomas Jefferson Middle School, Arlington, VA.

Rivenes, R. S. (Ed.). (1978). *Foundations of physical education: A scientific approach.* Boston: Houghton Mifflin.

RMC Research Corporation. (1993). *National study of before and after school programs: Final report.* Washington, DC: U.S. Department of Education.

Roach, V., Ascroft, J., & Stamp, A. (1995). *Winning ways: Creating inclusive schools, classrooms and communities.* Alexander, VA: National Association of State Boards of Education.

Rodriguez, A. (1975). Introduction. *Inequality in education, 19*(3), 91–105.

Rogers, C. (1942). *Counseling and psychotherapy: Newer concepts in practice.* Boston: Houghton Mifflin.

Rogers, J. (1993). The inclusive revolution. (Research Report No. 11). Bloomington, IN: Phi Delta Kappa.

Romano, L. G., & Georgiady, N. P. (1994). *Building an effective middle school.* Madison, WI: WCB Brown & Benchmark Publishers.

Rose, S. (1996). The sexual politics of the religious right: Sex-ed and the public schools. *Religion and Education, 23*(2), 77–83.

Rosenberg, J. A. (1988). The reflection of the past helps the future. *The Florida Nurse, 36*(10), 12.

Rosenfield, S. (1987). *Instructional consultation.* Hillsdale, NJ: Erlbaum.

Ross, P. O. (1993). *National excellence: A case for developing America's talent.* Washington, DC: U.S. Department of Education, Office of Educational Research and Improvement.

Rossell, C. H., & Baker, K. (1996). The educational effectiveness of bilingual education. *Research in the Teaching of English, 30*(1), 7–74.

Roth, J., & Hendrickson, J. M. (1991). Schools and youth agencies. *Phi Delta Kappan, 72*(8), 619–622.

Rude, H. A., & Anderson, R. E. (1992). Administrator effectiveness in support of inclusive schools. *Case in Point, 7*(1), 31–37.

Safford, P. L., & Safford, E. J. (1996). A history of childhood disability. New York: Teachers College Press.

Sagor, R. (1996). Building resiliency in students. *Educational Leadership, 54*(1), 38–43.

Saldate, M. W., Mishra, S. P., & Medina, M., Jr. (1985). Bilingual instruction and academic achievement: A longitudinal study. *Journal of Instructional Psychology, 12*(1), 24–30.

Salmon, M. E. (1994). School (health) nursing in the era of health care reform: What is the outlook? *Journal of School Health, 64*(4), 137–140.

Sanborn, M. A., & Hartman, B. G. (1982). *Issues in physical education* (3rd ed.). Philadelphia: Lea & Febiger.

Sandler, L., & Vandegrift, J. A. (1993). Community service and service learning in Arizona: 1993 evaluation report for Arizona's Serve-America Program. Tempe, AZ: Arizona State University, Morrison Institute for Public Policy.

Sapon-Shevin, M. (1994). *Playing favorites: Gifted education and the disruption of community.* Albany, NY: State University of New York Press.

Savitch, J., & Serling, L. (1995). Paving a path through untracked territory. *Educational Leadership, 52*(4), 72–74.

Scherer, M. (1994). On schools where students want to be: A conversation with Deborah Meier. *Educational Leadership, 52*(1), 4–8.

Schinke, S., & Cole, K. (1995). Prevention in community settings. In G. J. Botvin, S. Schinke, & M. A. Orlandi (Eds.), *Drug abuse prevention with multiethnic youth* (pp. 215–232). Thousand Oaks, CA: Sage.

Schmidt, J. J. (1993a). *Counseling in schools: Essential services and comprehensive programs.* Needham Heights, MA: Allyn and Bacon.

Schmidt, J. J. (1993b). Becoming an "able" counselor. *Elementary School Guidance and Counseling, 21*(1), 16–22.

Schoen, T. M., Arien, J., & Arvanitis, M. A. (1997). Children blossom in a special and general education integration program: A private child care center and a public school collaborative. *Young Children, 52*(2), 58–63.

School-to-Work Opportunities Act of 1994, Pub. L. No. 103-239, 108 Stat. 568.

Schwartz, L. L. (1994). *Why give "gifts" to the gifted?: Investing in a national resource.* Thousand Oaks, CA: Corwin Press.

Seaton, D. C. (1992). *Physical education handbook* (8th ed.). Englewood Cliffs, NJ: Prentice-Hall.

Secada, W. G. (1990). Research, politics, and bilingual education. *The Annals of the American Academy of Political & Social Science, 99.*

Section 504 of the Rehabilitation Act of 1973, as amended, 29 U.S.C. sec. 794.

Shepard, L. (1991). The influence of standardized tests on the early childhood curriculum, teachers, and children. In B. Spodek & N. Saracho (Eds.), *Issues in early childhood curriculum* (pp. 166–189). New York: Teachers College Press.

Sheppo, K. G., Hartsfield, S. J., Ruff, S., Jones, C. A., & Holinga, M. (1995). How an urban school promotes inclusion. *Educational Leadership, 52*(4), 82–84.

Siedentop, D., & Locke, L. (1997). Making a difference for physical education: What professors and practices must build together. *JOPERD, 68*(4), 25–33.

Siegel, J. A., & Cole, E. (1990). Role expansion for school psychologists: Challenges and future directions. In E. Cole and J. A. (Eds.), *Effective consultation in school psychology* (pp. 3–17). Toronto, Ontario: Hogrefe & Huber Publishers.

Silcox, H. (1993). School-based community service programs—An imperative for effective schools. *NASSP Bulletin, 77*(550), 58–61.

Skidmore, R. A., Thackery, M. G., & Farley, O. W. (1997). *Introduction to social work* (7th ed.). Needham Heights, MA: Allyn and Bacon.

Smith-Hughes Vocational Education Act (Vocational Education Act of 1917), Pub. L. No. 86-70, 73 Stat. 144.

Social Security Act (Old Age Pension Act) of 1935, Pub. L. No. 531, 49 Stat. 620.

Solomon, G. B. (1997). Fair play in the gymnasium: Improving social skills among elementary school students. *JOPERD, 68*(5), 22–25.

South Carolina Department of Education. (1994). *Serving to learn: High school manual.* Columbia, SC: South Carolina Department of Education.

Spodek, B. (Ed.). (1993). *Handbook of research on the education of young children.* New York: Macmillan.

Spodek, B., & Brown, P. C. (1993). Curriculum alternatives in early childhood education: A historical perspective. In B. Spodek (Ed.), *Handbook of research on the education of young children* (pp. 91–104). New York: Macmillan.

Stanciak, L. A. (1995). Reforming the high school counselor's role: A look at developmental guidance. *NASSP Bulletin, 79*(570), 60–63.

Stanley, J. C. (1980). On educating the gifted. *Educational Researcher, 9,* 8–12.

Staub, D., & Peck, C. A. (1995). What are the outcomes for nondisabled students? *Educational Leadership, 52*(4), 36–39.

Steinhardt, M. A. (1992). Physical education. In P. W. Jackson (Ed.), *Handbook of research on curriculum* (pp. 964–1001). New York: MacMillan.

Steirer v. Bethlehem Area School District, 1993: 987 F. ld 989.

Stern, H., Burstall, C., & Harley, B. (1975). *French from age eight, or eleven?* Toronto, Canada: Ontario Ministry of Education.

Sternberg, R. J. (1985). *Beyond IQ: A triarchic theory of human intelligence.* Cambridge, NY: Cambridge University Press.

Subotnik, R., Kassan, L., Summers, E., & Wasser, A. (1993). *Genius revisited: High IQ children grown up.* Norwood, NJ: Ablex Publishing.

Super, D. E. (1976). *Career education and the meaning of work.* Washington, DC: Department of Health, Education, and Welfare, Office of Education.

Swap, S. M. (1993). *Developing home-school partnerships: From concepts to practice.* New York: Teachers College Press.

Terman, D. L., Larner, M. B., Stevenson, C. S., & Behrman, R. E. (1996, Spring). Special education for students with disabilities: Analysis and recommendations. In Behrman, R. E. (Ed.), *The future of children, 6*(1) (pp. 4–24). Los Altos, CA: Center for the Future of Children and The David and Lucile Packard Foundation.

Terman, L. (1925). *Genetic studies of genius.* Stanford, CA: Stanford University Press.

Terman, L. M., & Oden, M. H. (1959). *The gifted group at mid-life: Thirty-five years' follow-up of the superior child.* Stanford, CA: Stanford University Press.

Testerman, J. (1996). Holding at-risk students: The secret is one-to-one. *Phi Delta Kappan, 77*(5), 364–365.

Texas Education Agency. (1990). *The comprehensive guidance program for Texas Public Schools: A guide for program development pre-K–12th grade.* Austin, TX: Author.

Thomas, S. B., & Russo, C. J. (1995). *Special education law: Issues and implications for the '90s.* Topeka, KS: National Organization on Legal Problems in Education.

Thompson, S. (1995). The community as a classroom. *Educational Leadership, 52*(1), 17–20.

Thompson, S. (1996). How action research can put teachers and parents on the same team. *Educational Horizons, 74*(2), 70–76.

Tindall, R. H. (1979). School psychology: The development of a profession. In G. D. Phye and D. J. Reschly (Eds.), *School psychology: Perspectives and issues* (pp. 3–24). New York: Academic Press.

Tocqueville, Alexis de. (1830). *Democracy in America.* New York: Knopf.

Tolbert, E. L. (1982). *An introduction to guidance: The professional counselor* (2nd ed.). Boston: Little, Brown and Company.

Torres, S., Jr. (1996). The status of school social workers in America. *Social Work in Education, 18*(1), 62–83.

Townsend, K. K., & O'Neil, M. (1993). *The courage to care: The strength to serve.* Annapolis, MD: Maryland Student Service Alliance.

Trent, W. T., & Braddock, J. H. II. (1992). Extracurricular activities in secondary schools. In M. C. Alkin (Ed.), *Encyclopedia of educational research* (pp. 476–481). New York: Macmillan.

Trump, L. (1953). Extraclass activities and the needs of youth. In N. B. Henry (Ed.), *Adapting the secondary school program to the needs of youth* (pp. 160–179). Chicago: University of Chicago Press.

Tweedie, J. (1983). The politics of legalization in special education reform. In J. G. Chambers & W. T. Hartman (Eds.), *Special education policies: Their history, implementation, and finance* (pp. 48–73). Philadelphia: Temple University Press.

Unks, G. (1996, March/April). Will schools risk teaching about the risk of AIDS? *The Clearing House,* 205–210.

Urbinati, D., Steele, P., Harter, B. J. E., & Harrell, D. (1996). The evolution of the school nurse practitioner: Past, present, and future. *The Journal of School Nursing, 12*(2), 6–9.

U.S. Department of Education. (1992). *What works: Schools without drugs.* Washington, DC: Author.

U.S. Department of Education. (1994). The improving America's schools Act of 1994: Summary sheets. Washington, DC: U.S. Department of Education.

U.S. Department of Education. (1995). *The Seventeenth Annual Report to Congress on the Implementation of the Individuals with Disabilities Act.* Washington, DC: Government Printing Office.

U.S. Department of Education, Office for Civil Rights. (1995). *The Civil Rights of Students with Hidden Disabilities under Section 504 of the Rehabilitation Act of 1973.* Washington, DC: Government Printing Office.

U.S. Department of Education, Office of Educational Research and Improvement. (1988). National Education Longitudinal Study on Gifted and Talented Education, unpublished study, Washington, DC.

U.S. Department of Health and Human Services. (1990). *Healthy people 2000: National health promotion and disease prevention objectives* (DHHS Publication No. PHS 91-50212). Washington, DC: U.S. Government Printing Office.

U.S. Department of Health, Education and Welfare. (1976). *Title IX and physical education: A compliance overview.* Washington, DC: Government Printing Office.

Villa, R. A., & Thousand, J. S. (1992). How one district integrated special and general education. *Educational Leadership, 50*(2), 39–41.

Violas, P. C. (1978). *The training of the urban working class: A history of twentieth century American education.* Chicago: Rand McNally.

Vocational Education Act of 1946 (George-Barden Act; George-Deen Vocational Education Act; Vocational Education Act of 1936), Pub. L. No. 85-864, 72 Stat. 1597.

VonVillas, B. A. (1995). The changing role of high school guidance: Career counseling and school-to-work. *NASSP Bulletin, 79*(573), 81–86.

Wagner-Peyser Act (National Employment Service Act) of 1933, Pub. L. No. 97-300, 96 Stat. 1392.

Walberg, H. J. (1994). Families as partners in educational productivity. *Phi Delta Kappan, 65*(6), 397–400.

Walker, D., & Soltis, J. (1997). *Curriculum and aims* (3rd ed.). New York: Teachers College Press.

Ward, W. (1930). *Creative dramatics for the upper grades and junior high school.* New York: D. Appleton-Century.

Watkins, J., & Wilkes, D. (1993). *Sharing success in the Southeast: Promising service-learning program.* U.S. Department of Education: SERVE SouthEastern Regional Vision for Education and the School of Education at the University of North Carolina at Greensboro.

Webb, C. W. (1997). Working with parents from cradle to preschool: A university collaborative with an urban public school. *Young Children, 52*(4), 15–19.

Weissberg, R. P., Shriver, T. P., Bose, S., & De Falco, K. (1997). Creating a district-wide social development project. *Educational Leadership, 54*(8), 37–39.

Wheeler, P. T., & Loesch, L. (1981). Program evaluation and counseling: Yesterday, today, and tomorrow. *The Personnel and Guidance Journal, 59*(9), 573–578.

White, M. A., & Harris, M. W. (1961). *The school psychologist.* New York: Harper and Brothers.

Will, M. C. (1986). Educating children with learning problems: A shared responsibility. *Exceptional Children,* 411–415.

Willgoose, C. E. (1984). *The curriculum in physical education* (4th ed.). Englewood Cliffs, NJ: Prentice-Hall.

William T. Grant Foundation. Commission on Work, Family, and Citizenship. (1988). *The forgotten half: Pathways to success for America's youth and young families final report.* Washington, DC: Author.

Winters, P. A. (1990). Getting high: Components of successful drug education programs. *Journal of Alcohol and Drug Education, 35*(2), 20–23.

Winters, W. G., & Easton, F. (1983). *The practice of social work in schools: An ecological perspective.* New York: The Free Press.

Wisconsin Department of Public Instruction. (1987). *A guide to curriculum planning in marketing education.* Madison, WI: Wisconsin Department of Public Education.

Witmer, J. J., & Anderson, C. S. (1994). *How to establish a high school service learning program.* Alexandria, PA: Association for Supervision and Curriculum Development.

Wold, S. J. *School nursing: A framework for practice.* North Branch, MN: Sunrise River Press.

Worsnop, R. I. (1993). Bilingual education. *CQ Researcher, 3*(2), 699–715.

Wrenn, C. G. (1968). The movement into counseling in the elementary school In V. Faust (Ed.), *The counselor–consultant in the elementary school* (pp. 1–30). Boston: Houghton Mifflin.

Yniguez v. Mofford, 1995: 69 F. 3d 920.

Zanga, J. R., & Oda, D. S. (1991). School health services. In B. W. Spradley (Ed.), *Readings in community health nursing* (4th ed., pp. 435–443). Philadelphia: J. B. Lippincott.

Zastrow, C. (1996). *Introduction to social work and social welfare* (6th ed.). Pacific Grove, CA: Brooks/Cole.

Zeigler, E. F. (1968). *Problems in the history and philosophy of physical education and sport.* Englewood Cliffs, NJ: Prentice-Hall.

Zeigler, E. F. (1979). *History of physical education and sport.* Englewood Cliffs, NJ: Prentice-Hall.

Zigler, E. F., Finn-Stevenson, M., & Marsland, K. W. (1995). Child day care in the schools: The school of the 21st century. *Child Welfare: Journal of Policy, Practice, and Program, 74*(6), 1301–1326.

Zinser, J. (1992). Mandatory community service: Services or servitude? *State Legislatures,* 30–33.

Zirkel, P. A. (1977). The legal vicissitudes of bilingual education. *Phi Delta Kappan, 58,* 409–411.

Zunker, V. G. (1994). *Career counseling: Applied concepts of life planning* (4th ed.). Pacific Grove, CA: Brooks/Cole.

INDEX